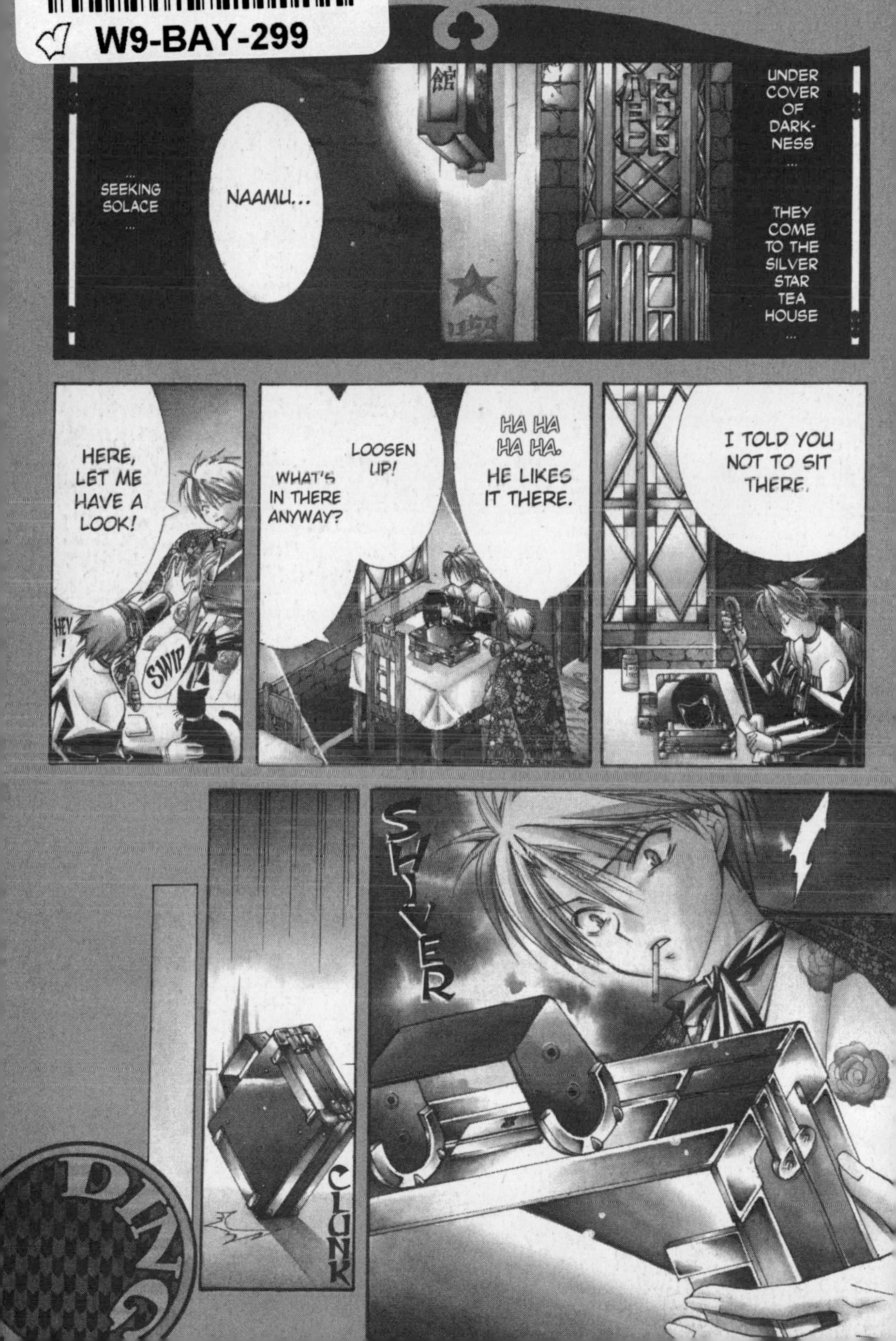
UNDER COVER OF DARKNESS ...
THEY COME TO THE SILVER STAR TEA HOUSE ...
NAAMU...
... SEEKING SOLACE ...
I TOLD YOU NOT TO SIT THERE.
HA HA HA HA. HE LIKES IT THERE.
LOOSEN UP!
WHAT'S IN THERE ANYWAY?
HERE, LET ME HAVE A LOOK!
HEY!
SWIP
SHIVER
CLUNK
DING

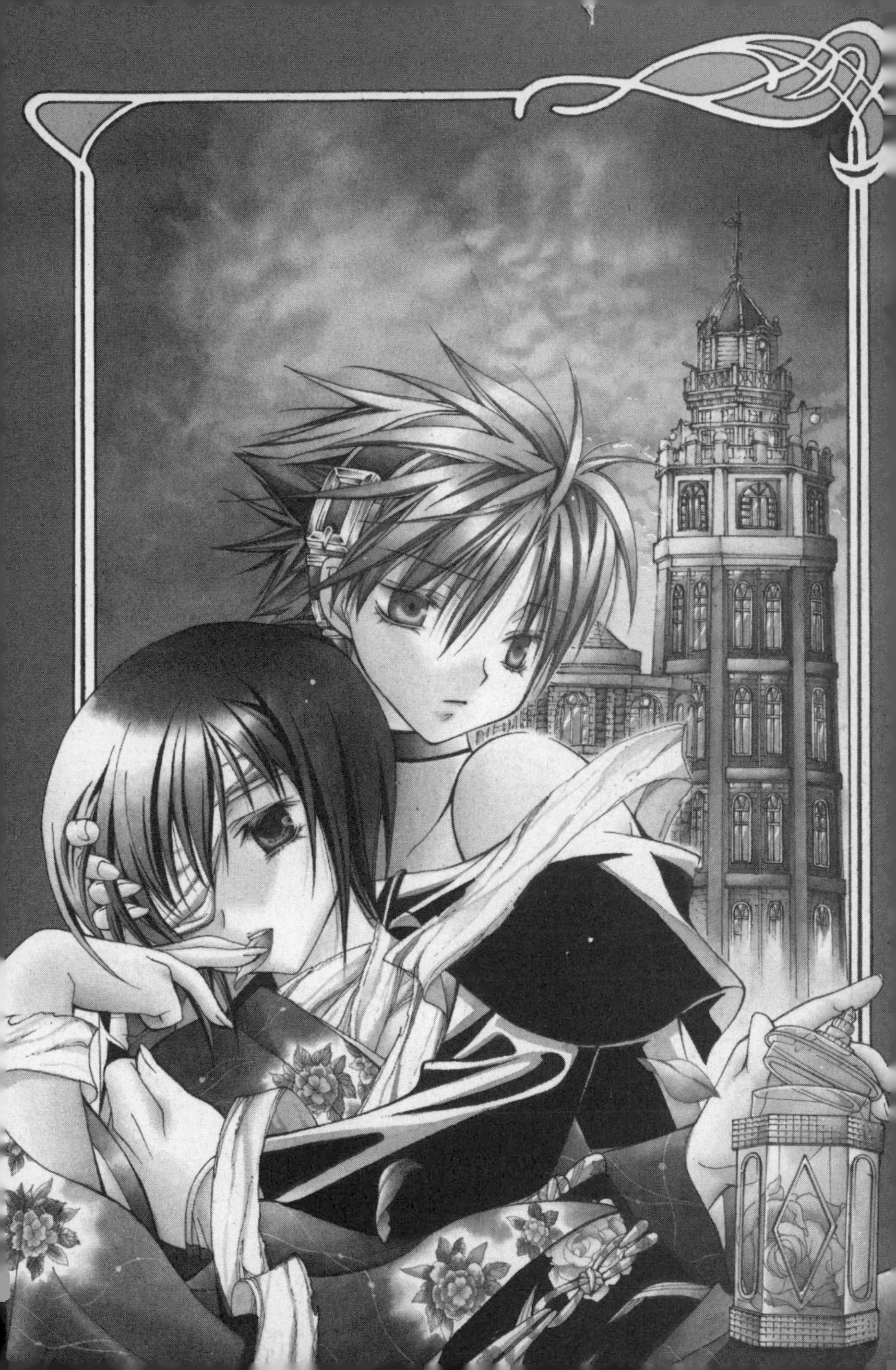

# THE FOURTEENTH NIGHT: CONTINUANCE

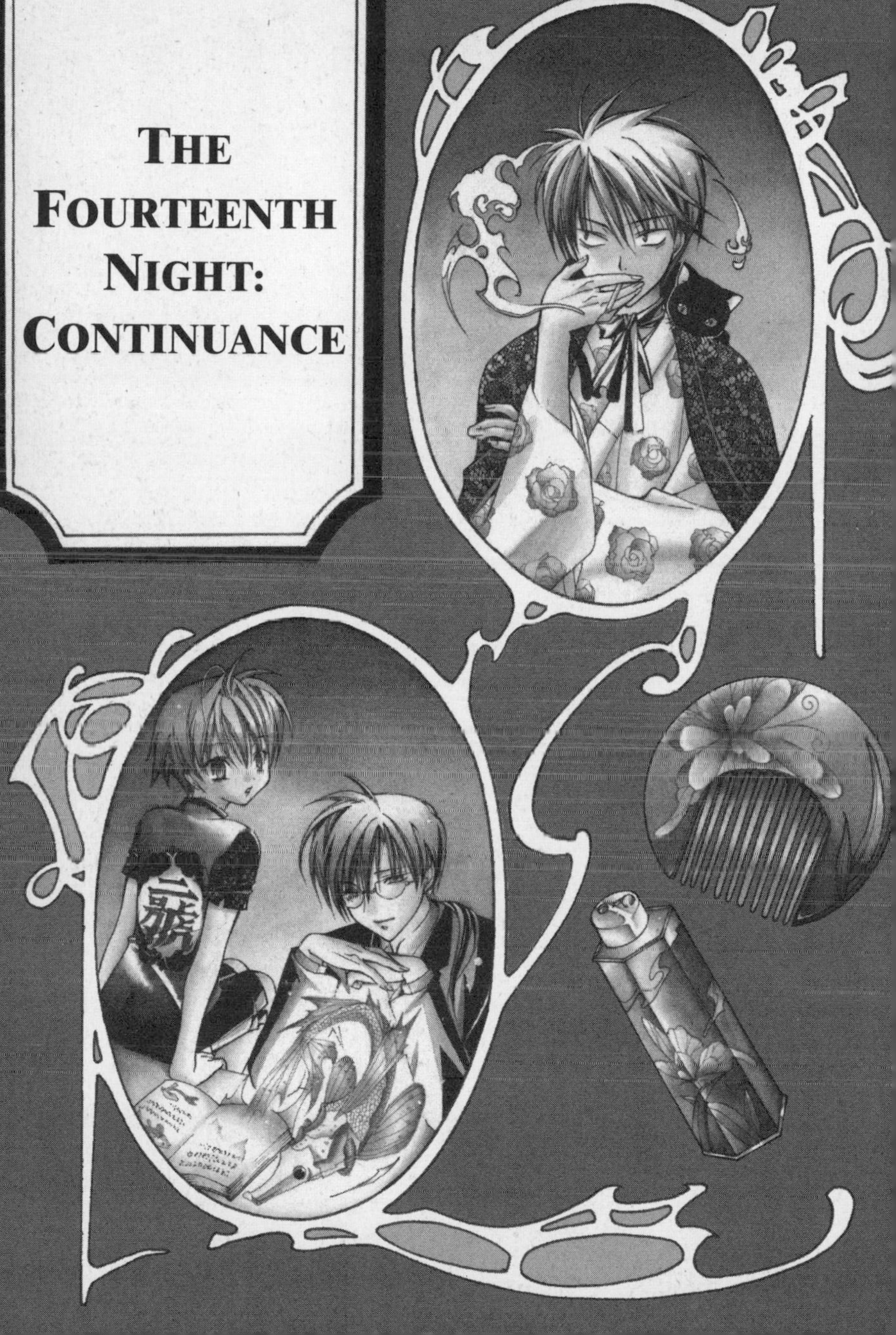

## SUPER POPULAR! GREAT ROMANTIC HOWAH...

# SHIN MASHIBA's friend, Wan Wan Shiroi.

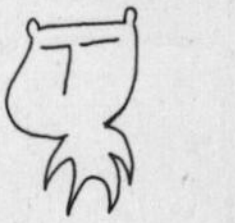

Hey again! Volume 3 already? Wow, congratulations!
I'm not sure if I'm a guest or just a space filler. This is my third time now! I have a feeling that the readers are going to start asking who the heck I am.

But considering I was asked to be here, what's going on?! Isn't this usually a leftover page? I'm getting shafted here! Was there ever a guest treated like this in the past?! This is outrageous! I have a feeling that my relationship with Mashiba may suffer a rift. So anyway, here I am again. Look forward to it!

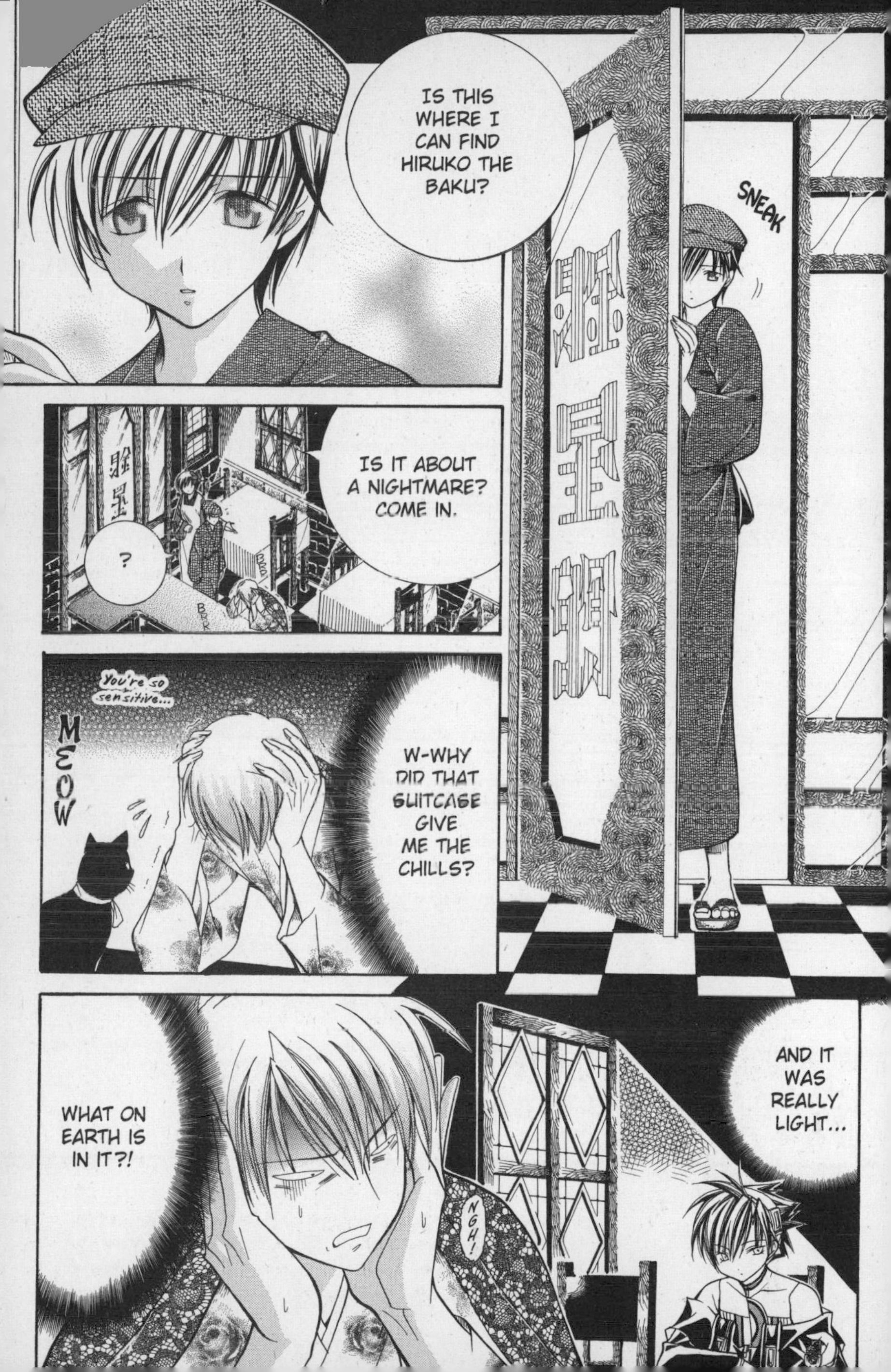

SNEAK
IS THIS WHERE I CAN FIND HIRUKO THE BAKU?
IS IT ABOUT A NIGHTMARE? COME IN.
?
W-WHY DID THAT SUITCASE GIVE ME THE CHILLS?
You're so sensitive...
MEOW
AND IT WAS REALLY LIGHT...
NGH!
WHAT ON EARTH IS IN IT?!

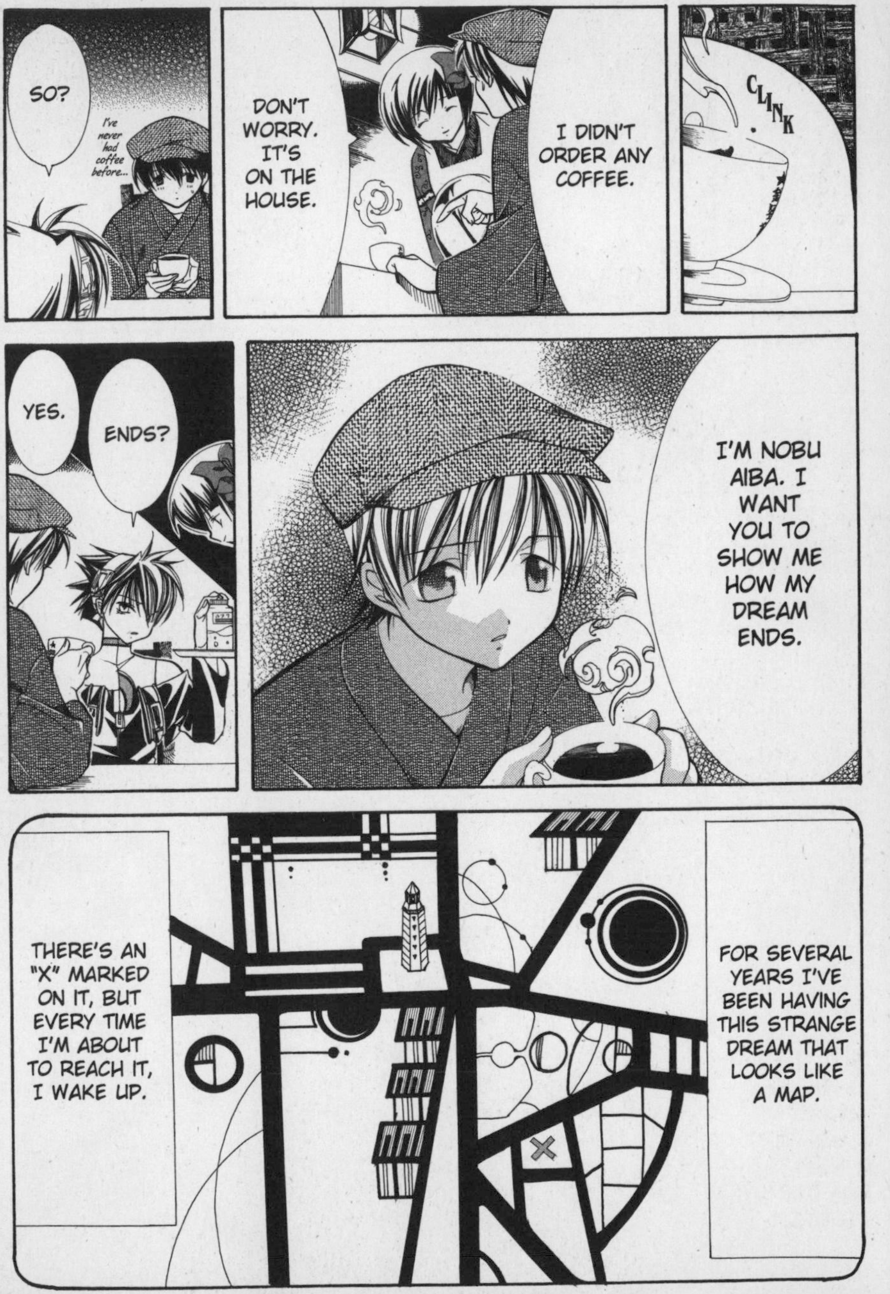
CLINK
I DIDN'T ORDER ANY COFFEE.
DON'T WORRY. IT'S ON THE HOUSE.
SO?
I've never had coffee before...
I'M NOBU AIBA. I WANT YOU TO SHOW ME HOW MY DREAM ENDS.
ENDS?
YES.
FOR SEVERAL YEARS I'VE BEEN HAVING THIS STRANGE DREAM THAT LOOKS LIKE A MAP.
THERE'S AN "X" MARKED ON IT, BUT EVERY TIME I'M ABOUT TO REACH IT, I WAKE UP.

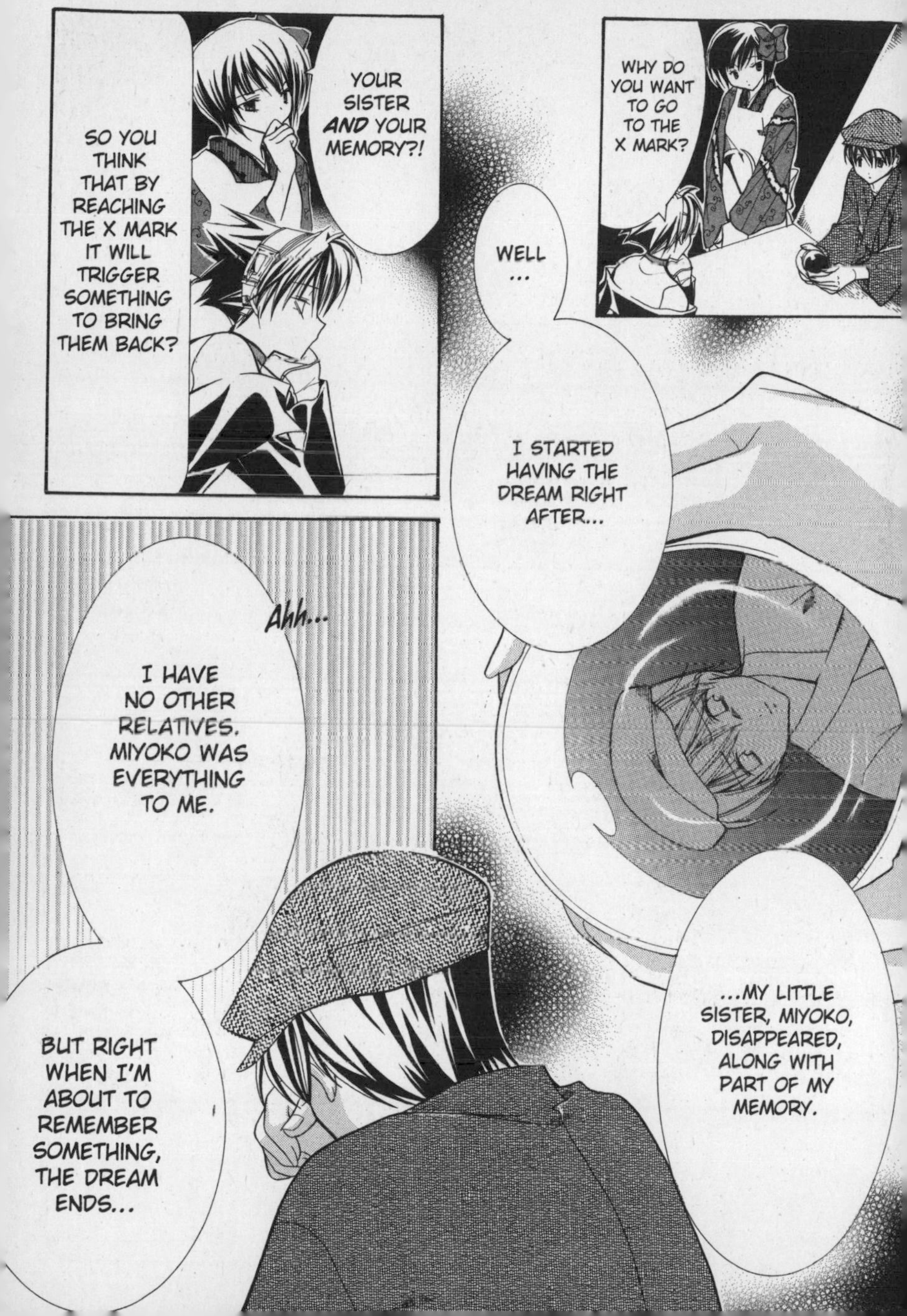
WHY DO YOU WANT TO GO TO THE X MARK?
WELL ...
I STARTED HAVING THE DREAM RIGHT AFTER...
...MY LITTLE SISTER, MIYOKO, DISAPPEARED, ALONG WITH PART OF MY MEMORY.
YOUR SISTER AND YOUR MEMORY?!
SO YOU THINK THAT BY REACHING THE X MARK IT WILL TRIGGER SOMETHING TO BRING THEM BACK?
Ahh...
I HAVE NO OTHER RELATIVES. MIYOKO WAS EVERYTHING TO ME.
BUT RIGHT WHEN I'M ABOUT TO REMEMBER SOMETHING, THE DREAM ENDS...

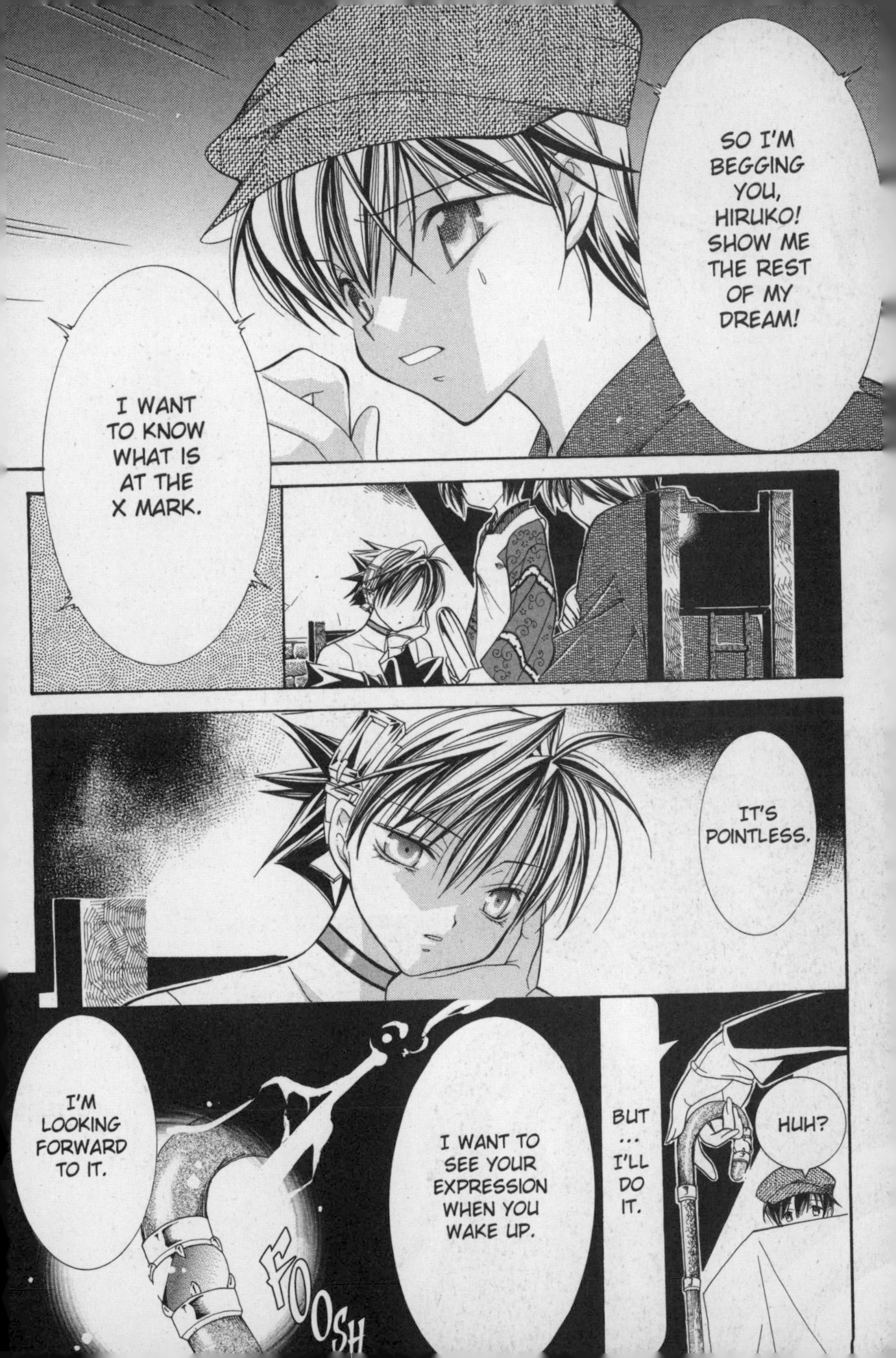
SO I'M BEGGING YOU, HIRUKO! SHOW ME THE REST OF MY DREAM!
I WANT TO KNOW WHAT IS AT THE X MARK.
IT'S POINTLESS.
HUH?
BUT... I'LL DO IT.
I WANT TO SEE YOUR EXPRESSION WHEN YOU WAKE UP.
I'M LOOKING FORWARD TO IT.
FOOSH

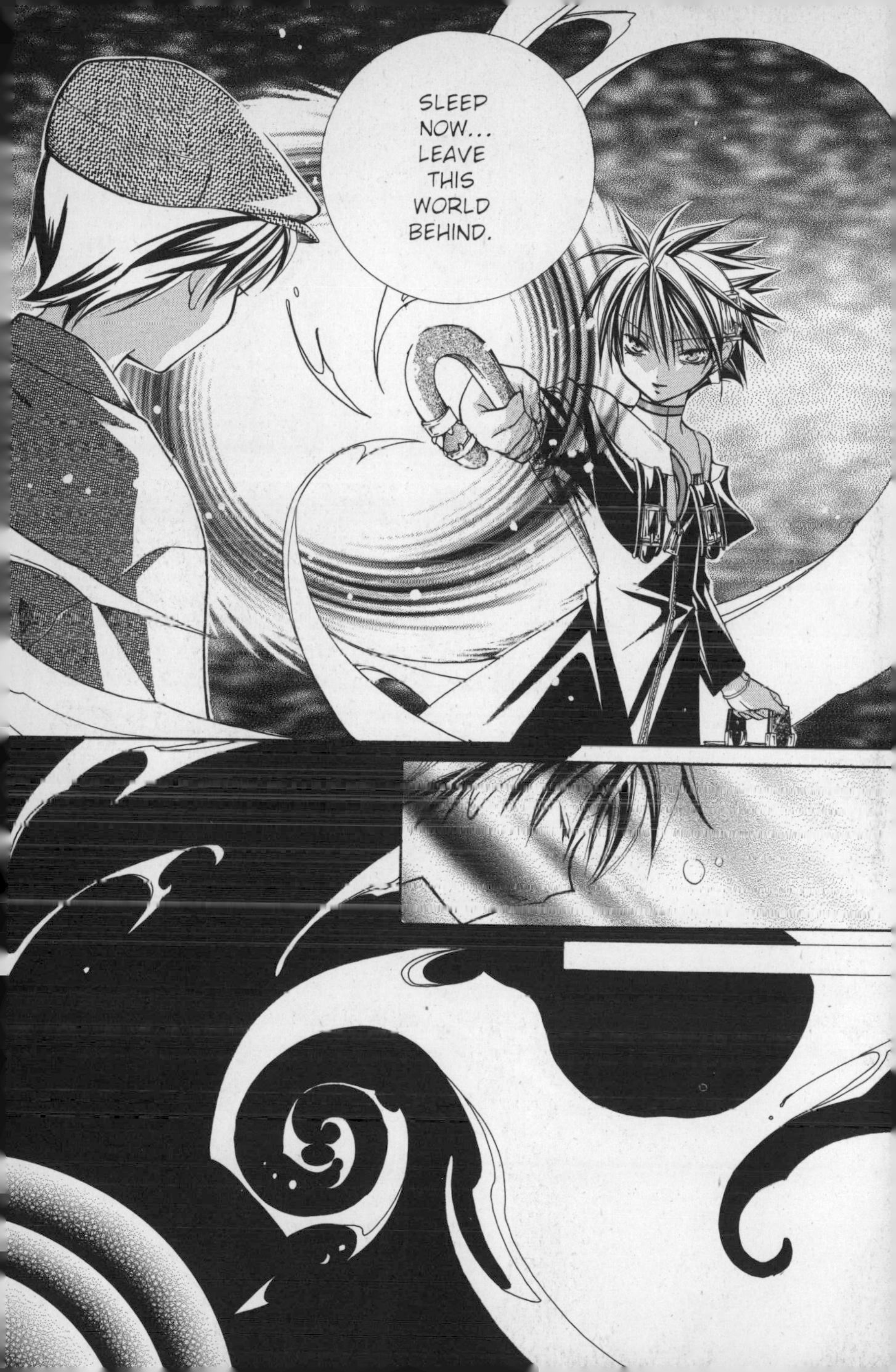
SLEEP NOW... LEAVE THIS WORLD BEHIND.

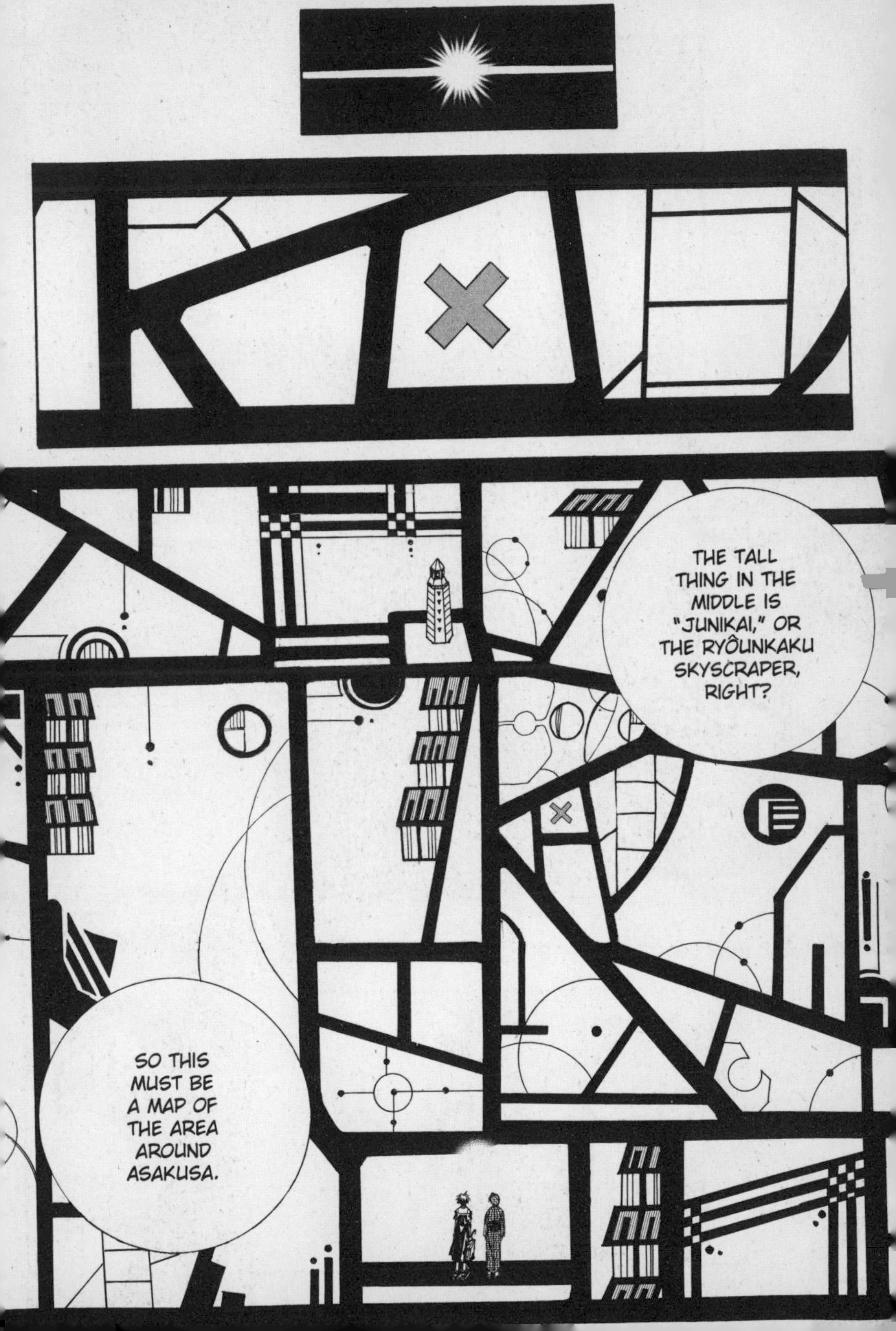
THE TALL THING IN THE MIDDLE IS "JUNIKAI," OR THE RYÔUNKAKU SKYSCRAPER, RIGHT?
SO THIS MUST BE A MAP OF THE AREA AROUND ASAKUSA.

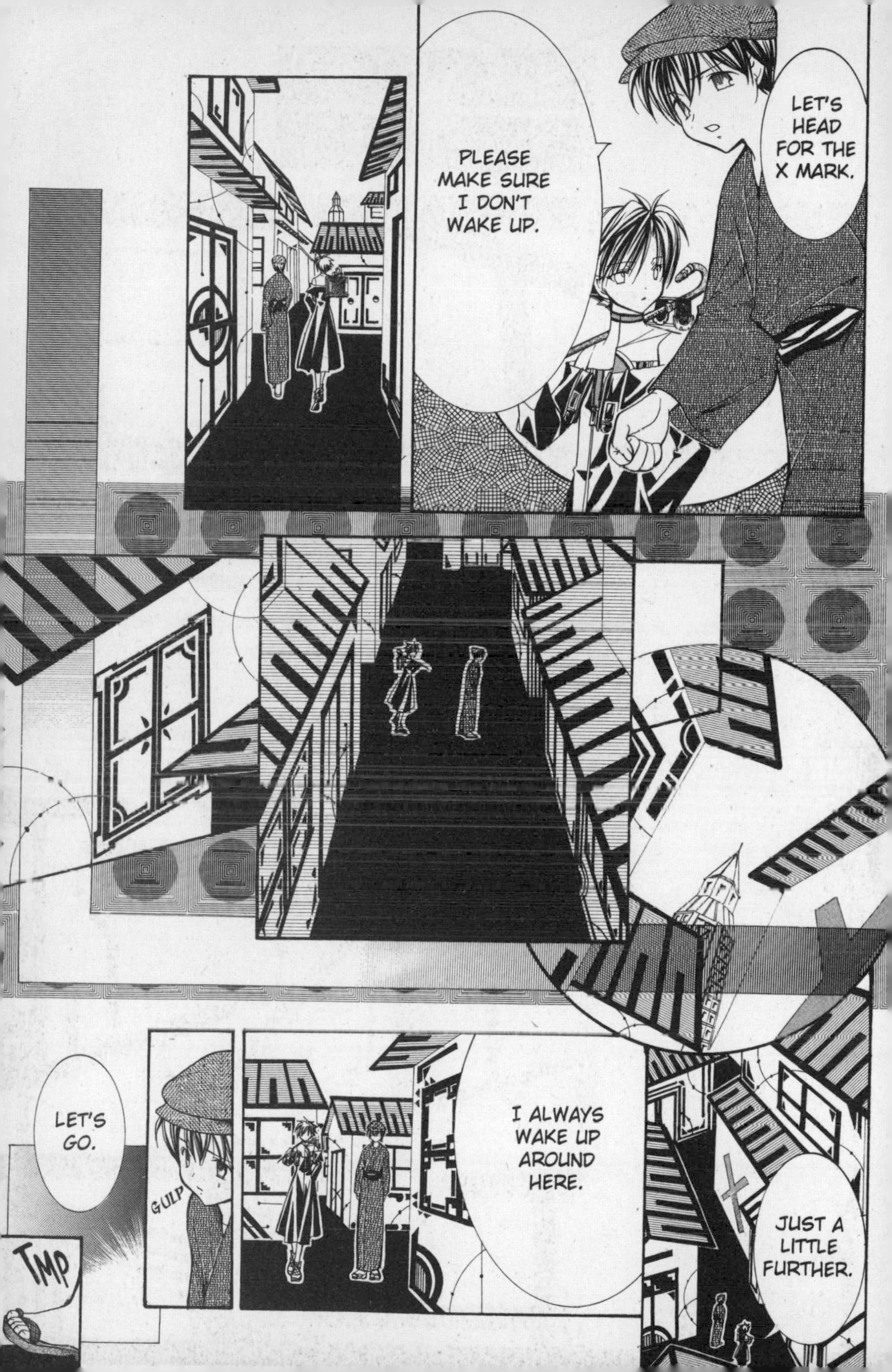
LET'S HEAD FOR THE X MARK.
PLEASE MAKE SURE I DON'T WAKE UP.
JUST A LITTLE FURTHER.
I ALWAYS WAKE UP AROUND HERE.
LET'S GO.
GULP
TMP

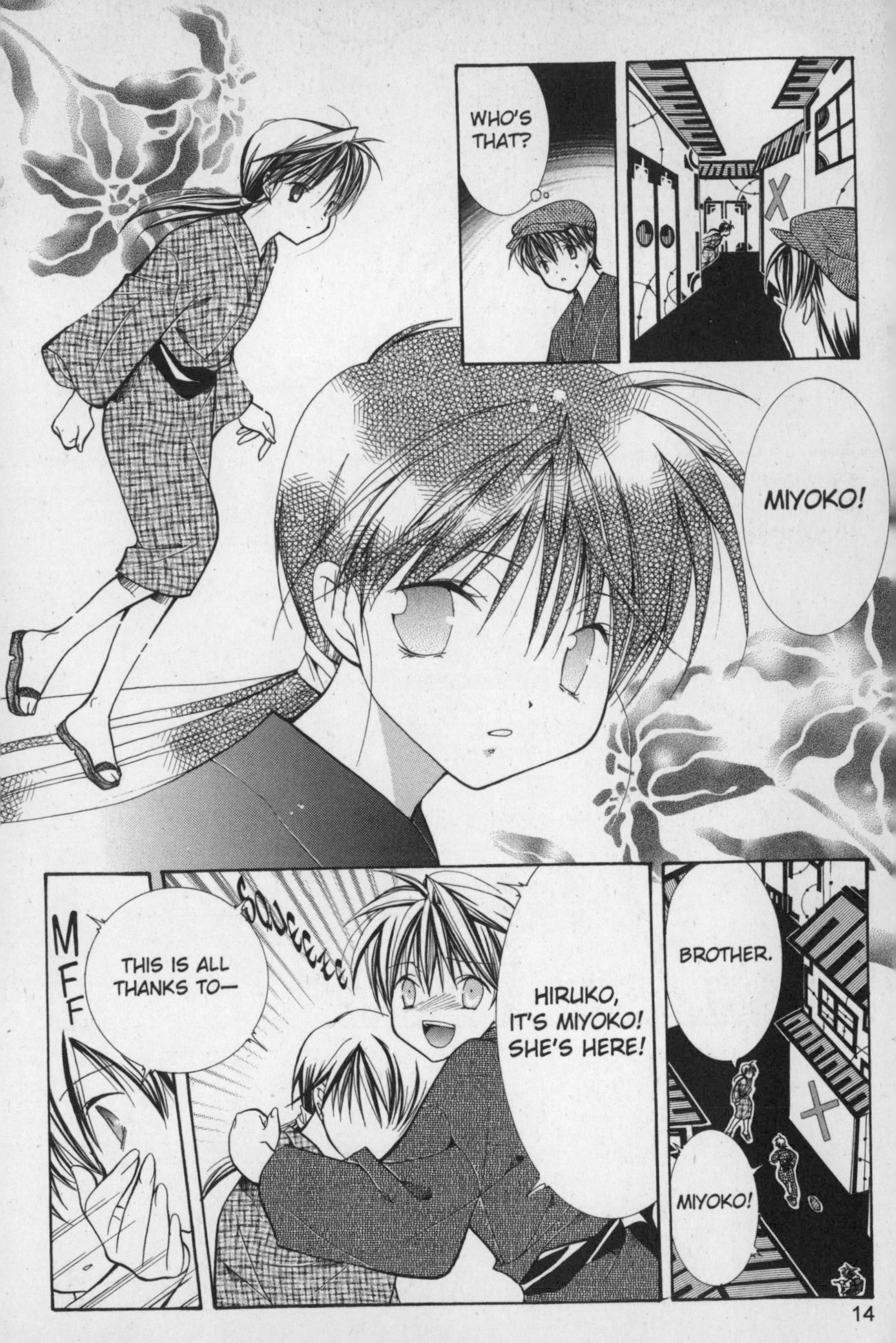
WHO'S THAT?
MIYOKO!
BROTHER.
MIYOKO!
HIRUKO, IT'S MIYOKO! SHE'S HERE!
THIS IS ALL THANKS TO—
MFF

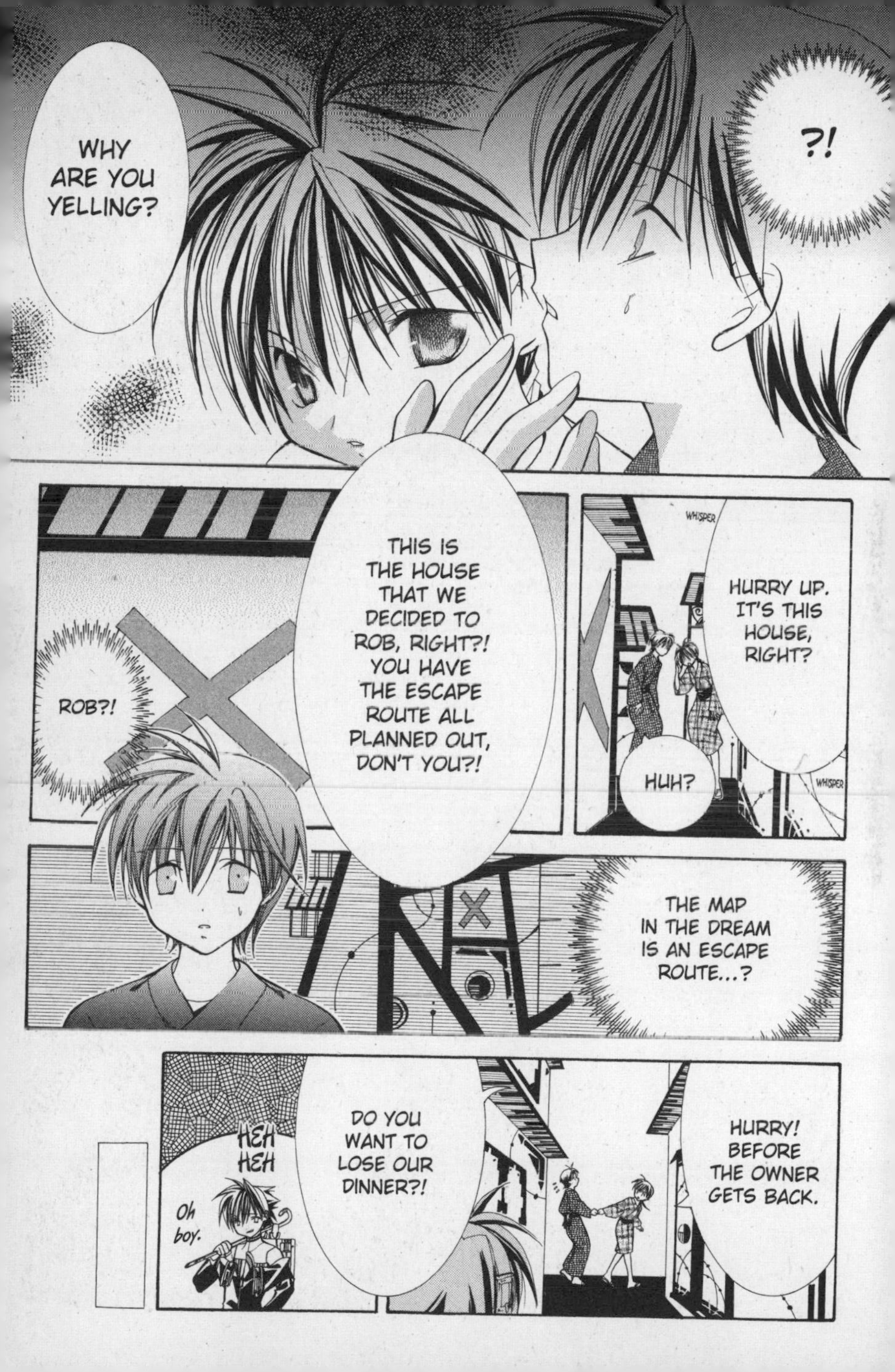
?!
WHY ARE YOU YELLING?
WHISPER
HURRY UP. IT'S THIS HOUSE, RIGHT?
WHISPER
HUH?
THIS IS THE HOUSE THAT WE DECIDED TO ROB, RIGHT?! YOU HAVE THE ESCAPE ROUTE ALL PLANNED OUT, DON'T YOU?!
ROB?!
THE MAP IN THE DREAM IS AN ESCAPE ROUTE...?
HURRY! BEFORE THE OWNER GETS BACK.
DO YOU WANT TO LOSE OUR DINNER?!
HEH HEH
Oh boy.

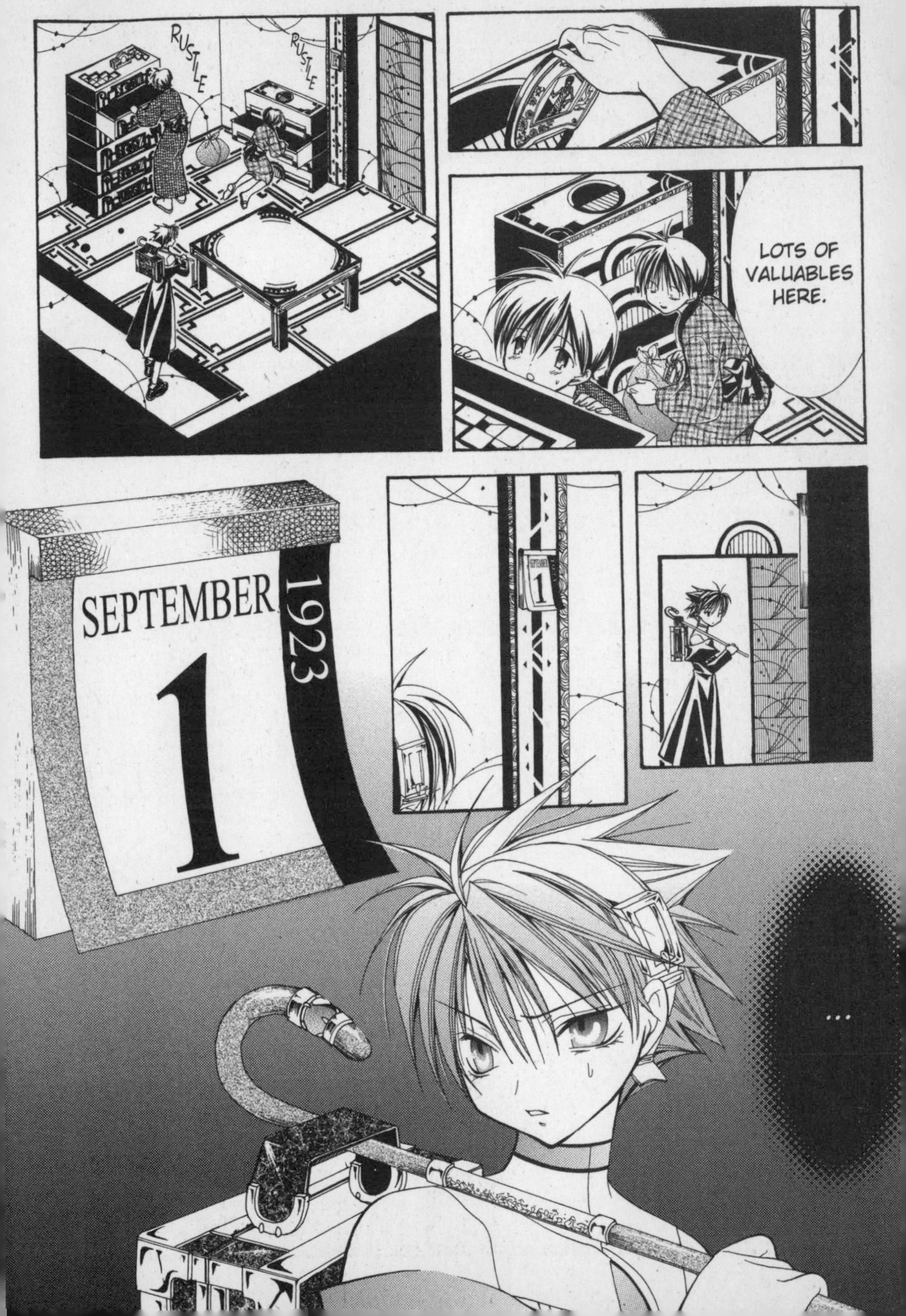
LOTS OF VALUABLES HERE.
RUSTLE
RUSTLE
SEPTEMBER
1
SEPTEMBER
1923
1
...

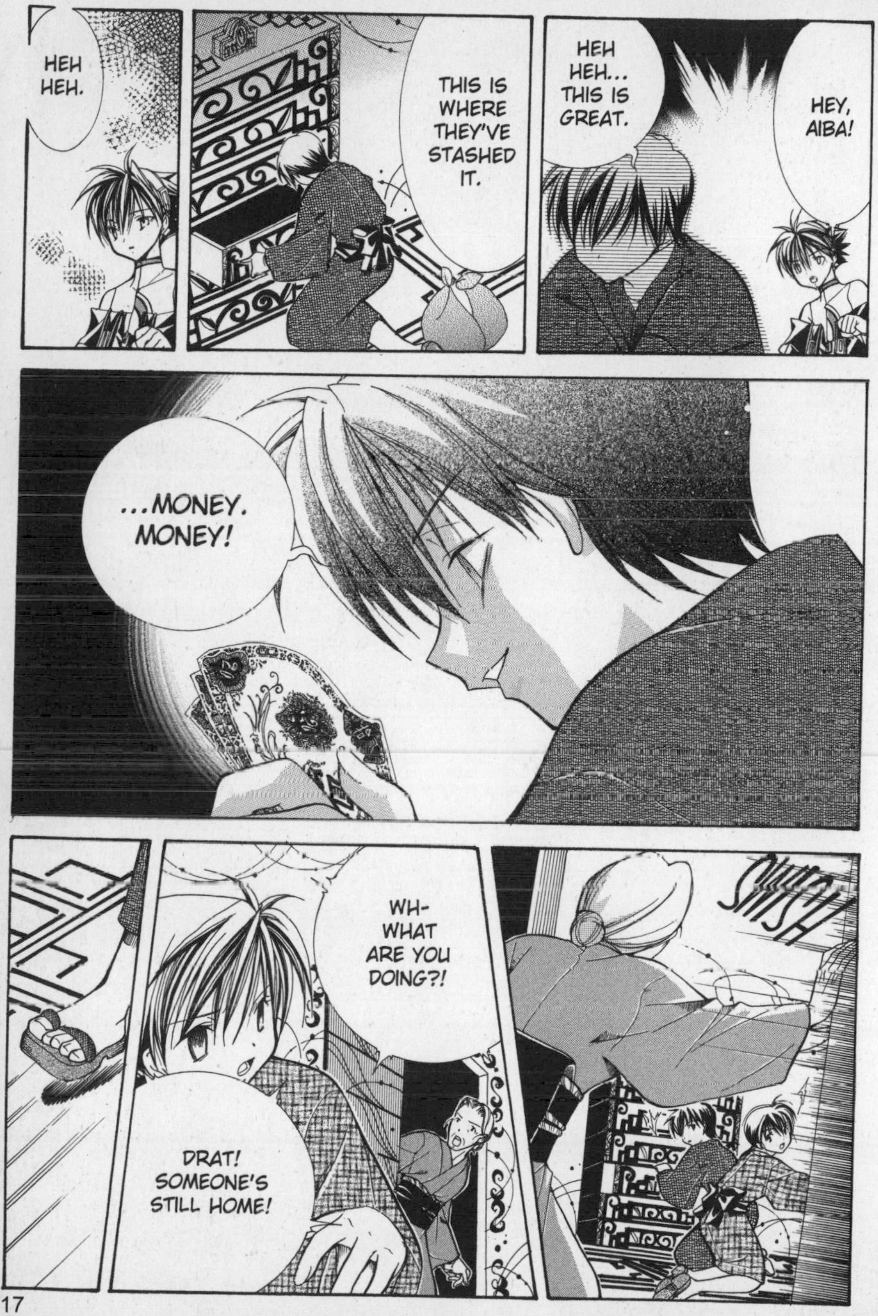
HEY, AIBA!
HEH HEH... THIS IS GREAT.
THIS IS WHERE THEY'VE STASHED IT.
HEH HEH.
...MONEY. MONEY!
WH- WHAT ARE YOU DOING?!
DRAT! SOMEONE'S STILL HOME!

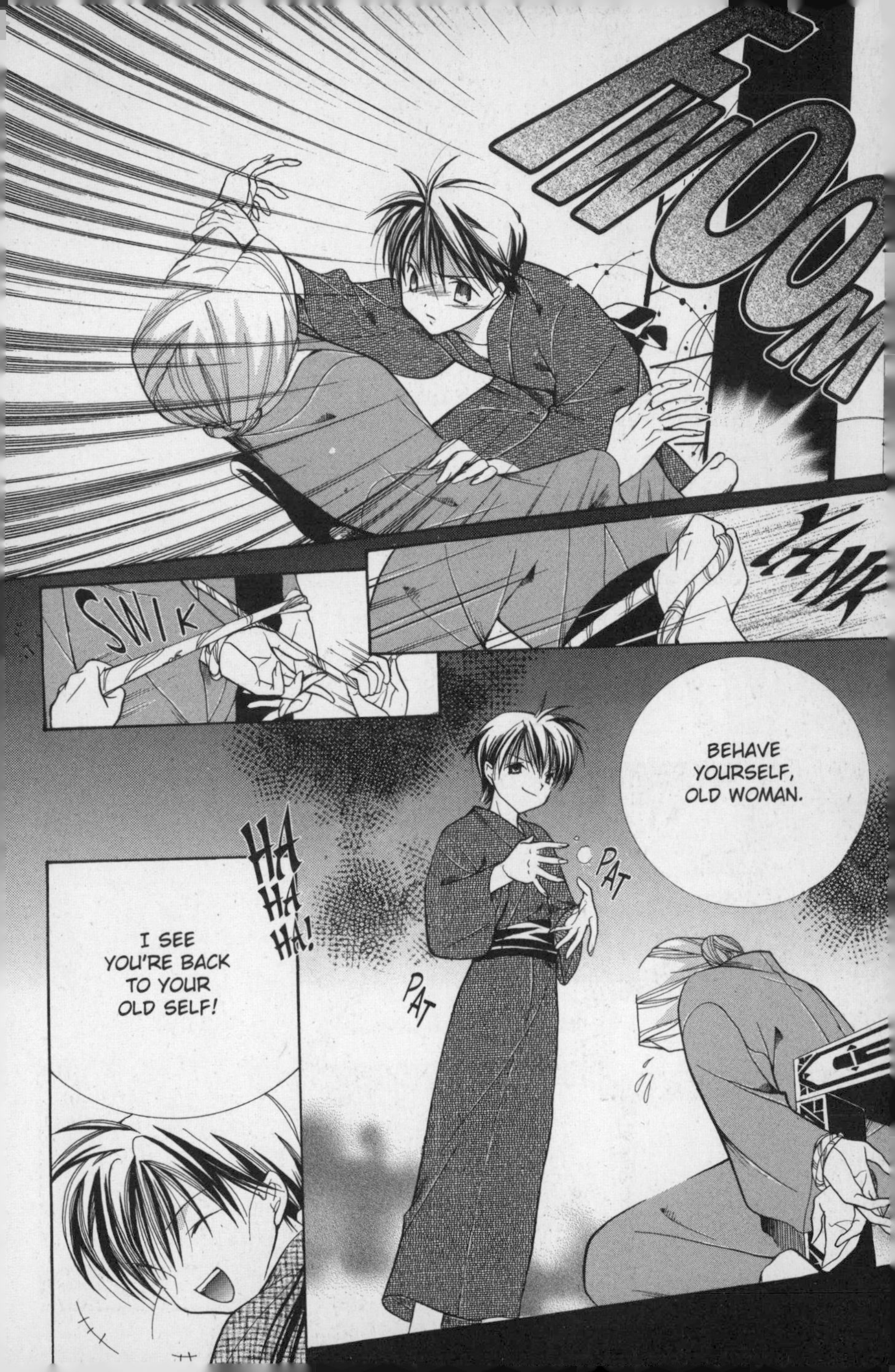
FWOOM
YANK
SWIK
BEHAVE YOURSELF, OLD WOMAN.
PAT
PAT
HA HA HA!
I SEE YOU'RE BACK TO YOUR OLD SELF!

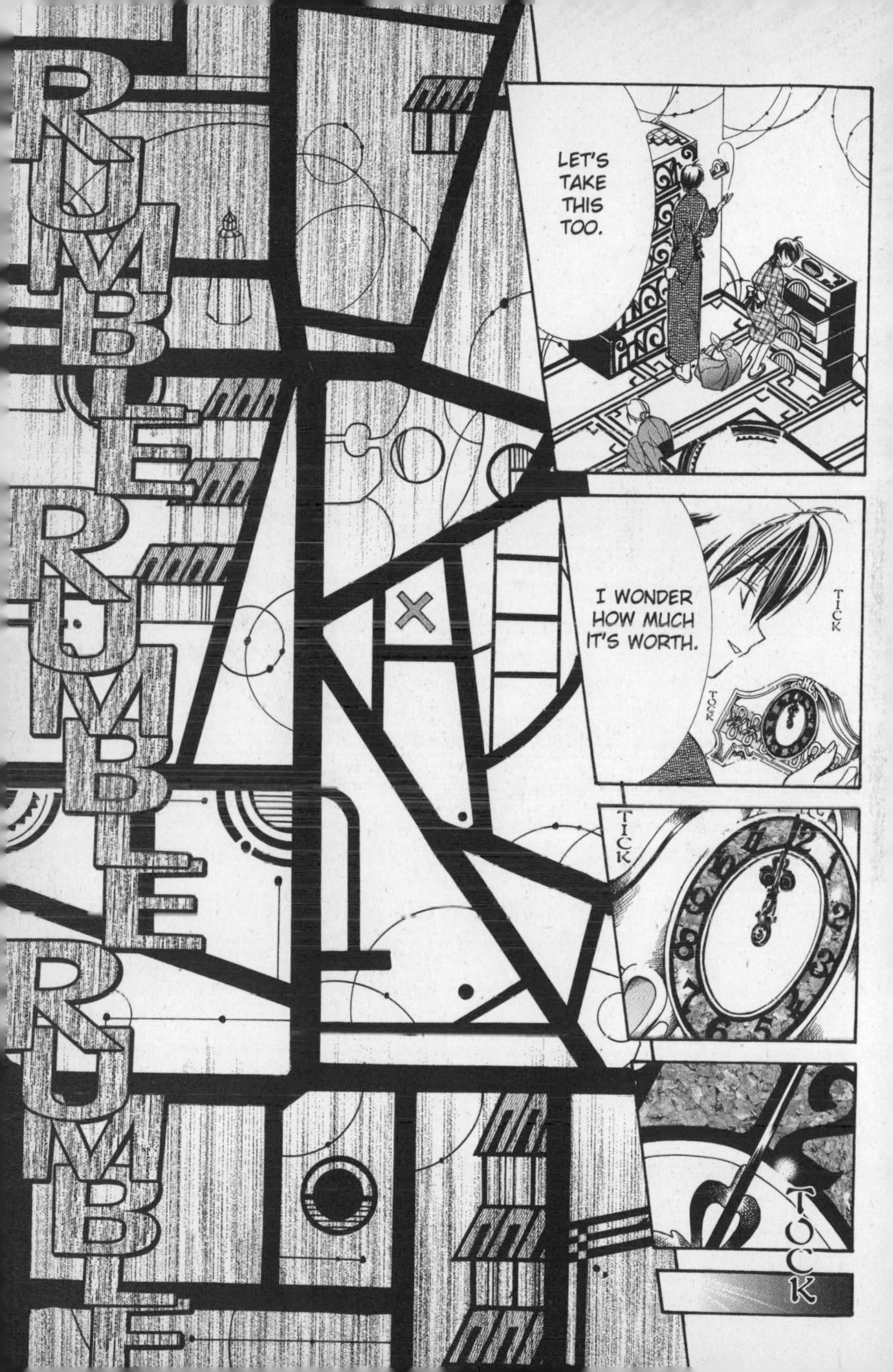

LET'S TAKE THIS TOO.
I WONDER HOW MUCH IT'S WORTH.
TICK
TOCK
TICK
TOCK
RUMBLE
RUMBLE
RUMBLE

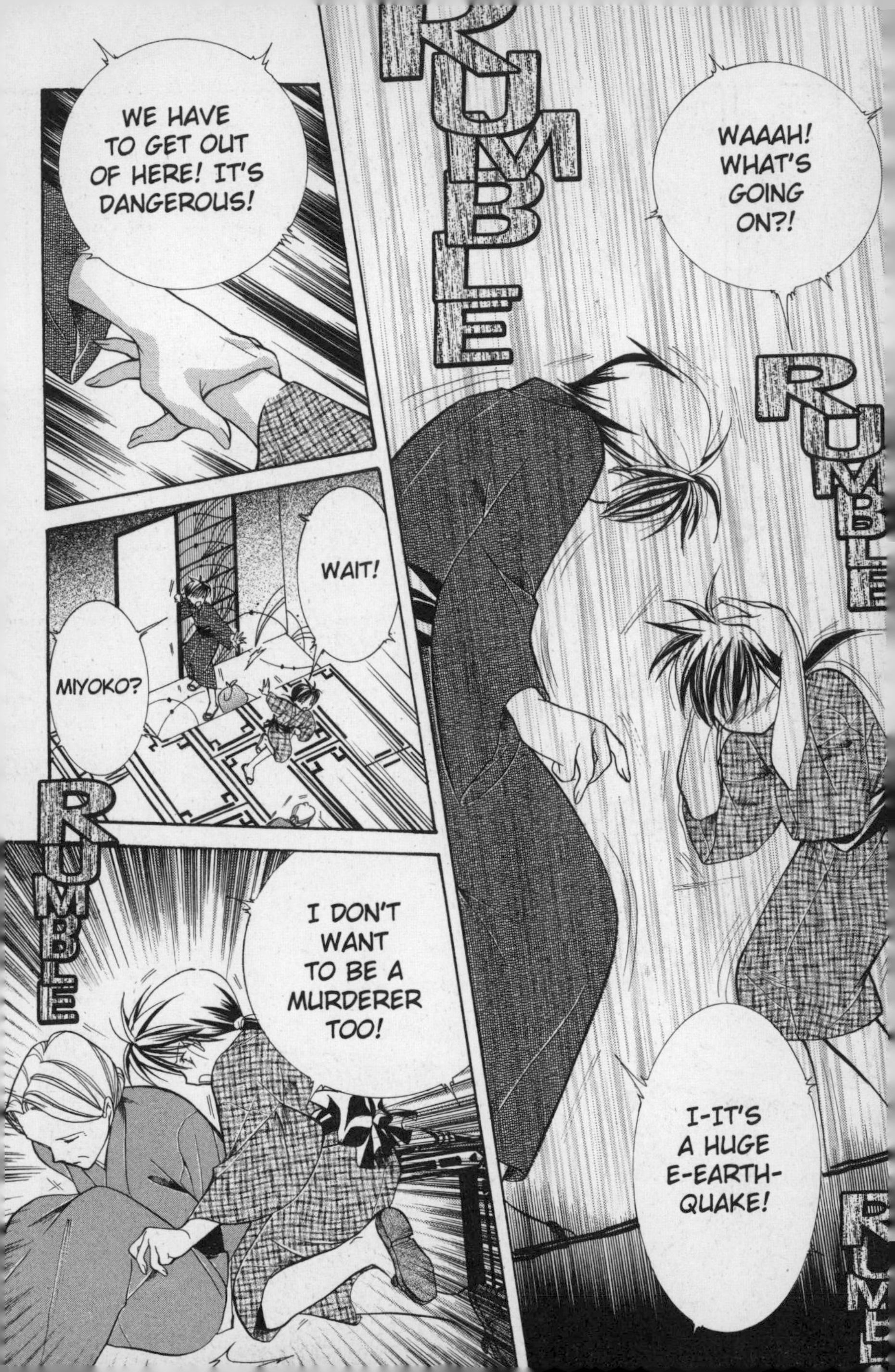
WAAAH! WHAT'S GOING ON?!
RUMBLE
RUMBLE
I-IT'S A HUGE E-EARTH-QUAKE!
RUMBL
WE HAVE TO GET OUT OF HERE! IT'S DANGEROUS!
WAIT!
MIYOKO?
RUMBLE
I DON'T WANT TO BE A MURDERER TOO!

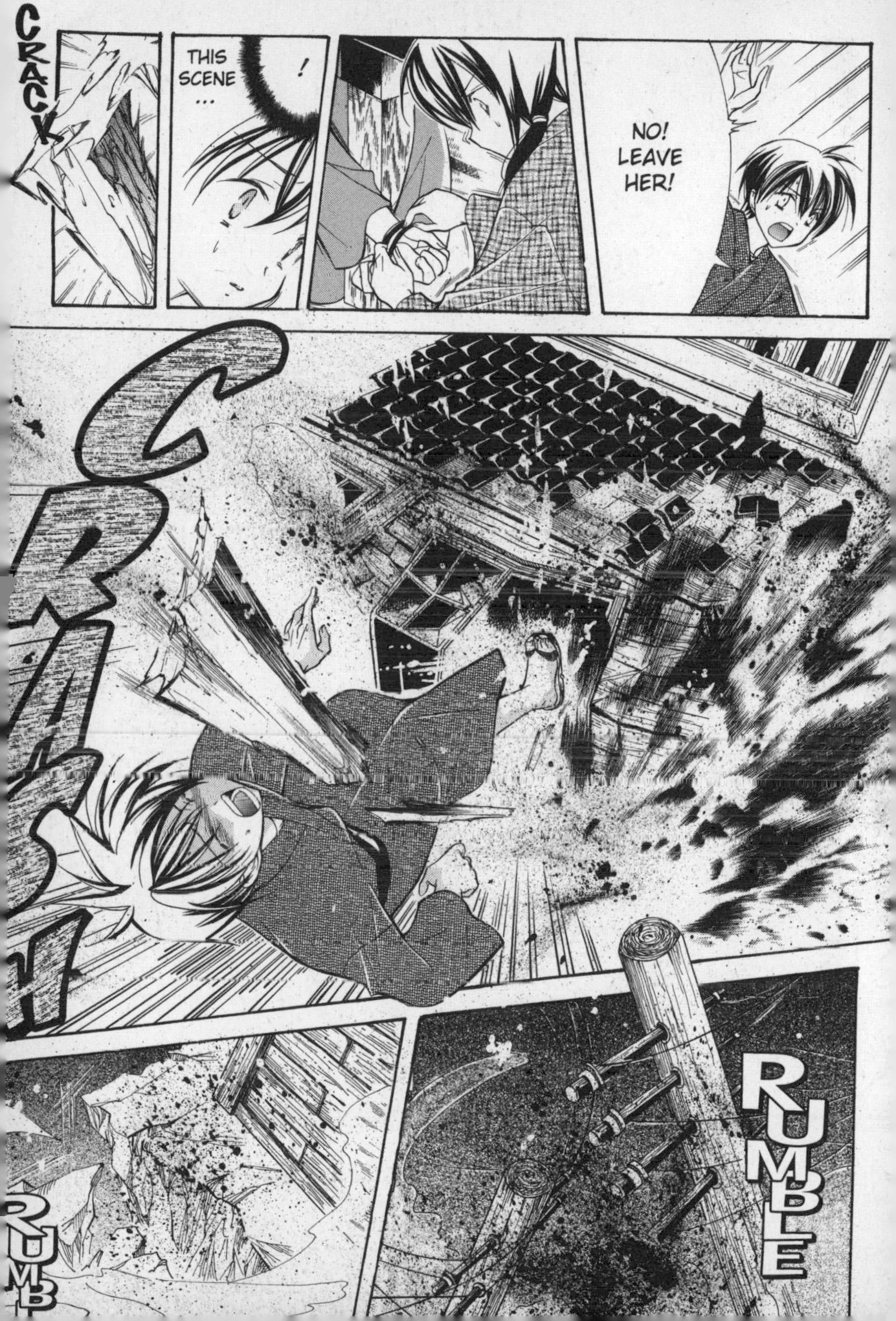

NO! LEAVE HER!
!
THIS SCENE ...
CRACK
CRASH
RUMBLE
RUMB

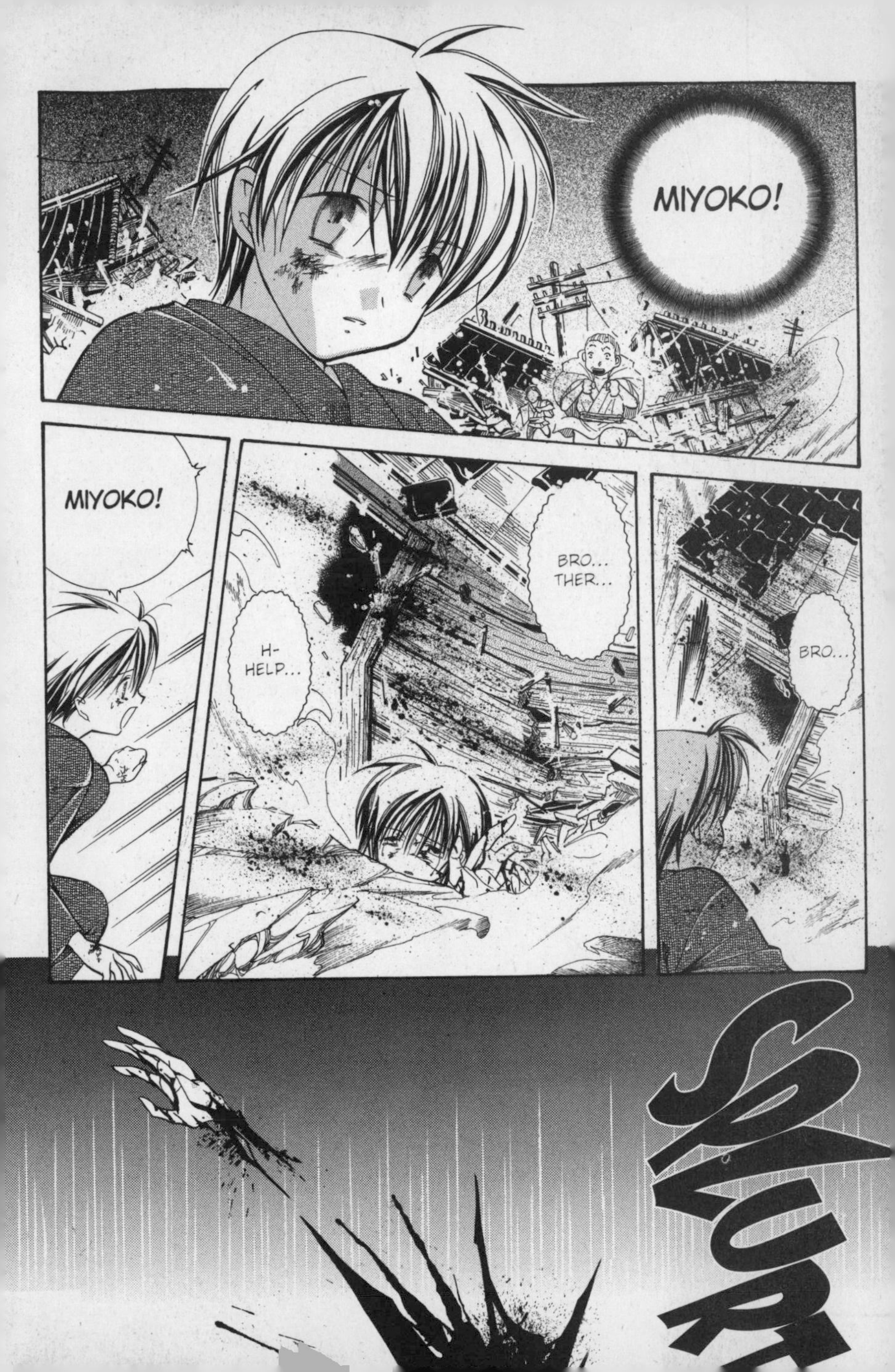
MIYOKO!
BRO...
BRO... THER...
H- HELP...
MIYOKO!
SPLURT

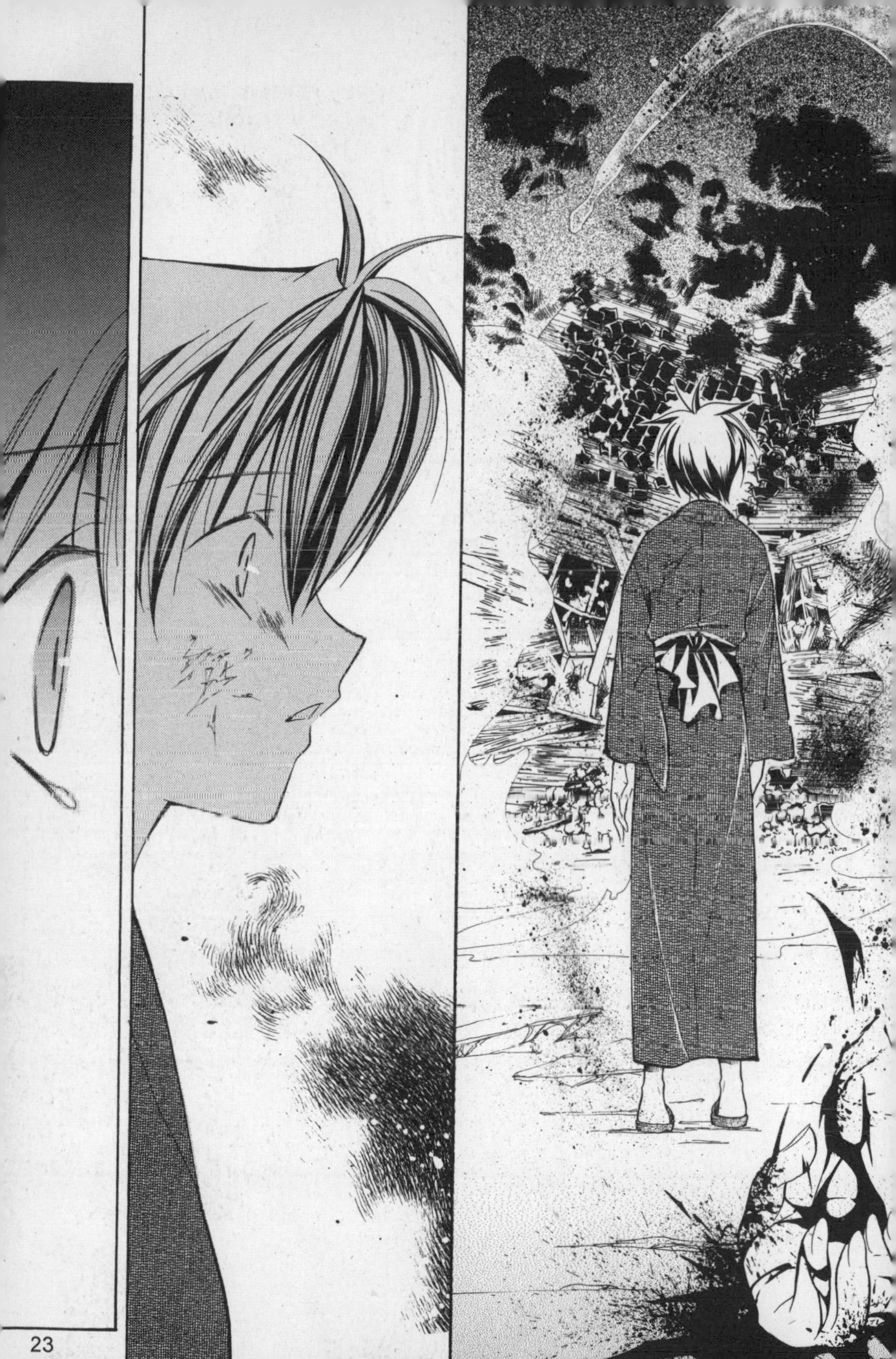

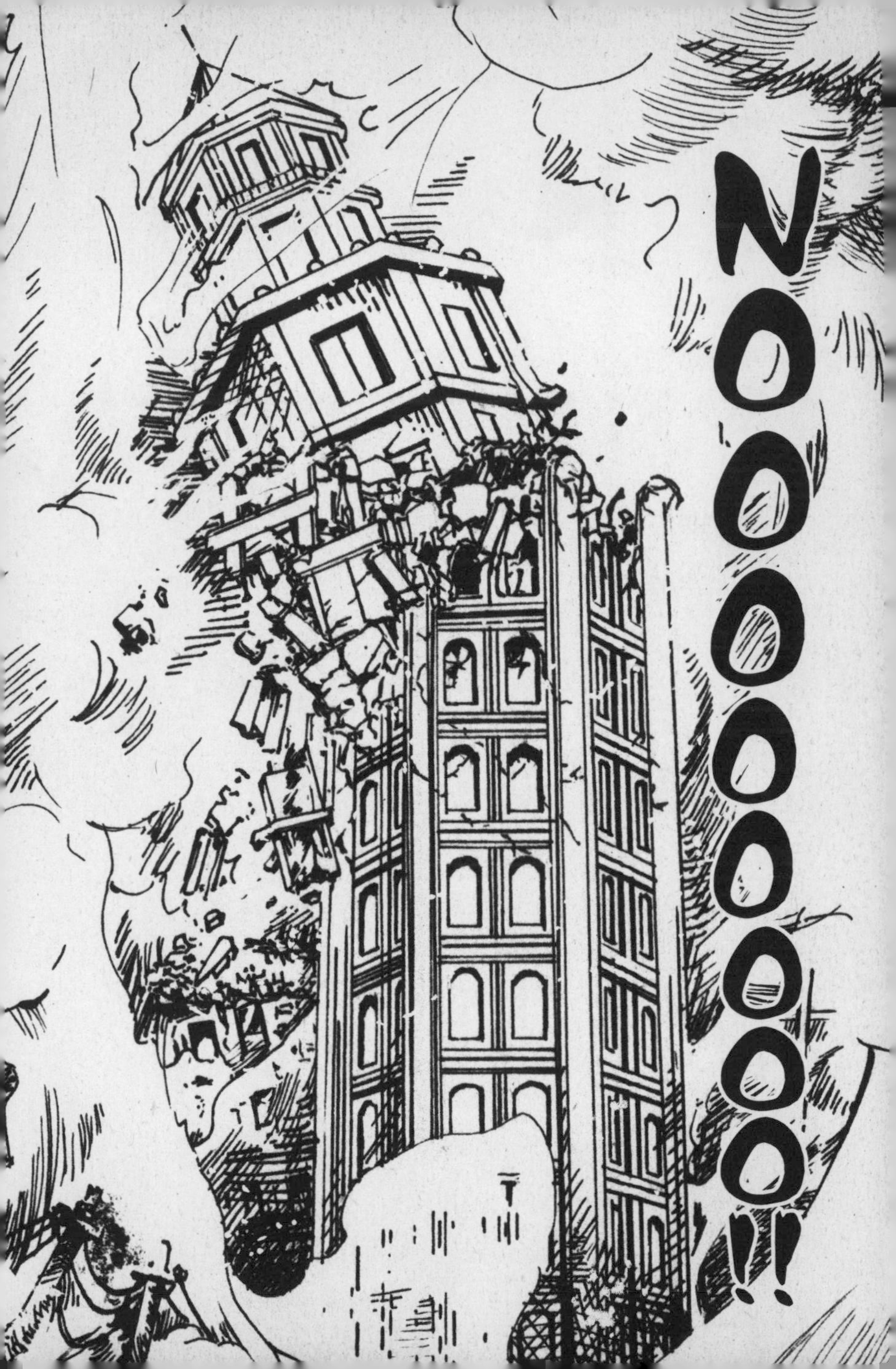
NOOOOOOOOO!!

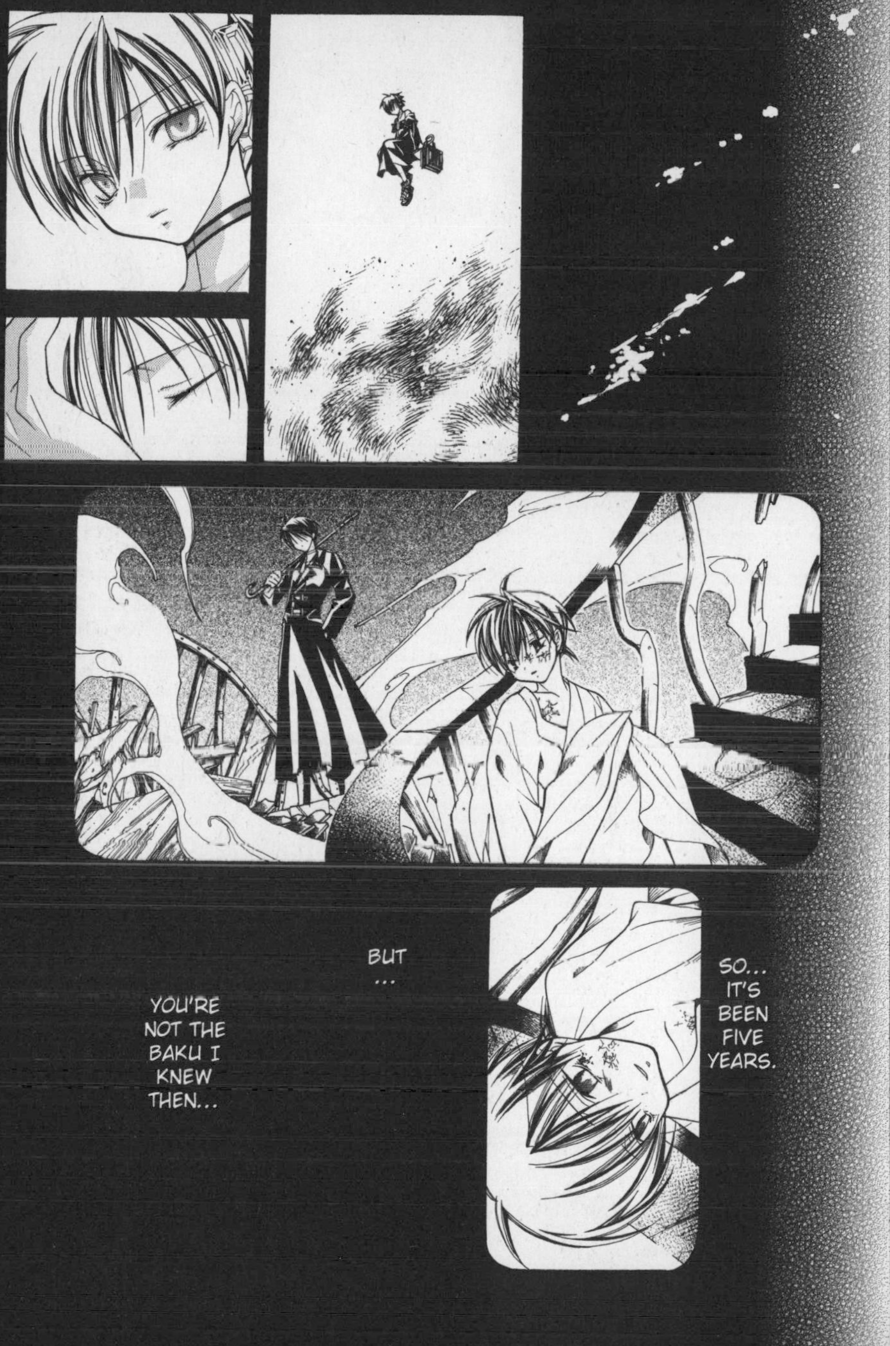
SO... IT'S BEEN FIVE YEARS.
BUT ...
YOU'RE NOT THE BAKU I KNEW THEN...

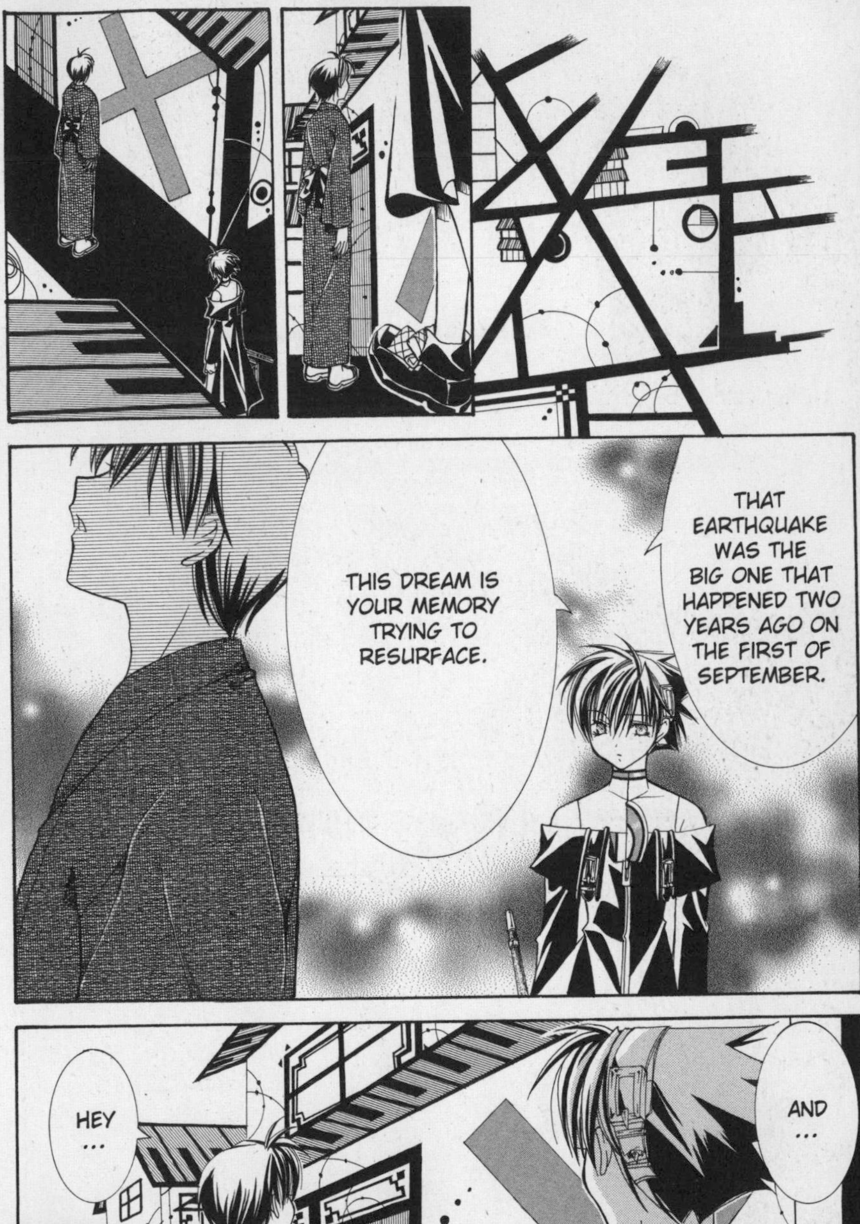
THAT EARTHQUAKE WAS THE BIG ONE THAT HAPPENED TWO YEARS AGO ON THE FIRST OF SEPTEMBER.
THIS DREAM IS YOUR MEMORY TRYING TO RESURFACE.
AND ...
HEY ...

※GREAT KANTO EARTHQUAKE OF 1923

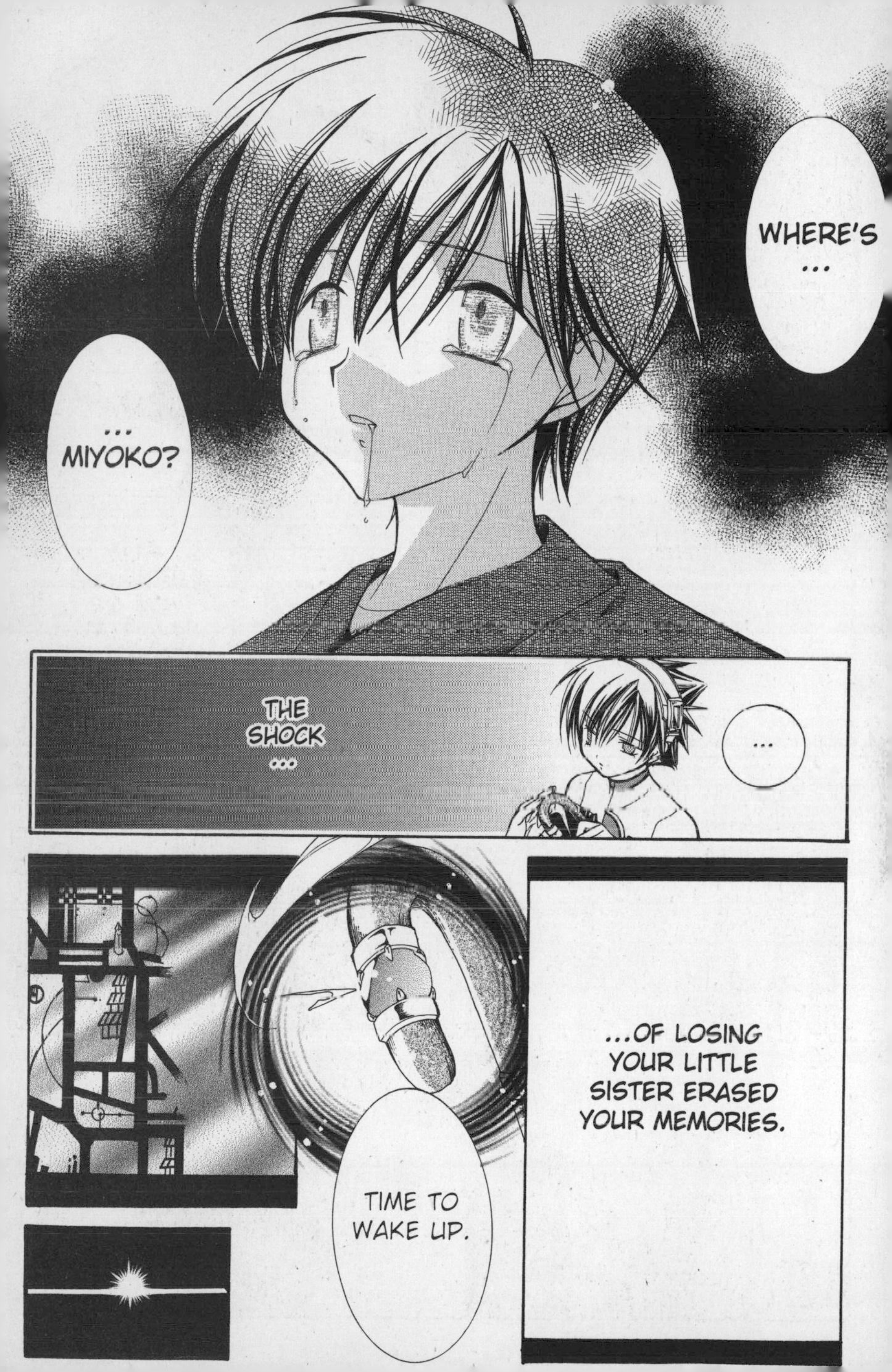
WHERE'S ...
... MIYOKO?
...
THE SHOCK ...
...OF LOSING YOUR LITTLE SISTER ERASED YOUR MEMORIES.
TIME TO WAKE UP.

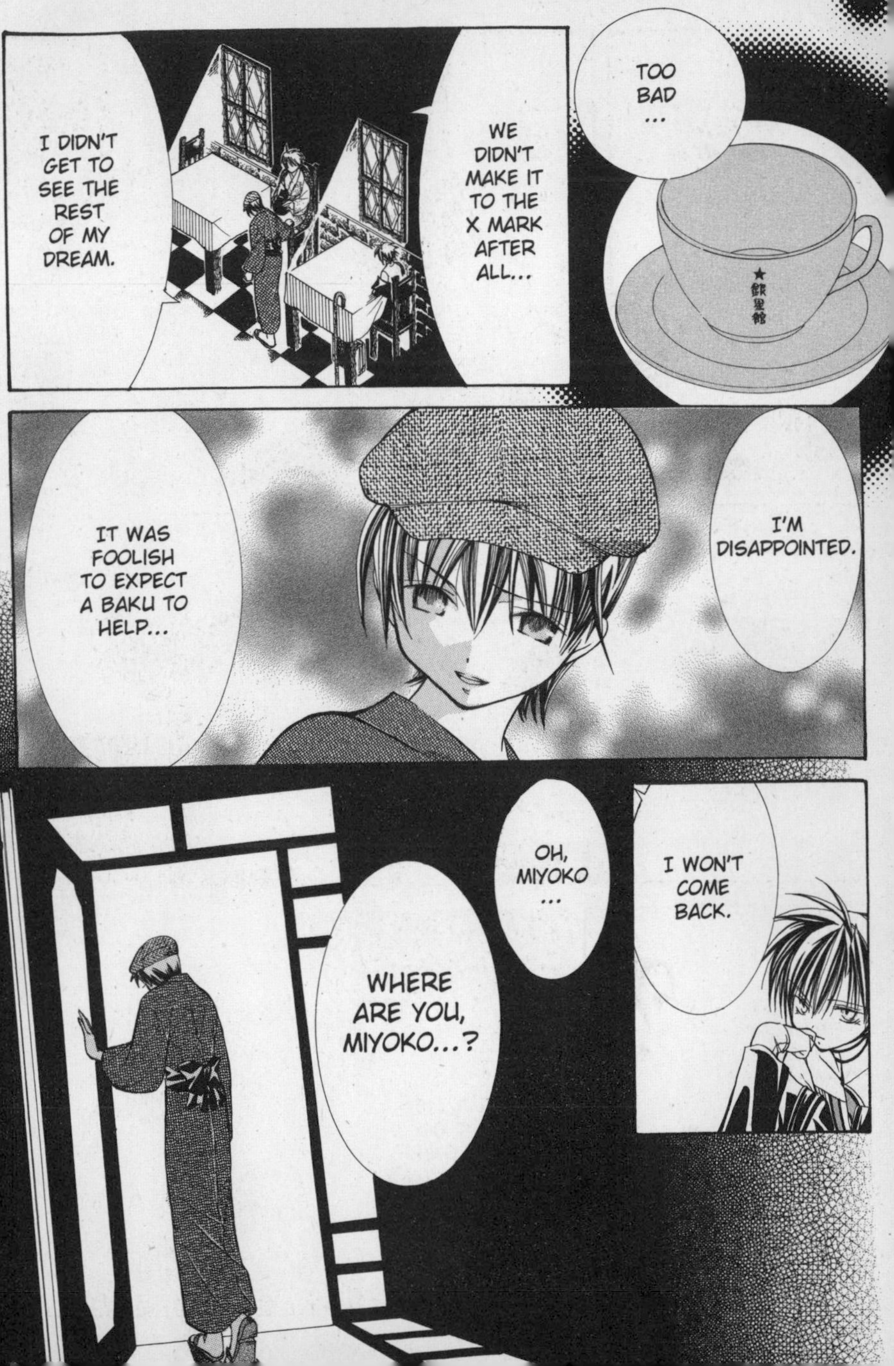
TOO BAD ...
WE DIDN'T MAKE IT TO THE X MARK AFTER ALL...
I DIDN'T GET TO SEE THE REST OF MY DREAM.
I'M DISAPPOINTED.
IT WAS FOOLISH TO EXPECT A BAKU TO HELP...
I WON'T COME BACK.
OH, MIYOKO ...
WHERE ARE YOU, MIYOKO...?

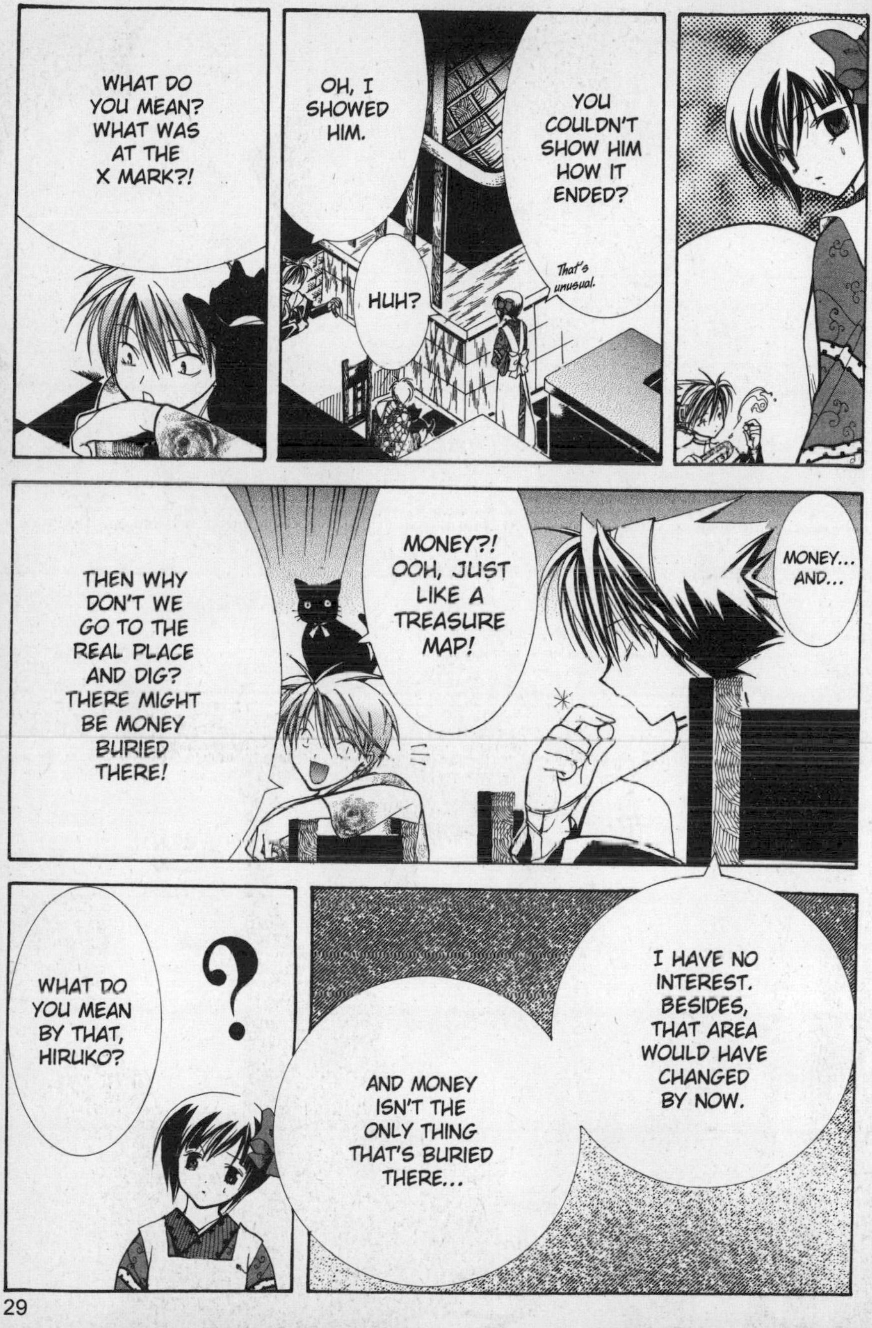
YOU COULDN'T SHOW HIM HOW IT ENDED?
That's unusual.
OH, I SHOWED HIM.
HUH?
WHAT DO YOU MEAN? WHAT WAS AT THE X MARK?!
MONEY... AND...
MONEY?! OOH, JUST LIKE A TREASURE MAP!
THEN WHY DON'T WE GO TO THE REAL PLACE AND DIG? THERE MIGHT BE MONEY BURIED THERE!
I HAVE NO INTEREST. BESIDES, THAT AREA WOULD HAVE CHANGED BY NOW.
AND MONEY ISN'T THE ONLY THING THAT'S BURIED THERE...
?
WHAT DO YOU MEAN BY THAT, HIRUKO?

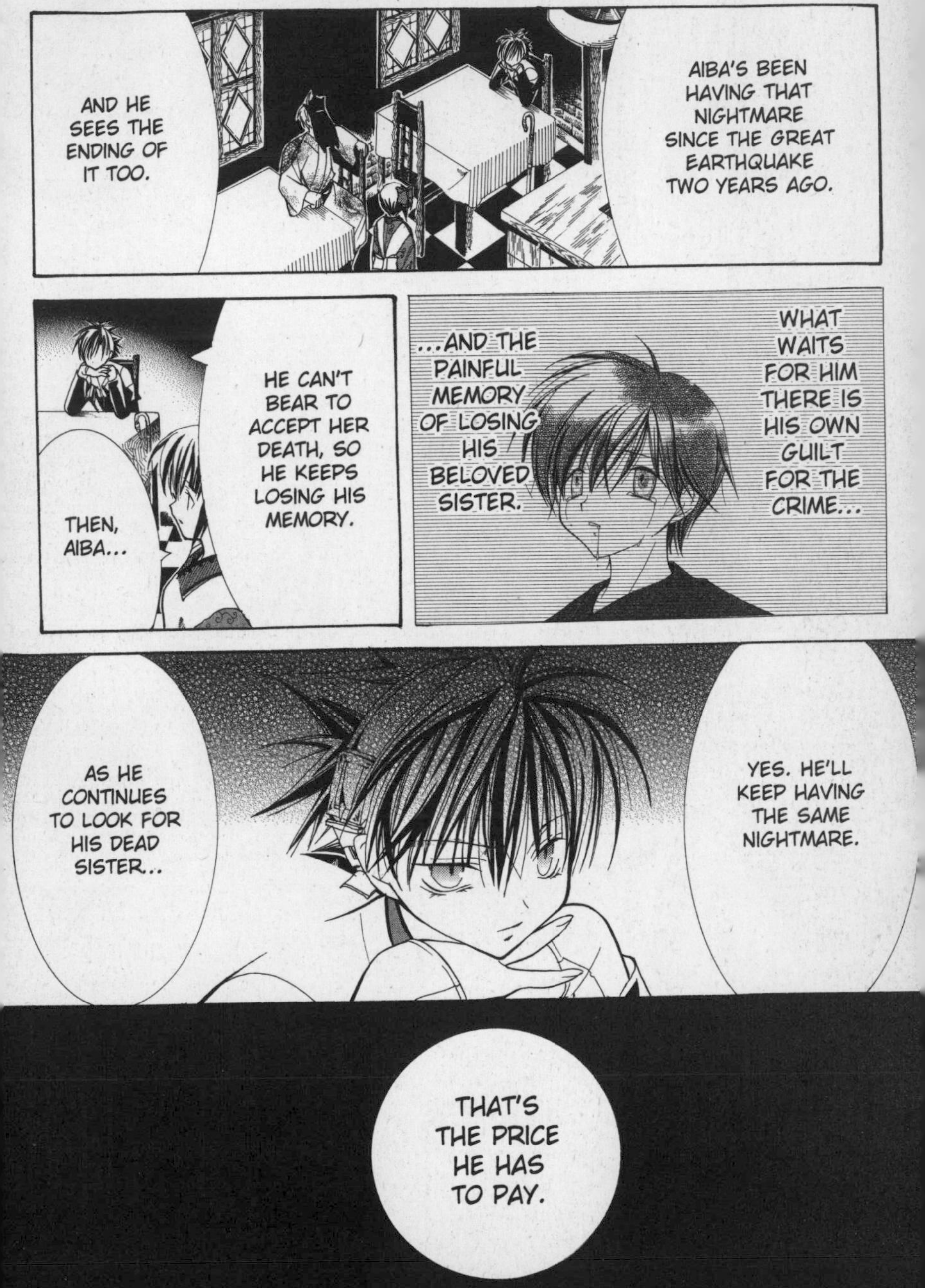
AIBA'S BEEN HAVING THAT NIGHTMARE SINCE THE GREAT EARTHQUAKE TWO YEARS AGO.
AND HE SEES THE ENDING OF IT TOO.
WHAT WAITS FOR HIM THERE IS HIS OWN GUILT FOR THE CRIME...
...AND THE PAINFUL MEMORY OF LOSING HIS BELOVED SISTER.
HE CAN'T BEAR TO ACCEPT HER DEATH, SO HE KEEPS LOSING HIS MEMORY.
THEN, AIBA...
YES. HE'LL KEEP HAVING THE SAME NIGHTMARE.
AS HE CONTINUES TO LOOK FOR HIS DEAD SISTER...
THAT'S THE PRICE HE HAS TO PAY.

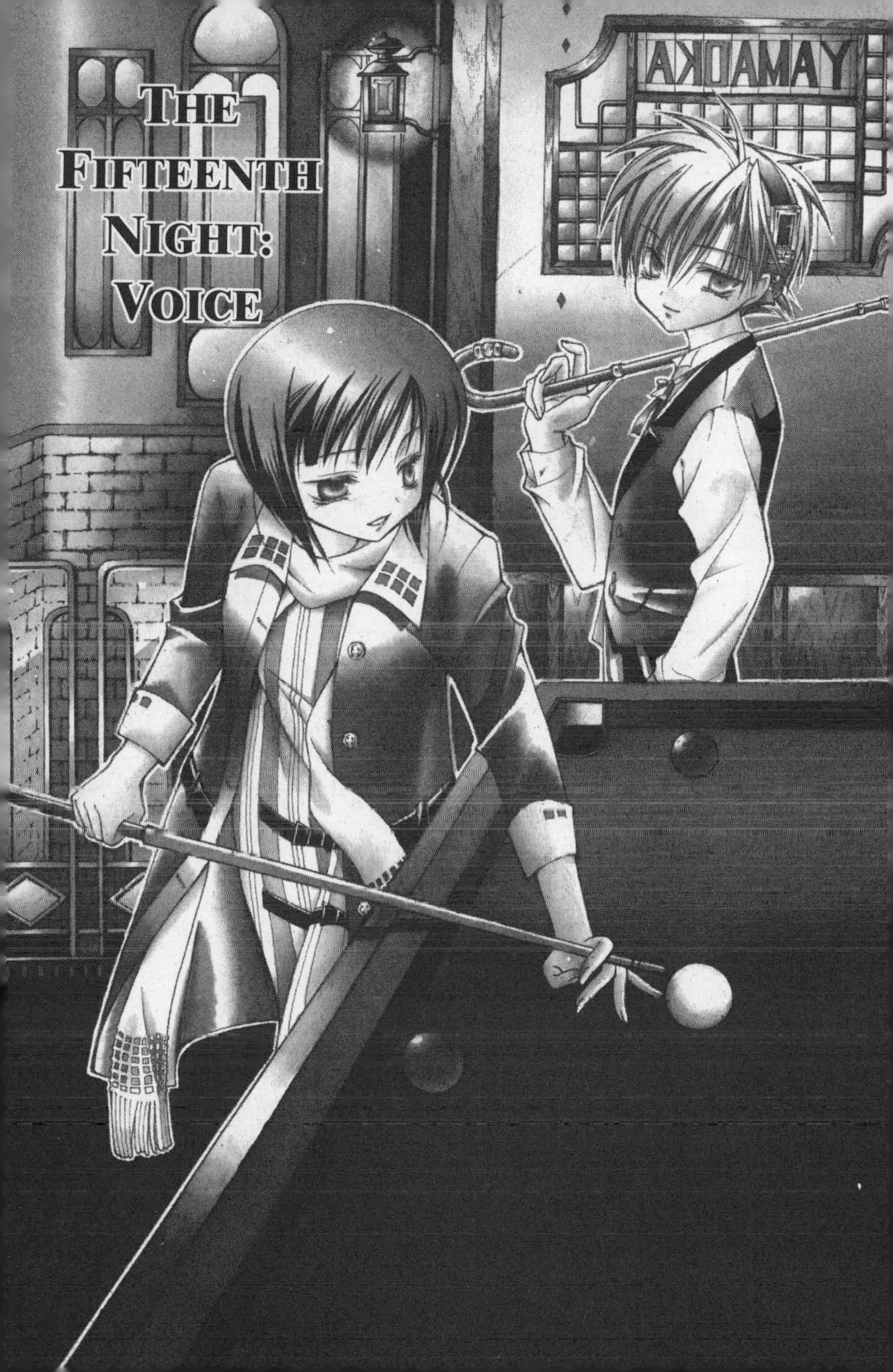
The Fifteenth Night: Voice

I really like this logo. What do you think? It looks like a sign for an Ear, Nose and Throat Clinic.

It's a play on the original logo.
I wish the magazine would use it at least once, because I think it's really fun. If the magazine readers would write "logo" five times in the margins of the readers' survey cards and send them in, it just might work. (laugh)
Please! There's strength in numbers! *Please, help!* (laugh)

I drew the logo on a mouse pad with a marker and gave it to Mashiba as a present, but the ink faded after only six months. It was so sad! If it looks like this at six months, I wonder what it will look like in three years! Probably really ripe!

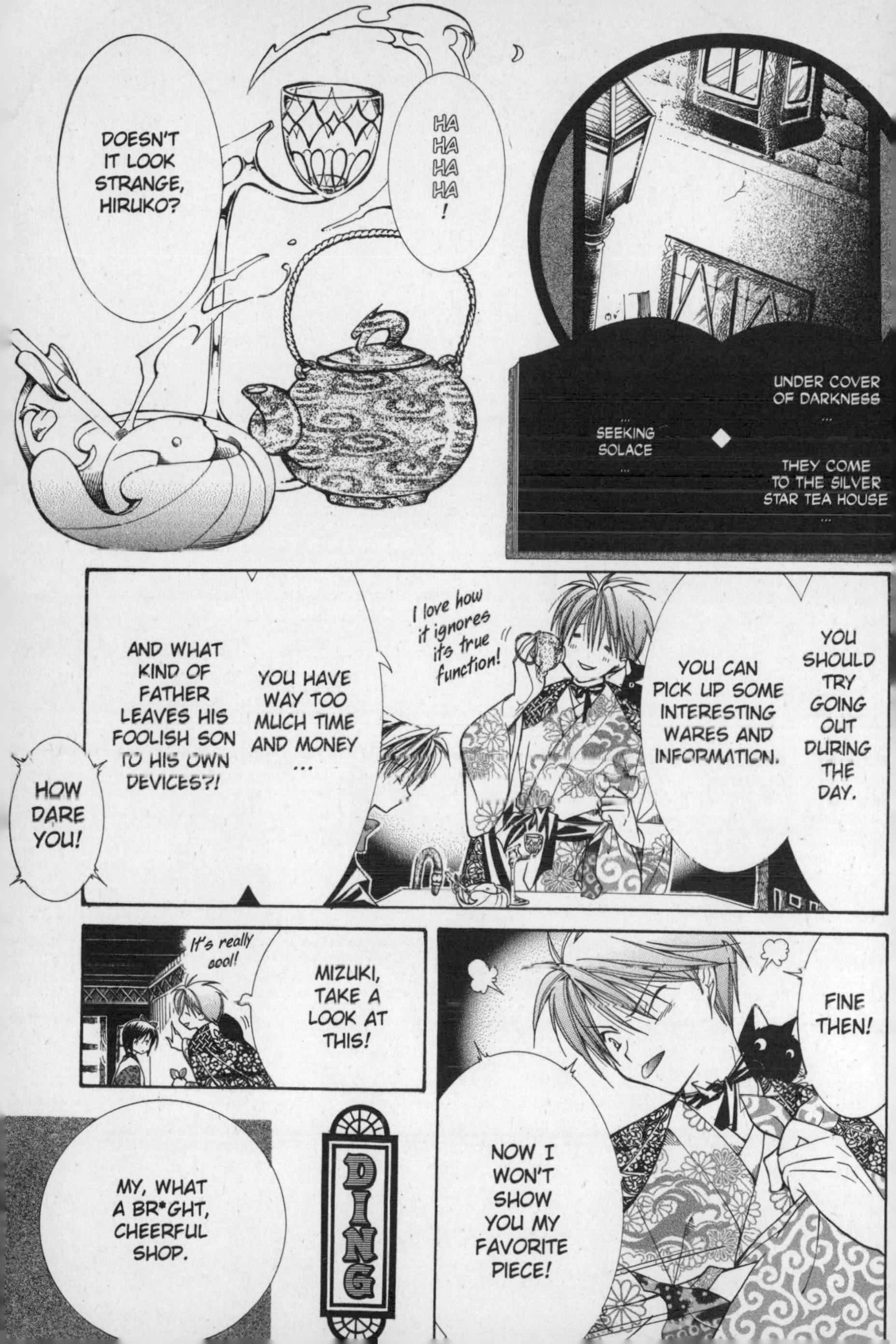
UNDER COVER OF DARKNESS ...
THEY COME TO THE SILVER STAR TEA HOUSE ...
... SEEKING SOLACE ...
HA HA HA HA!
DOESN'T IT LOOK STRANGE, HIRUKO?
YOU SHOULD TRY GOING OUT DURING THE DAY.
YOU CAN PICK UP SOME INTERESTING WARES AND INFORMATION.
I love how it ignores its true function!
YOU HAVE WAY TOO MUCH TIME AND MONEY ...
AND WHAT KIND OF FATHER LEAVES HIS FOOLISH SON TO HIS OWN DEVICES?!
HOW DARE YOU!
FINE THEN!
NOW I WON'T SHOW YOU MY FAVORITE PIECE!
MIZUKI, TAKE A LOOK AT THIS!
It's really cool!
DING
MY, WHAT A BR*GHT, CHEERFUL SHOP.

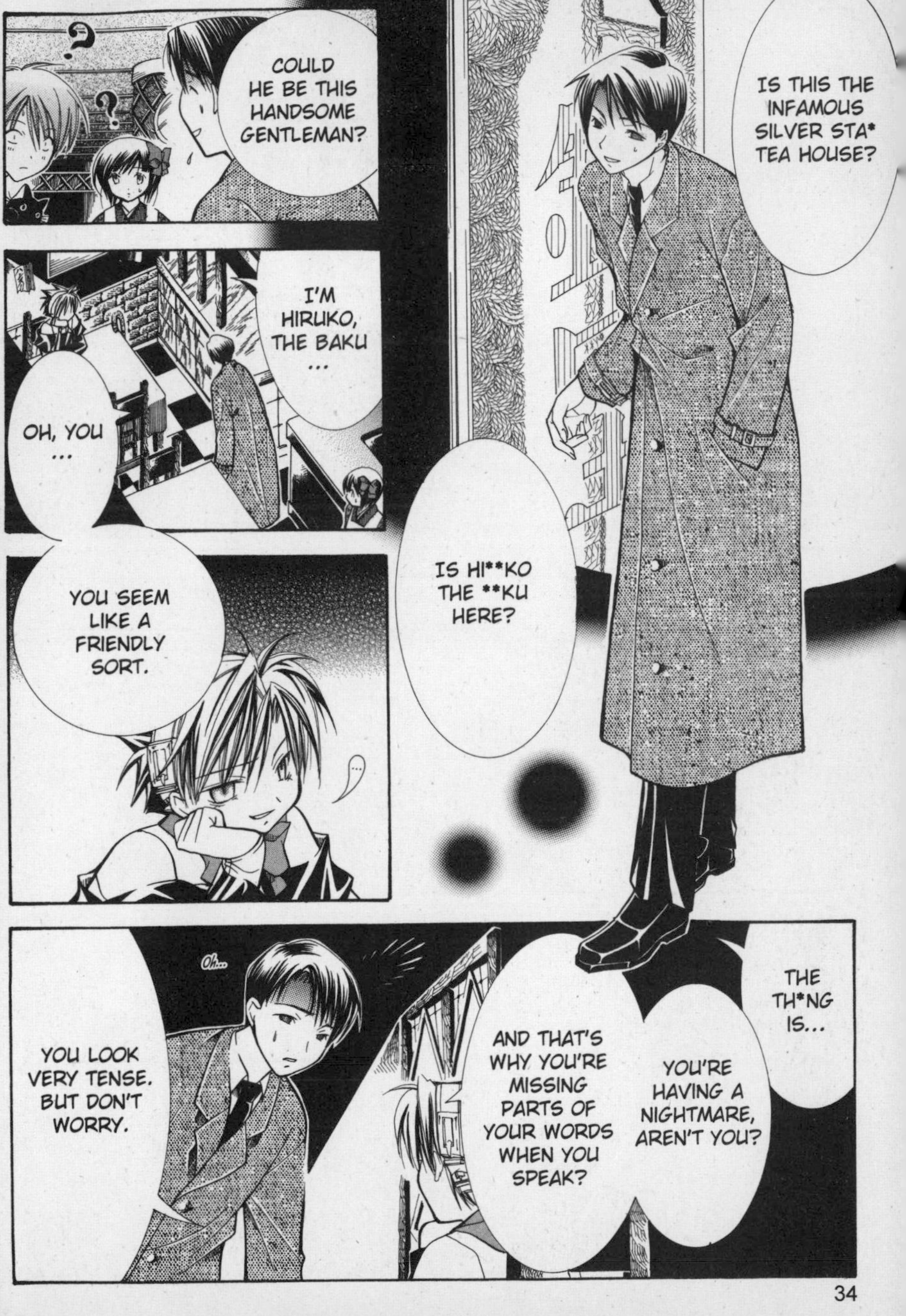
IS THIS THE INFAMOUS SILVER STA* TEA HOUSE?
IS HI**KO THE **KU HERE?
COULD HE BE THIS HANDSOME GENTLEMAN?
I'M HIRUKO, THE BAKU ...
OH, YOU ...
YOU SEEM LIKE A FRIENDLY SORT.
...
THE TH*NG IS...
YOU'RE HAVING A NIGHTMARE, AREN'T YOU?
AND THAT'S WHY YOU'RE MISSING PARTS OF YOUR WORDS WHEN YOU SPEAK?
Oh...
YOU LOOK VERY TENSE. BUT DON'T WORRY.

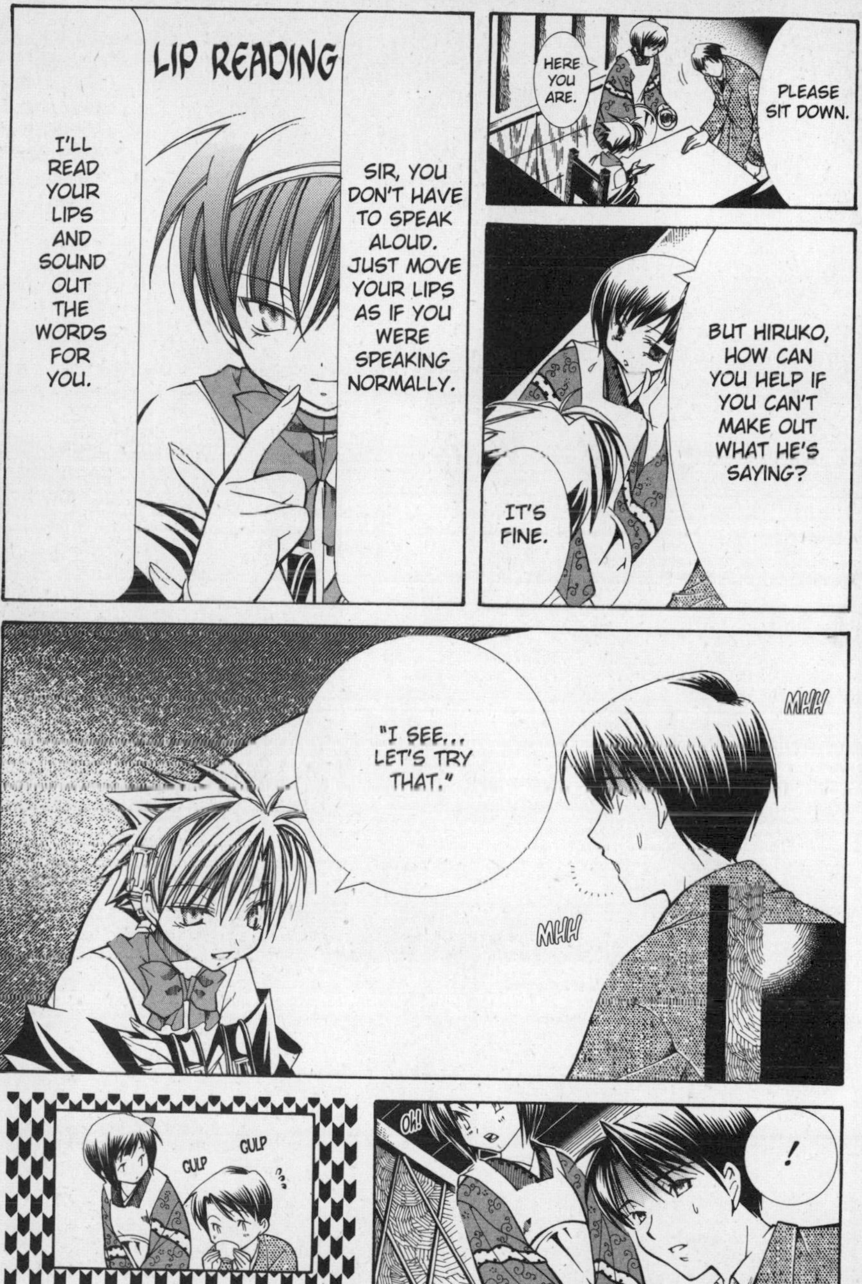
PLEASE SIT DOWN.
HERE YOU ARE.
BUT HIRUKO, HOW CAN YOU HELP IF YOU CAN'T MAKE OUT WHAT HE'S SAYING?
IT'S FINE.
LIP READING
SIR, YOU DON'T HAVE TO SPEAK ALOUD. JUST MOVE YOUR LIPS AS IF YOU WERE SPEAKING NORMALLY.
I'LL READ YOUR LIPS AND SOUND OUT THE WORDS FOR YOU.
MHH
"I SEE... LET'S TRY THAT."
MHH
!
OH!
GULP
GULP

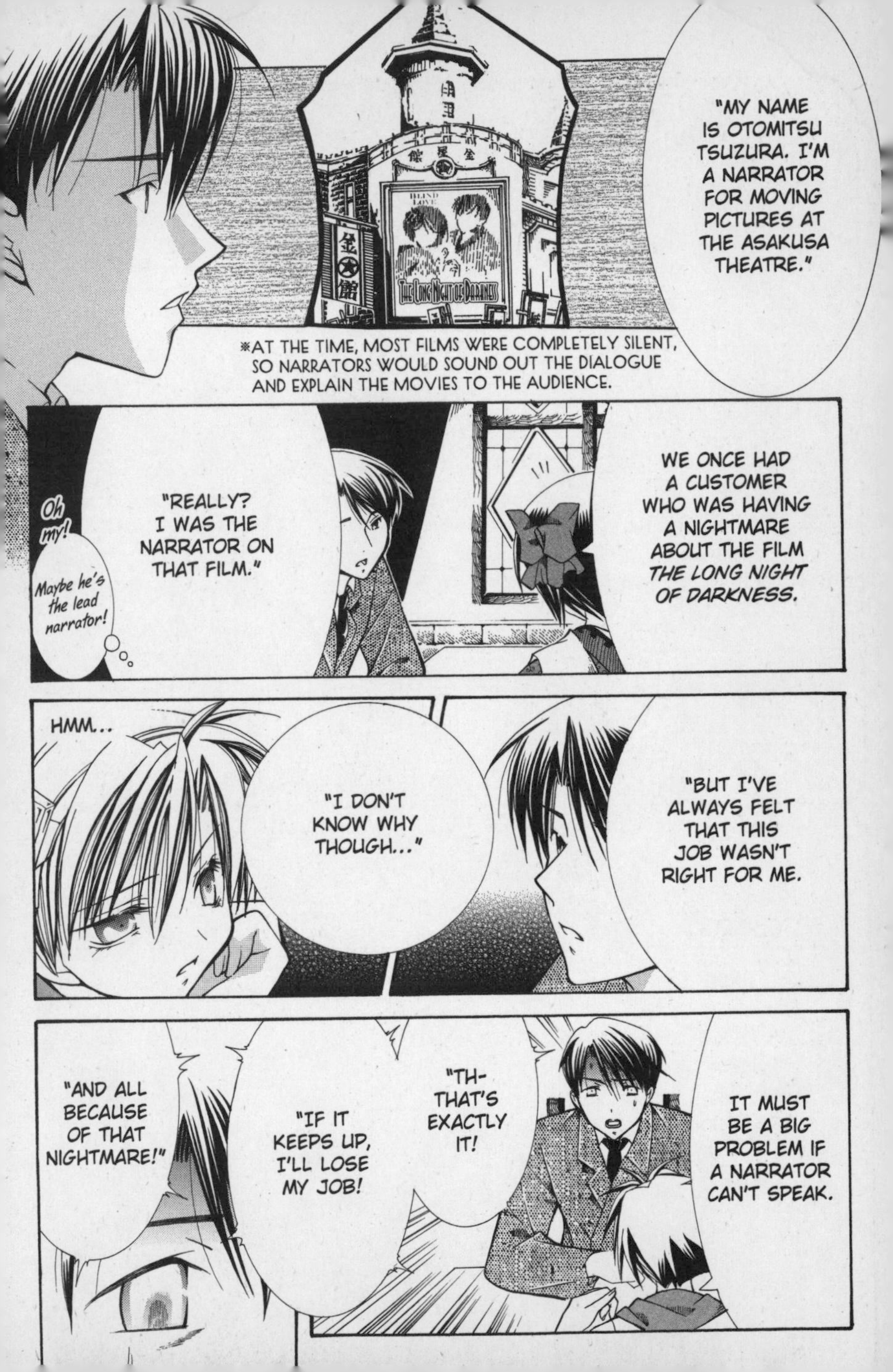
"MY NAME IS OTOMITSU TSUZURA. I'M A NARRATOR FOR MOVING PICTURES AT THE ASAKUSA THEATRE."
BLIND LOVE
THE LONG NIGHT OF DARKNESS
※AT THE TIME, MOST FILMS WERE COMPLETELY SILENT, SO NARRATORS WOULD SOUND OUT THE DIALOGUE AND EXPLAIN THE MOVIES TO THE AUDIENCE.
WE ONCE HAD A CUSTOMER WHO WAS HAVING A NIGHTMARE ABOUT THE FILM *THE LONG NIGHT OF DARKNESS.*
"REALLY? I WAS THE NARRATOR ON THAT FILM."
Oh my!
Maybe he's the lead narrator!
"BUT I'VE ALWAYS FELT THAT THIS JOB WASN'T RIGHT FOR ME.
"I DON'T KNOW WHY THOUGH..."
HMM...
IT MUST BE A BIG PROBLEM IF A NARRATOR CAN'T SPEAK.
"TH-THAT'S EXACTLY IT!
"IF IT KEEPS UP, I'LL LOSE MY JOB!
"AND ALL BECAUSE OF THAT NIGHTMARE!"

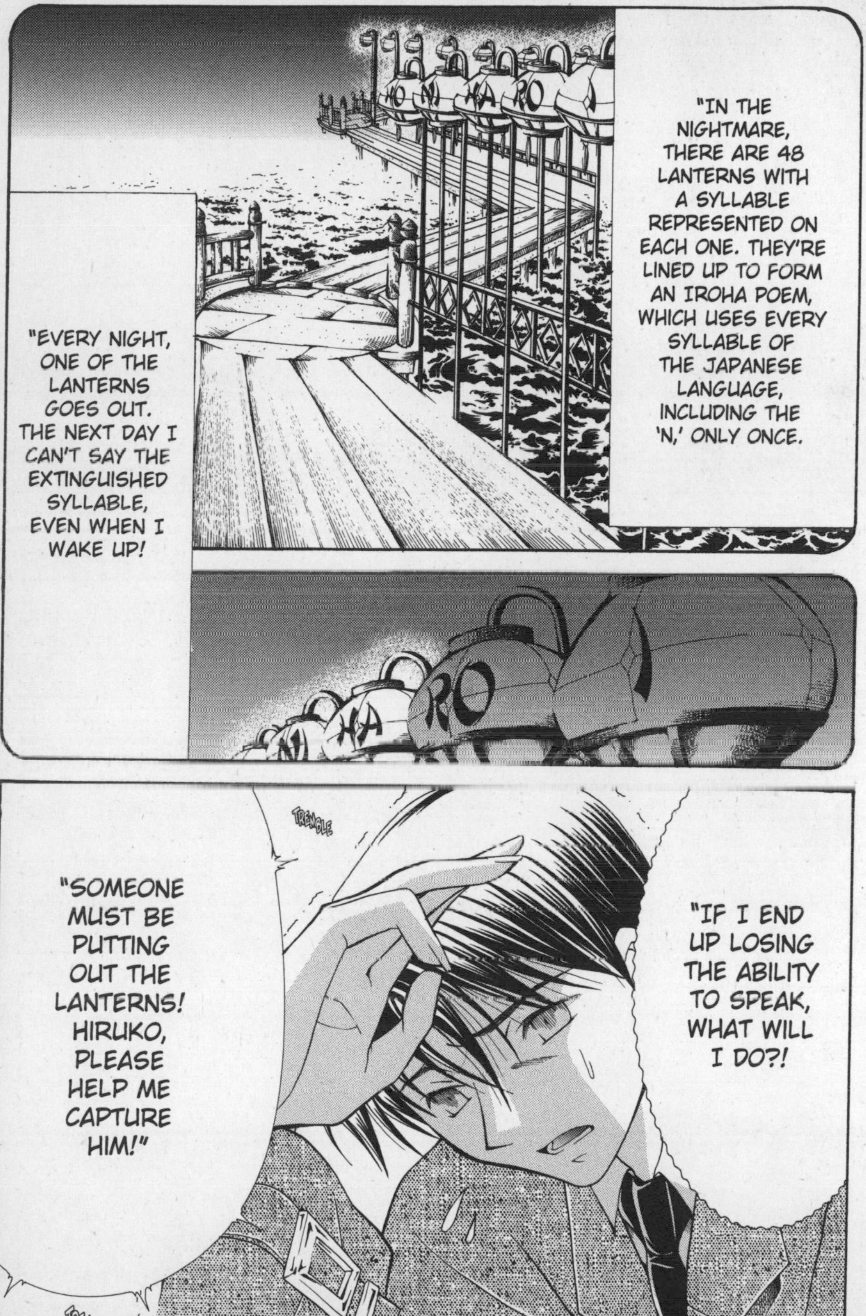
"IN THE NIGHTMARE, THERE ARE 48 LANTERNS WITH A SYLLABLE REPRESENTED ON EACH ONE. THEY'RE LINED UP TO FORM AN IROHA POEM, WHICH USES EVERY SYLLABLE OF THE JAPANESE LANGUAGE, INCLUDING THE 'N,' ONLY ONCE.
"EVERY NIGHT, ONE OF THE LANTERNS GOES OUT. THE NEXT DAY I CAN'T SAY THE EXTINGUISHED SYLLABLE, EVEN WHEN I WAKE UP!
"IF I END UP LOSING THE ABILITY TO SPEAK, WHAT WILL I DO?!
TREMBLE
"SOMEONE MUST BE PUTTING OUT THE LANTERNS! HIRUKO, PLEASE HELP ME CAPTURE HIM!"
TREMBLE

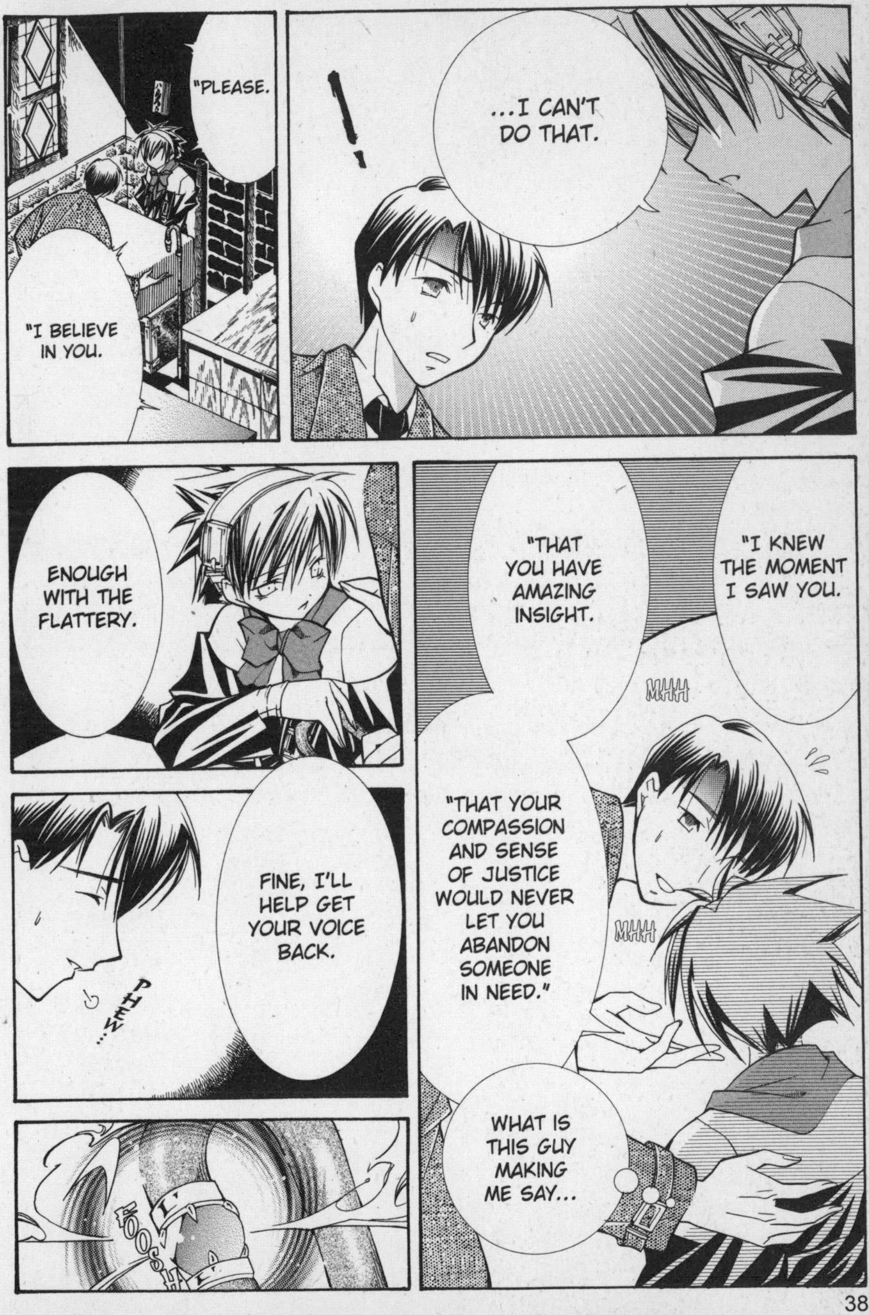
!
...I CAN'T DO THAT.
"PLEASE.
"I BELIEVE IN YOU.
"I KNEW THE MOMENT I SAW YOU.
"THAT YOU HAVE AMAZING INSIGHT.
MHH
"THAT YOUR COMPASSION AND SENSE OF JUSTICE WOULD NEVER LET YOU ABANDON SOMEONE IN NEED."
MHH
WHAT IS THIS GUY MAKING ME SAY...
ENOUGH WITH THE FLATTERY.
FINE, I'LL HELP GET YOUR VOICE BACK.
PHEW...
FOOSH

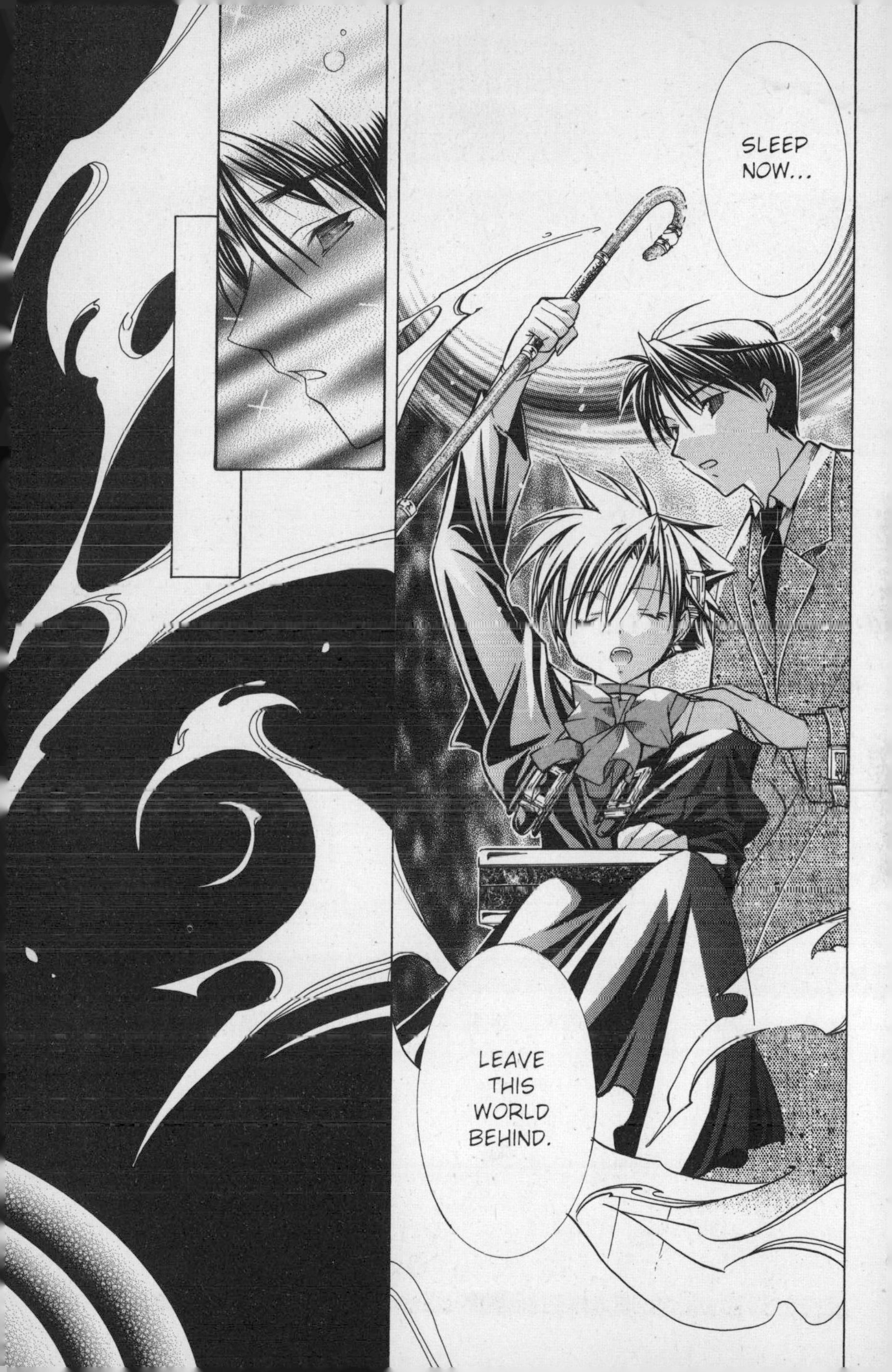
SLEEP NOW...
LEAVE THIS WORLD BEHIND.

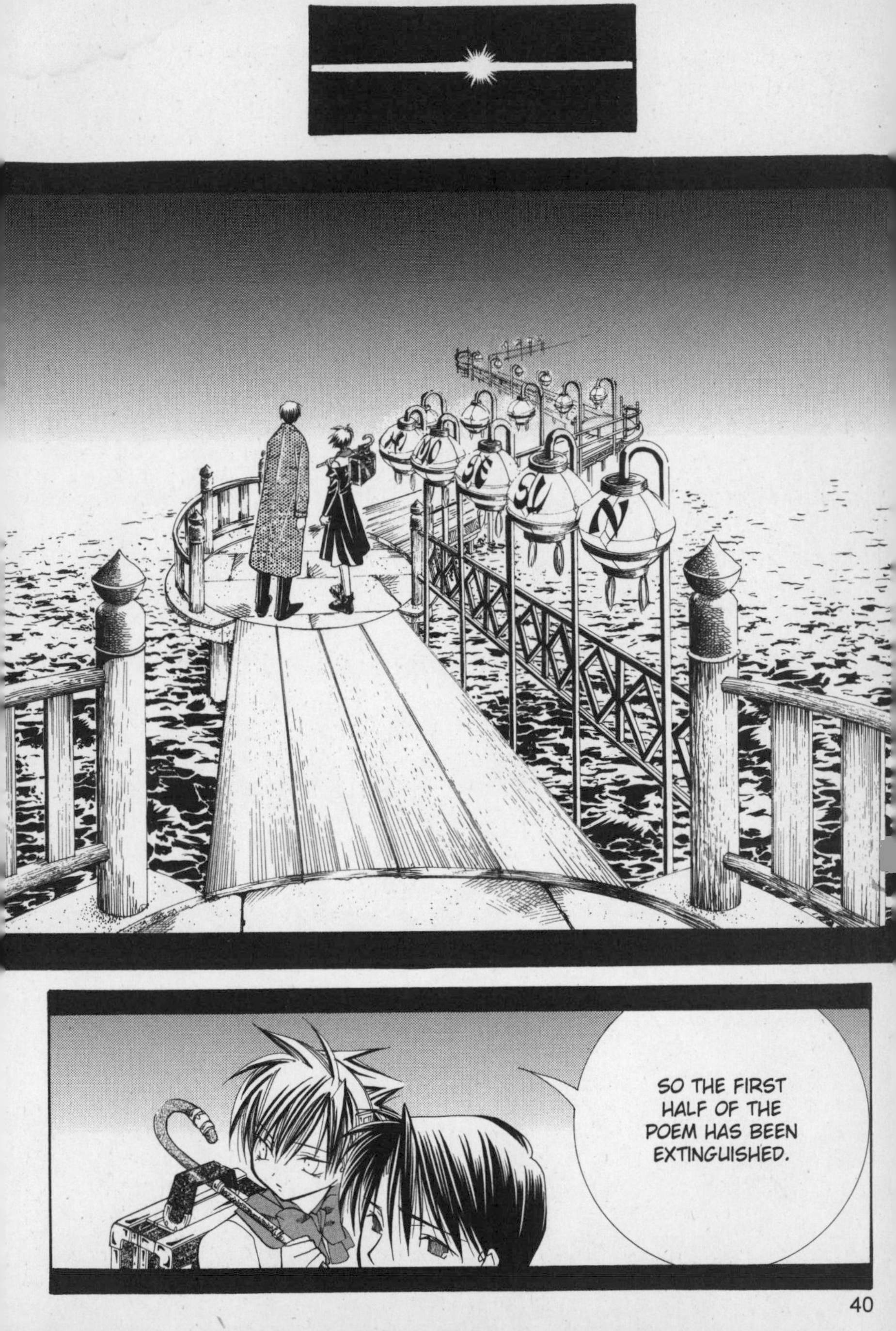
SO THE FIRST
HALF OF THE
POEM HAS BEEN
EXTINGUISHED.

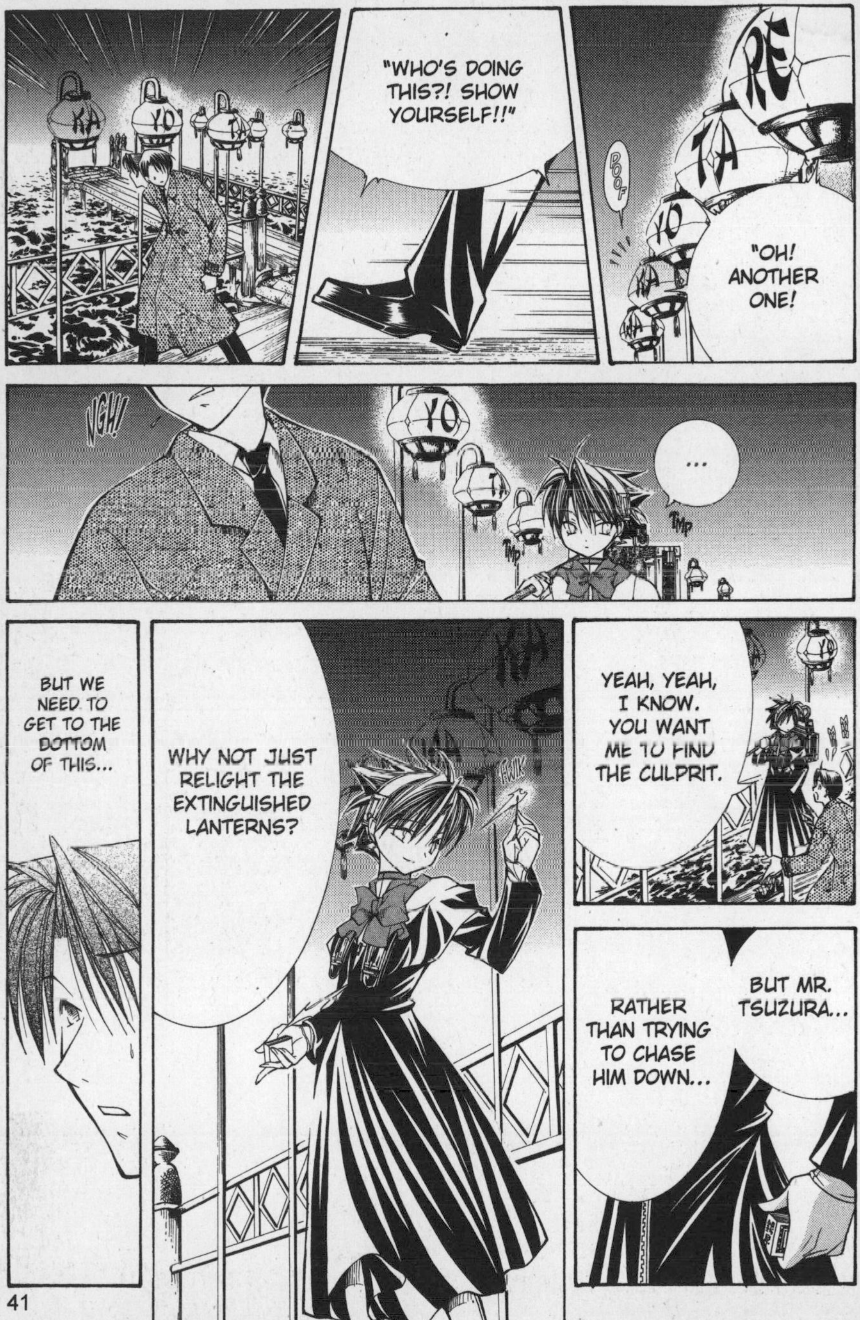
POOF
"OH! ANOTHER ONE!
"WHO'S DOING THIS?! SHOW YOURSELF!!"
NGH!
...
TMP
TMP
YEAH, YEAH, I KNOW. YOU WANT ME TO FIND THE CULPRIT.
BUT MR. TSUZURA...
RATHER THAN TRYING TO CHASE HIM DOWN...
WHY NOT JUST RELIGHT THE EXTINGUISHED LANTERNS?
BUT WE NEED TO GET TO THE BOTTOM OF THIS...

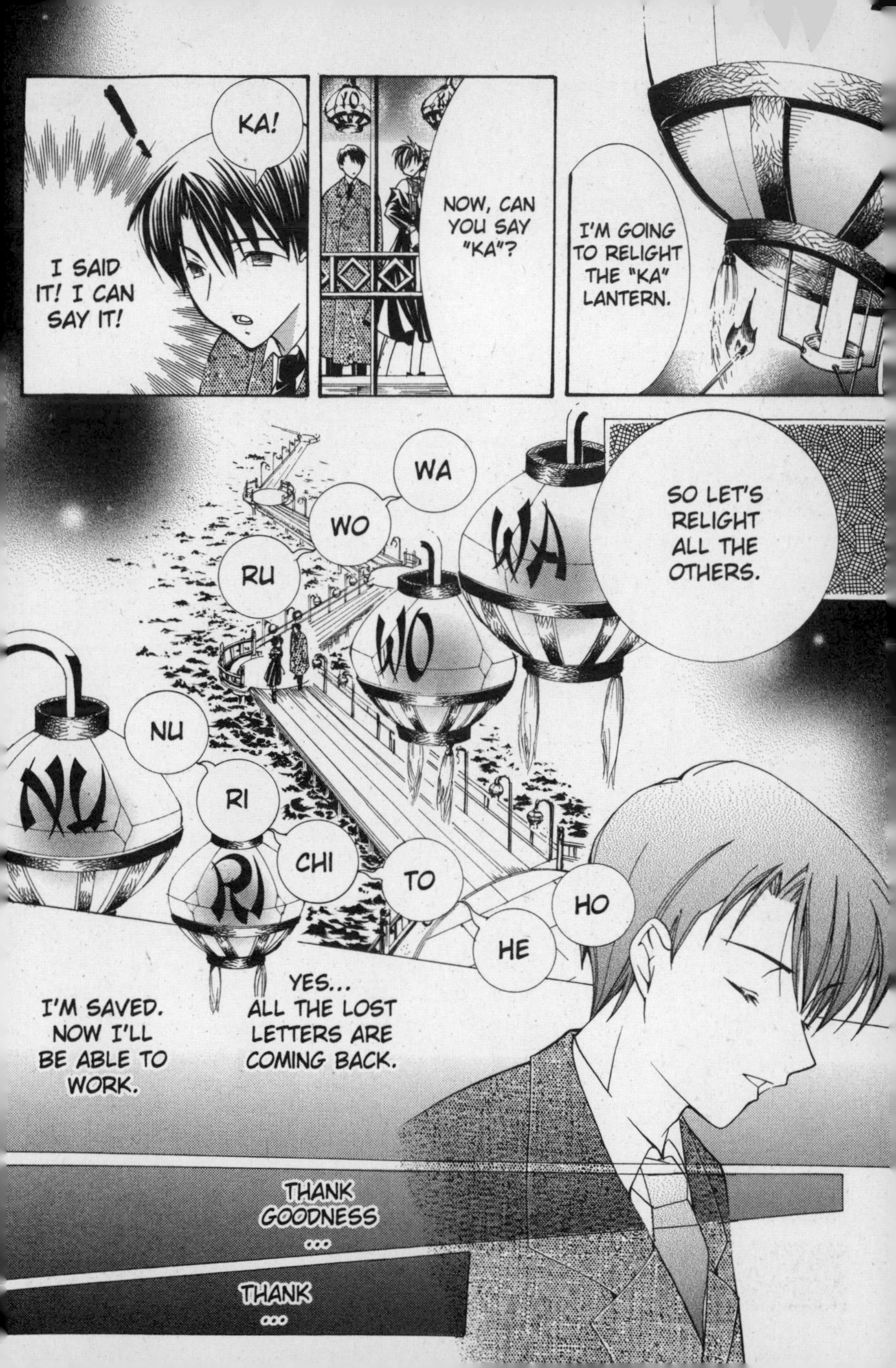
I'M GOING TO RELIGHT THE "KA" LANTERN.
NOW, CAN YOU SAY "KA"?
KA!
I SAID IT! I CAN SAY IT!
SO LET'S RELIGHT ALL THE OTHERS.
WA
WA
WO
WO
RU
NU
NU
RI
RI
CHI
TO
HE
HO
YES... ALL THE LOST LETTERS ARE COMING BACK.
I'M SAVED. NOW I'LL BE ABLE TO WORK.
THANK GOODNESS ...
THANK ...

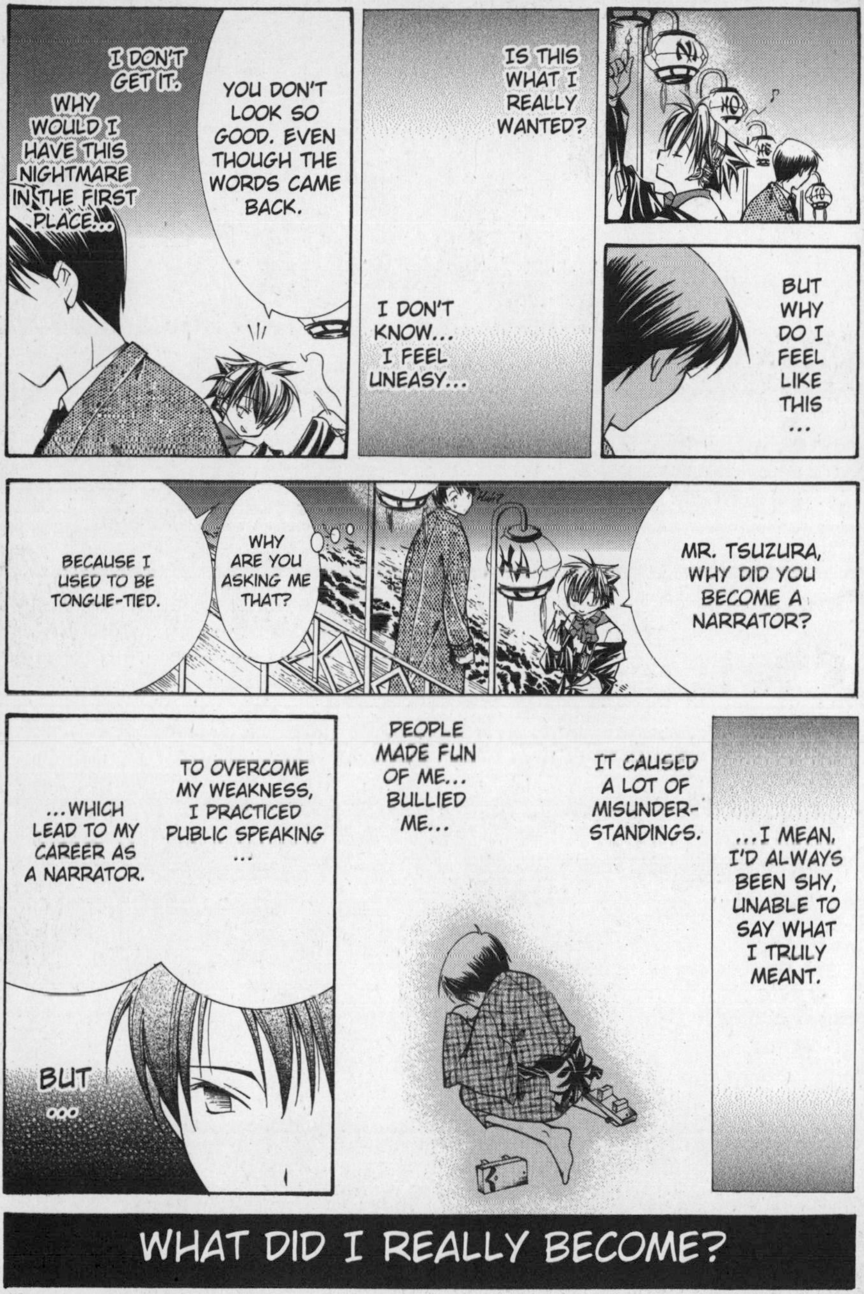
BUT WHY DO I FEEL LIKE THIS...
IS THIS WHAT I REALLY WANTED?
I DON'T KNOW... I FEEL UNEASY...
YOU DON'T LOOK SO GOOD. EVEN THOUGH THE WORDS CAME BACK.
I DON'T GET IT.
WHY WOULD I HAVE THIS NIGHTMARE IN THE FIRST PLACE...
MR. TSUZURA, WHY DID YOU BECOME A NARRATOR?
WHY ARE YOU ASKING ME THAT?
BECAUSE I USED TO BE TONGUE-TIED.
...I MEAN, I'D ALWAYS BEEN SHY, UNABLE TO SAY WHAT I TRULY MEANT.
IT CAUSED A LOT OF MISUNDERSTANDINGS.
PEOPLE MADE FUN OF ME... BULLIED ME...
TO OVERCOME MY WEAKNESS, I PRACTICED PUBLIC SPEAKING...
...WHICH LEAD TO MY CAREER AS A NARRATOR.
BUT...
WHAT DID I REALLY BECOME?

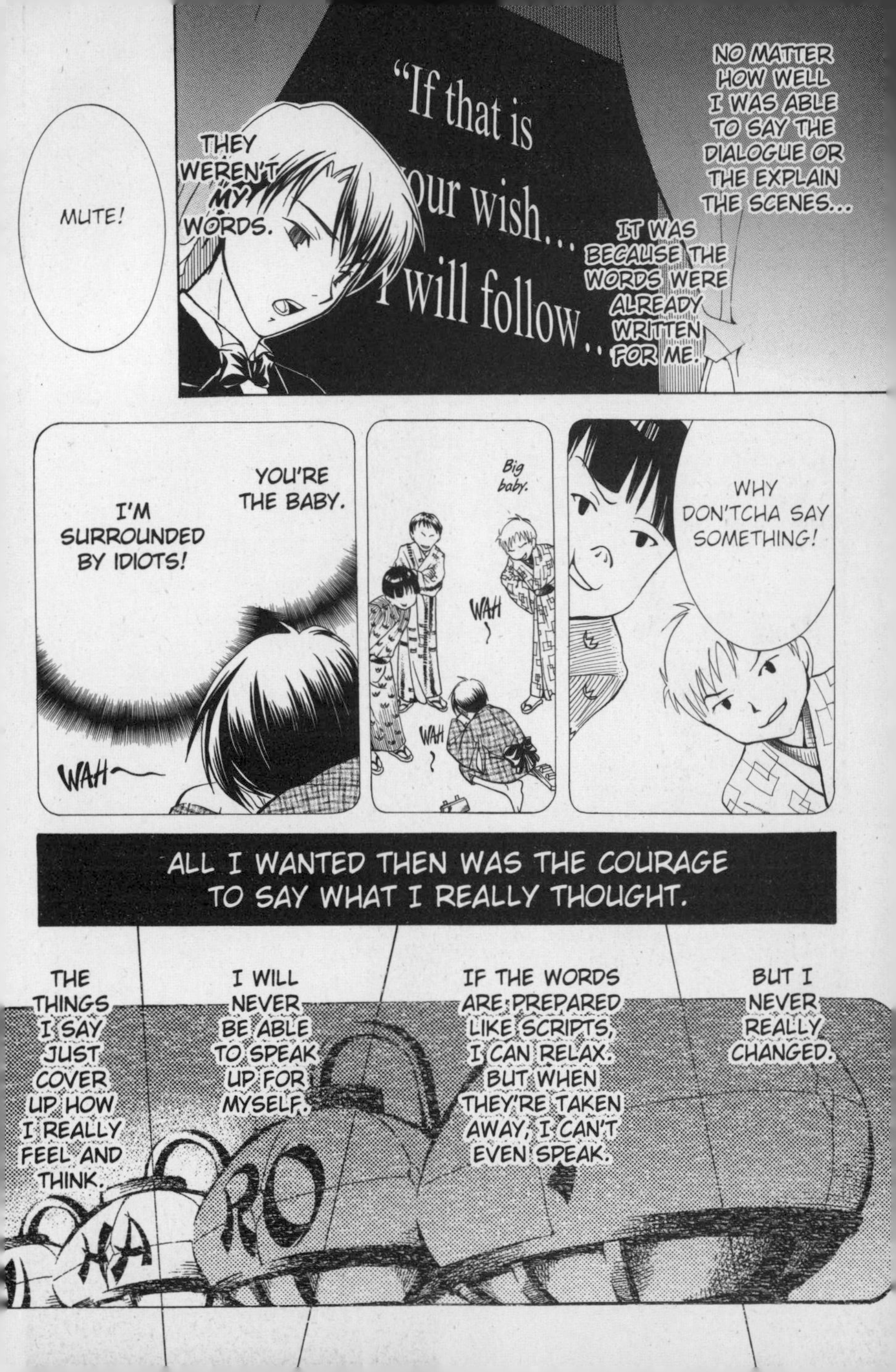

NO MATTER HOW WELL I WAS ABLE TO SAY THE DIALOGUE OR THE EXPLAIN THE SCENES...
IT WAS BECAUSE THE WORDS WERE ALREADY WRITTEN FOR ME.
“If that is
our wish....
I will follow...
THEY WEREN'T MY WORDS.
MUTE!
WHY DON'TCHA SAY SOMETHING!
Big baby.
WAH
WAH
YOU'RE THE BABY.
I'M SURROUNDED BY IDIOTS!
WAH~
ALL I WANTED THEN WAS THE COURAGE TO SAY WHAT I REALLY THOUGHT.
BUT I NEVER REALLY CHANGED.
IF THE WORDS ARE PREPARED LIKE SCRIPTS, I CAN RELAX. BUT WHEN THEY'RE TAKEN AWAY, I CAN'T EVEN SPEAK.
I WILL NEVER BE ABLE TO SPEAK UP FOR MYSELF.
THE THINGS I SAY JUST COVER UP HOW I REALLY FEEL AND THINK.
RO
HA

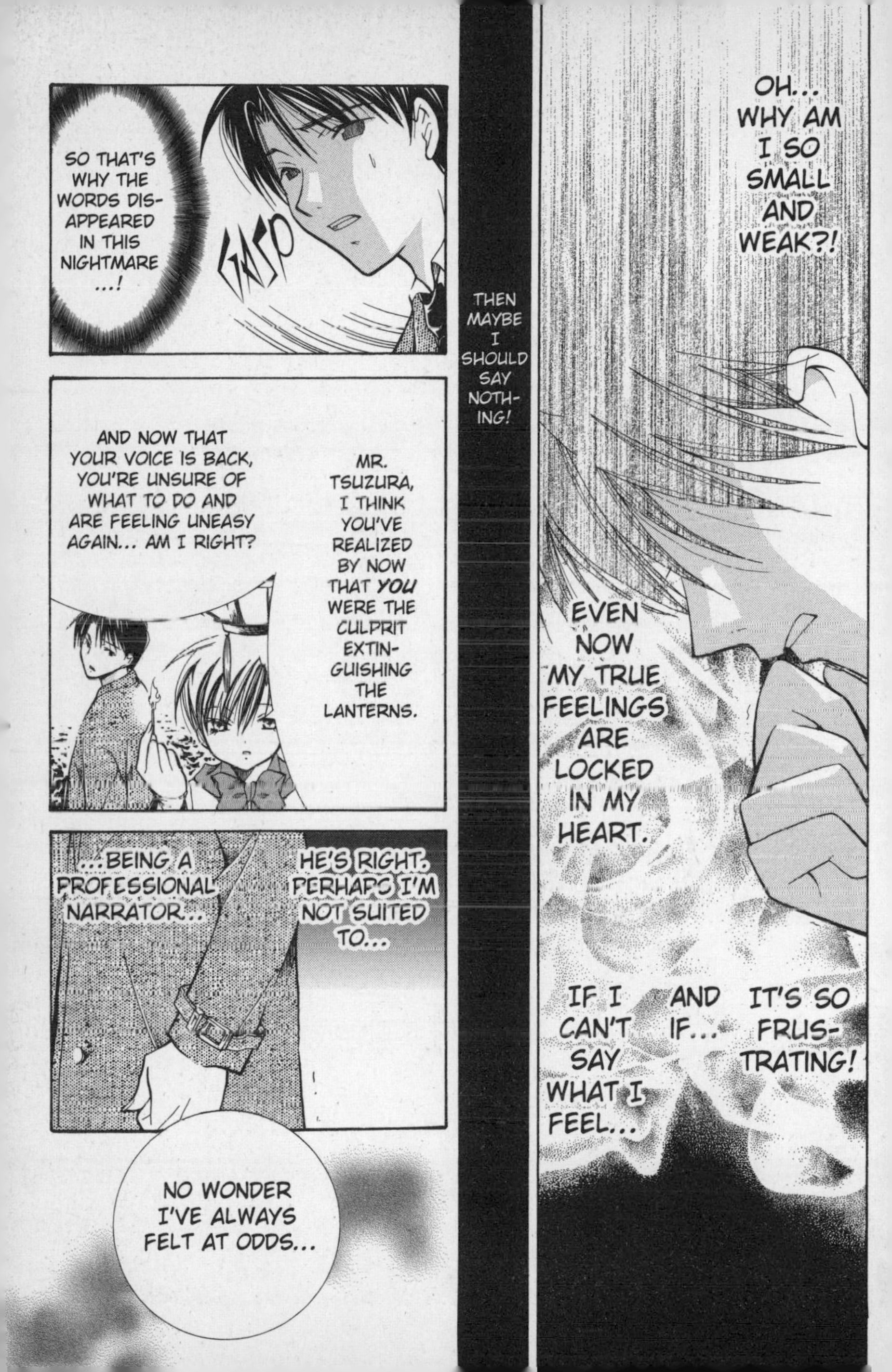
OH... WHY AM I SO SMALL AND WEAK?!
EVEN NOW MY TRUE FEELINGS ARE LOCKED IN MY HEART.
IT'S SO FRUS-TRATING!
AND IF...
IF I CAN'T SAY WHAT I FEEL...
THEN MAYBE I SHOULD SAY NOTH-ING!
SO THAT'S WHY THE WORDS DIS-APPEARED IN THIS NIGHTMARE ...!
GASP
MR. TSUZURA, I THINK YOU'VE REALIZED BY NOW THAT *YOU* WERE THE CULPRIT EXTIN-GUISHING THE LANTERNS.
AND NOW THAT YOUR VOICE IS BACK, YOU'RE UNSURE OF WHAT TO DO AND ARE FEELING UNEASY AGAIN... AM I RIGHT?
HE'S RIGHT. PERHAPS I'M NOT SUITED TO...
...BEING A PROFESSIONAL NARRATOR...
NO WONDER I'VE ALWAYS FELT AT ODDS...

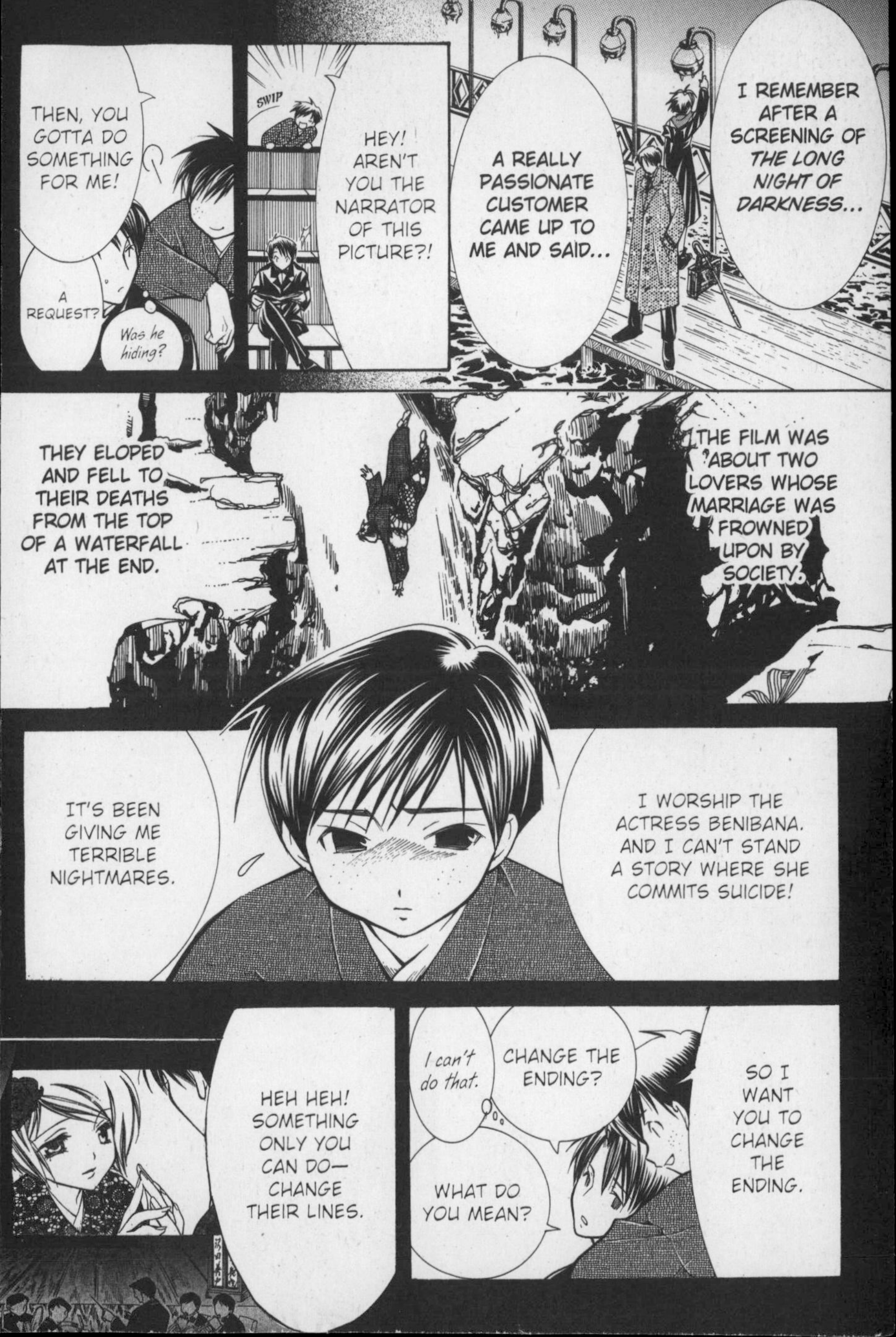
I REMEMBER AFTER A SCREENING OF *THE LONG NIGHT OF DARKNESS*...
A REALLY PASSIONATE CUSTOMER CAME UP TO ME AND SAID...
SWIP
HEY! AREN'T YOU THE NARRATOR OF THIS PICTURE?!
THEN, YOU GOTTA DO SOMETHING FOR ME!
A REQUEST?
*Was he hiding?*
THE FILM WAS ABOUT TWO LOVERS WHOSE MARRIAGE WAS FROWNED UPON BY SOCIETY.
THEY ELOPED AND FELL TO THEIR DEATHS FROM THE TOP OF A WATERFALL AT THE END.
I WORSHIP THE ACTRESS BENIBANA. AND I CAN'T STAND A STORY WHERE SHE COMMITS SUICIDE!
IT'S BEEN GIVING ME TERRIBLE NIGHTMARES.
SO I WANT YOU TO CHANGE THE ENDING.
CHANGE THE ENDING?
*I can't do that.*
WHAT DO YOU MEAN?
HEH HEH! SOMETHING ONLY YOU CAN DO—CHANGE THEIR LINES.

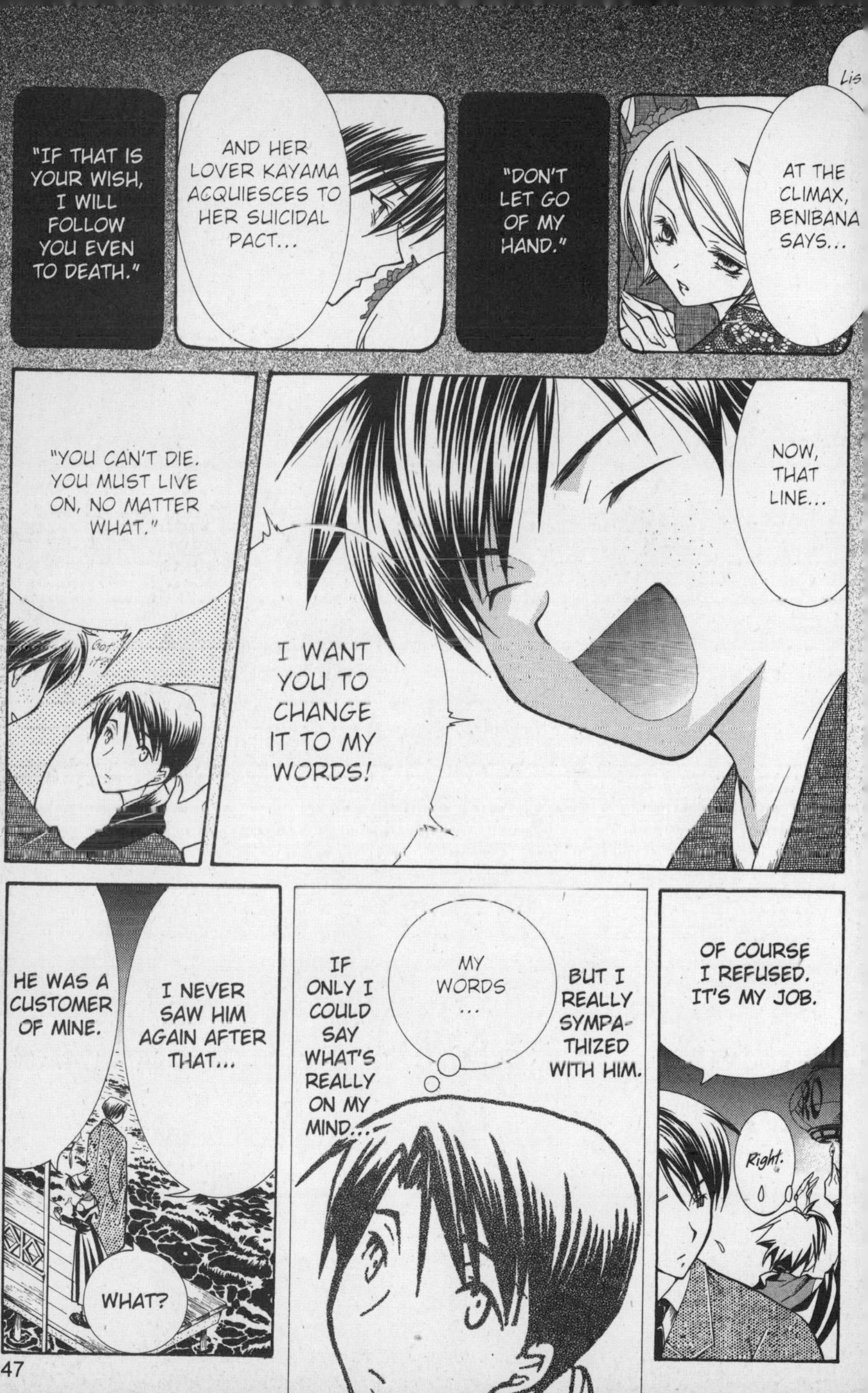
Lis
AT THE CLIMAX, BENIBANA SAYS...
"DON'T LET GO OF MY HAND."
AND HER LOVER KAYAMA ACQUIESCES TO HER SUICIDAL PACT...
"IF THAT IS YOUR WISH, I WILL FOLLOW YOU EVEN TO DEATH."
NOW, THAT LINE...
I WANT YOU TO CHANGE IT TO MY WORDS!
"YOU CAN'T DIE. YOU MUST LIVE ON, NO MATTER WHAT."
OF COURSE I REFUSED. IT'S MY JOB.
Right.
BUT I REALLY SYMPA-THIZED WITH HIM.
MY WORDS...
IF ONLY I COULD SAY WHAT'S REALLY ON MY MIND...
I NEVER SAW HIM AGAIN AFTER THAT...
HE WAS A CUSTOMER OF MINE.
WHAT?

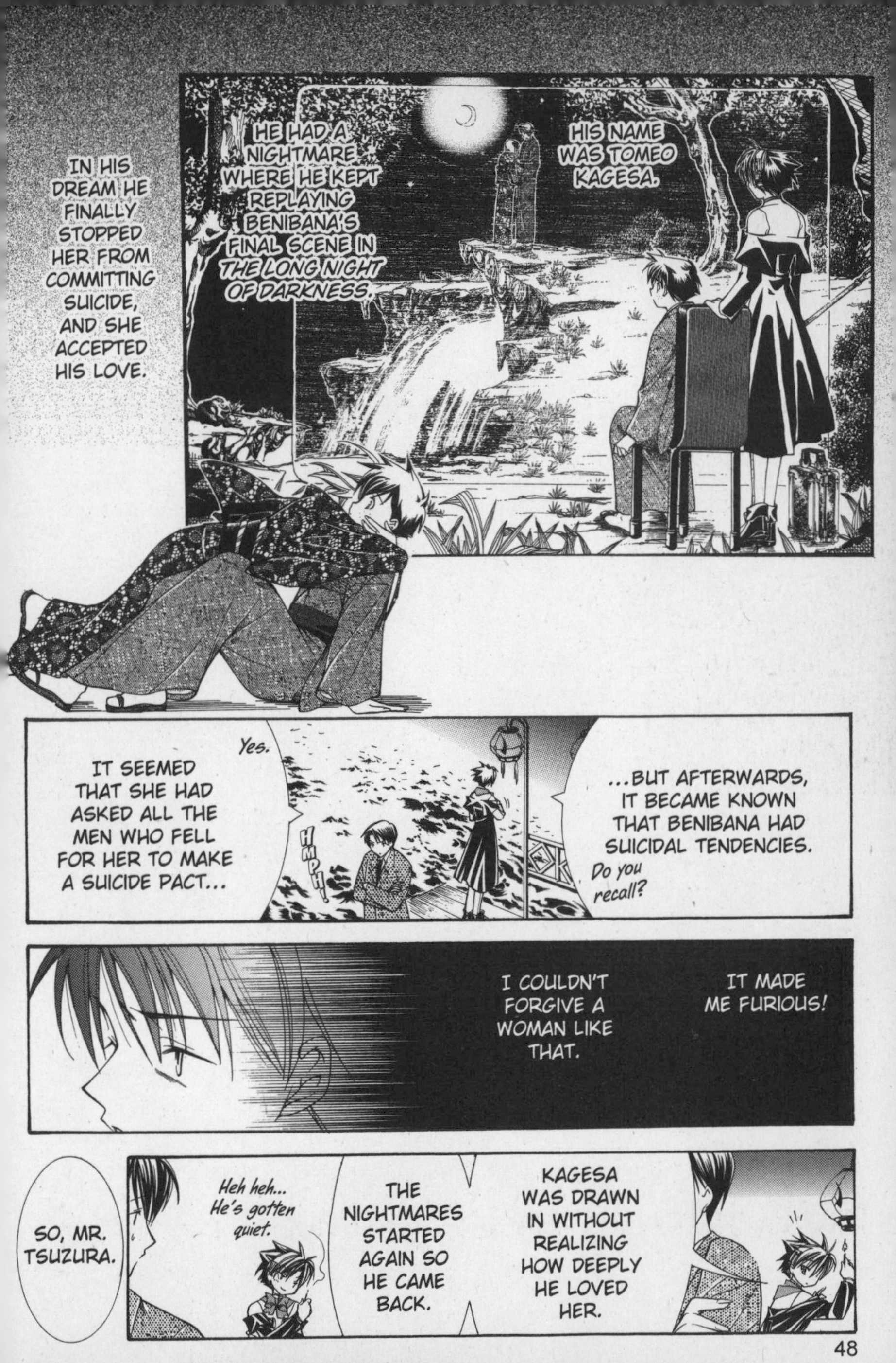
HIS NAME WAS TOMEO KAGESA.
HE HAD A NIGHTMARE WHERE HE KEPT REPLAYING BENIBANA'S FINAL SCENE IN THE LONG NIGHT OF DARKNESS.
IN HIS DREAM HE FINALLY STOPPED HER FROM COMMITTING SUICIDE, AND SHE ACCEPTED HIS LOVE.
...BUT AFTERWARDS, IT BECAME KNOWN THAT BENIBANA HAD SUICIDAL TENDENCIES.
Do you recall?
HMPH!
Yes.
IT SEEMED THAT SHE HAD ASKED ALL THE MEN WHO FELL FOR HER TO MAKE A SUICIDE PACT...
IT MADE ME FURIOUS!
I COULDN'T FORGIVE A WOMAN LIKE THAT.
KAGESA WAS DRAWN IN WITHOUT REALIZING HOW DEEPLY HE LOVED HER.
THE NIGHTMARES STARTED AGAIN SO HE CAME BACK.
Heh heh... He's gotten quiet.
SO, MR. TSUZURA.

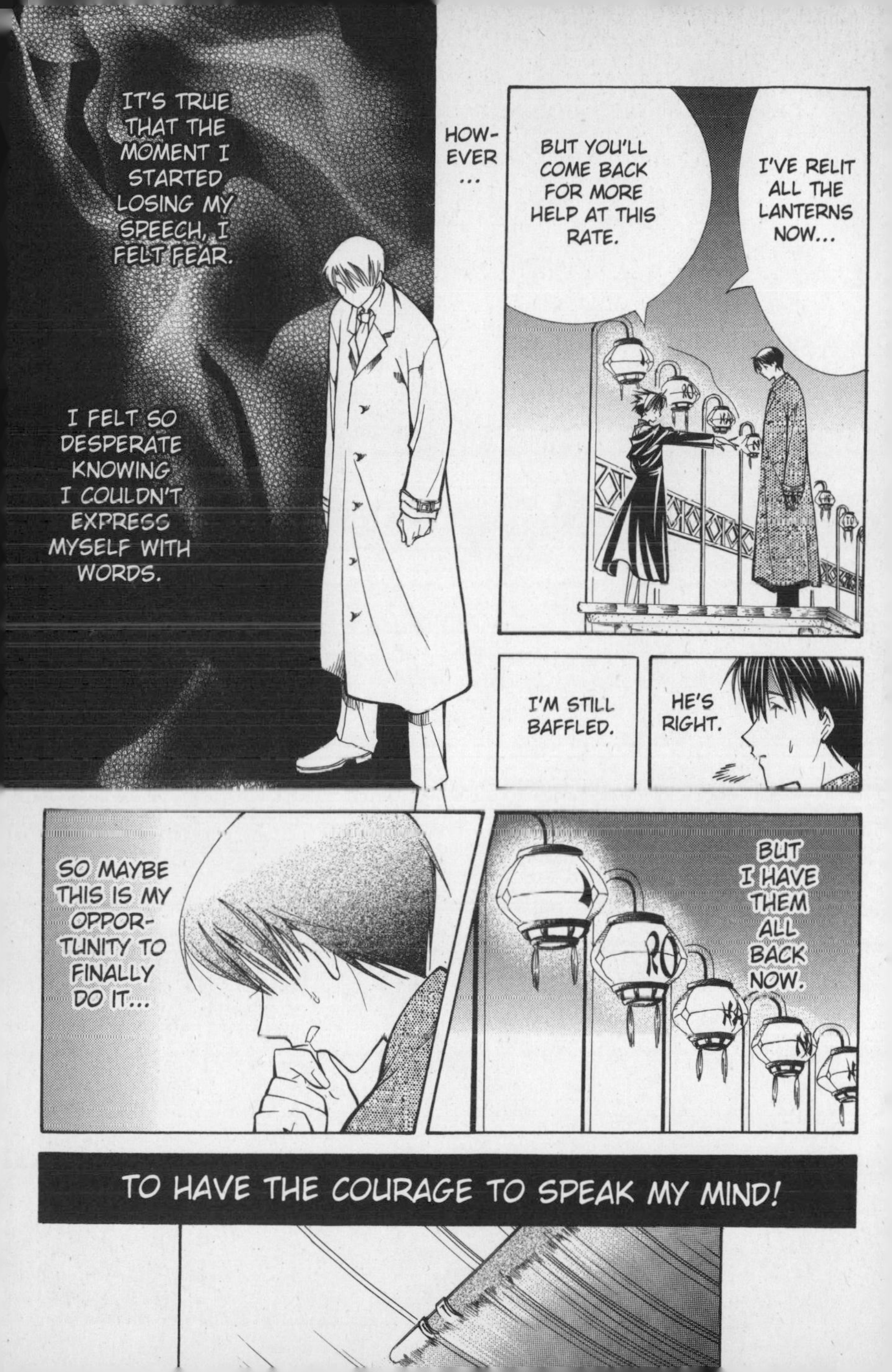

I'VE RELIT ALL THE LANTERNS NOW...
BUT YOU'LL COME BACK FOR MORE HELP AT THIS RATE.
HOW-EVER...
HE'S RIGHT.
I'M STILL BAFFLED.
IT'S TRUE THAT THE MOMENT I STARTED LOSING MY SPEECH, I FELT FEAR.
I FELT SO DESPERATE KNOWING I COULDN'T EXPRESS MYSELF WITH WORDS.
BUT I HAVE THEM ALL BACK NOW.
SO MAYBE THIS IS MY OPPOR-TUNITY TO FINALLY DO IT...
TO HAVE THE COURAGE TO SPEAK MY MIND!

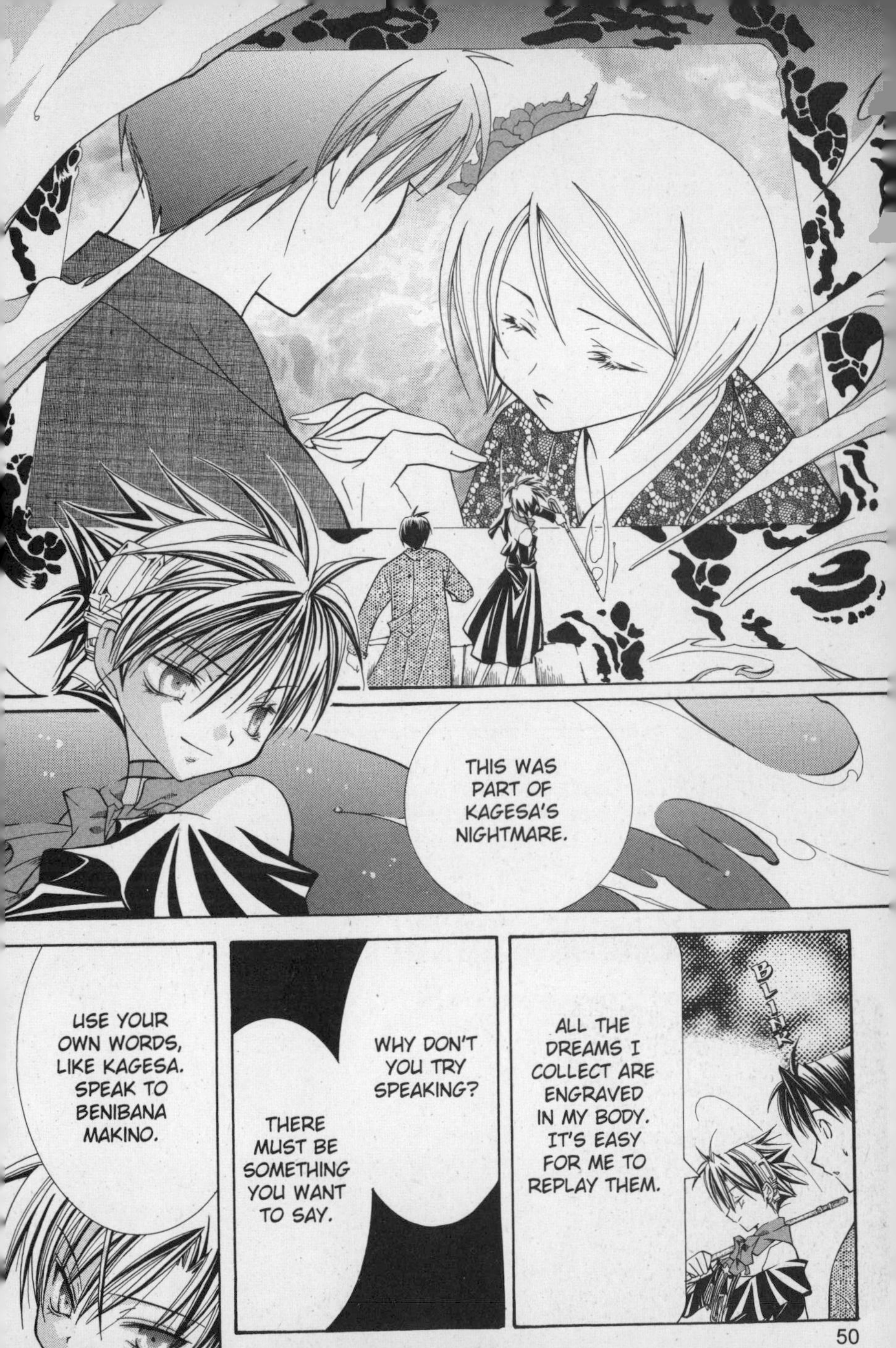
THIS WAS PART OF KAGESA'S NIGHTMARE.
BLINK
ALL THE DREAMS I COLLECT ARE ENGRAVED IN MY BODY. IT'S EASY FOR ME TO REPLAY THEM.
WHY DON'T YOU TRY SPEAKING?
THERE MUST BE SOMETHING YOU WANT TO SAY.
USE YOUR OWN WORDS, LIKE KAGESA. SPEAK TO BENIBANA MAKINO.

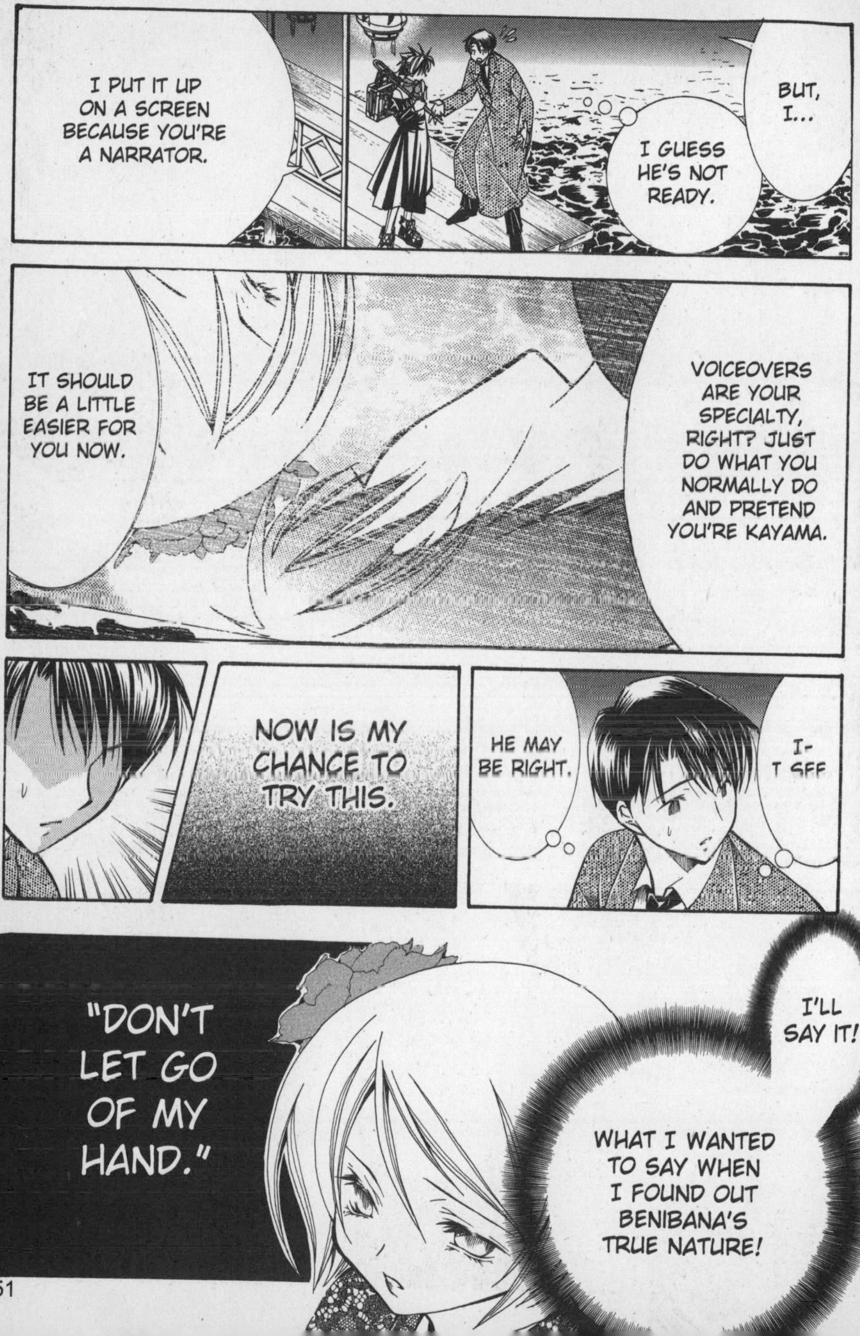
BUT, I...
I GUESS HE'S NOT READY.
I PUT IT UP ON A SCREEN BECAUSE YOU'RE A NARRATOR.
VOICEOVERS ARE YOUR SPECIALTY, RIGHT? JUST DO WHAT YOU NORMALLY DO AND PRETEND YOU'RE KAYAMA.
IT SHOULD BE A LITTLE EASIER FOR YOU NOW.
I- I SEE
HE MAY BE RIGHT.
NOW IS MY CHANCE TO TRY THIS.
I'LL SAY IT!
WHAT I WANTED TO SAY WHEN I FOUND OUT BENIBANA'S TRUE NATURE!
"DON'T LET GO OF MY HAND."

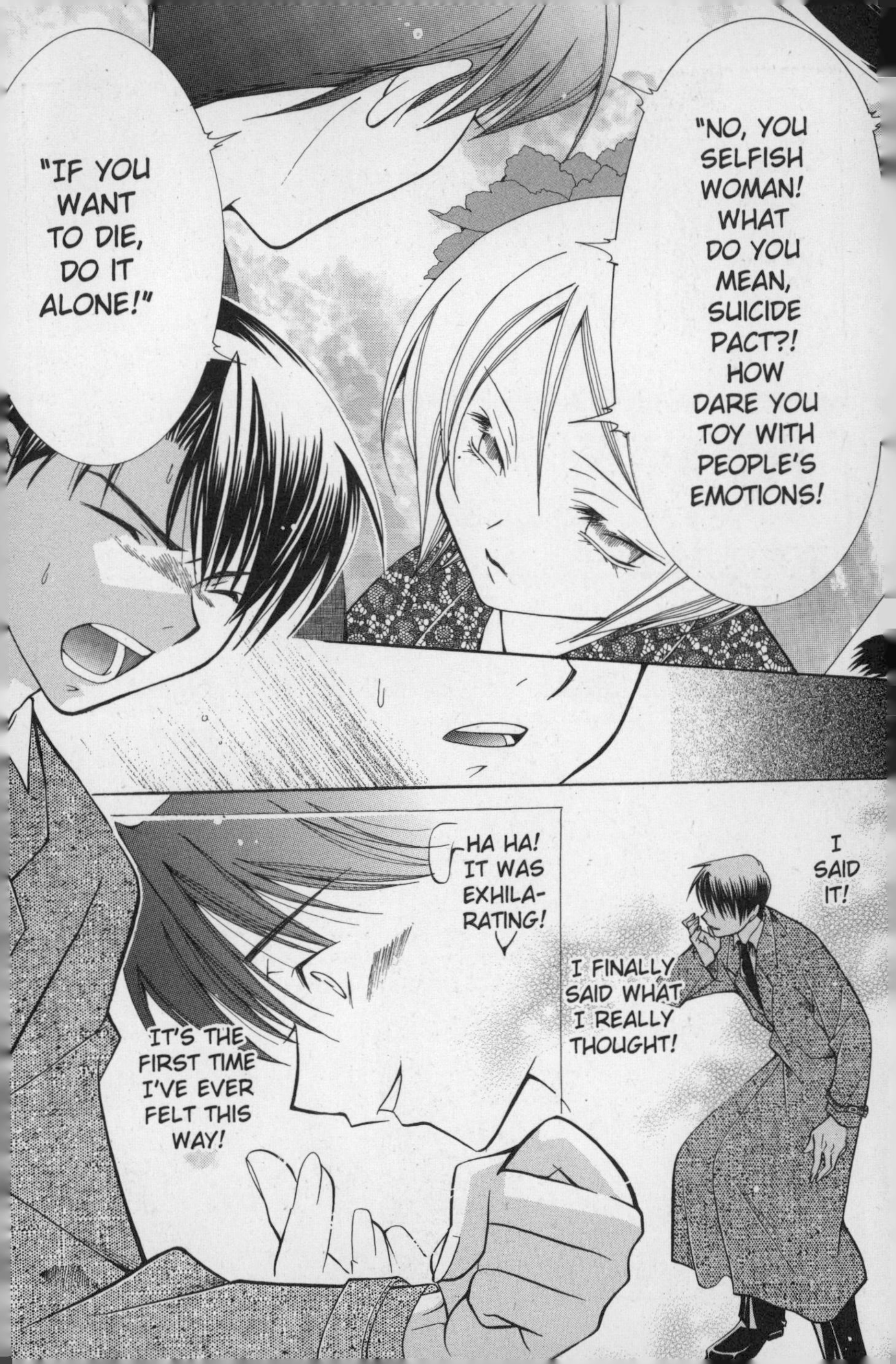
"NO, YOU SELFISH WOMAN! WHAT DO YOU MEAN, SUICIDE PACT?! HOW DARE YOU TOY WITH PEOPLE'S EMOTIONS!
"IF YOU WANT TO DIE, DO IT ALONE!"
I SAID IT!
I FINALLY SAID WHAT I REALLY THOUGHT!
HA HA! IT WAS EXHILA-RATING!
IT'S THE FIRST TIME I'VE EVER FELT THIS WAY!

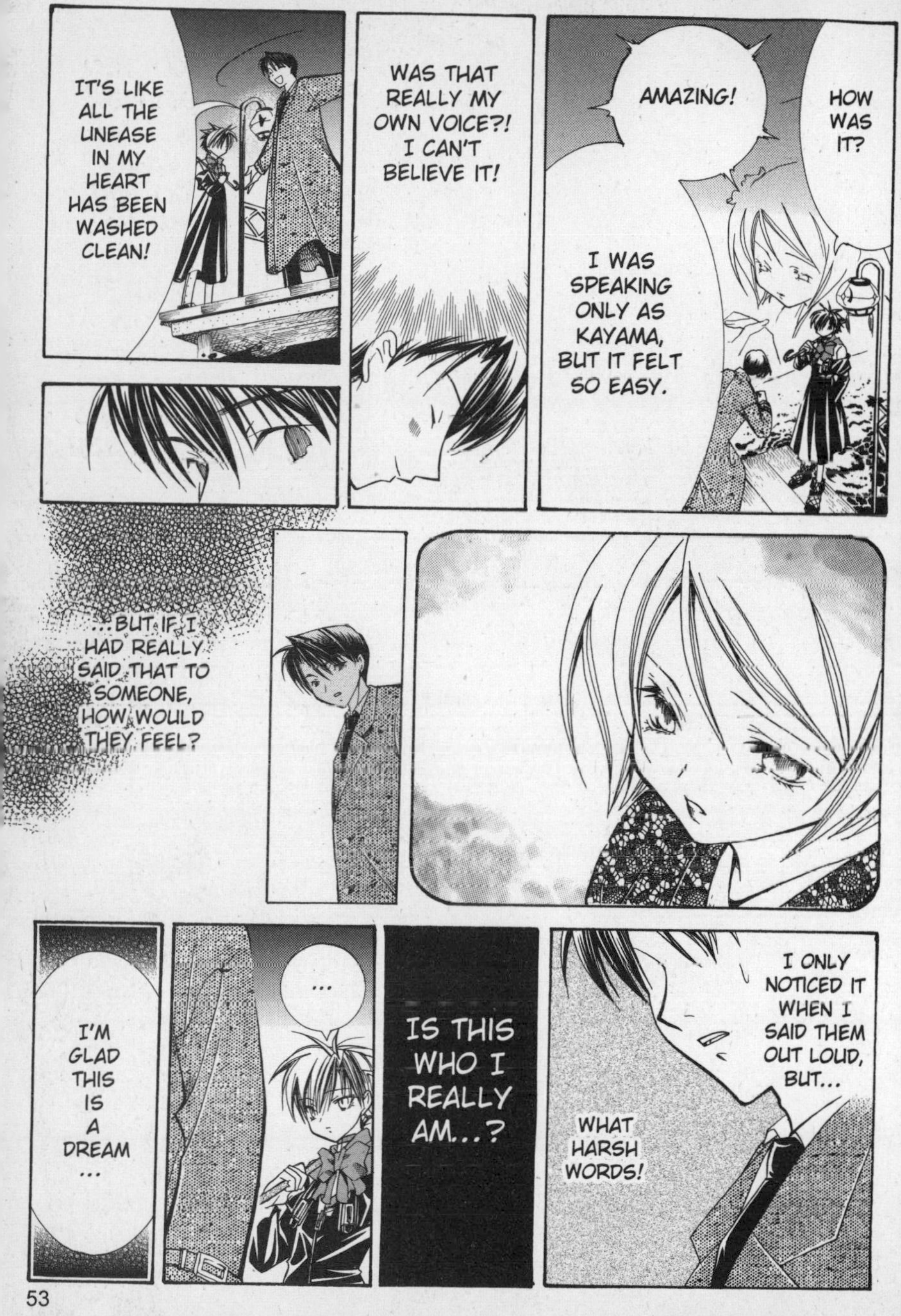
HOW WAS IT?
AMAZING!
I WAS SPEAKING ONLY AS KAYAMA, BUT IT FELT SO EASY.
WAS THAT REALLY MY OWN VOICE?! I CAN'T BELIEVE IT!
IT'S LIKE ALL THE UNEASE IN MY HEART HAS BEEN WASHED CLEAN!
...BUT IF I HAD REALLY SAID THAT TO SOMEONE, HOW WOULD THEY FEEL?
I ONLY NOTICED IT WHEN I SAID THEM OUT LOUD, BUT...
WHAT HARSH WORDS!
IS THIS WHO I REALLY AM...?
...
I'M GLAD THIS IS A DREAM...

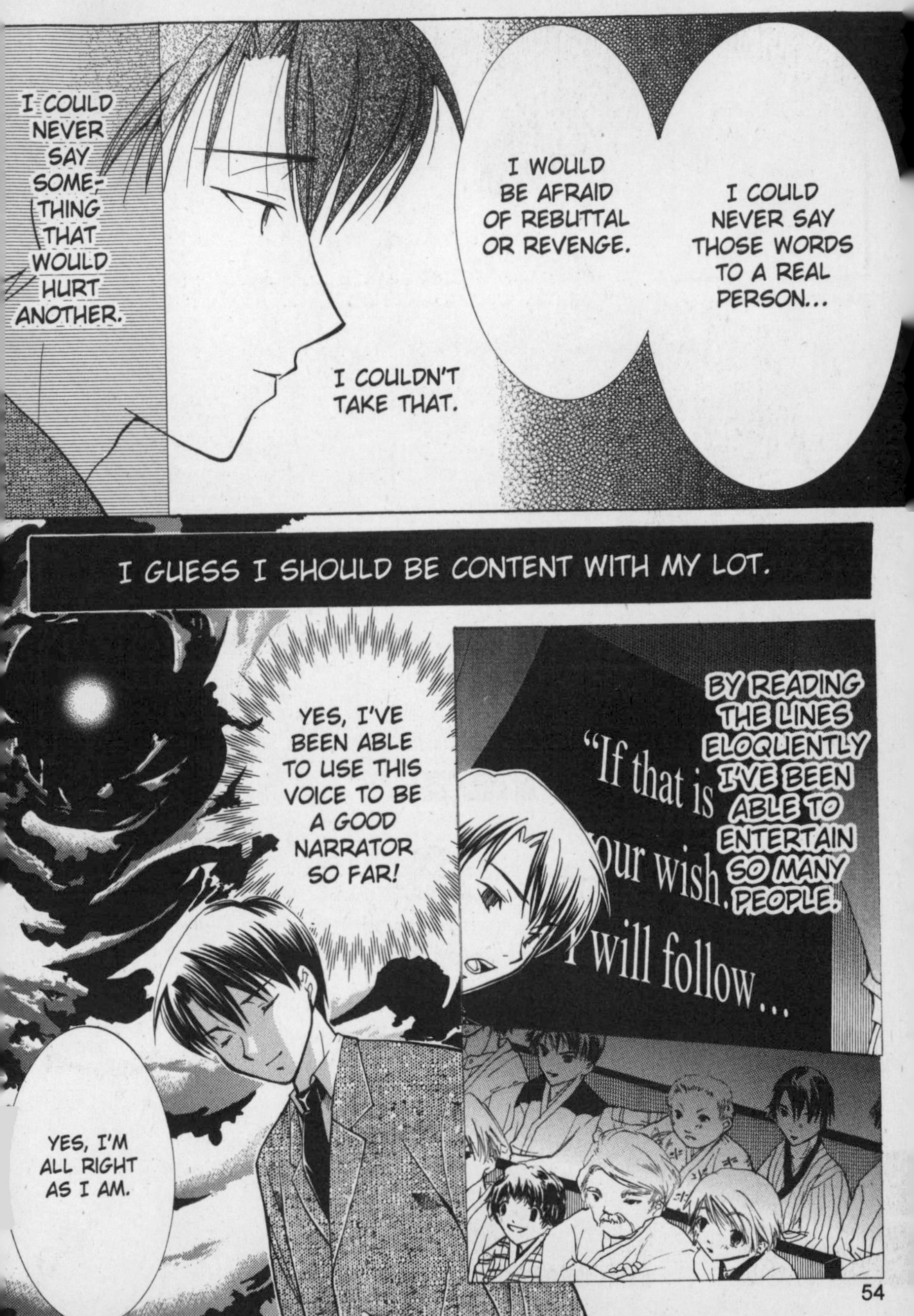
I COULD NEVER SAY THOSE WORDS TO A REAL PERSON...
I WOULD BE AFRAID OF REBUTTAL OR REVENGE.
I COULDN'T TAKE THAT.
I COULD NEVER SAY SOME-THING THAT WOULD HURT ANOTHER.
I GUESS I SHOULD BE CONTENT WITH MY LOT.
BY READING THE LINES ELOQUENTLY I'VE BEEN ABLE TO ENTERTAIN SO MANY PEOPLE.
"If that is
our wish.
will follow...
YES, I'VE BEEN ABLE TO USE THIS VOICE TO BE A GOOD NARRATOR SO FAR!
YES, I'M ALL RIGHT AS I AM.

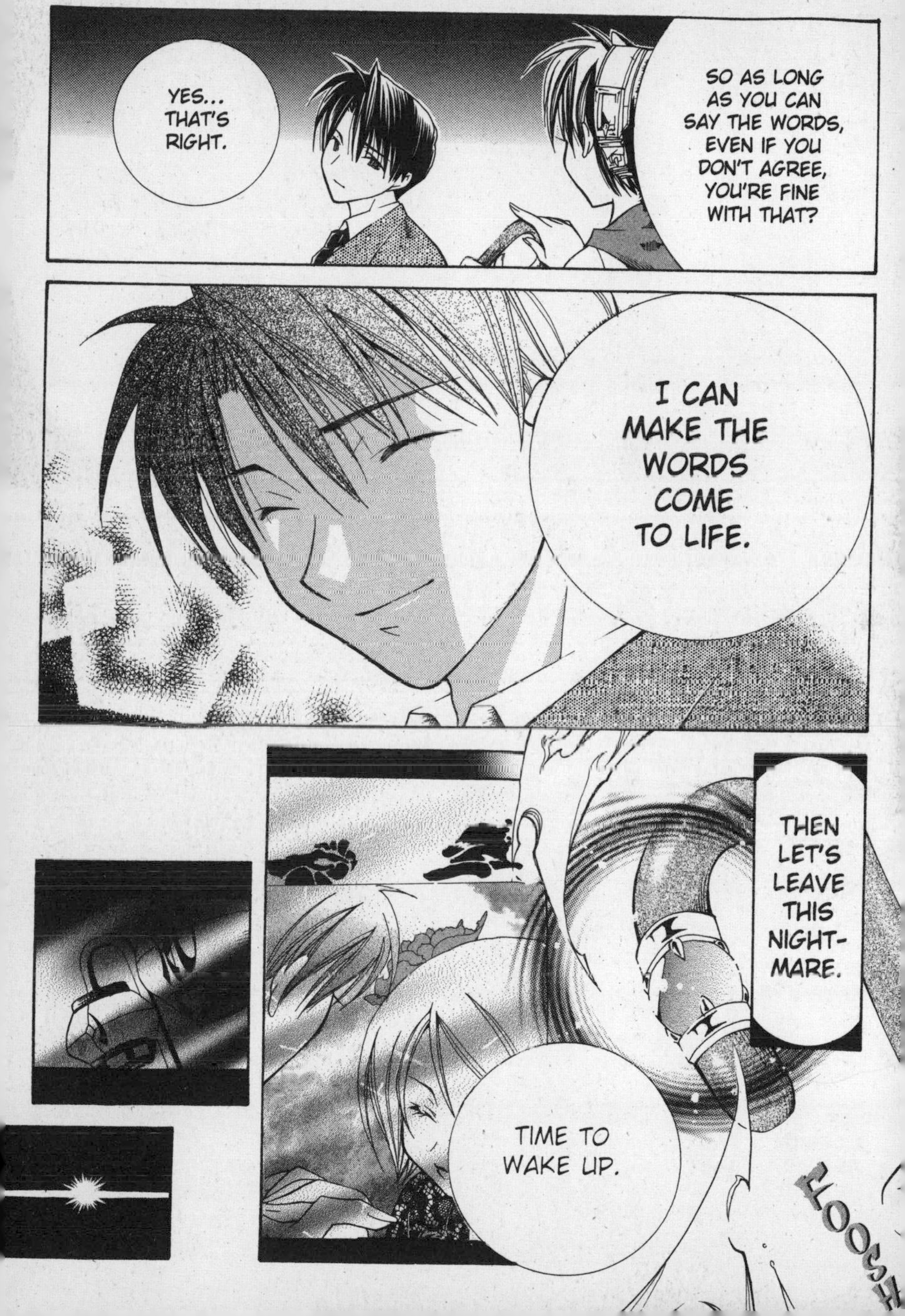
SO AS LONG AS YOU CAN SAY THE WORDS, EVEN IF YOU DON'T AGREE, YOU'RE FINE WITH THAT?
YES... THAT'S RIGHT.
I CAN MAKE THE WORDS COME TO LIFE.
THEN LET'S LEAVE THIS NIGHT-MARE.
TIME TO WAKE UP.
FOOSH

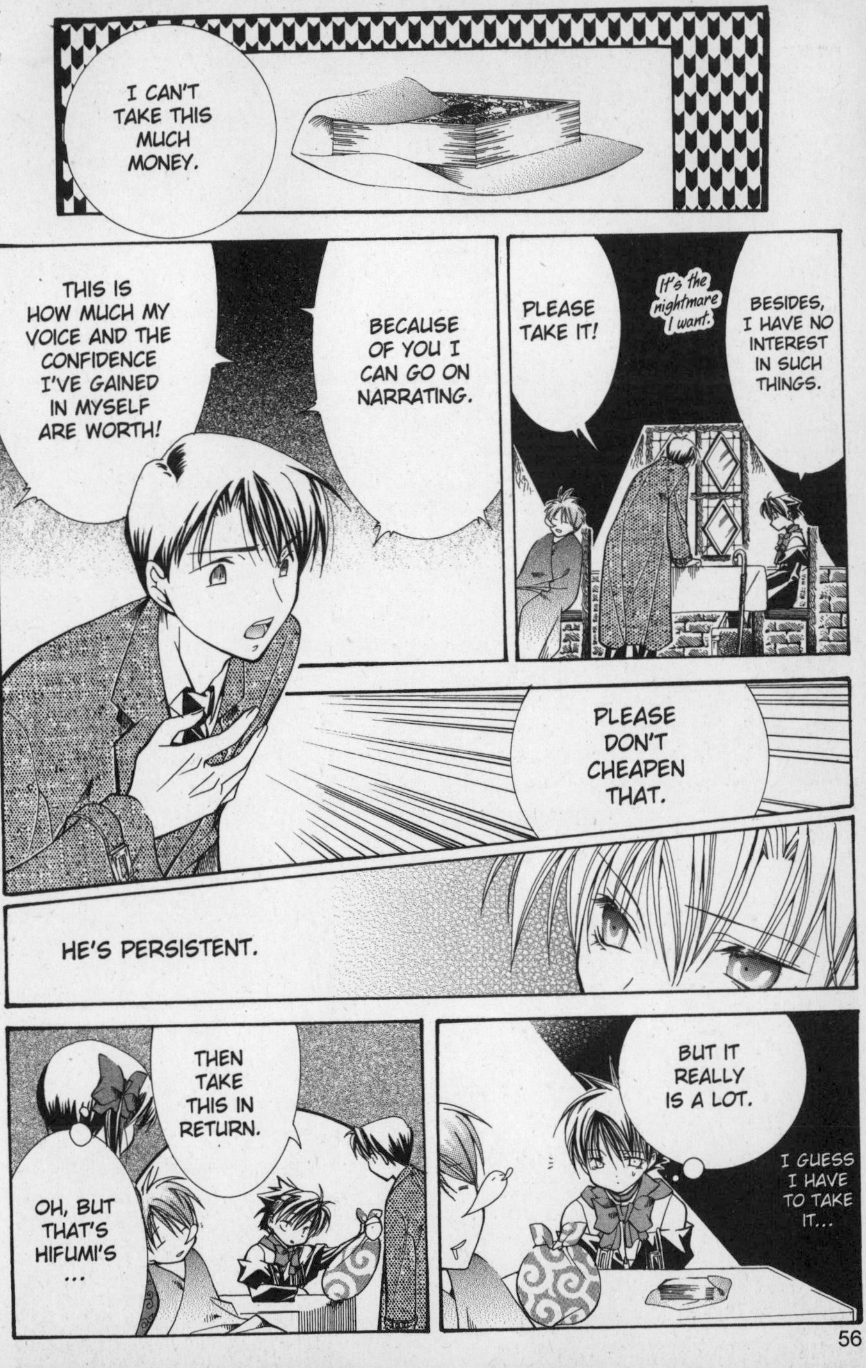

I CAN'T TAKE THIS MUCH MONEY.
BESIDES, I HAVE NO INTEREST IN SUCH THINGS.
It's the nightmare I want.
PLEASE TAKE IT!
BECAUSE OF YOU I CAN GO ON NARRATING.
THIS IS HOW MUCH MY VOICE AND THE CONFIDENCE I'VE GAINED IN MYSELF ARE WORTH!
PLEASE DON'T CHEAPEN THAT.
HE'S PERSISTENT.
BUT IT REALLY IS A LOT.
I GUESS I HAVE TO TAKE IT...
THEN TAKE THIS IN RETURN.
OH, BUT THAT'S HIFUMI'S ...

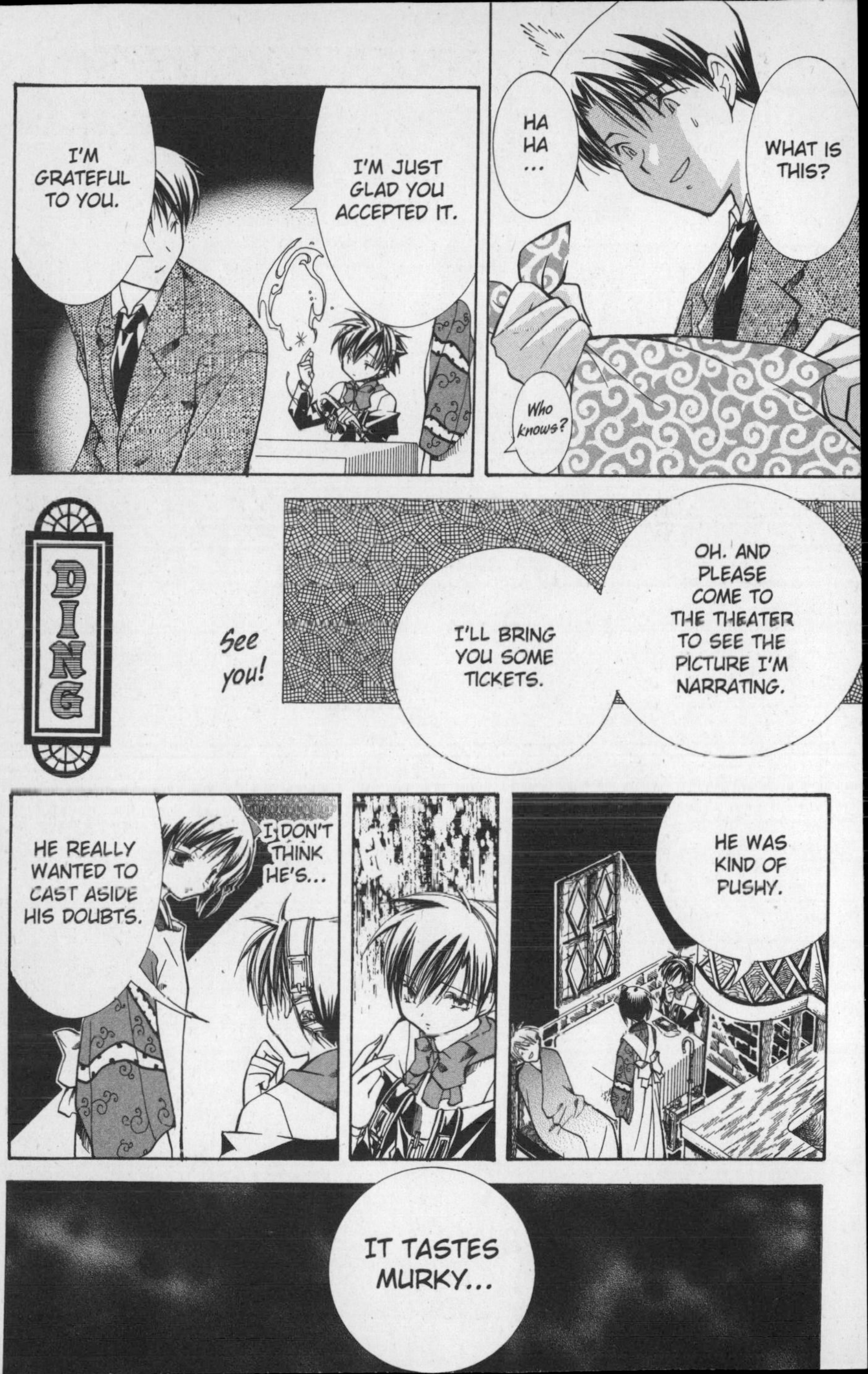
WHAT IS THIS?
HA HA ...
Who knows?
I'M JUST GLAD YOU ACCEPTED IT.
I'M GRATEFUL TO YOU.
OH. AND PLEASE COME TO THE THEATER TO SEE THE PICTURE I'M NARRATING.
I'LL BRING YOU SOME TICKETS.
See you!
DING
HE WAS KIND OF PUSHY.
I DON'T THINK HE'S...
HE REALLY WANTED TO CAST ASIDE HIS DOUBTS.
IT TASTES MURKY...

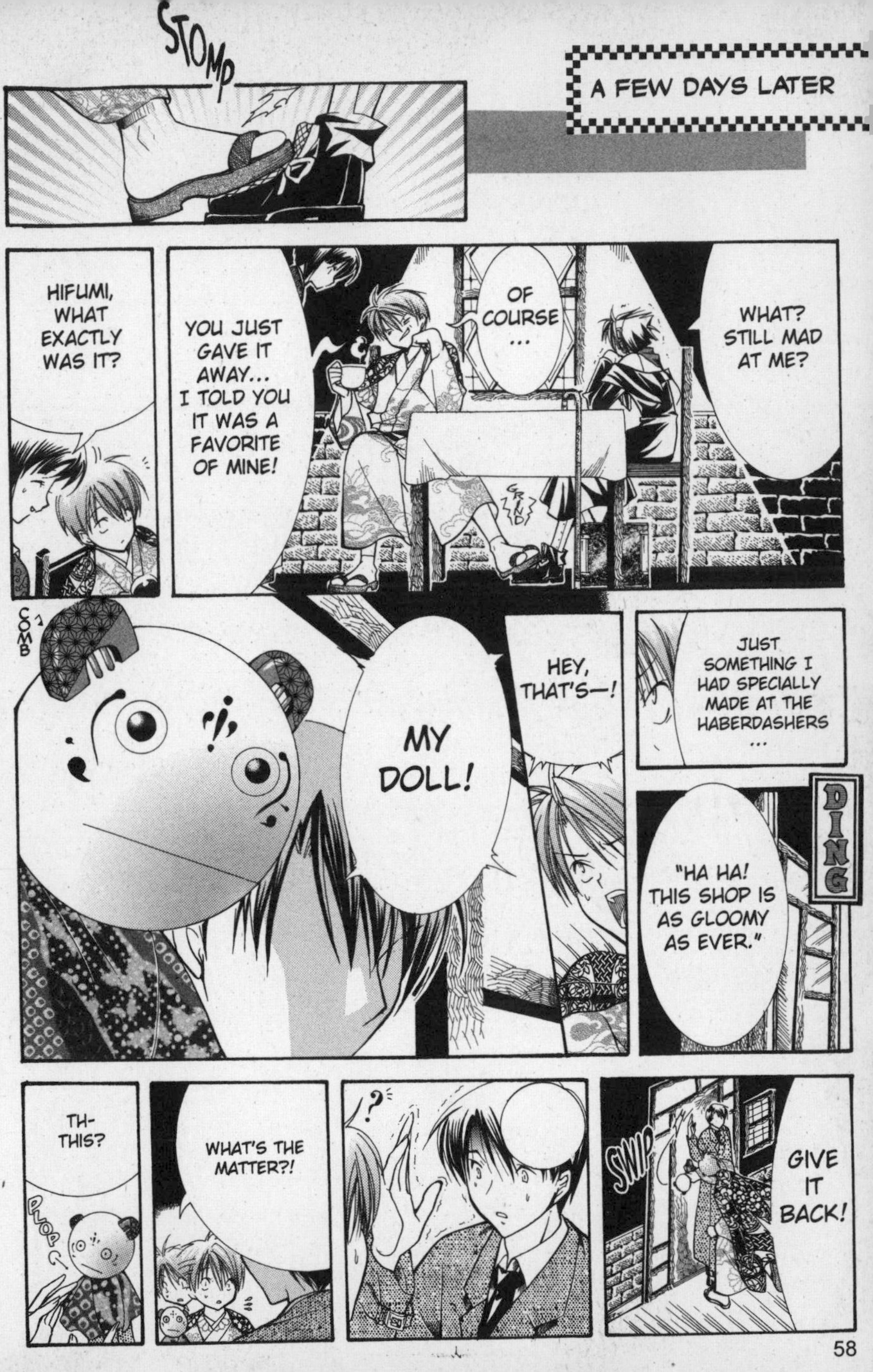
A FEW DAYS LATER
STOMP
WHAT? STILL MAD AT ME?
OF COURSE...
GRIND
YOU JUST GAVE IT AWAY... I TOLD YOU IT WAS A FAVORITE OF MINE!
HIFUMI, WHAT EXACTLY WAS IT?
JUST SOMETHING I HAD SPECIALLY MADE AT THE HABERDASHERS...
DING
"HA HA! THIS SHOP IS AS GLOOMY AS EVER."
HEY, THAT'S—!
MY DOLL!
COMB
GIVE IT BACK!
SWIP
?!
WHAT'S THE MATTER?!
TH- THIS?
PLOP

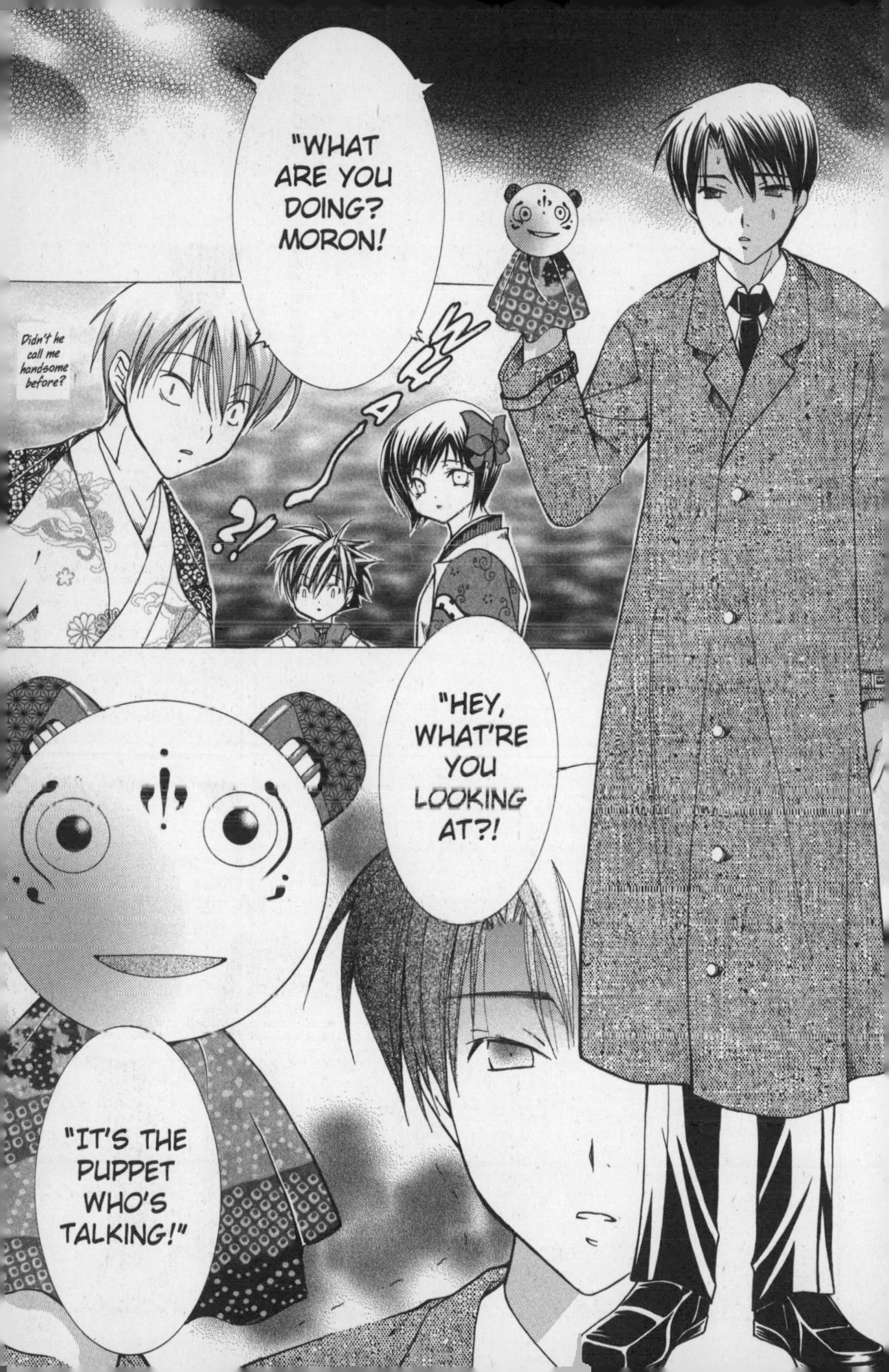
"WHAT ARE YOU DOING? MORON!
WHA—
?!
Didn't he call me handsome before?
"HEY, WHAT'RE YOU LOOKING AT?!
"IT'S THE PUPPET WHO'S TALKING!"

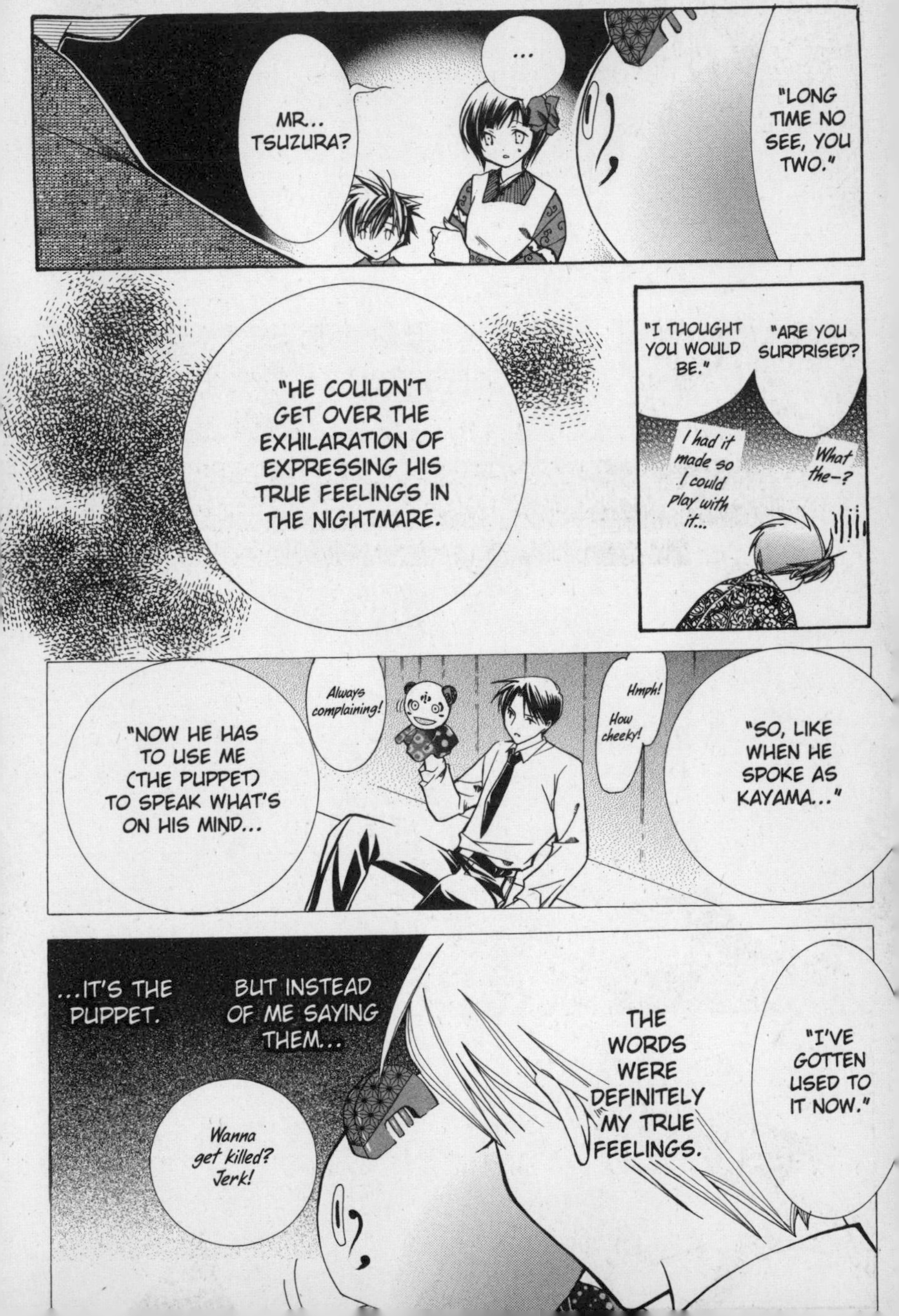
"LONG TIME NO SEE, YOU TWO."
...
MR... TSUZURA?
"ARE YOU SURPRISED?
"I THOUGHT YOU WOULD BE."
What the-?
I had it made so I could play with it...
"HE COULDN'T GET OVER THE EXHILARATION OF EXPRESSING HIS TRUE FEELINGS IN THE NIGHTMARE.
"SO, LIKE WHEN HE SPOKE AS KAYAMA..."
Hmph! How cheeky!
Always complaining!
"NOW HE HAS TO USE ME (THE PUPPET) TO SPEAK WHAT'S ON HIS MIND...
"I'VE GOTTEN USED TO IT NOW."
THE WORDS WERE DEFINITELY MY TRUE FEELINGS.
BUT INSTEAD OF ME SAYING THEM...
...IT'S THE PUPPET.
Wanna get killed? Jerk!

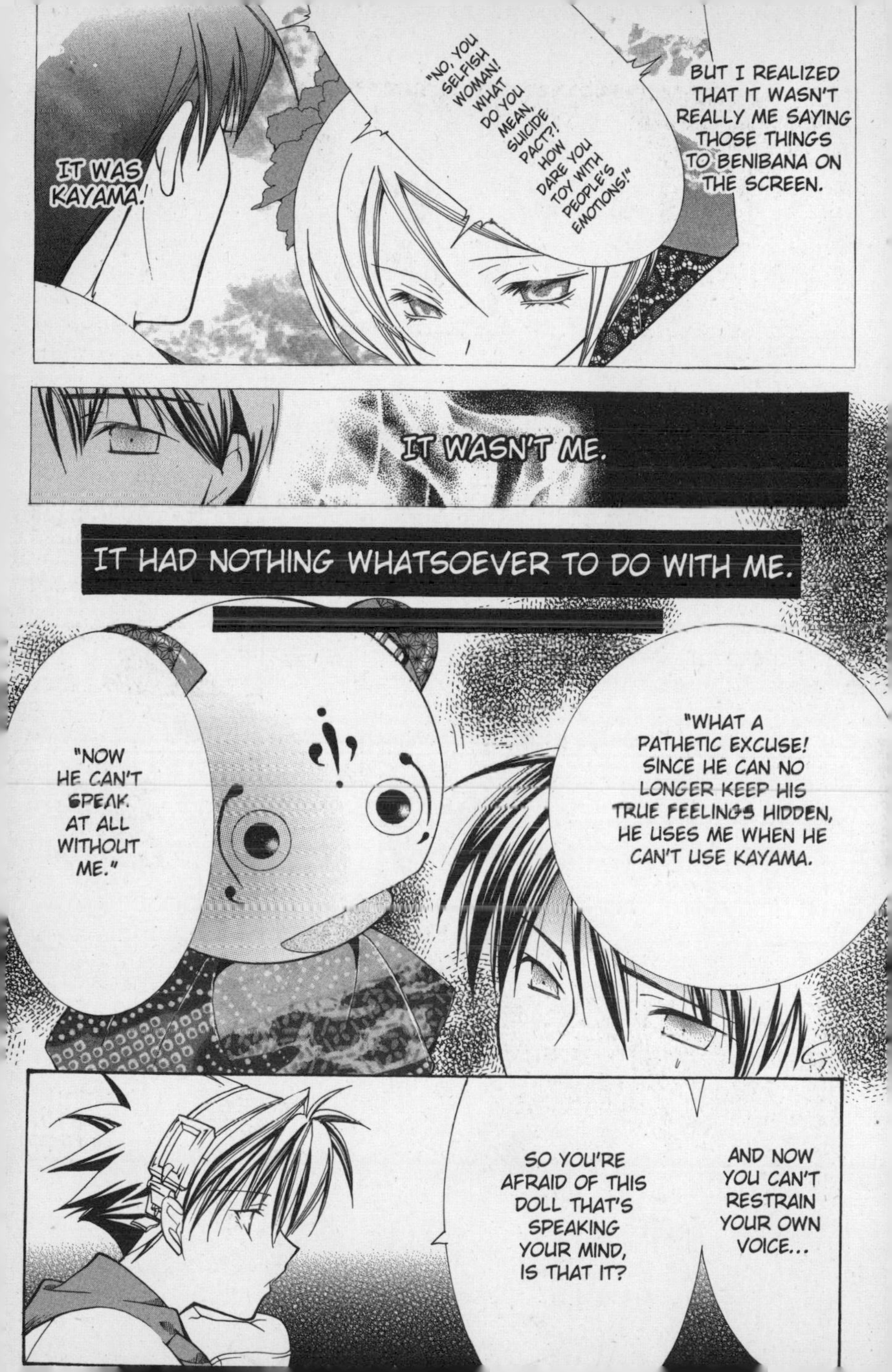
BUT I REALIZED THAT IT WASN'T REALLY ME SAYING THOSE THINGS TO BENIBANA ON THE SCREEN.
"NO, YOU SELFISH WOMAN! WHAT DO YOU MEAN, SUICIDE PACT?! HOW DARE YOU TOY WITH PEOPLE'S EMOTIONS!"
IT WAS KAYAMA.
IT WASN'T ME.
IT HAD NOTHING WHATSOEVER TO DO WITH ME.
"WHAT A PATHETIC EXCUSE! SINCE HE CAN NO LONGER KEEP HIS TRUE FEELINGS HIDDEN, HE USES ME WHEN HE CAN'T USE KAYAMA.
"NOW HE CAN'T SPEAK AT ALL WITHOUT ME."
AND NOW YOU CAN'T RESTRAIN YOUR OWN VOICE...
SO YOU'RE AFRAID OF THIS DOLL THAT'S SPEAKING YOUR MIND, IS THAT IT?

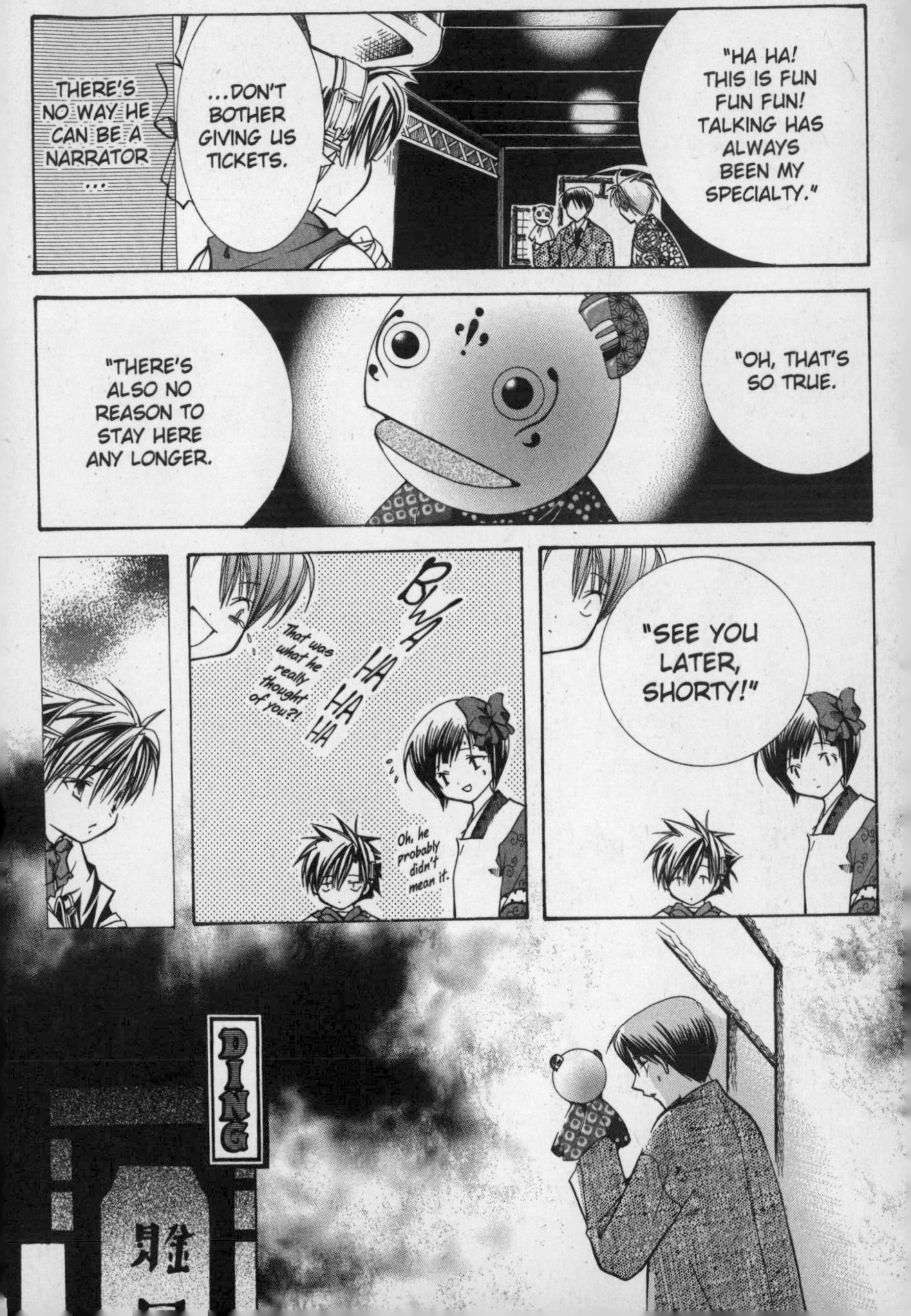
"HA HA! THIS IS FUN FUN FUN! TALKING HAS ALWAYS BEEN MY SPECIALTY."
...DON'T BOTHER GIVING US TICKETS.
THERE'S NO WAY HE CAN BE A NARRATOR...
"OH, THAT'S SO TRUE.
"THERE'S ALSO NO REASON TO STAY HERE ANY LONGER.
"SEE YOU LATER, SHORTY!"
BWAHAHAHA
That was what he really thought of you?!
Oh, he probably didn't mean it.
DING

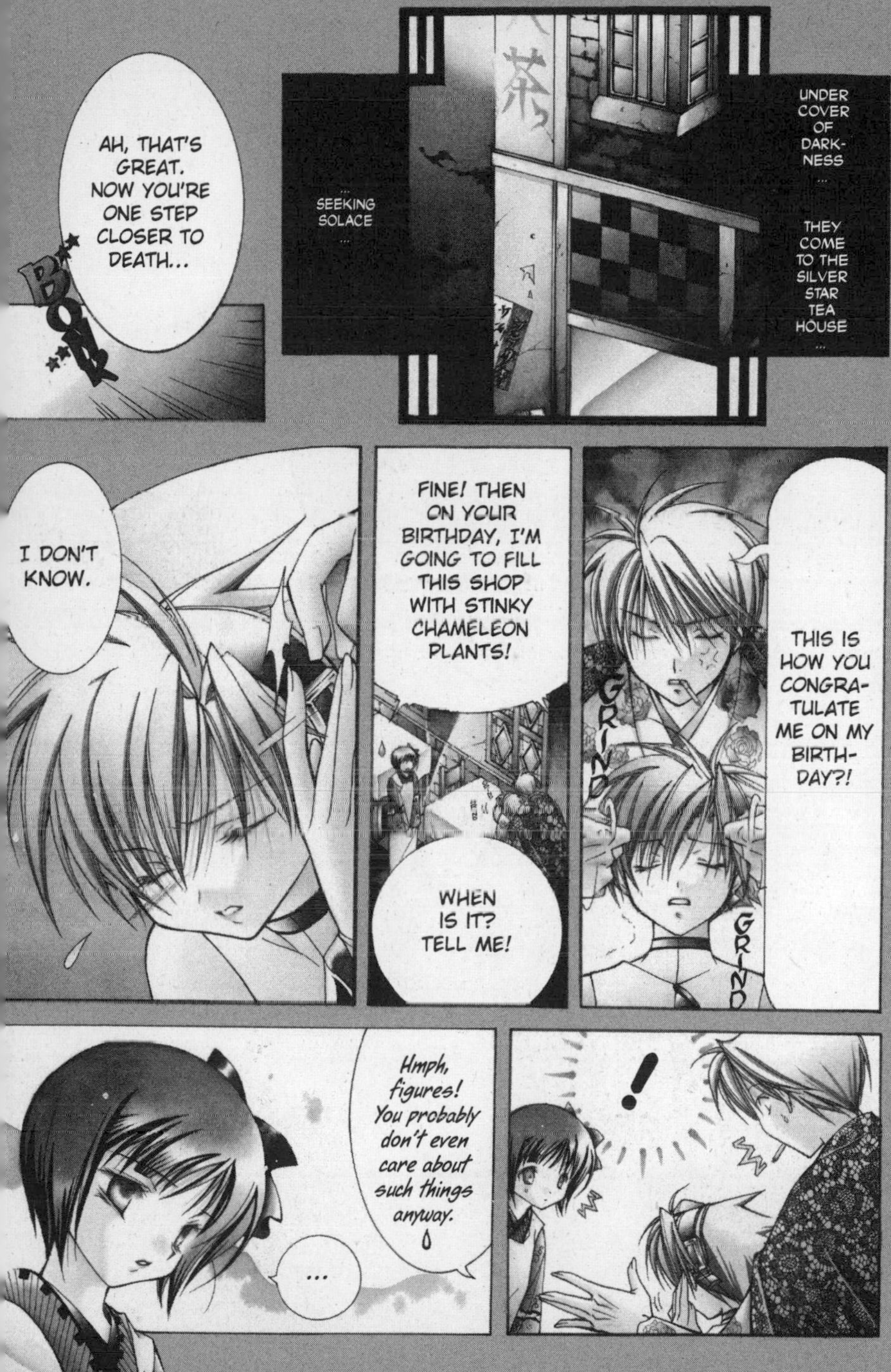
UNDER COVER OF DARKNESS ...
THEY COME TO THE SILVER STAR TEA HOUSE ...
... SEEKING SOLACE ...
AH, THAT'S GREAT. NOW YOU'RE ONE STEP CLOSER TO DEATH...
BONK
THIS IS HOW YOU CONGRATULATE ME ON MY BIRTHDAY?!
GRIND
GRIND
FINE! THEN ON YOUR BIRTHDAY, I'M GOING TO FILL THIS SHOP WITH STINKY CHAMELEON PLANTS!
WHEN IS IT? TELL ME!
I DON'T KNOW.
!
Hmph, figures! You probably don't even care about such things anyway.
...

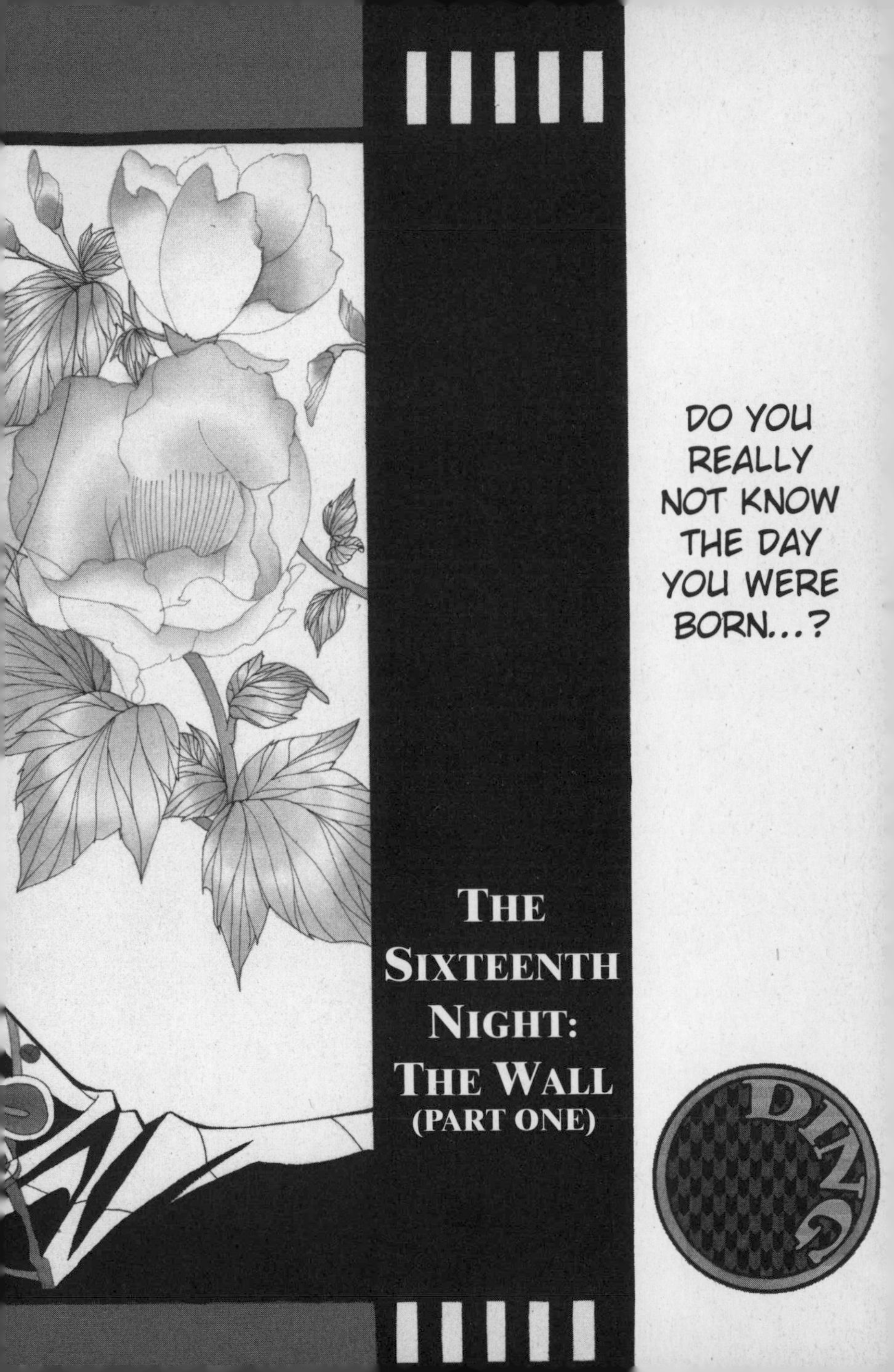
DO YOU REALLY NOT KNOW THE DAY YOU WERE BORN...?
DING
THE SIXTEENTH NIGHT: THE WALL
(PART ONE)

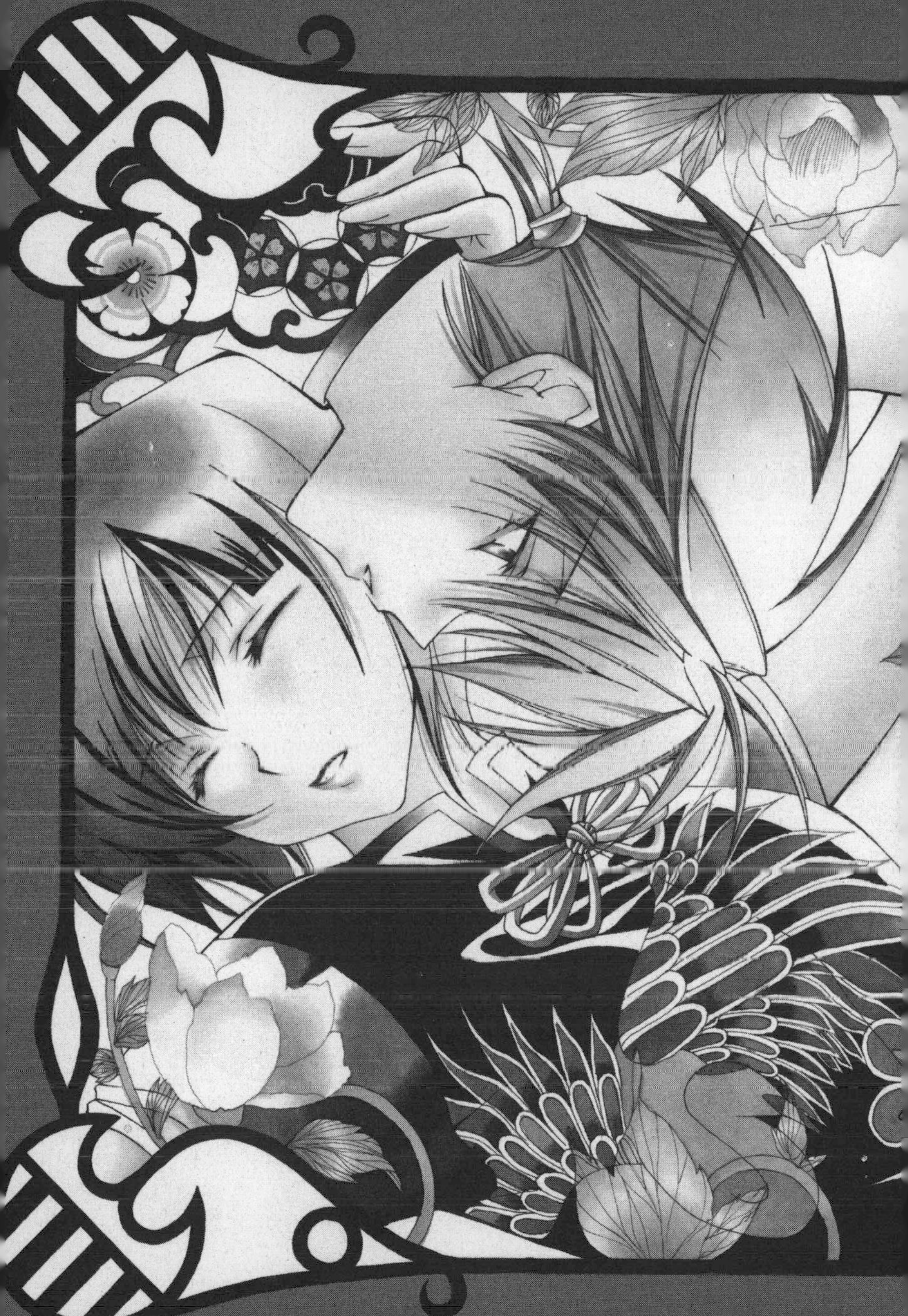

## WAN WAN SHIROI'S CONTEST ~Comedy Quiz~

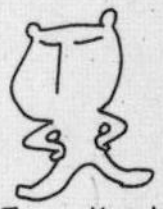

Send your answers to Mashiba! Be creative! The one that makes me laugh the most will get a Formalin plastic board autographed by Mashiba and me. (Limited to one winner.)

(written in marker)

Q1: The Silver Star Tea House's delicious coffee has a secret ingredient. What ingredient is used to give it that special flavor? (For instance, seaweed.)

Q2: It is well known that Hifumi's cat, Naamu, doesn't like him. What three things in particular does he hate about Hifumi?

Q3: Hifumi is well known for his couture. What's the one thing he wouldn't wear unless he was dying?

Q4: There's a seat in the Silver Star Tea House that no one wants to sit in. Why is that?

Q5: The Silver Star Tea House has a bell on the door that makes a "ding" sound when someone enters. But it's not really a bell. What is it?

Continued on PAGE 144...

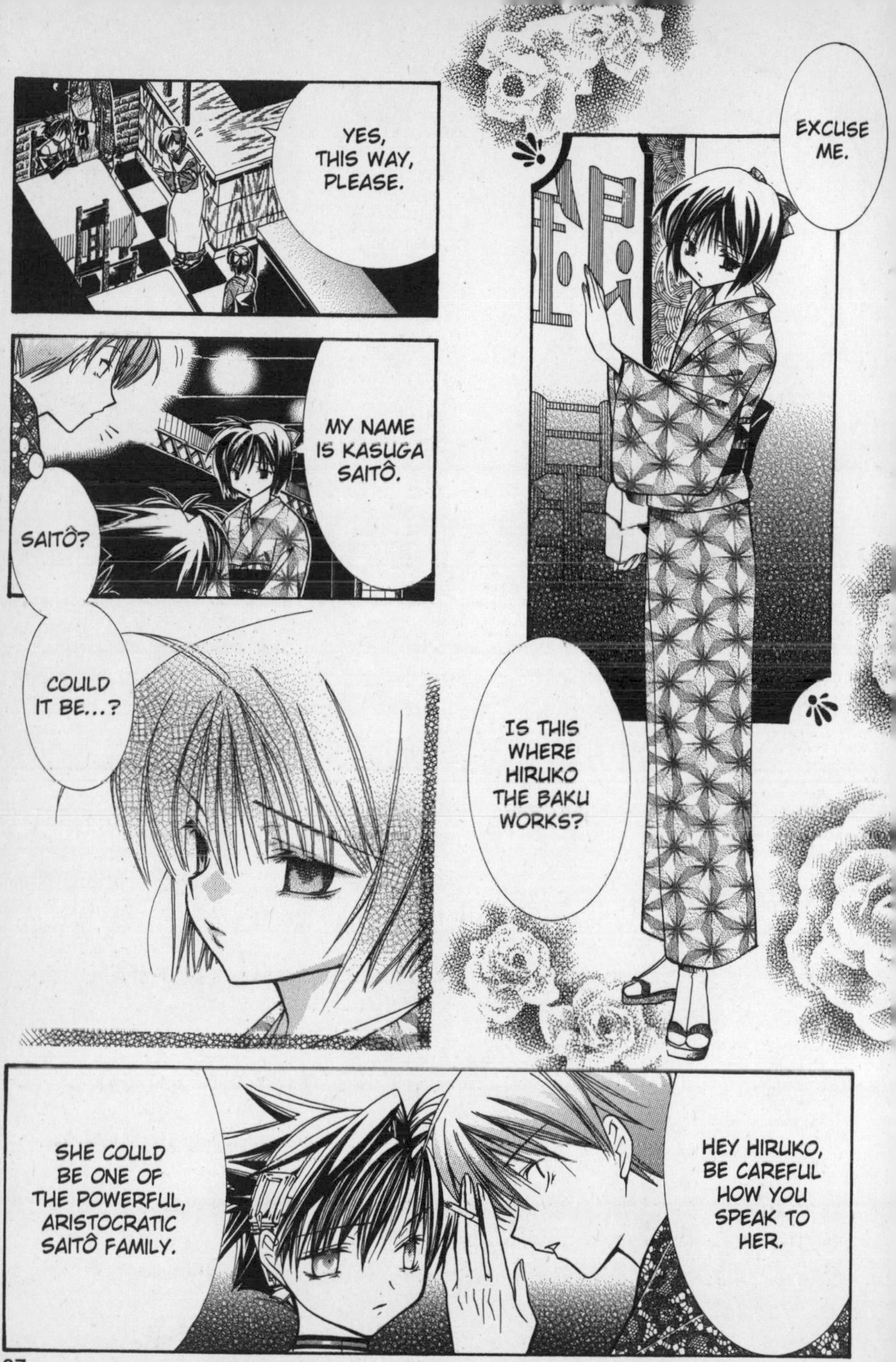
EXCUSE ME.
IS THIS WHERE HIRUKO THE BAKU WORKS?
YES, THIS WAY, PLEASE.
MY NAME IS KASUGA SAITÔ.
SAITÔ?
COULD IT BE...?
HEY HIRUKO, BE CAREFUL HOW YOU SPEAK TO HER.
SHE COULD BE ONE OF THE POWERFUL, ARISTOCRATIC SAITÔ FAMILY.

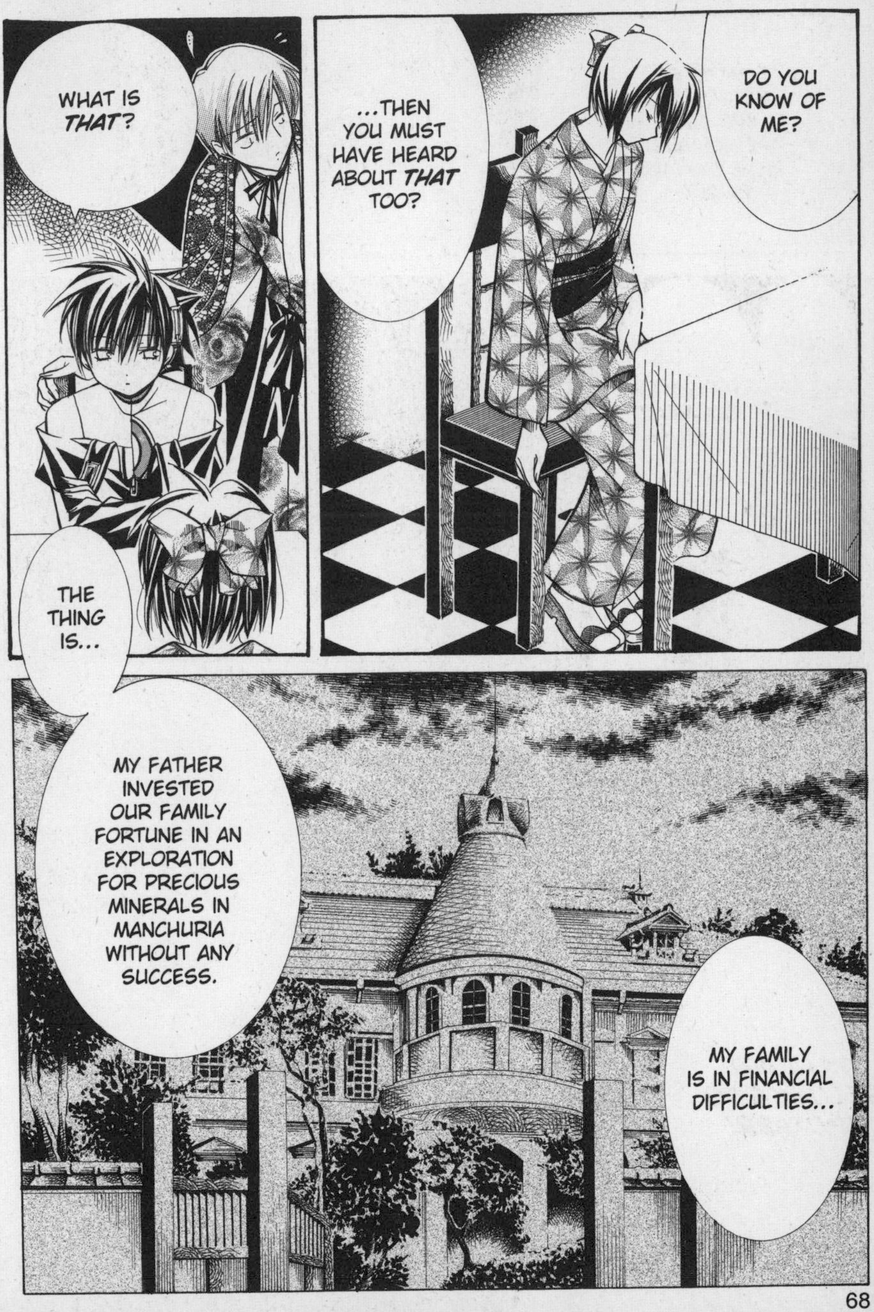
DO YOU KNOW OF ME?
...THEN YOU MUST HAVE HEARD ABOUT *THAT* TOO?
WHAT IS *THAT*?
THE THING IS...
MY FATHER INVESTED OUR FAMILY FORTUNE IN AN EXPLORATION FOR PRECIOUS MINERALS IN MANCHURIA WITHOUT ANY SUCCESS.
MY FAMILY IS IN FINANCIAL DIFFICULTIES...

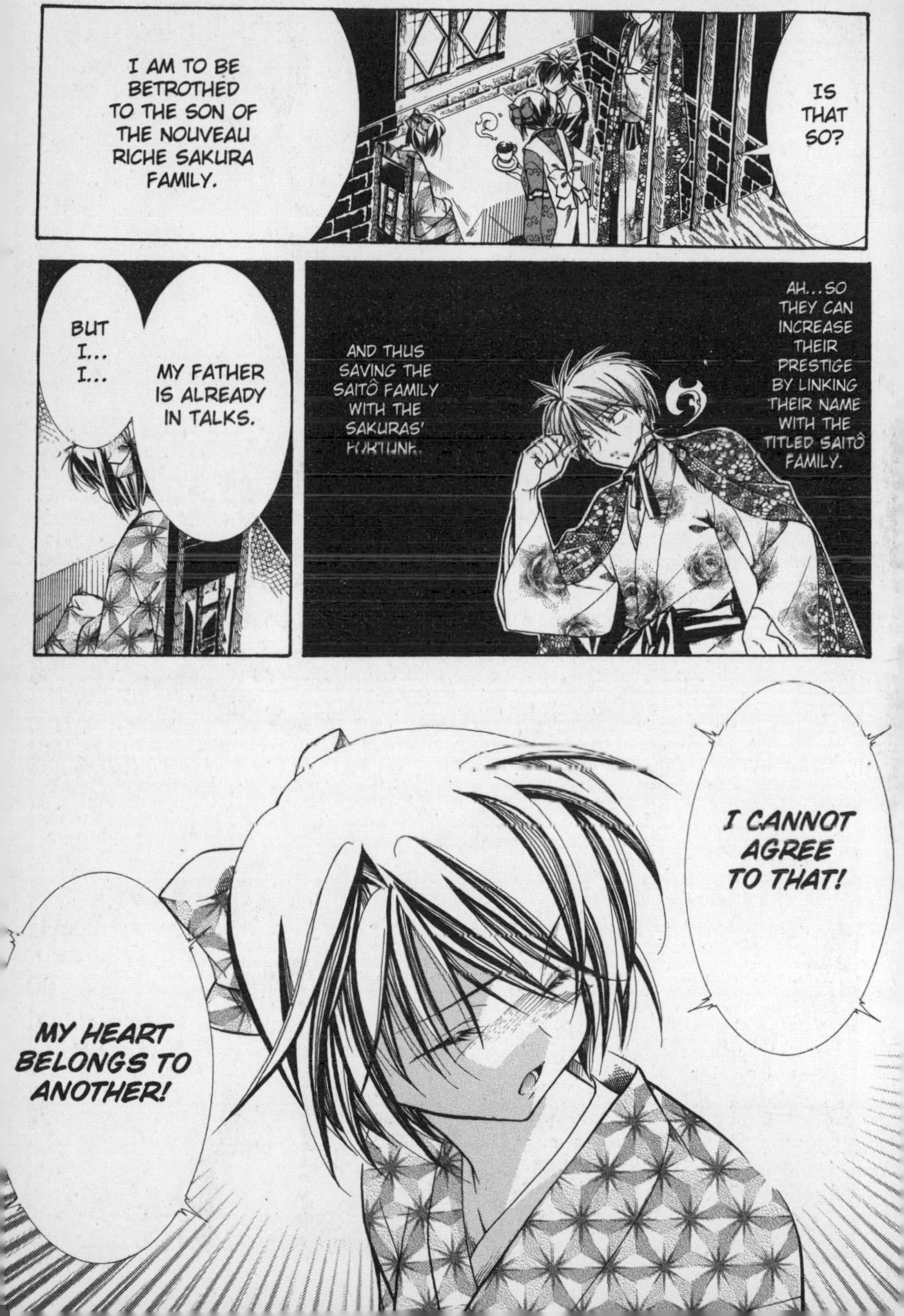
I AM TO BE BETROTHED TO THE SON OF THE NOUVEAU RICHE SAKURA FAMILY.
IS THAT SO?
AH...SO THEY CAN INCREASE THEIR PRESTIGE BY LINKING THEIR NAME WITH THE TITLED SAITÔ FAMILY.
AND THUS SAVING THE SAITÔ FAMILY WITH THE SAKURAS' FORTUNE.
MY FATHER IS ALREADY IN TALKS.
BUT I... I...
I CANNOT AGREE TO THAT!
MY HEART BELONGS TO ANOTHER!

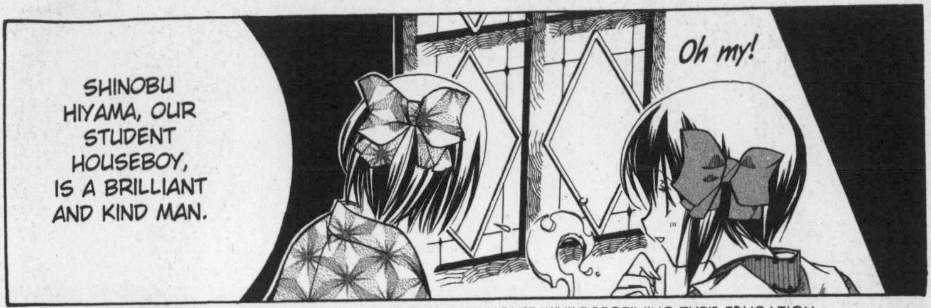
Oh my!
SHINOBU HIYAMA, OUR STUDENT HOUSEBOY, IS A BRILLIANT AND KIND MAN.

※STUDENT HOUSEBOYS LIVED AND WORKED IN SOMEONE'S HOUSE WHILE RECEIVING THEIR EDUCATION.

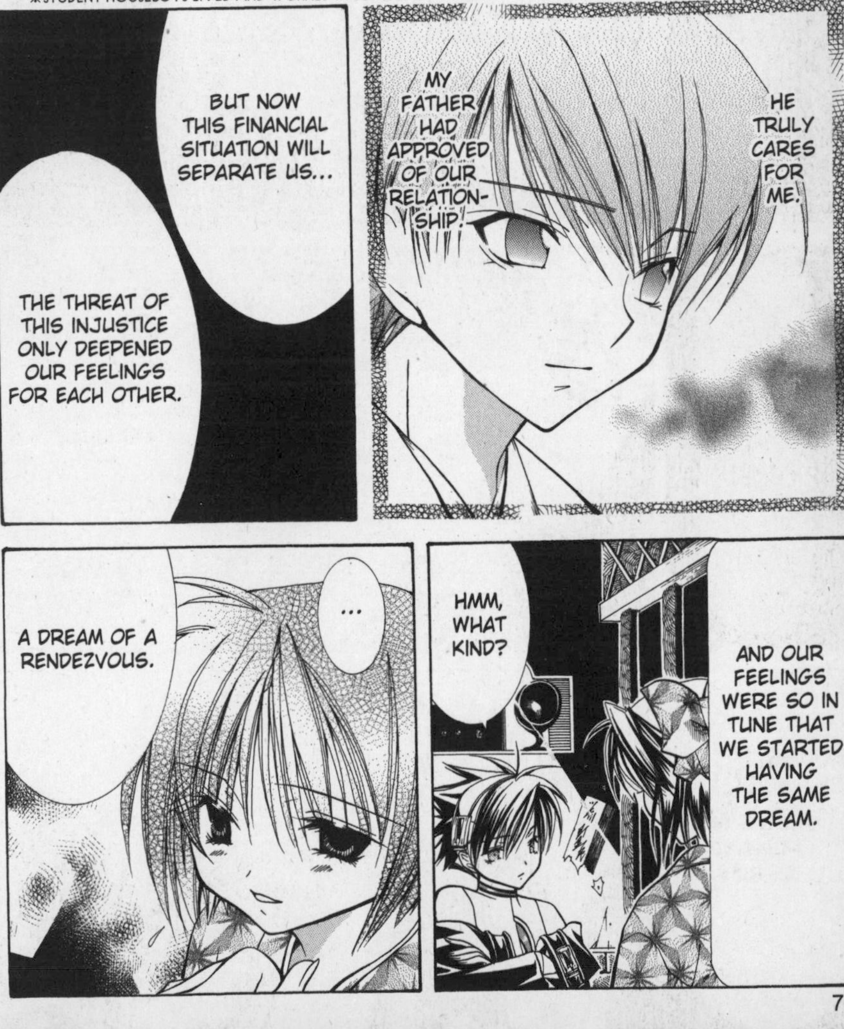
HE TRULY CARES FOR ME.
MY FATHER HAD APPROVED OF OUR RELATION-SHIP.
BUT NOW THIS FINANCIAL SITUATION WILL SEPARATE US...
THE THREAT OF THIS INJUSTICE ONLY DEEPENED OUR FEELINGS FOR EACH OTHER.
AND OUR FEELINGS WERE SO IN TUNE THAT WE STARTED HAVING THE SAME DREAM.
HMM, WHAT KIND?
...
A DREAM OF A RENDEZVOUS.

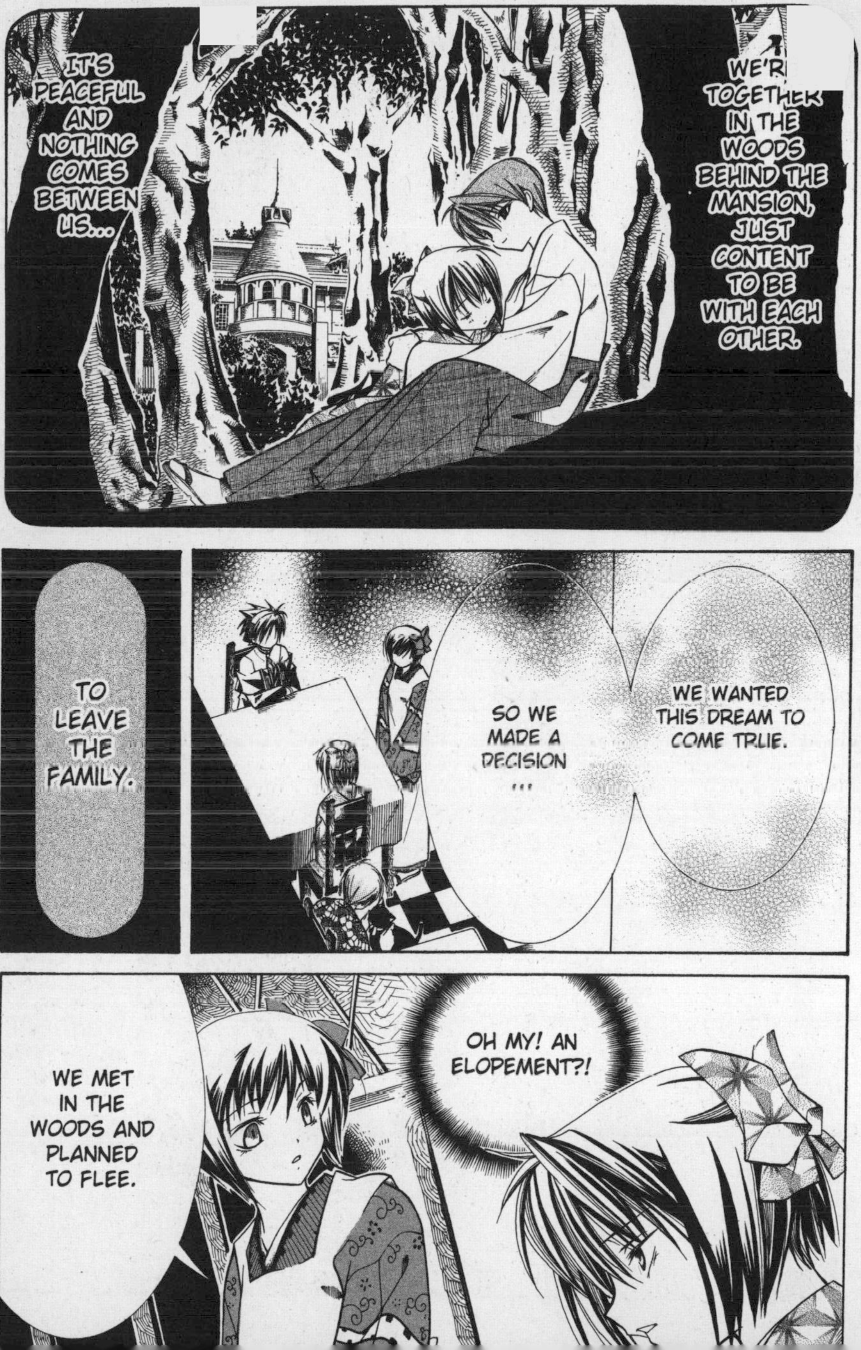

WE'R TOGETHER IN THE WOODS BEHIND THE MANSION, JUST CONTENT TO BE WITH EACH OTHER.
IT'S PEACEFUL AND NOTHING COMES BETWEEN US...
WE WANTED THIS DREAM TO COME TRUE.
SO WE MADE A DECISION ...
TO LEAVE THE FAMILY.
OH MY! AN ELOPEMENT?!
WE MET IN THE WOODS AND PLANNED TO FLEE.

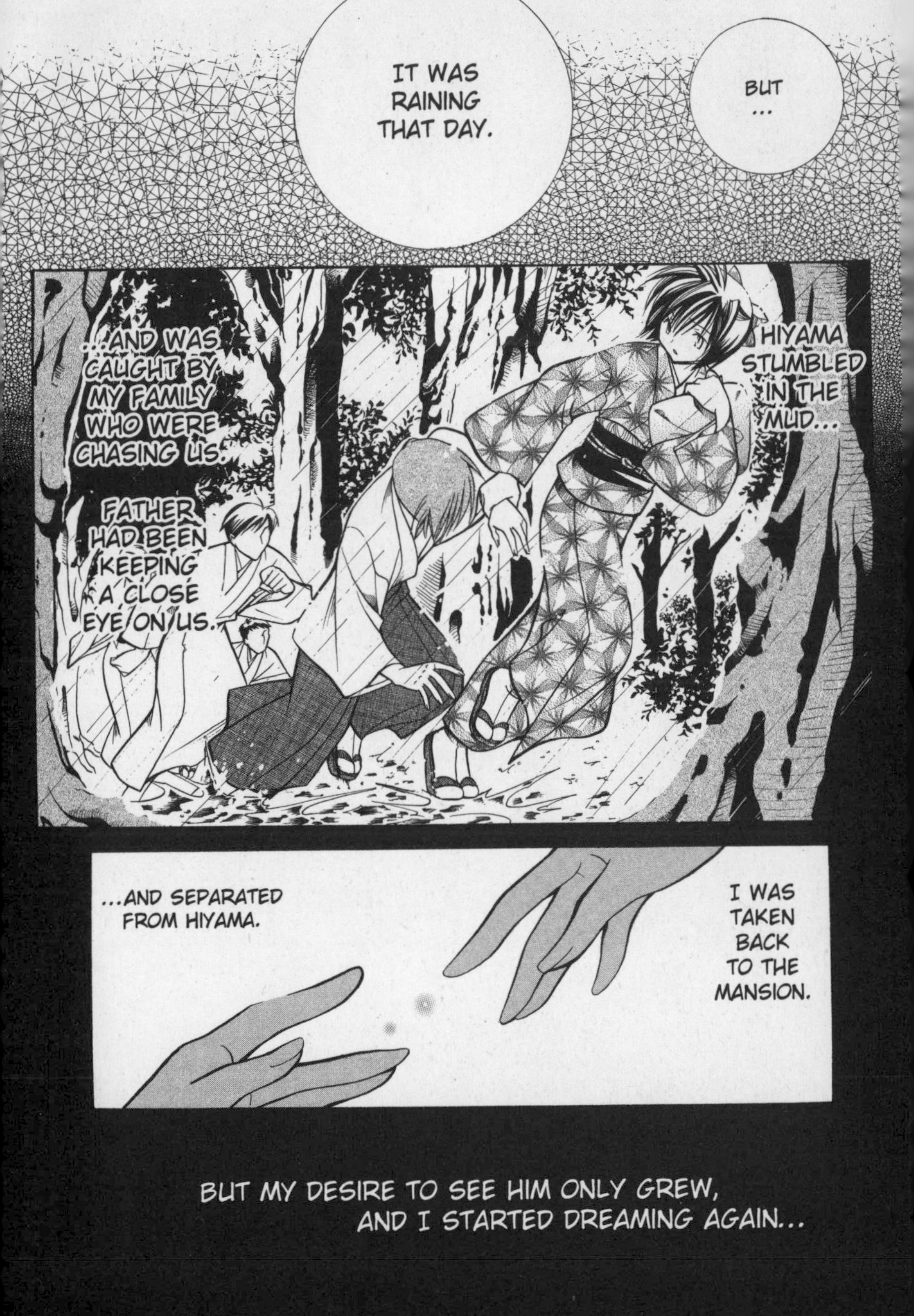
IT WAS RAINING THAT DAY.
BUT ...
HIYAMA STUMBLED IN THE MUD...
...AND WAS CAUGHT BY MY FAMILY WHO WERE CHASING US.
FATHER HAD BEEN KEEPING A CLOSE EYE ON US.
I WAS TAKEN BACK TO THE MANSION.
...AND SEPARATED FROM HIYAMA.
BUT MY DESIRE TO SEE HIM ONLY GREW,
AND I STARTED DREAMING AGAIN...

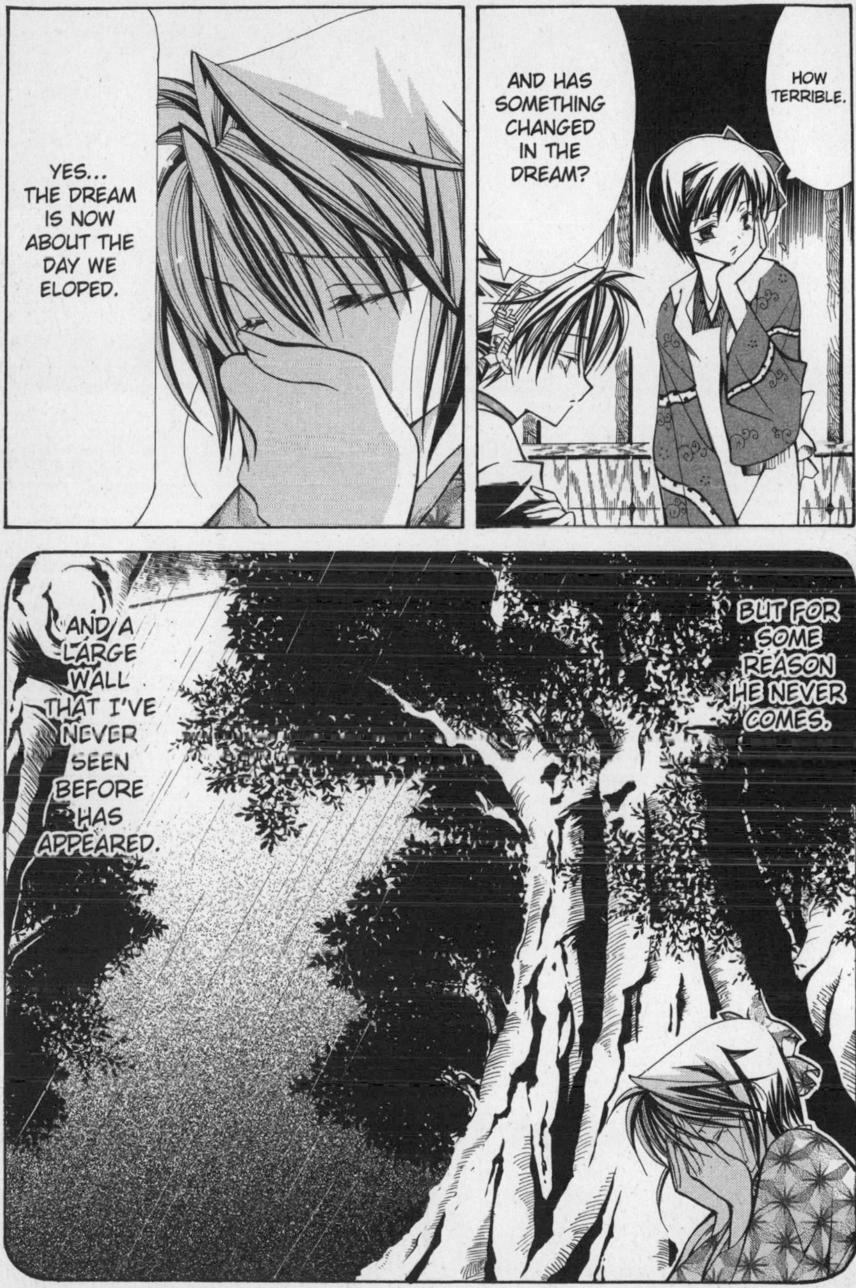
HOW TERRIBLE.
AND HAS SOMETHING CHANGED IN THE DREAM?
YES... THE DREAM IS NOW ABOUT THE DAY WE ELOPED.
BUT FOR SOME REASON HE NEVER COMES.
AND A LARGE WALL THAT I'VE NEVER SEEN BEFORE HAS APPEARED.

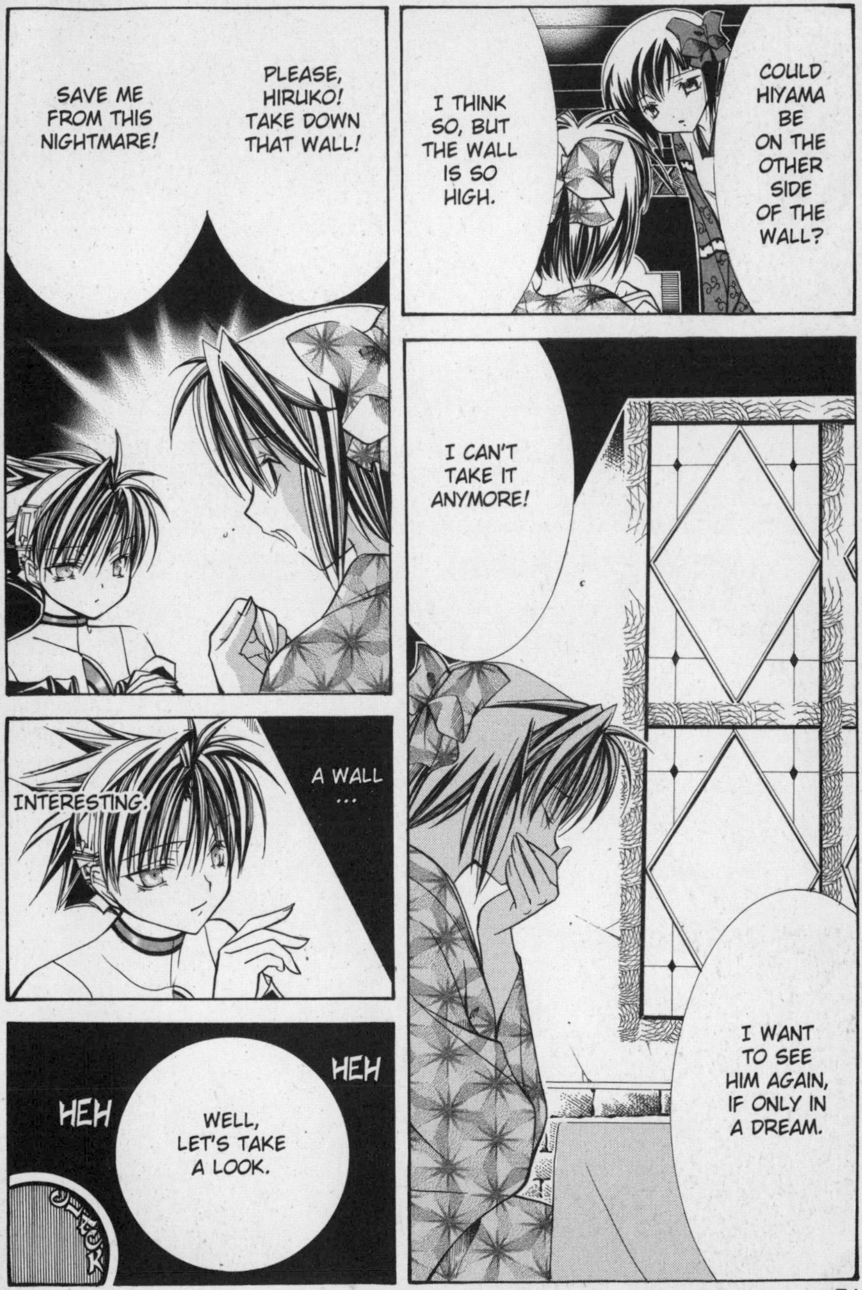

COULD HIYAMA BE ON THE OTHER SIDE OF THE WALL?
I THINK SO, BUT THE WALL IS SO HIGH.
PLEASE, HIRUKO! TAKE DOWN THAT WALL!
SAVE ME FROM THIS NIGHTMARE!
I CAN'T TAKE IT ANYMORE!
I WANT TO SEE HIM AGAIN, IF ONLY IN A DREAM.
A WALL ...
INTERESTING.
HEH
HEH
WELL, LET'S TAKE A LOOK.

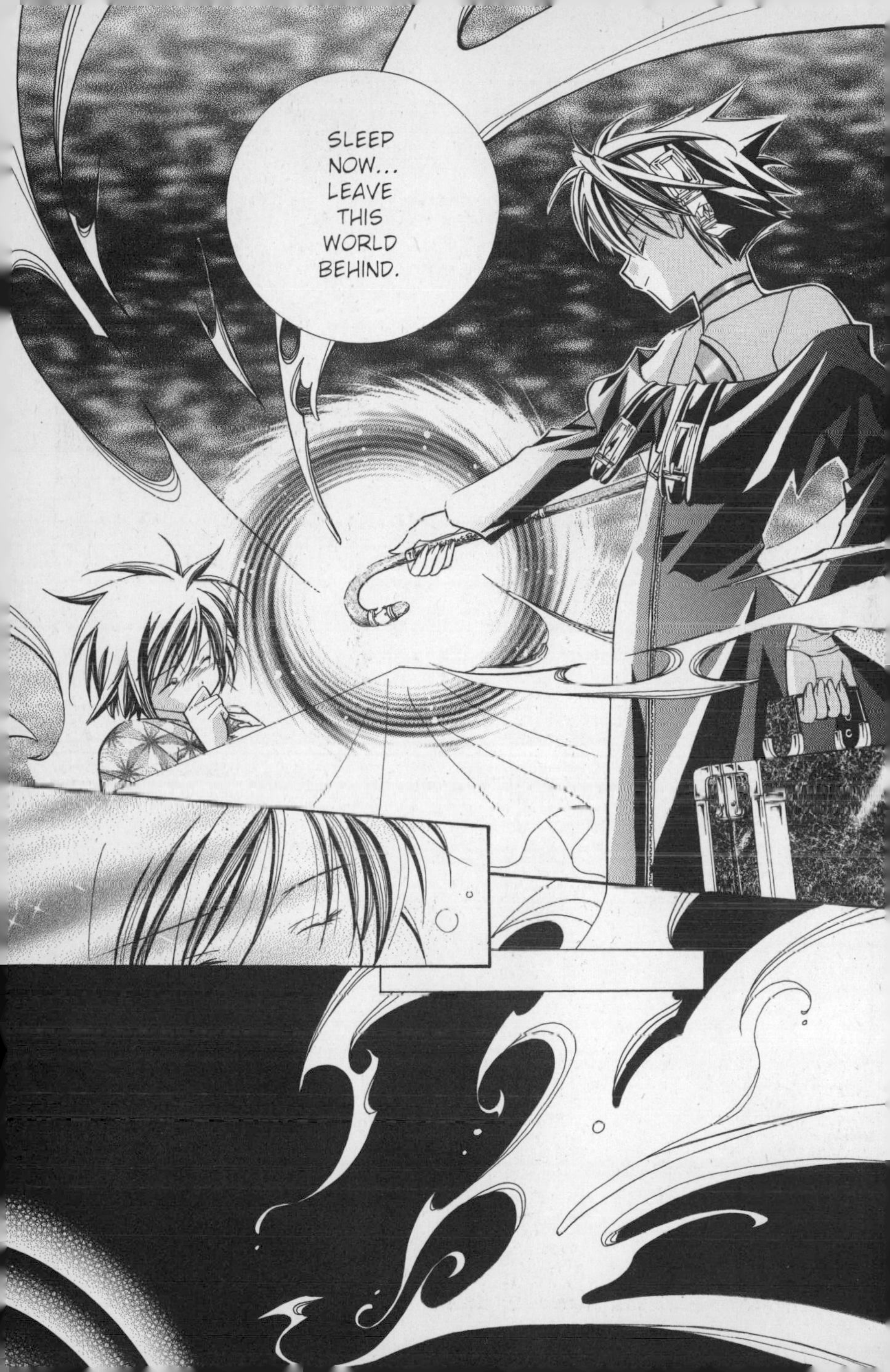
SLEEP NOW... LEAVE THIS WORLD BEHIND.

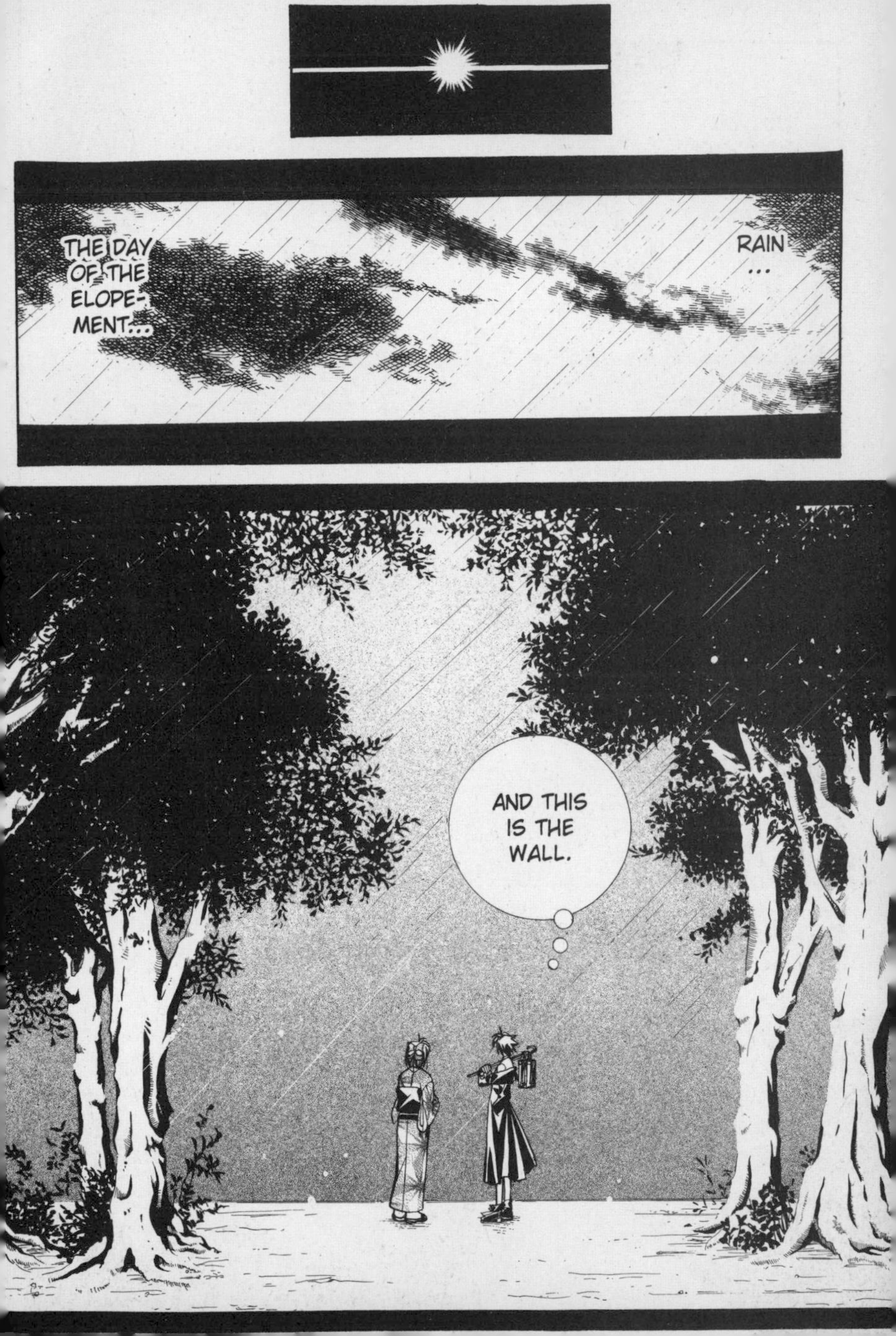
RAIN ...
THE DAY OF THE ELOPEMENT...
AND THIS IS THE WALL.

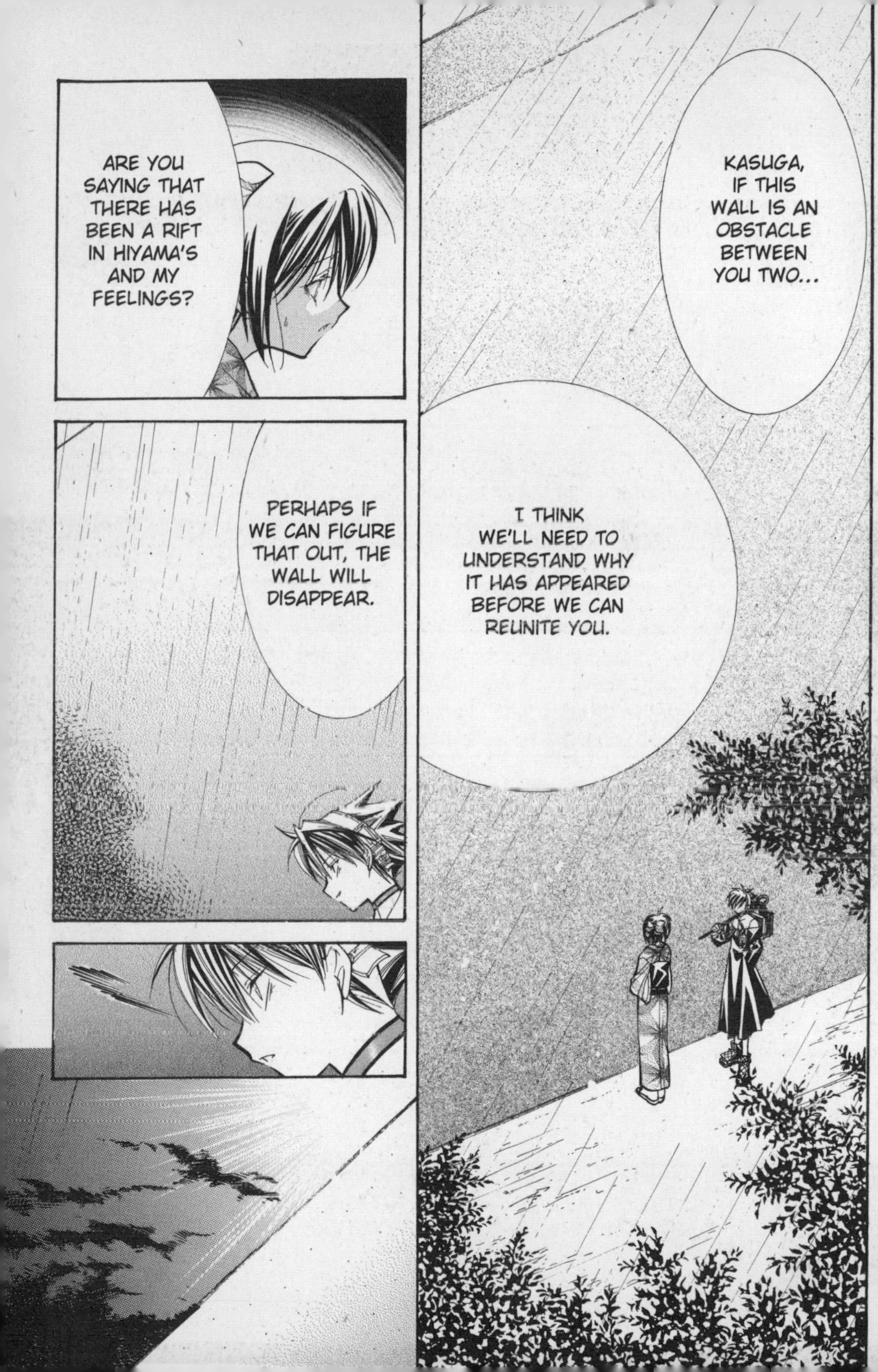
KASUGA, IF THIS WALL IS AN OBSTACLE BETWEEN YOU TWO...
I THINK WE'LL NEED TO UNDERSTAND WHY IT HAS APPEARED BEFORE WE CAN REUNITE YOU.
ARE YOU SAYING THAT THERE HAS BEEN A RIFT IN HIYAMA'S AND MY FEELINGS?
PERHAPS IF WE CAN FIGURE THAT OUT, THE WALL WILL DISAPPEAR.

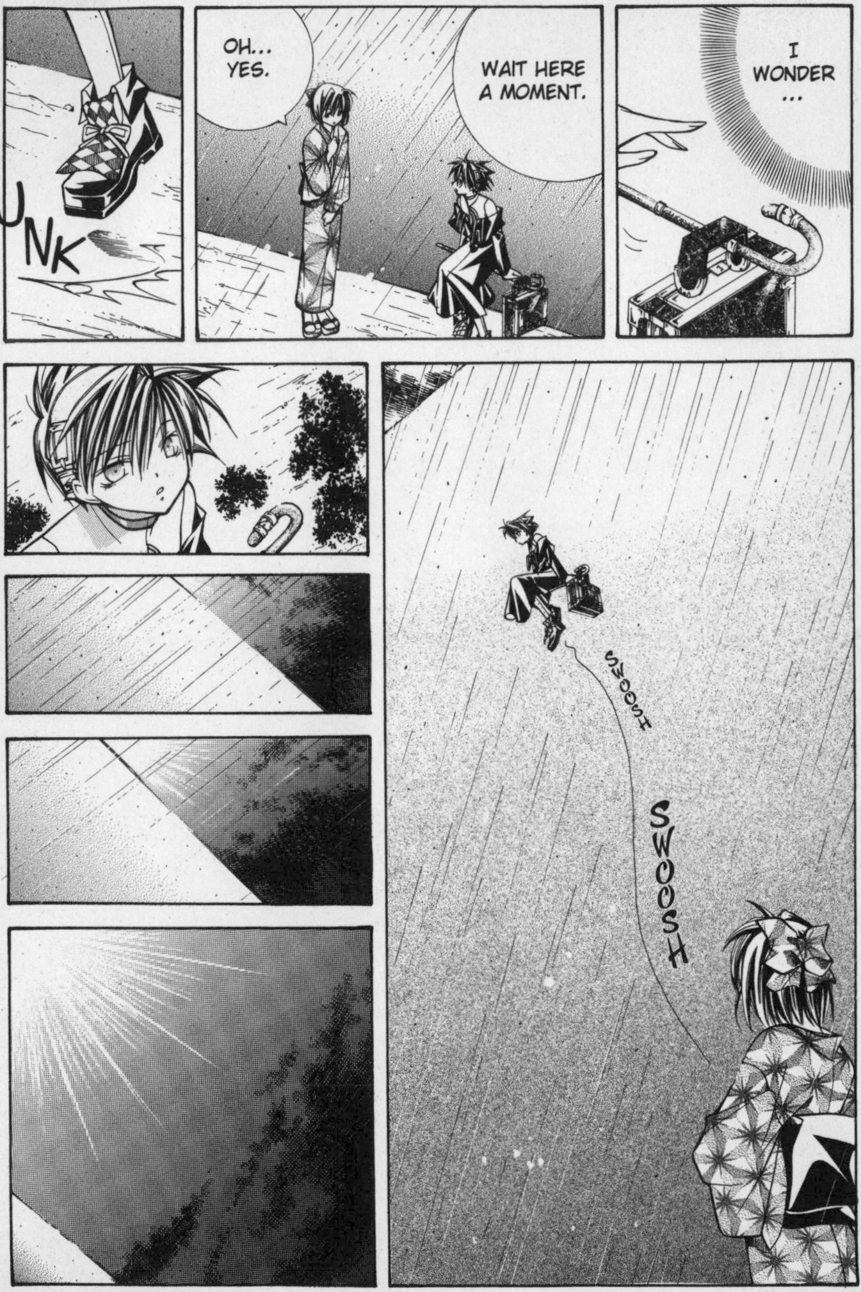
I WONDER ...
WAIT HERE A MOMENT.
OH... YES.
HUNK
SWOOSH
SWOOSH

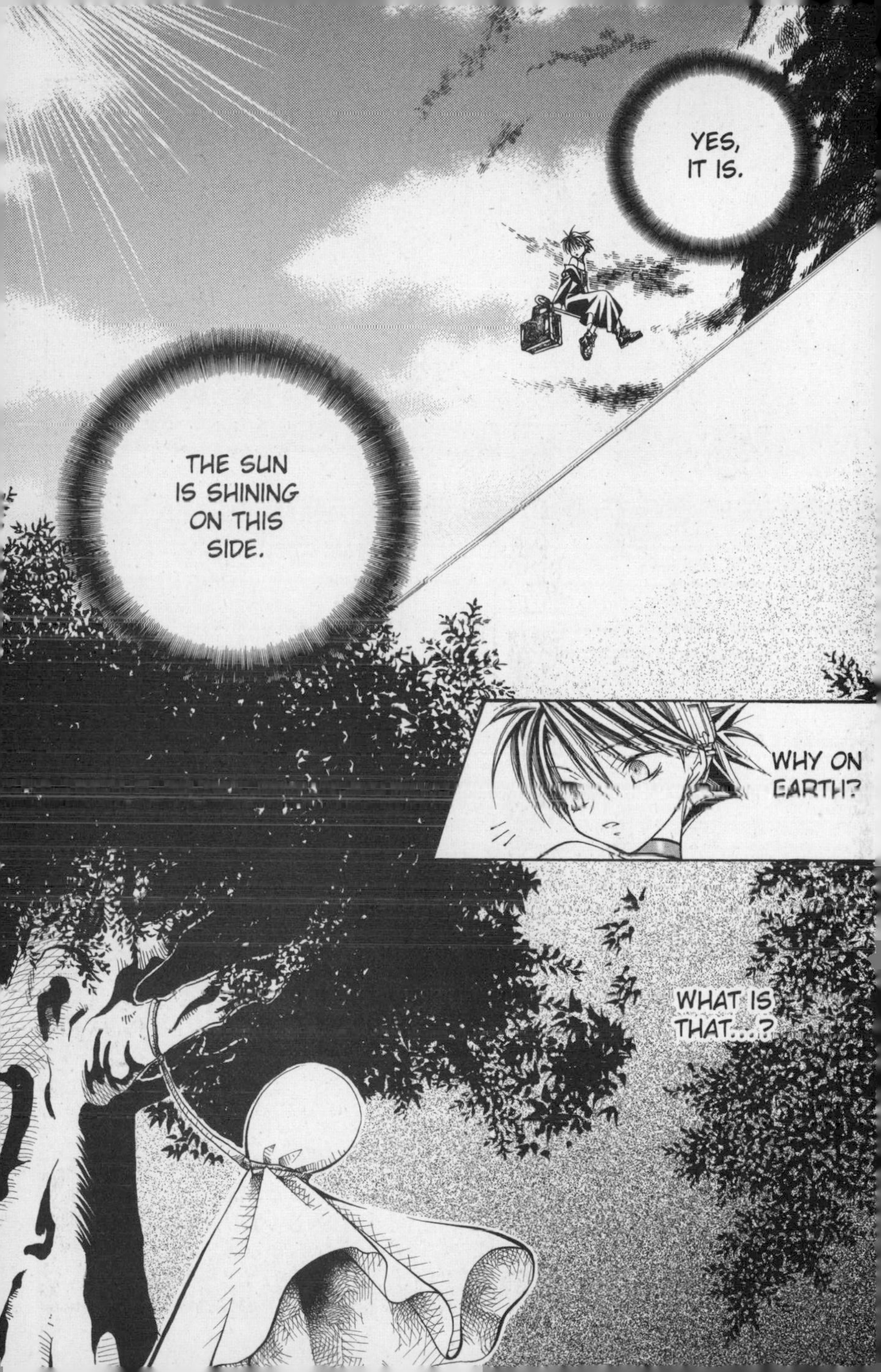
YES, IT IS.
THE SUN IS SHINING ON THIS SIDE.
WHY ON EARTH?
WHAT IS THAT...?

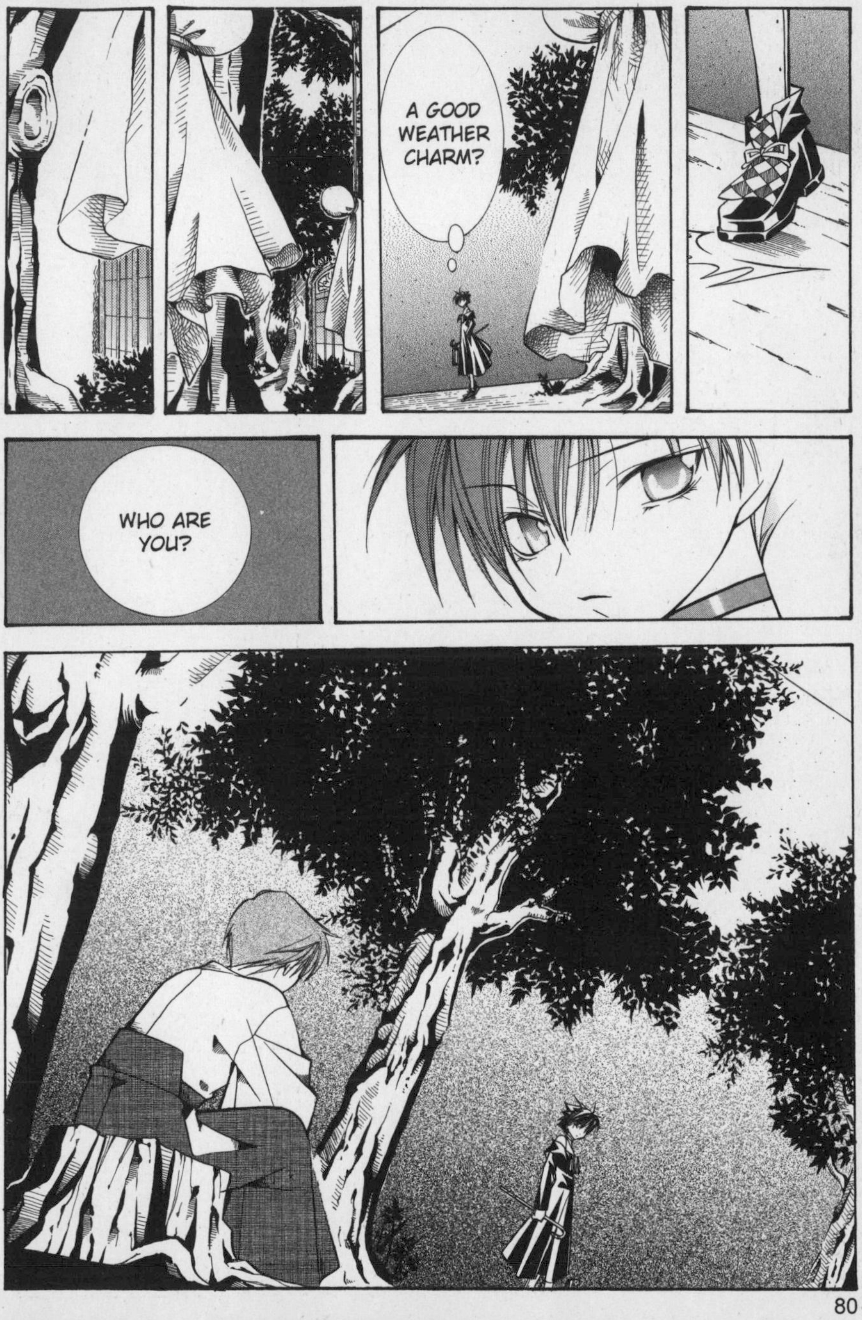
A GOOD WEATHER CHARM?
WHO ARE YOU?

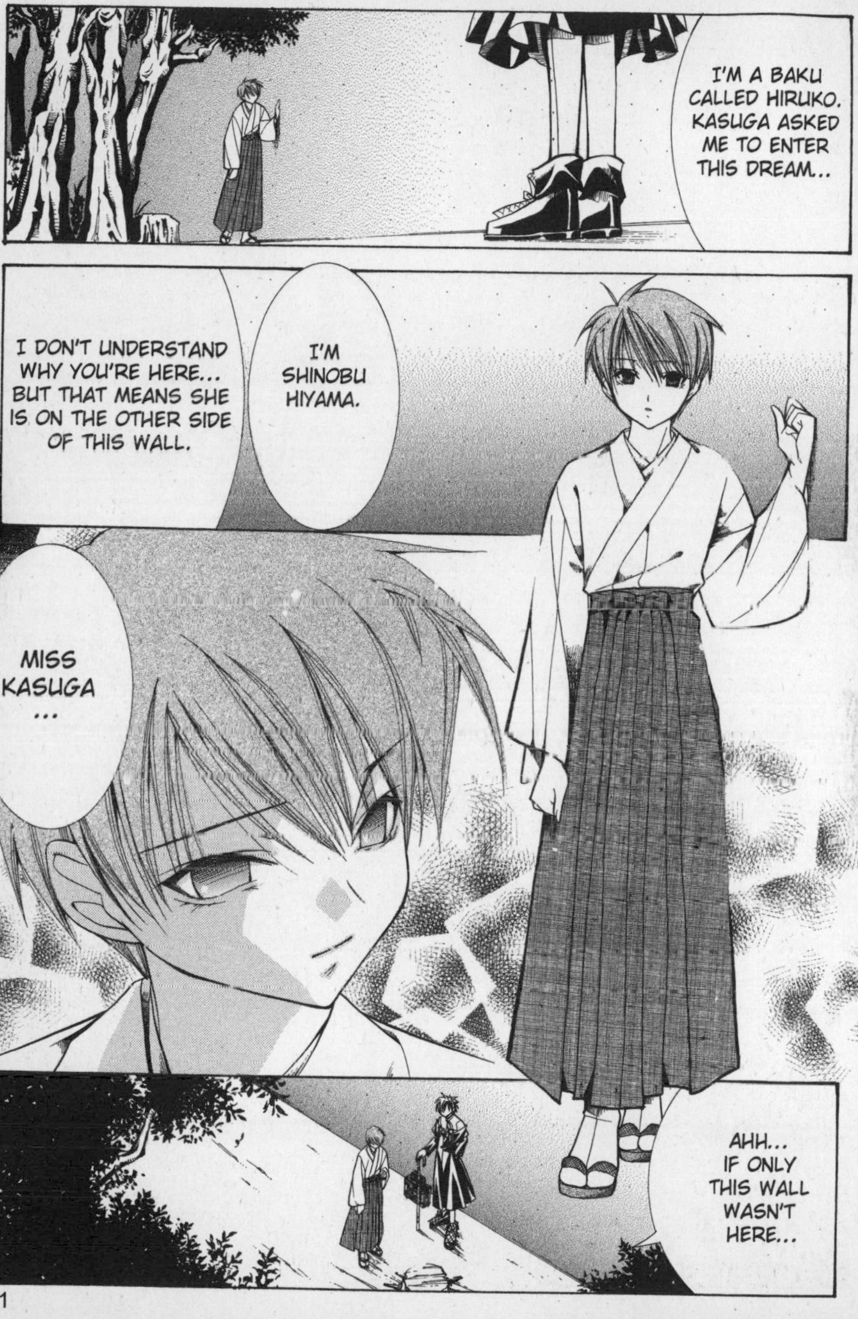
I'M A BAKU CALLED HIRUKO. KASUGA ASKED ME TO ENTER THIS DREAM...
I'M SHINOBU HIYAMA.
I DON'T UNDERSTAND WHY YOU'RE HERE... BUT THAT MEANS SHE IS ON THE OTHER SIDE OF THIS WALL.
MISS KASUGA ...
AHH... IF ONLY THIS WALL WASN'T HERE...

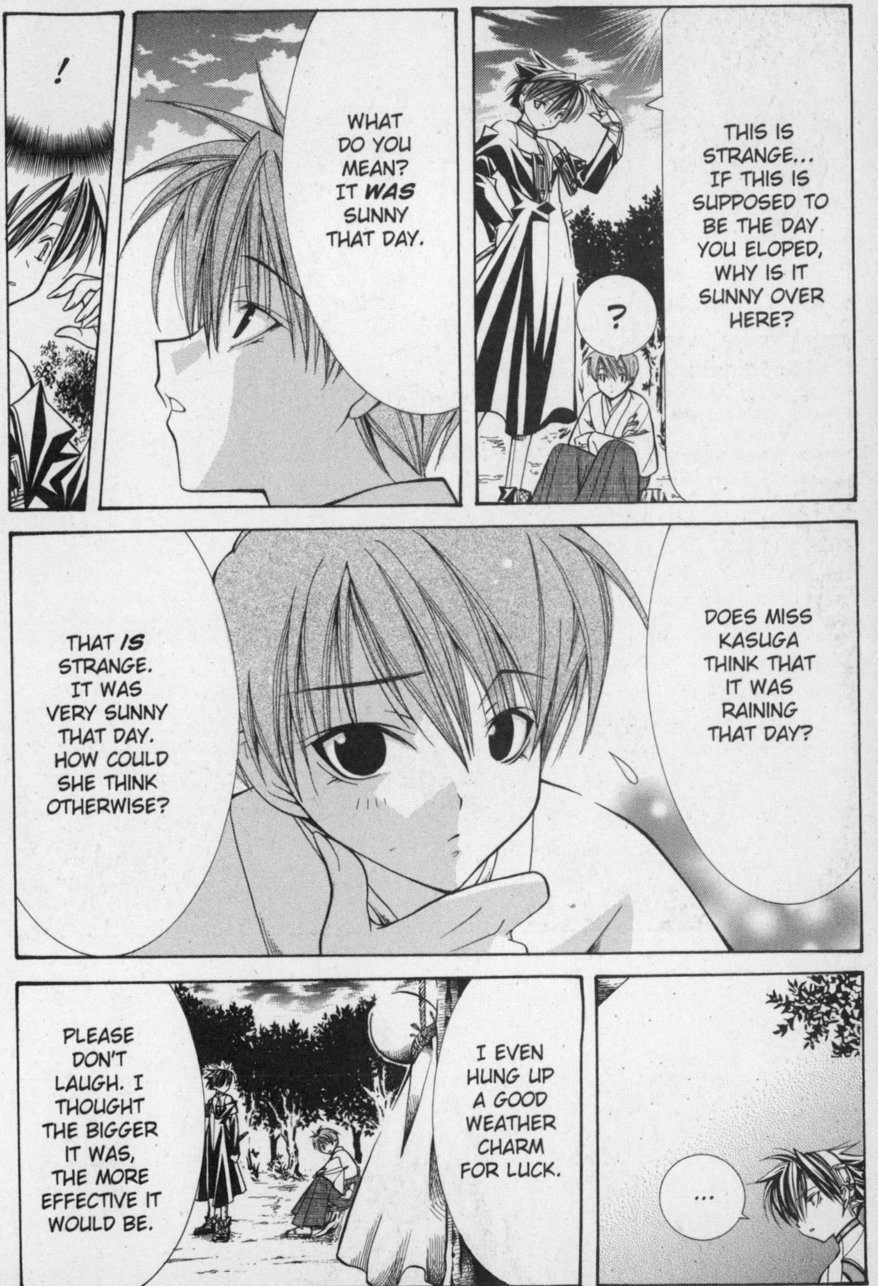
THIS IS STRANGE... IF THIS IS SUPPOSED TO BE THE DAY YOU ELOPED, WHY IS IT SUNNY OVER HERE?
?
WHAT DO YOU MEAN? IT *WAS* SUNNY THAT DAY.
!
DOES MISS KASUGA THINK THAT IT WAS RAINING THAT DAY?
THAT *IS* STRANGE. IT WAS VERY SUNNY THAT DAY. HOW COULD SHE THINK OTHERWISE?
...
I EVEN HUNG UP A GOOD WEATHER CHARM FOR LUCK.
PLEASE DON'T LAUGH. I THOUGHT THE BIGGER IT WAS, THE MORE EFFECTIVE IT WOULD BE.

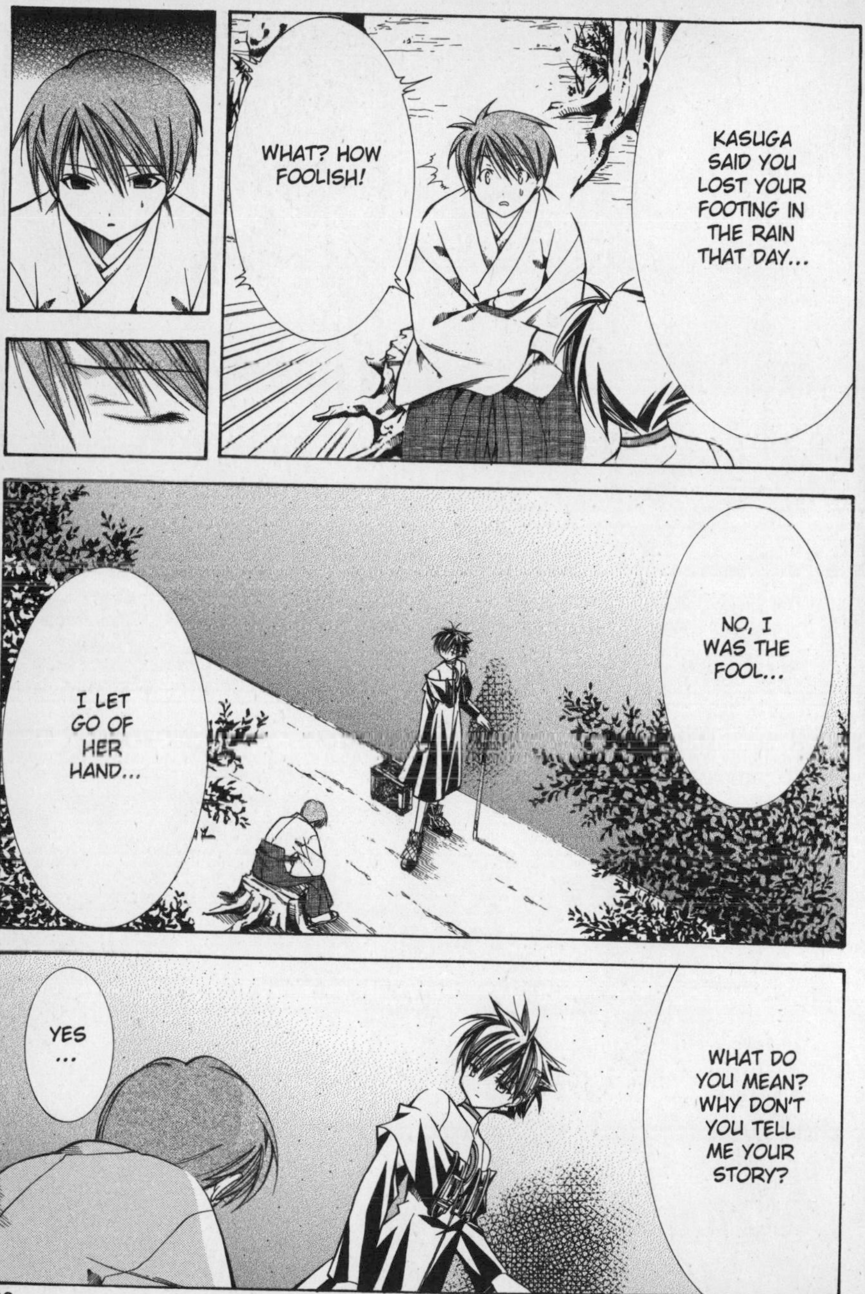
KASUGA SAID YOU LOST YOUR FOOTING IN THE RAIN THAT DAY...
WHAT? HOW FOOLISH!
NO, I WAS THE FOOL...
I LET GO OF HER HAND...
WHAT DO YOU MEAN? WHY DON'T YOU TELL ME YOUR STORY?
YES ...

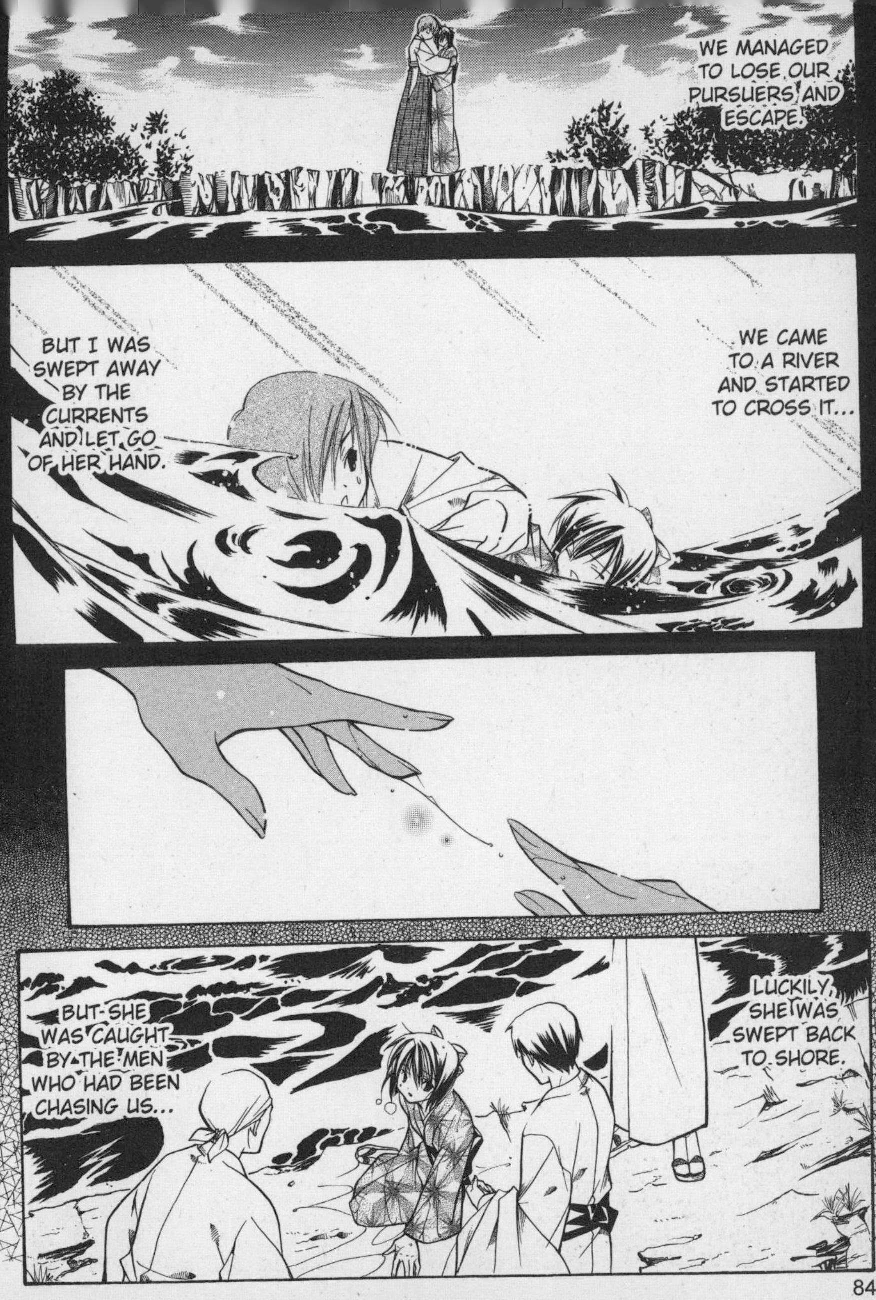
WE MANAGED TO LOSE OUR PURSUERS AND ESCAPE.
WE CAME TO A RIVER AND STARTED TO CROSS IT...
BUT I WAS SWEPT AWAY BY THE CURRENTS AND LET GO OF HER HAND.
LUCKILY, SHE WAS SWEPT BACK TO SHORE.
BUT SHE WAS CAUGHT BY THE MEN WHO HAD BEEN CHASING US...

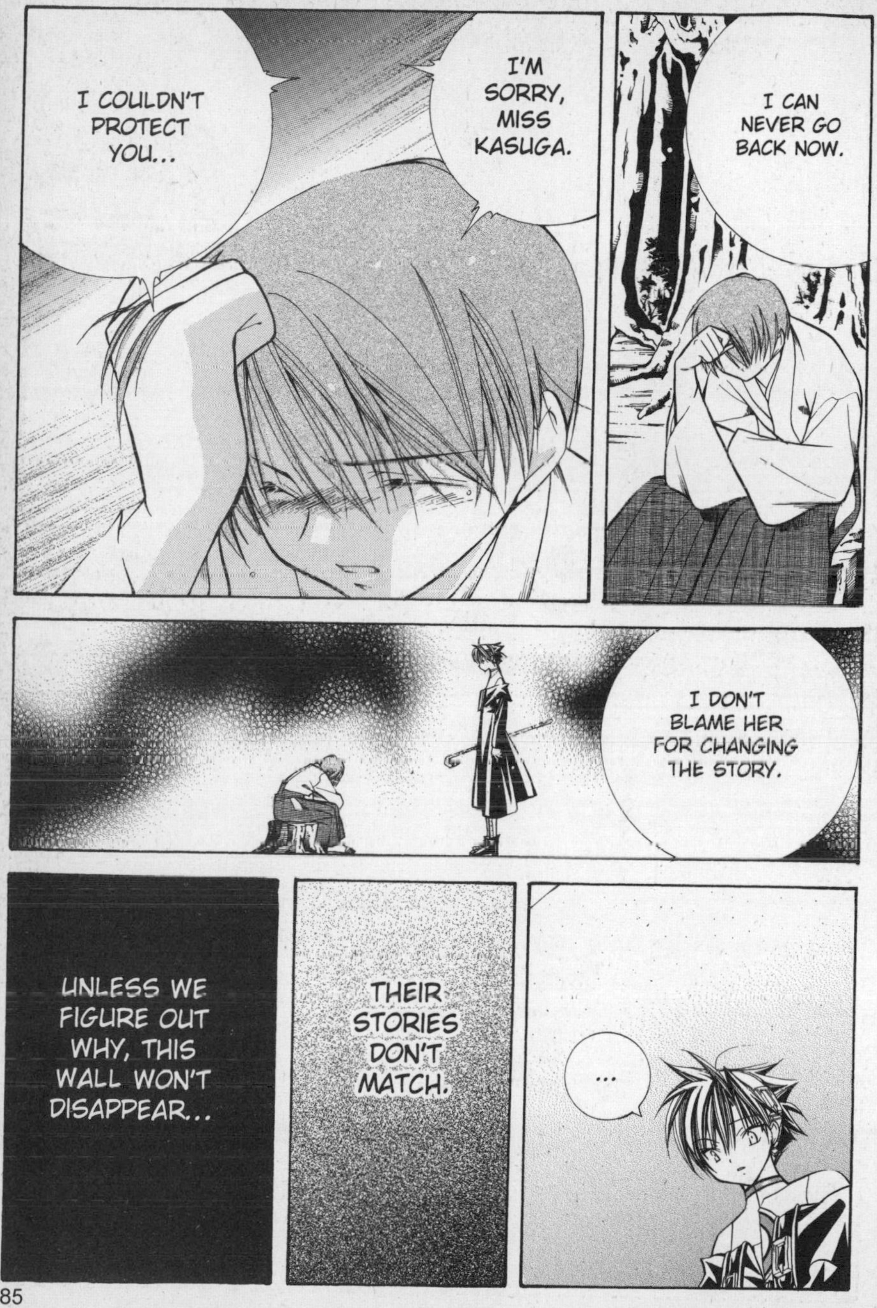
I CAN NEVER GO BACK NOW.
I'M SORRY, MISS KASUGA.
I COULDN'T PROTECT YOU...
I DON'T BLAME HER FOR CHANGING THE STORY.
...
THEIR STORIES DON'T MATCH.
UNLESS WE FIGURE OUT WHY, THIS WALL WON'T DISAPPEAR...

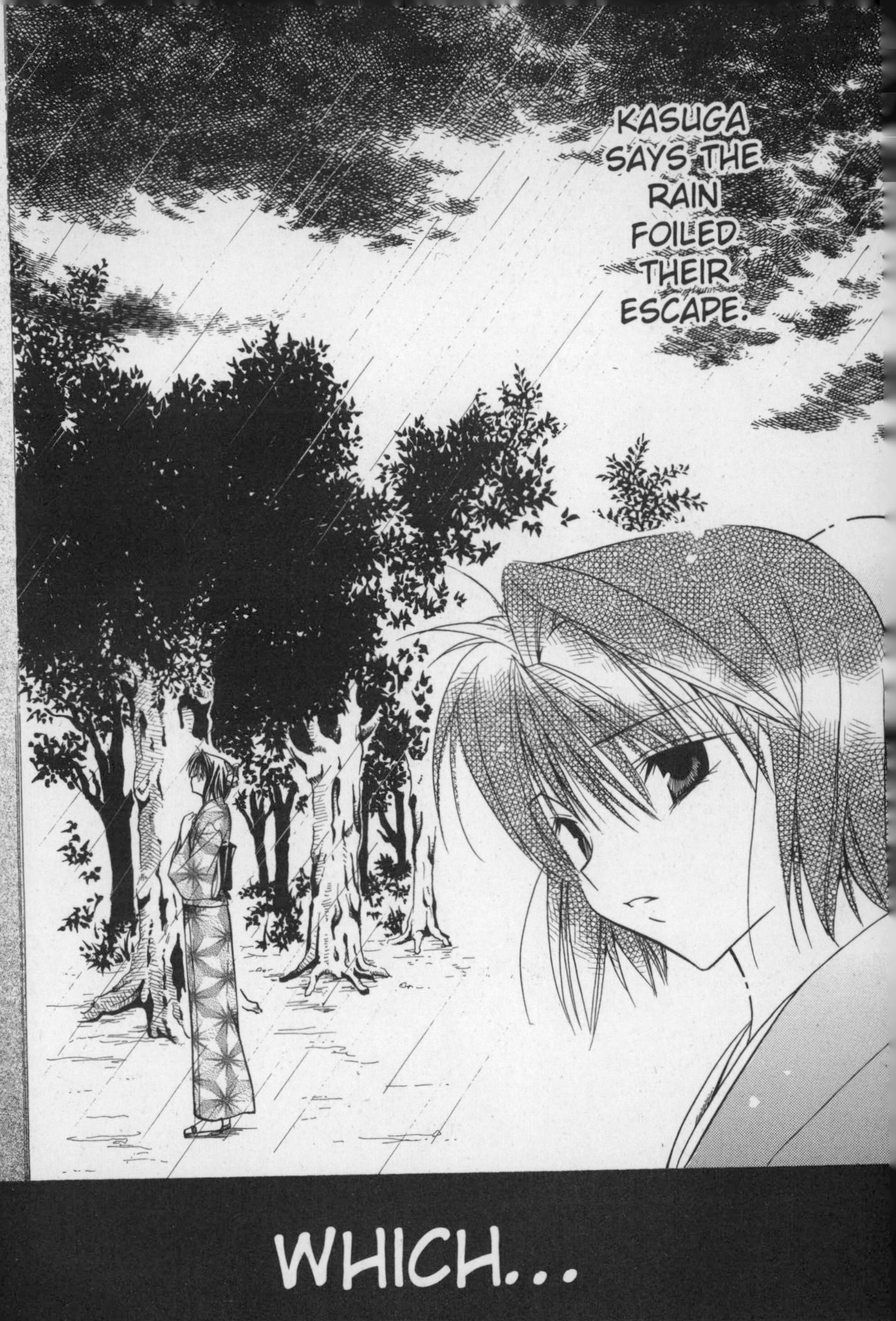
KASUGA SAYS THE RAIN FOILED THEIR ESCAPE.
WHICH...

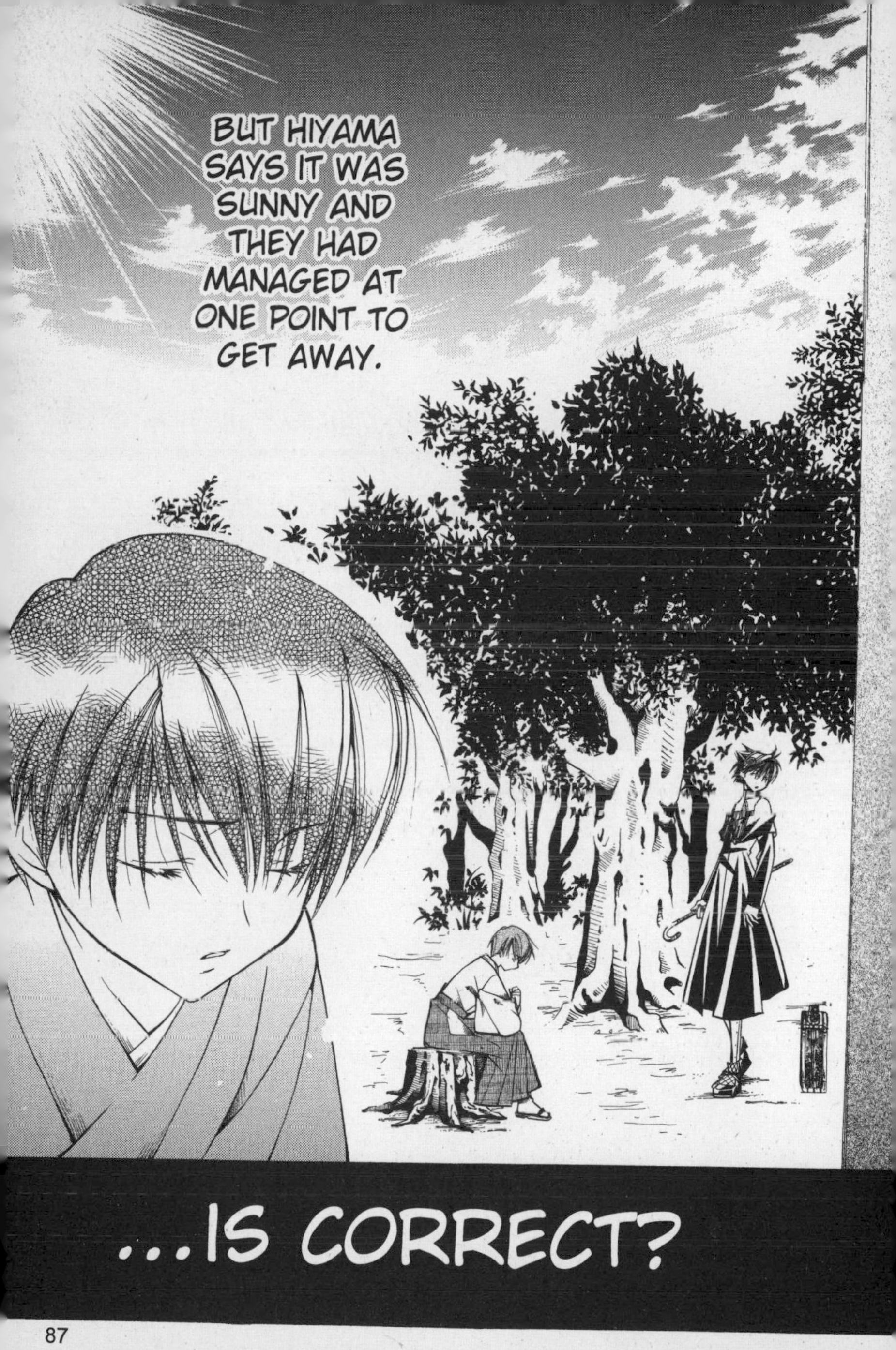
BUT HIYAMA SAYS IT WAS SUNNY AND THEY HAD MANAGED AT ONE POINT TO GET AWAY.
...IS CORRECT?

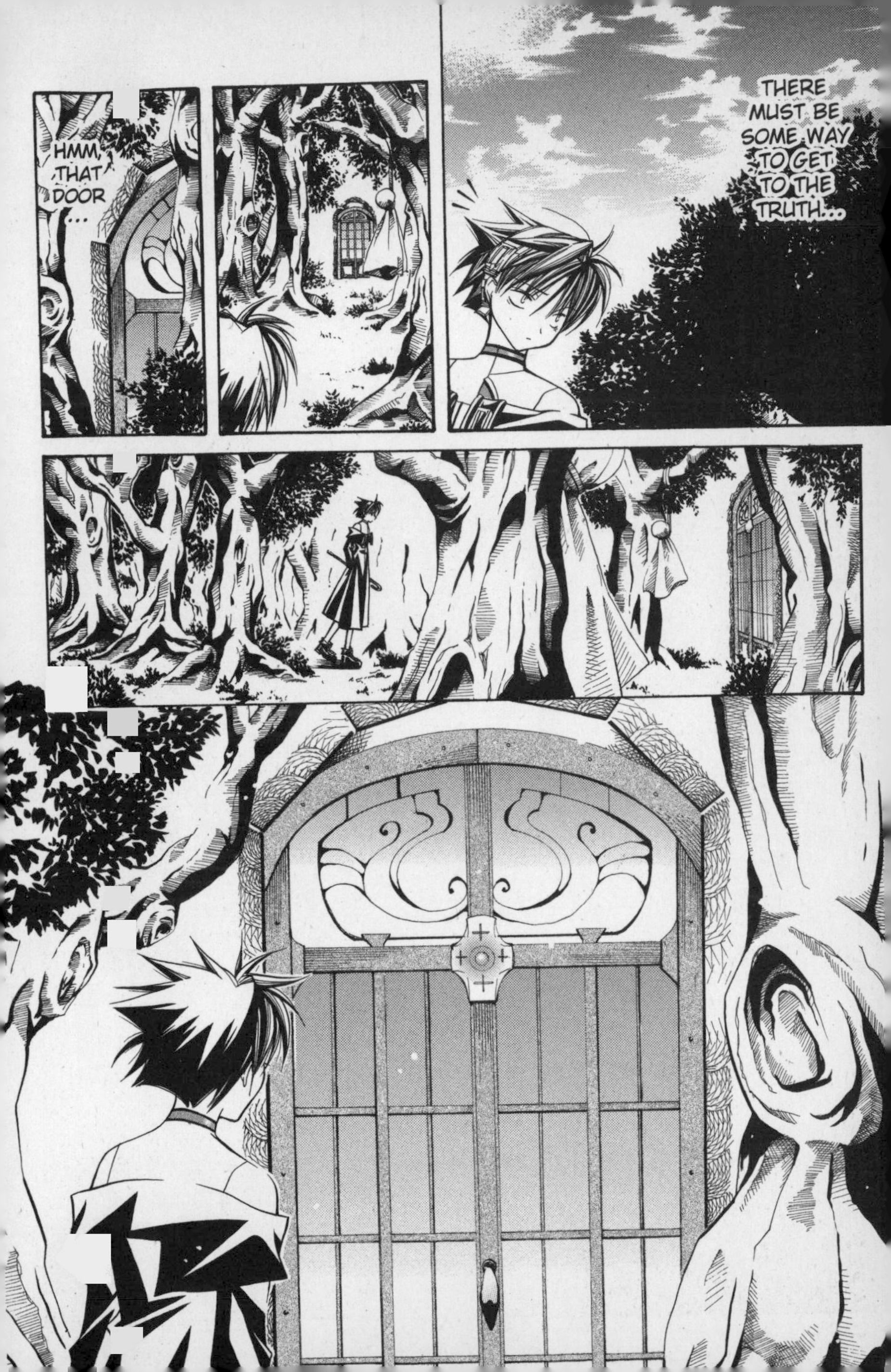
THERE MUST BE SOME WAY TO GET TO THE TRUTH...
HMM, THAT DOOR...

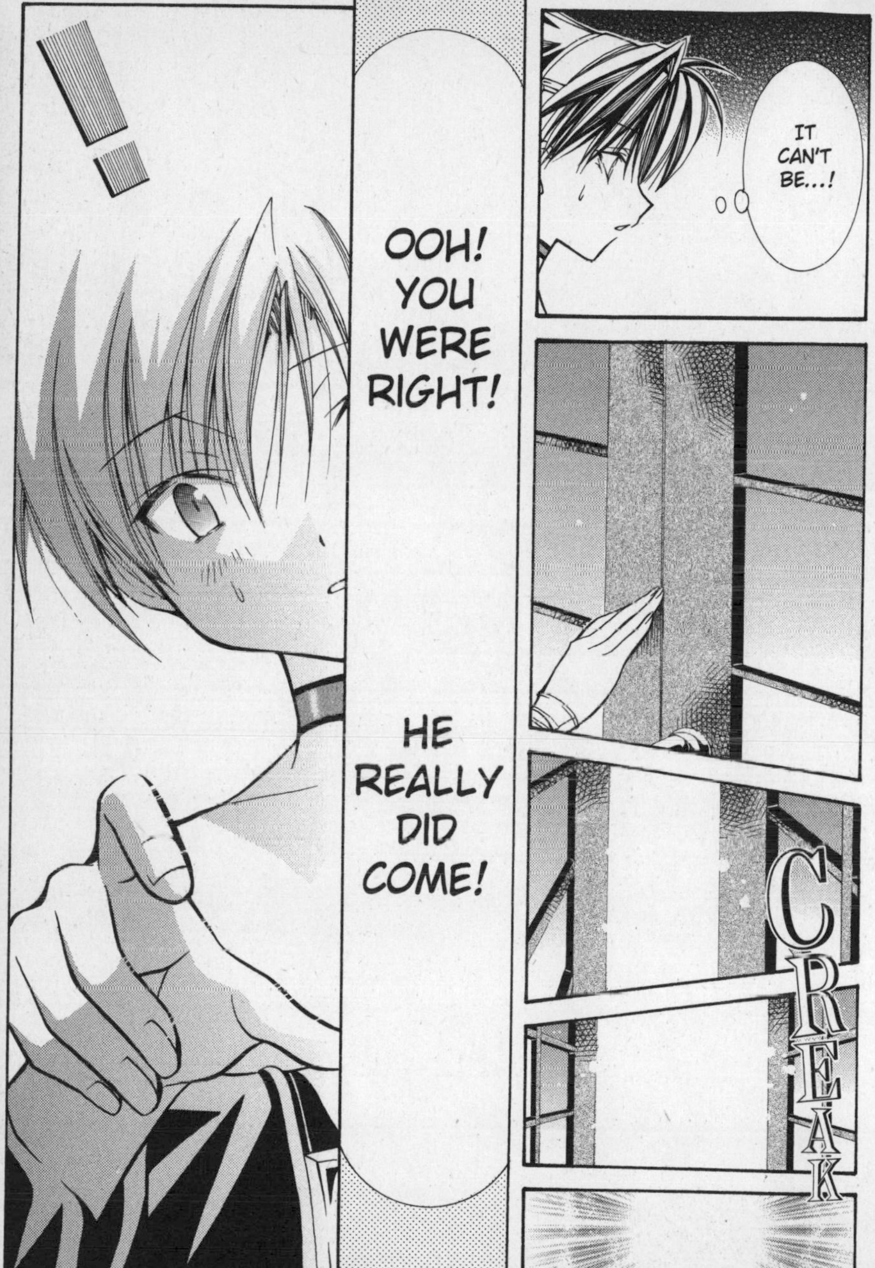
IT CAN'T BE...!
CREAK
OOH! YOU WERE RIGHT!
HE REALLY DID COME!

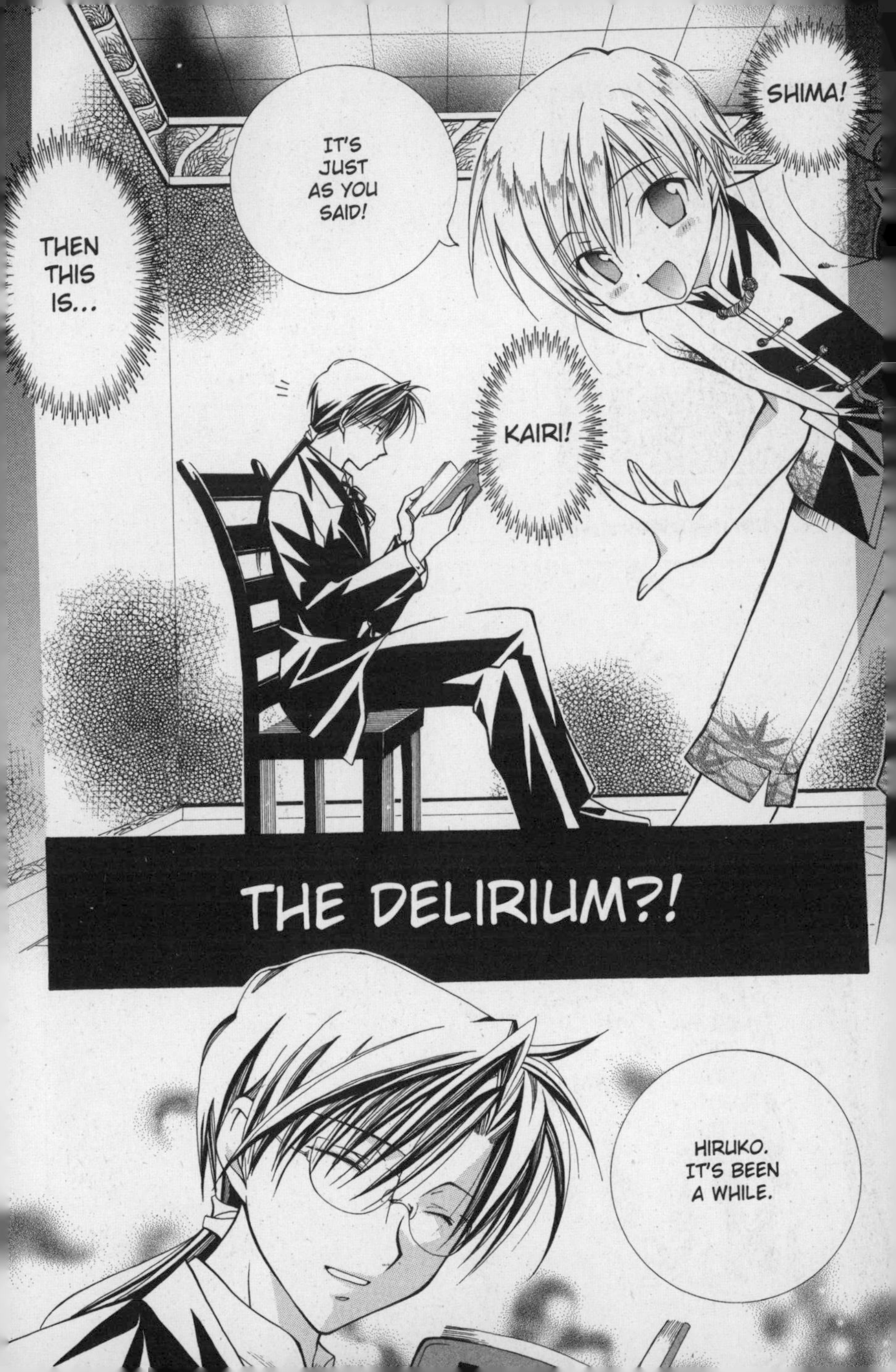
SHIMA!
IT'S JUST AS YOU SAID!
THEN THIS IS...
KAIRI!
THE DELIRIUM?!
HIRUKO. IT'S BEEN A WHILE.

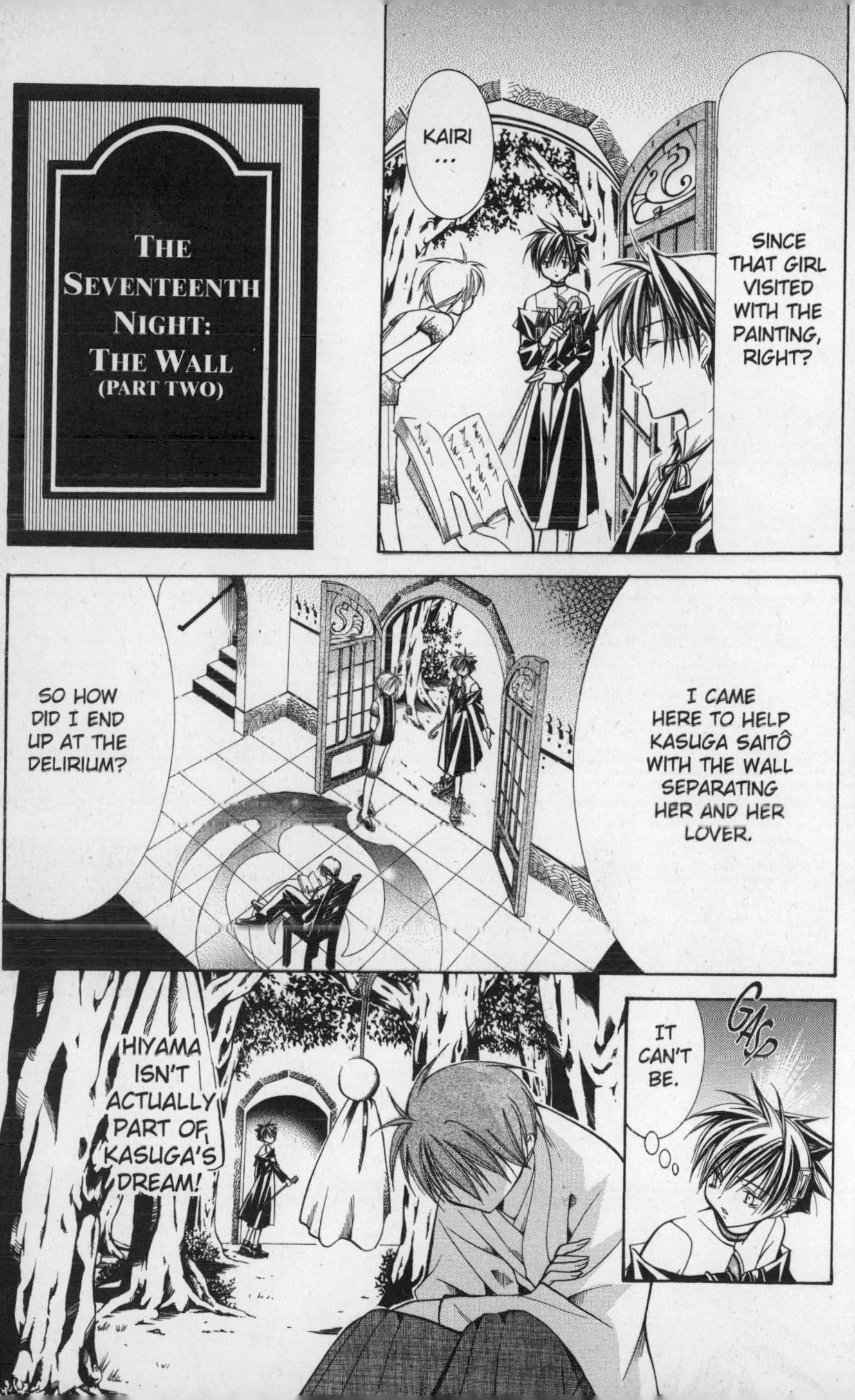
SINCE THAT GIRL VISITED WITH THE PAINTING, RIGHT?
KAIRI ...
THE SEVENTEENTH NIGHT: THE WALL (PART TWO)
I CAME HERE TO HELP KASUGA SAITÔ WITH THE WALL SEPARATING HER AND HER LOVER.
SO HOW DID I END UP AT THE DELIRIUM?
GASP
IT CAN'T BE.
HIYAMA ISN'T ACTUALLY PART OF KASUGA'S DREAM!

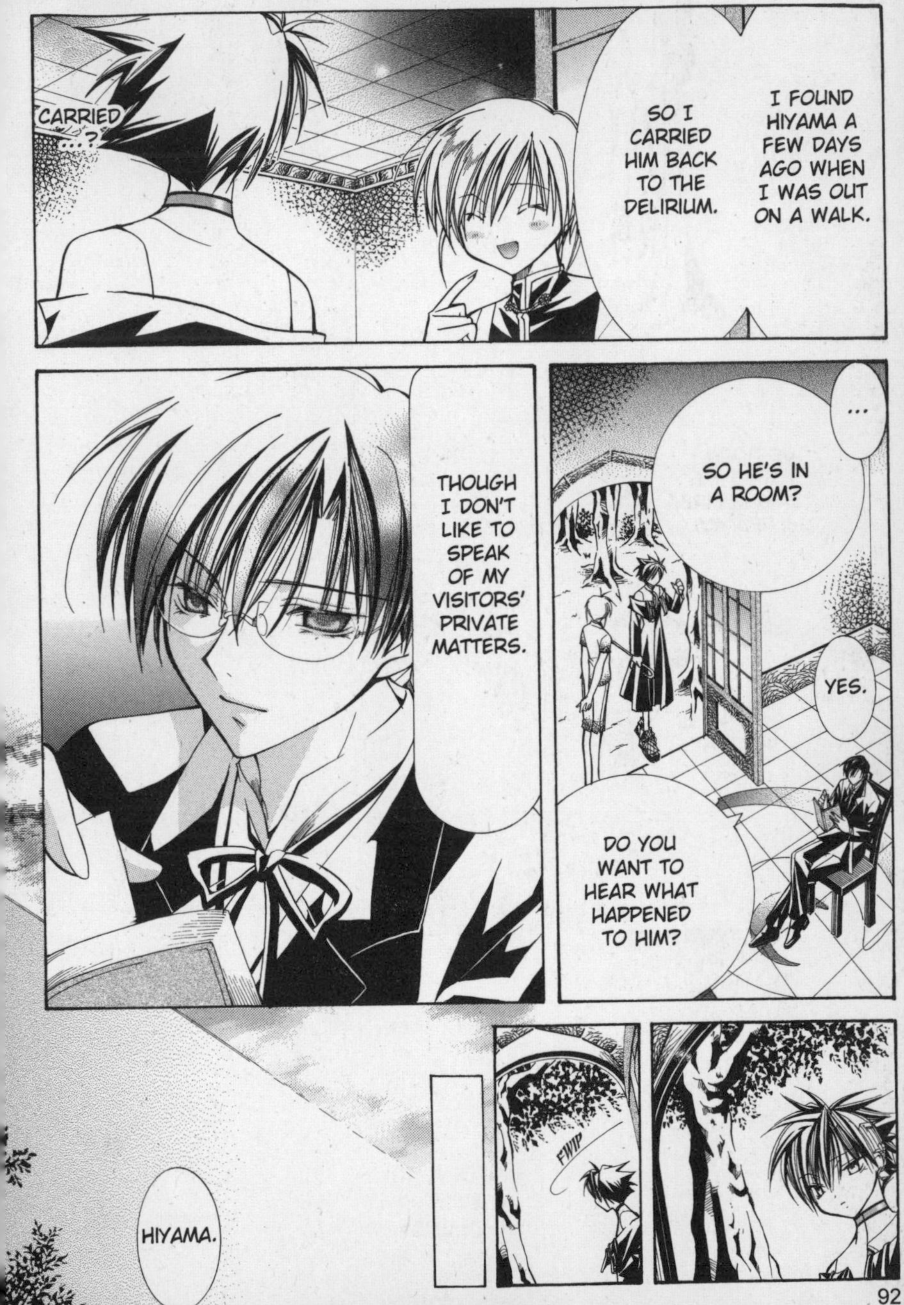
I FOUND HIYAMA A FEW DAYS AGO WHEN I WAS OUT ON A WALK.
SO I CARRIED HIM BACK TO THE DELIRIUM.
CARRIED ...?
...
SO HE'S IN A ROOM?
YES.
DO YOU WANT TO HEAR WHAT HAPPENED TO HIM?
THOUGH I DON'T LIKE TO SPEAK OF MY VISITORS' PRIVATE MATTERS.
FWIP
HIYAMA.

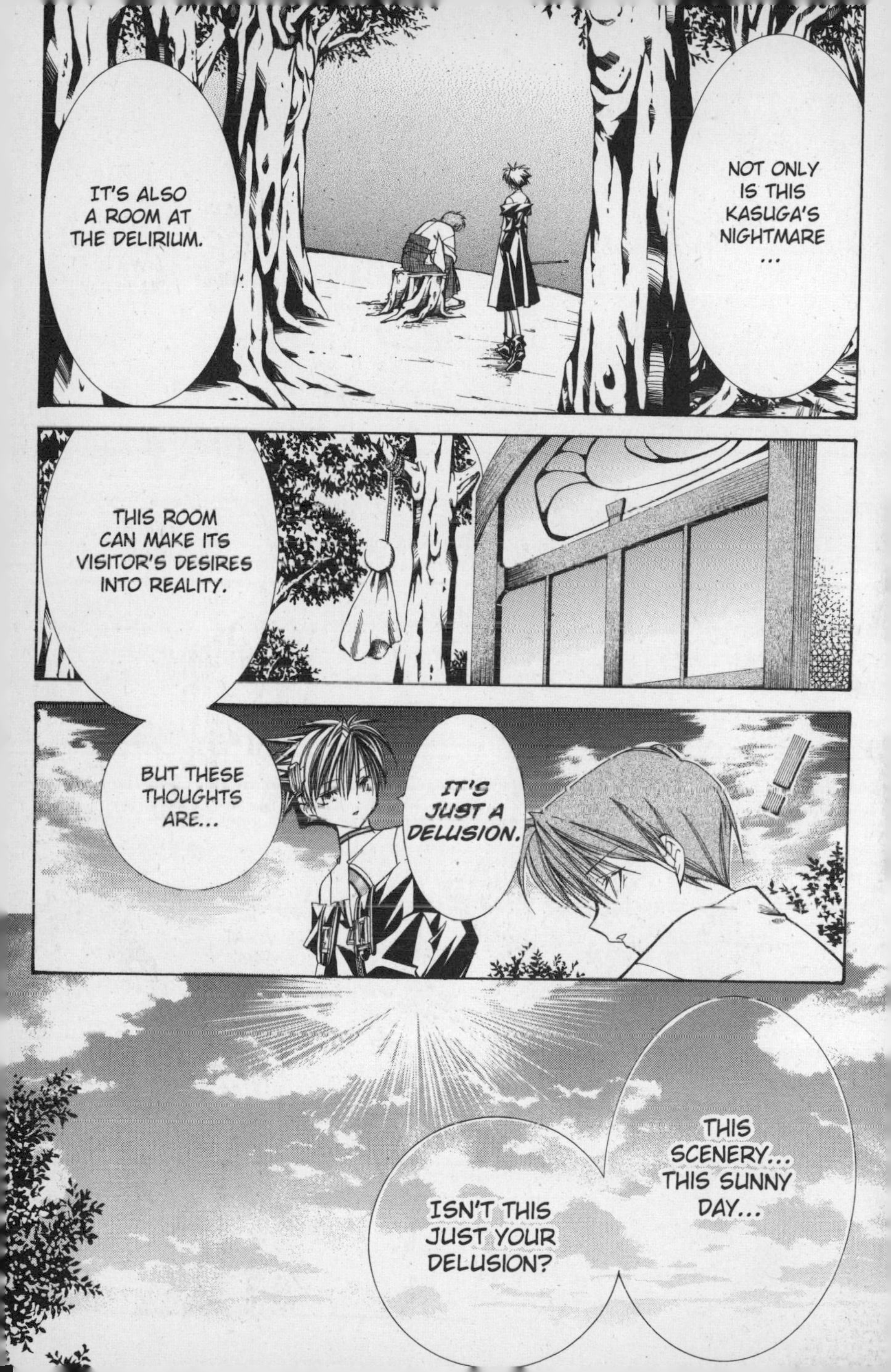
NOT ONLY IS THIS KASUGA'S NIGHTMARE ...
IT'S ALSO A ROOM AT THE DELIRIUM.
THIS ROOM CAN MAKE ITS VISITOR'S DESIRES INTO REALITY.
BUT THESE THOUGHTS ARE...
IT'S JUST A DELUSION.
THIS SCENERY... THIS SUNNY DAY...
ISN'T THIS JUST YOUR DELUSION?

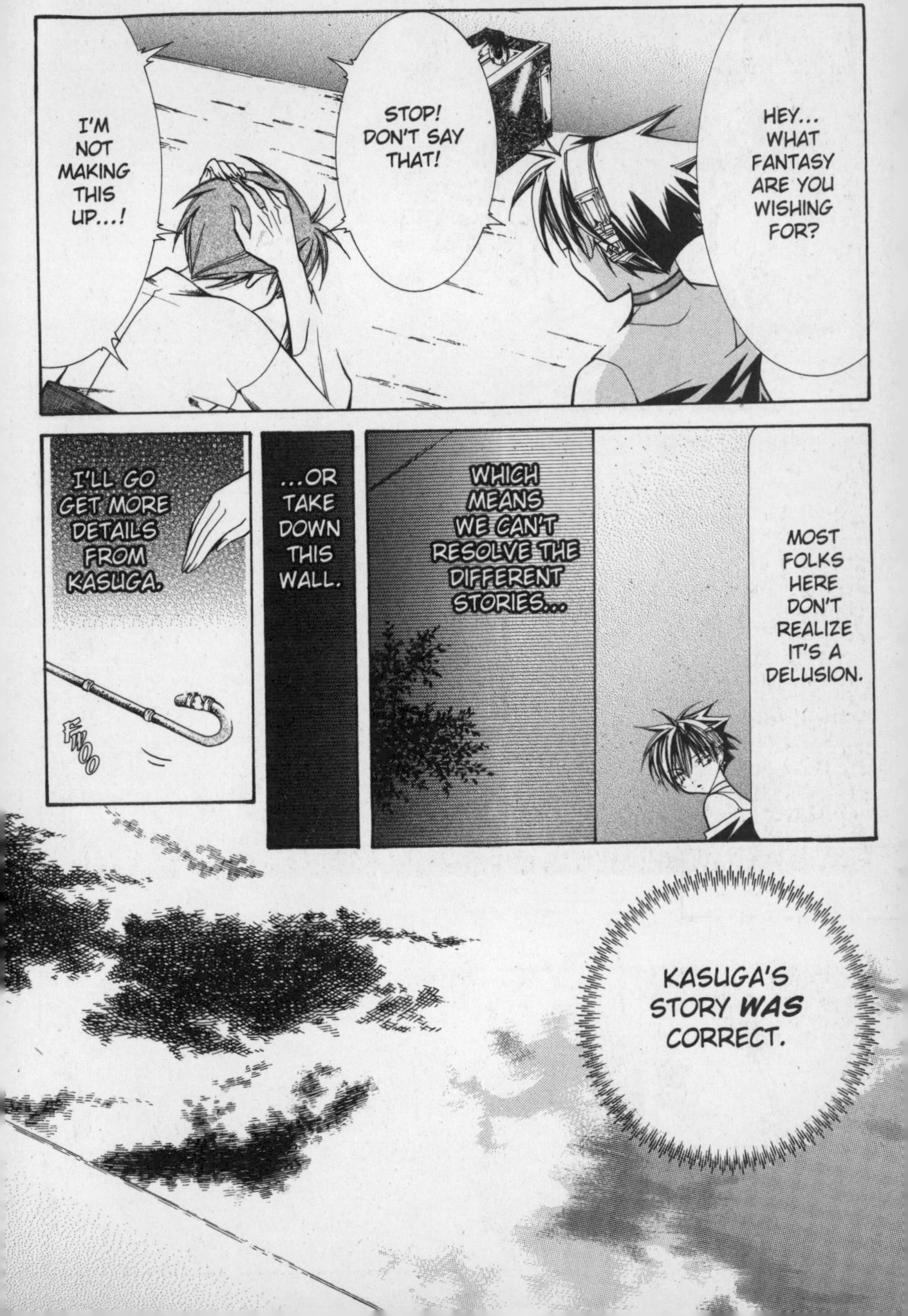
HEY... WHAT FANTASY ARE YOU WISHING FOR?
STOP! DON'T SAY THAT!
I'M NOT MAKING THIS UP...!
MOST FOLKS HERE DON'T REALIZE IT'S A DELUSION.
WHICH MEANS WE CAN'T RESOLVE THE DIFFERENT STORIES...
...OR TAKE DOWN THIS WALL.
I'LL GO GET MORE DETAILS FROM KASUGA.
FWOO
KASUGA'S STORY **WAS** CORRECT.

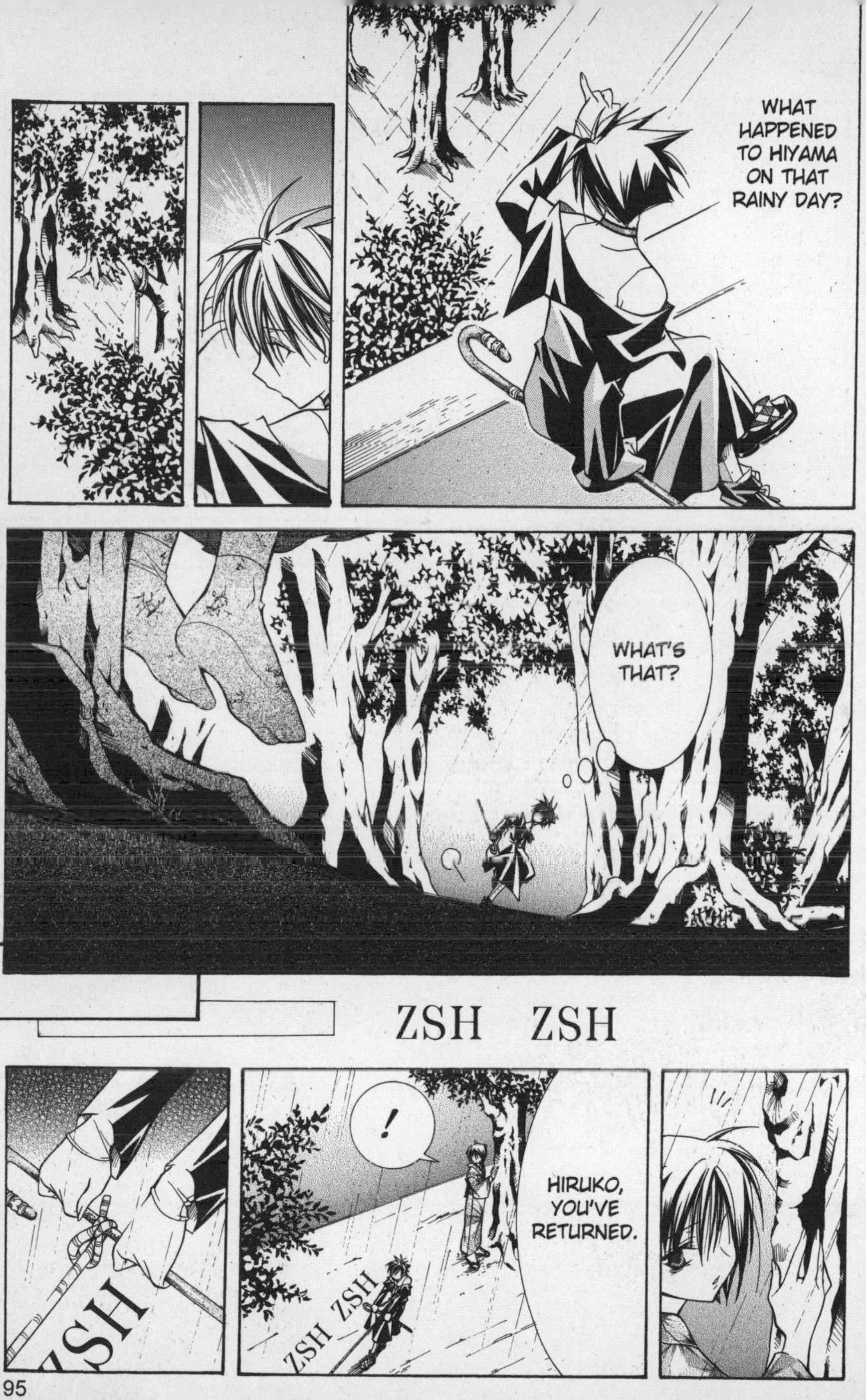
WHAT HAPPENED TO HIYAMA ON THAT RAINY DAY?
WHAT'S THAT?
ZSH ZSH
HIRUKO, YOU'VE RETURNED.
!
ZSH ZSH
ZSH

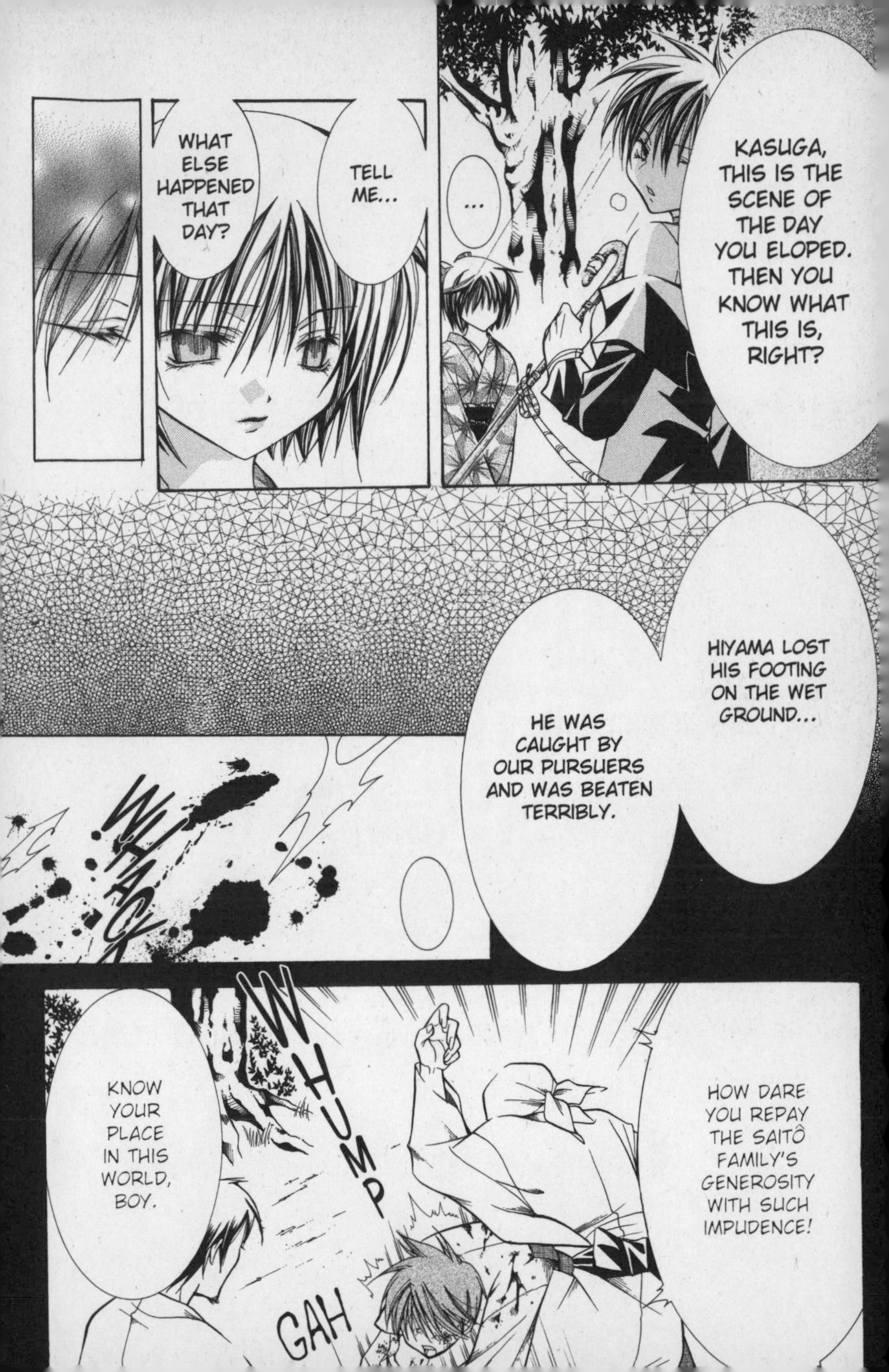
KASUGA, THIS IS THE SCENE OF THE DAY YOU ELOPED. THEN YOU KNOW WHAT THIS IS, RIGHT?
...
TELL ME...
WHAT ELSE HAPPENED THAT DAY?
HIYAMA LOST HIS FOOTING ON THE WET GROUND...
HE WAS CAUGHT BY OUR PURSUERS AND WAS BEATEN TERRIBLY.
WHACK
HOW DARE YOU REPAY THE SAITÔ FAMILY'S GENEROSITY WITH SUCH IMPUDENCE!
WHUMP
KNOW YOUR PLACE IN THIS WORLD, BOY.
GAH

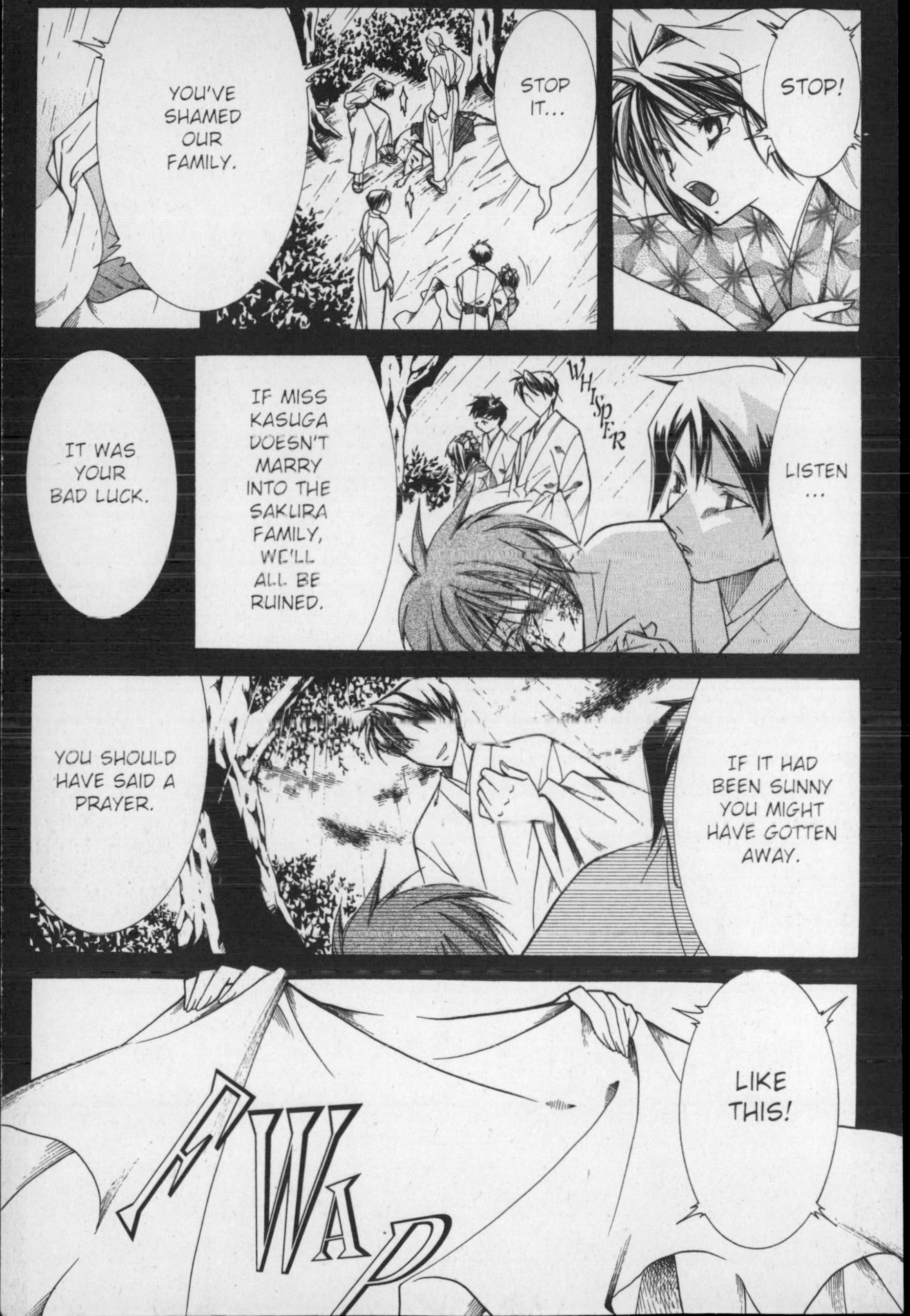
STOP!
STOP IT...
YOU'VE SHAMED OUR FAMILY.
LISTEN ...
WHISPER
IF MISS KASUGA DOESN'T MARRY INTO THE SAKURA FAMILY, WE'LL ALL BE RUINED.
IT WAS YOUR BAD LUCK.
IF IT HAD BEEN SUNNY YOU MIGHT HAVE GOTTEN AWAY.
YOU SHOULD HAVE SAID A PRAYER.
LIKE THIS!
SWAP

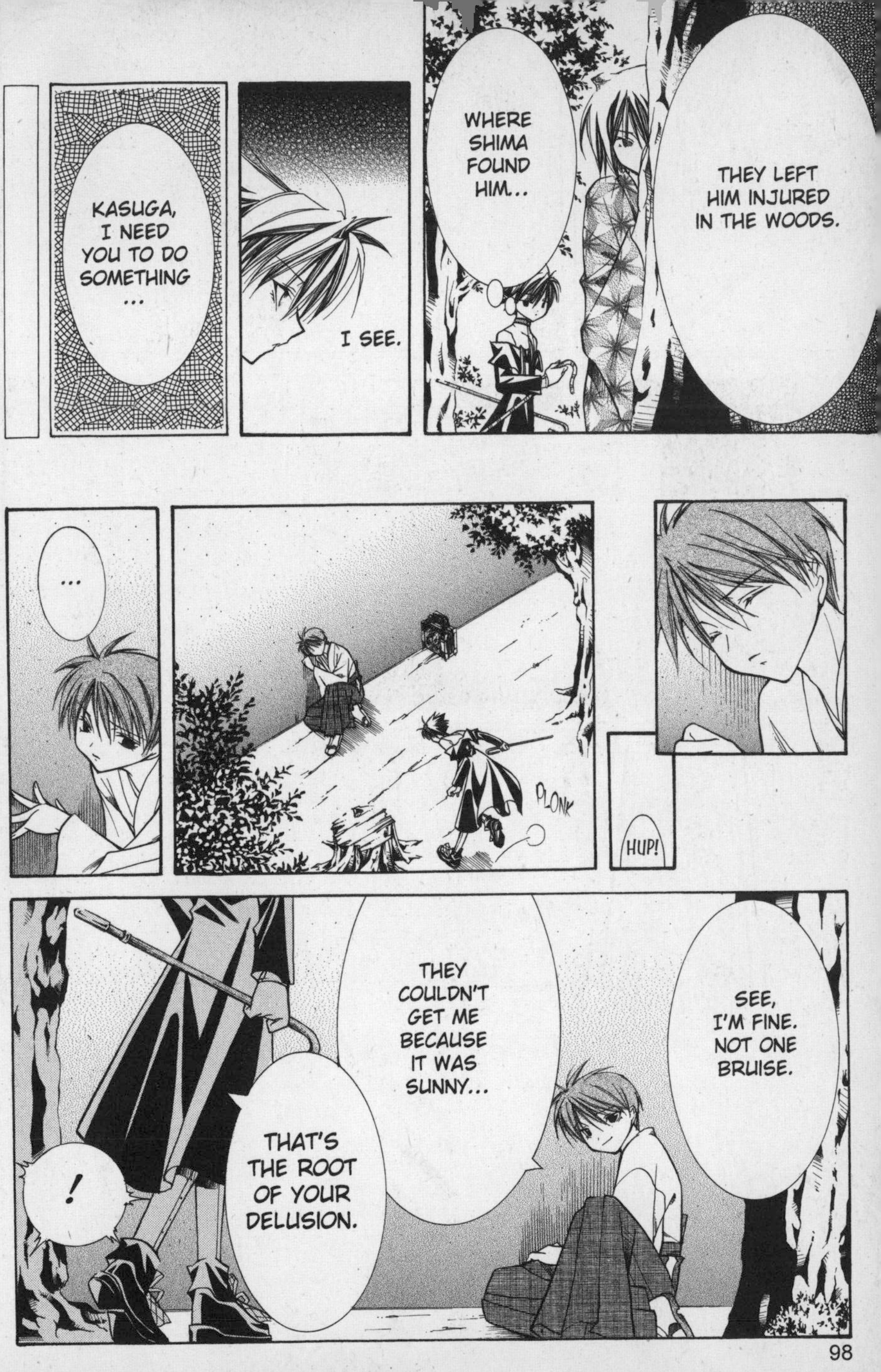
THEY LEFT HIM INJURED IN THE WOODS.
WHERE SHIMA FOUND HIM...
I SEE.
KASUGA, I NEED YOU TO DO SOMETHING ...
HUP!
PLONK
...
SEE, I'M FINE. NOT ONE BRUISE.
THEY COULDN'T GET ME BECAUSE IT WAS SUNNY...
THAT'S THE ROOT OF YOUR DELUSION.
!

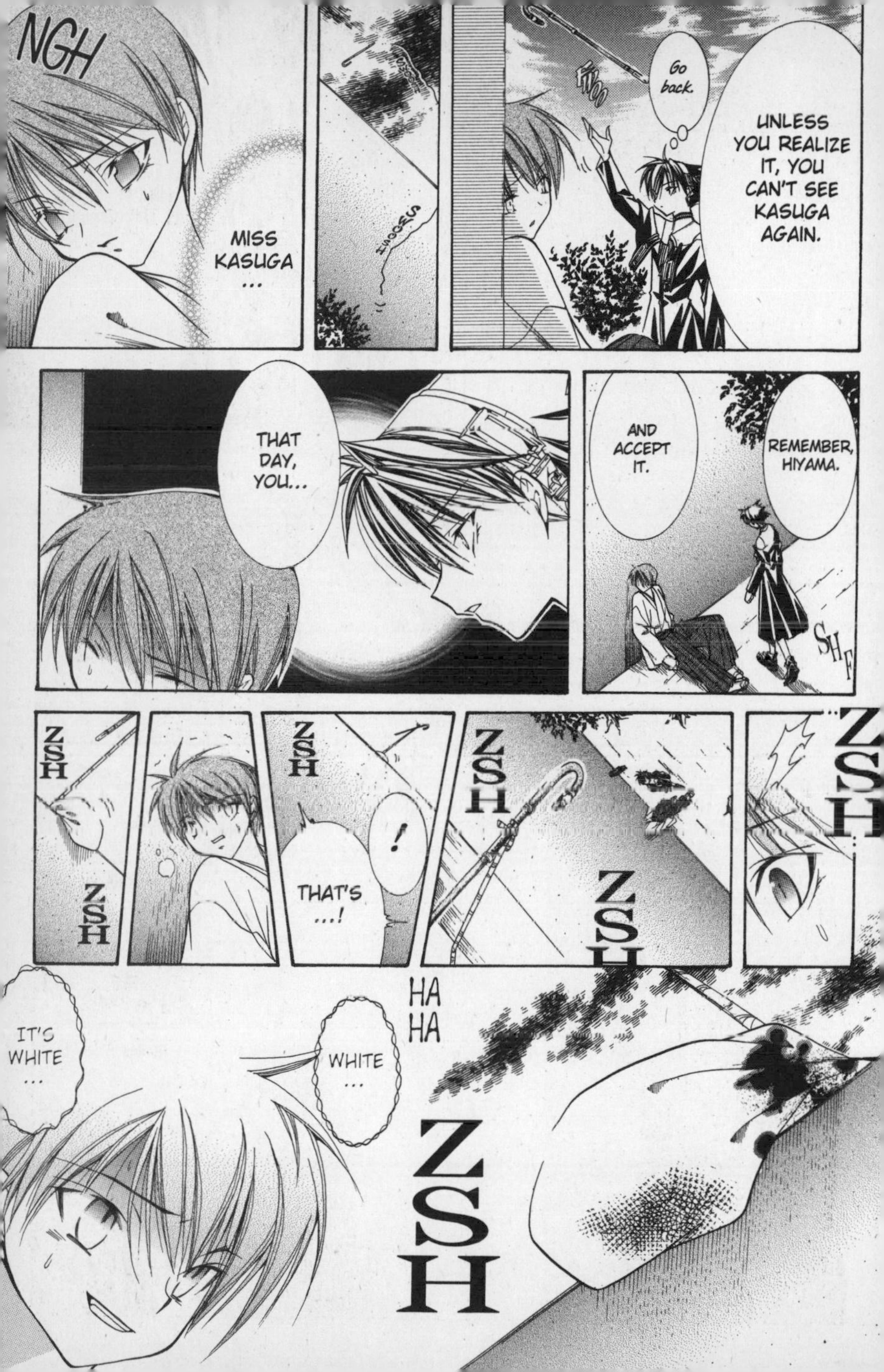
UNLESS YOU REALIZE IT, YOU CAN'T SEE KASUGA AGAIN.
Go back.
FWOO
NGH
MISS KASUGA ...
REMEMBER, HIYAMA.
AND ACCEPT IT.
SHF
THAT DAY, YOU...
ZSH
ZSH
ZSH
ZSH
!
THAT'S ...!
ZSH
ZSH
HA HA
ZSH
WHITE ...
IT'S WHITE ...

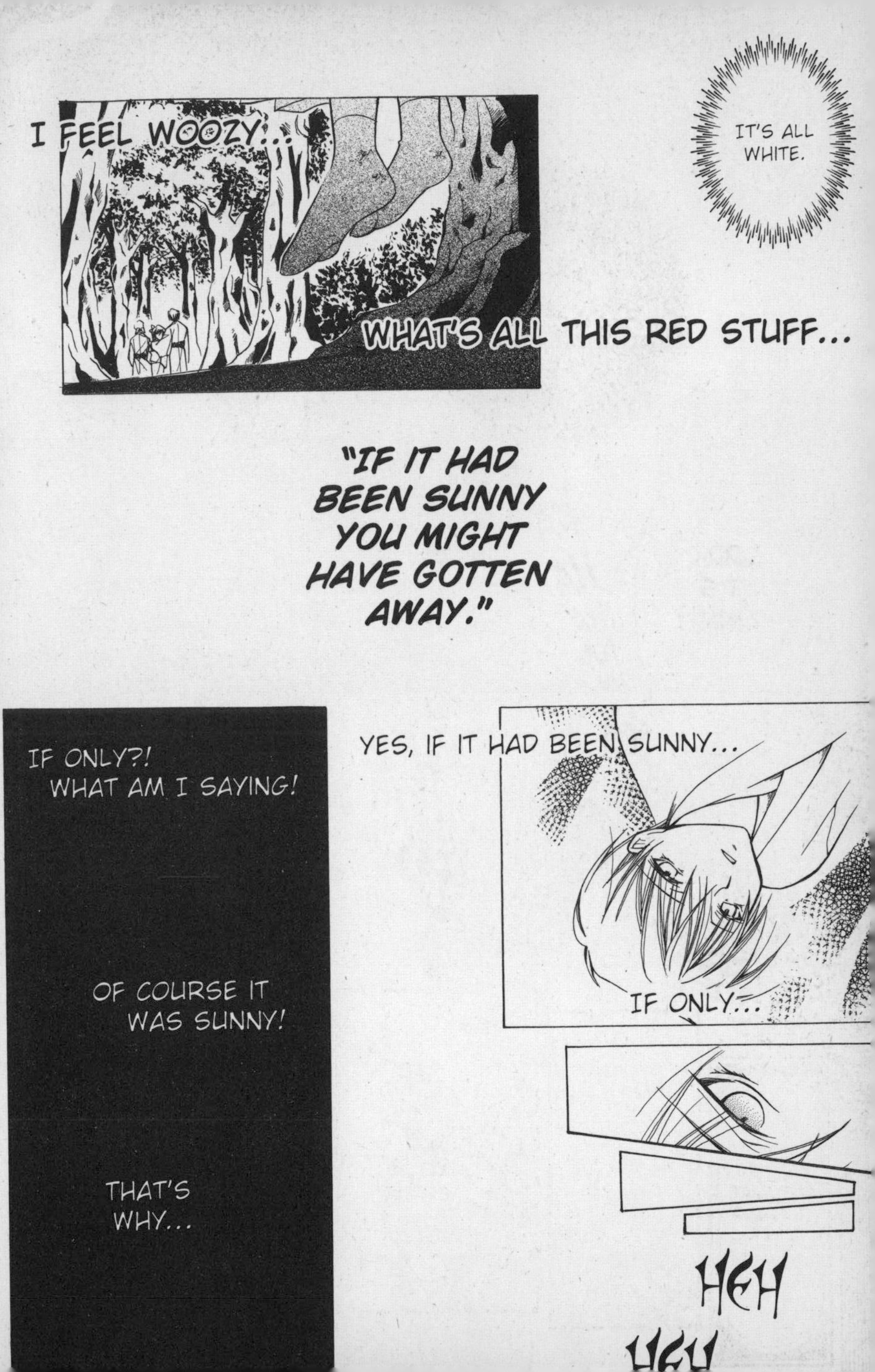

IT'S ALL WHITE.
I FEEL WOOZY...
WHAT'S ALL THIS RED STUFF...
"IF IT HAD BEEN SUNNY YOU MIGHT HAVE GOTTEN AWAY."
YES, IF IT HAD BEEN SUNNY...
IF ONLY...
HEH
IF ONLY?! WHAT AM I SAYING!
OF COURSE IT WAS SUNNY!
THAT'S WHY...

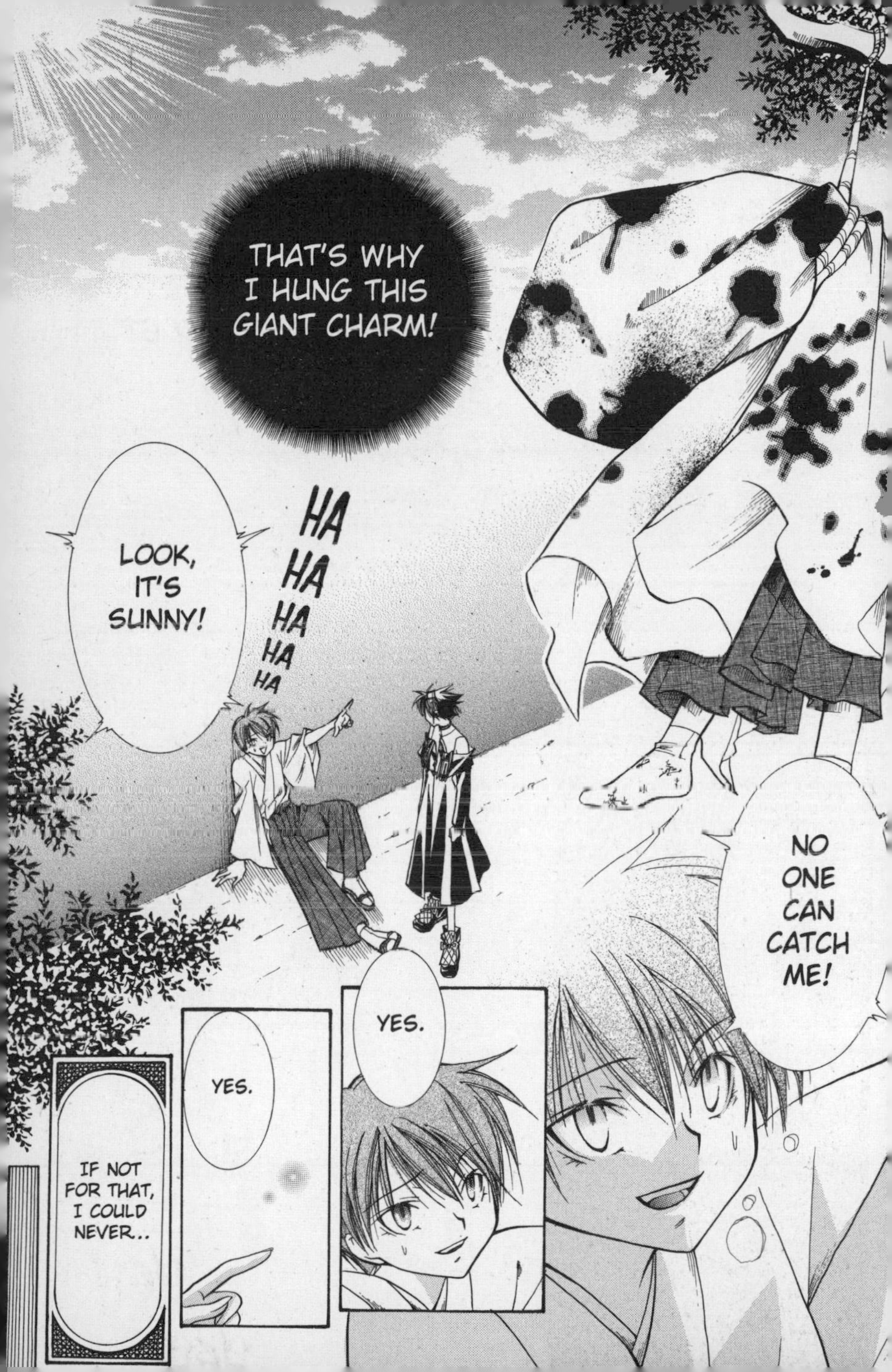
THAT'S WHY I HUNG THIS GIANT CHARM!
LOOK, IT'S SUNNY!
HA HA HA HA HA
NO ONE CAN CATCH ME!
YES.
YES.
IF NOT FOR THAT, I COULD NEVER...

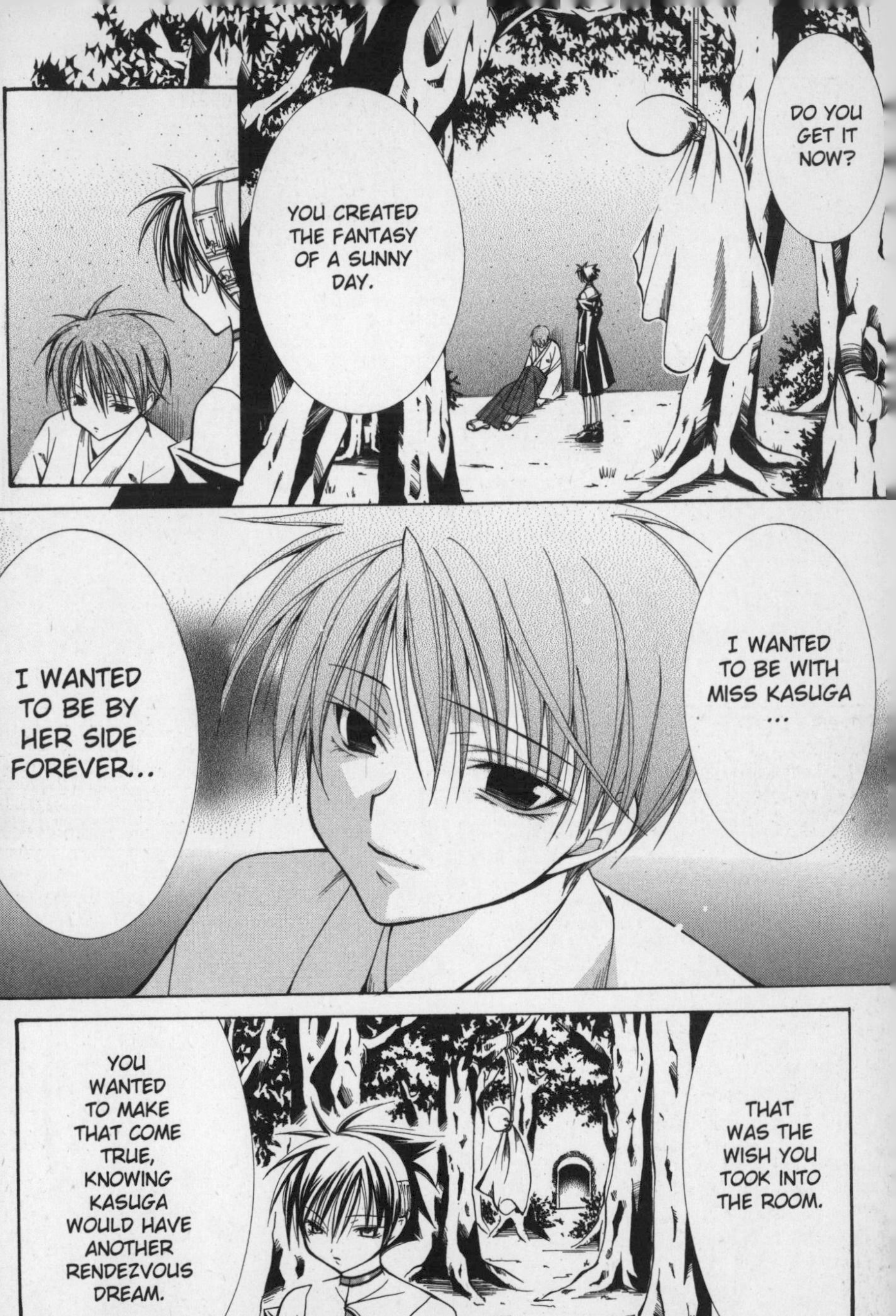
DO YOU GET IT NOW?
YOU CREATED THE FANTASY OF A SUNNY DAY.
I WANTED TO BE WITH MISS KASUGA ...
I WANTED TO BE BY HER SIDE FOREVER...
THAT WAS THE WISH YOU TOOK INTO THE ROOM.
YOU WANTED TO MAKE THAT COME TRUE, KNOWING KASUGA WOULD HAVE ANOTHER RENDEZVOUS DREAM.

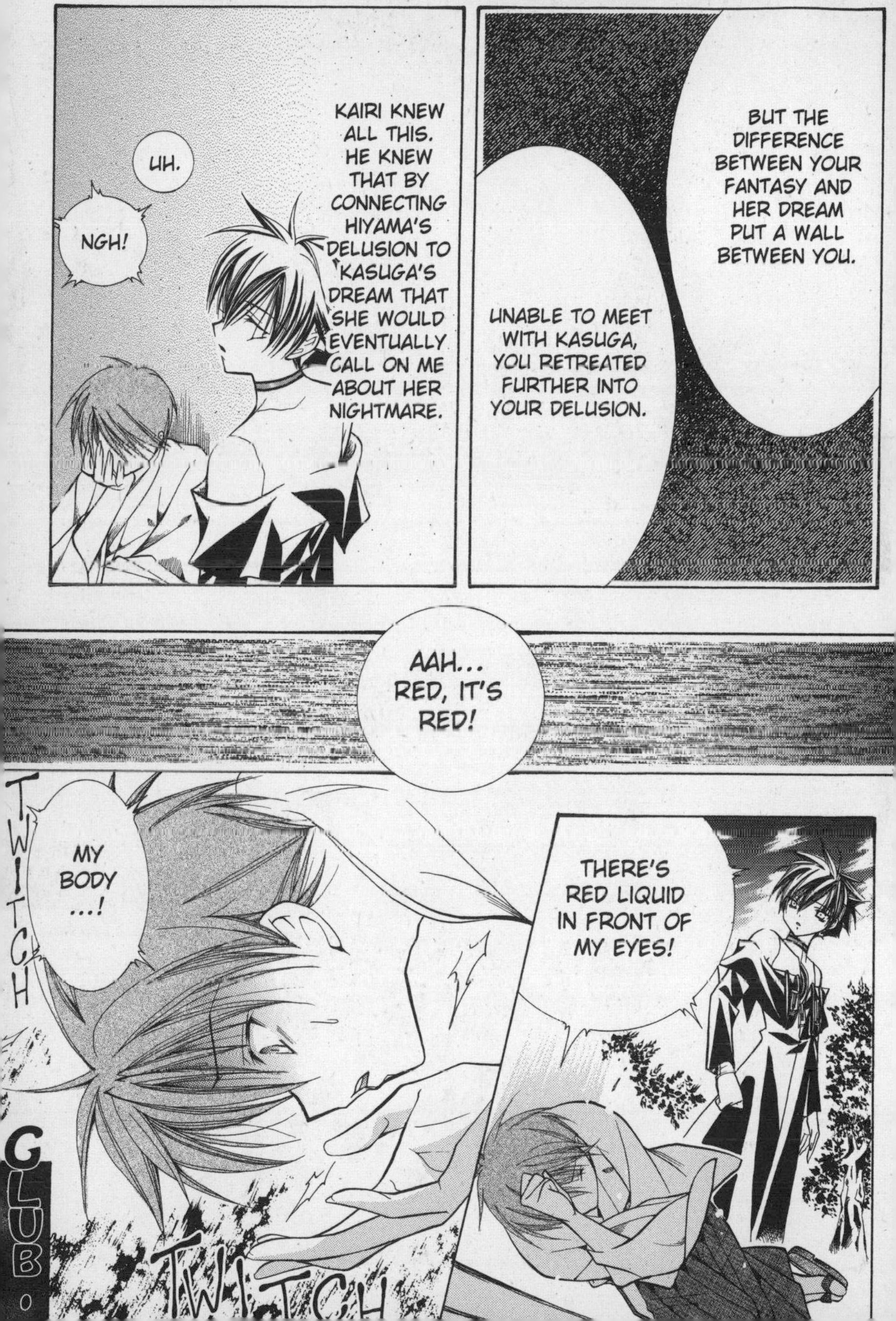
BUT THE DIFFERENCE BETWEEN YOUR FANTASY AND HER DREAM PUT A WALL BETWEEN YOU.
UNABLE TO MEET WITH KASUGA, YOU RETREATED FURTHER INTO YOUR DELUSION.
KAIRI KNEW ALL THIS. HE KNEW THAT BY CONNECTING HIYAMA'S DELUSION TO KASUGA'S DREAM THAT SHE WOULD EVENTUALLY CALL ON ME ABOUT HER NIGHTMARE.
UH.
NGH!
AAH... RED, IT'S RED!
THERE'S RED LIQUID IN FRONT OF MY EYES!
MY BODY ...!
TWITCH
TWITCH

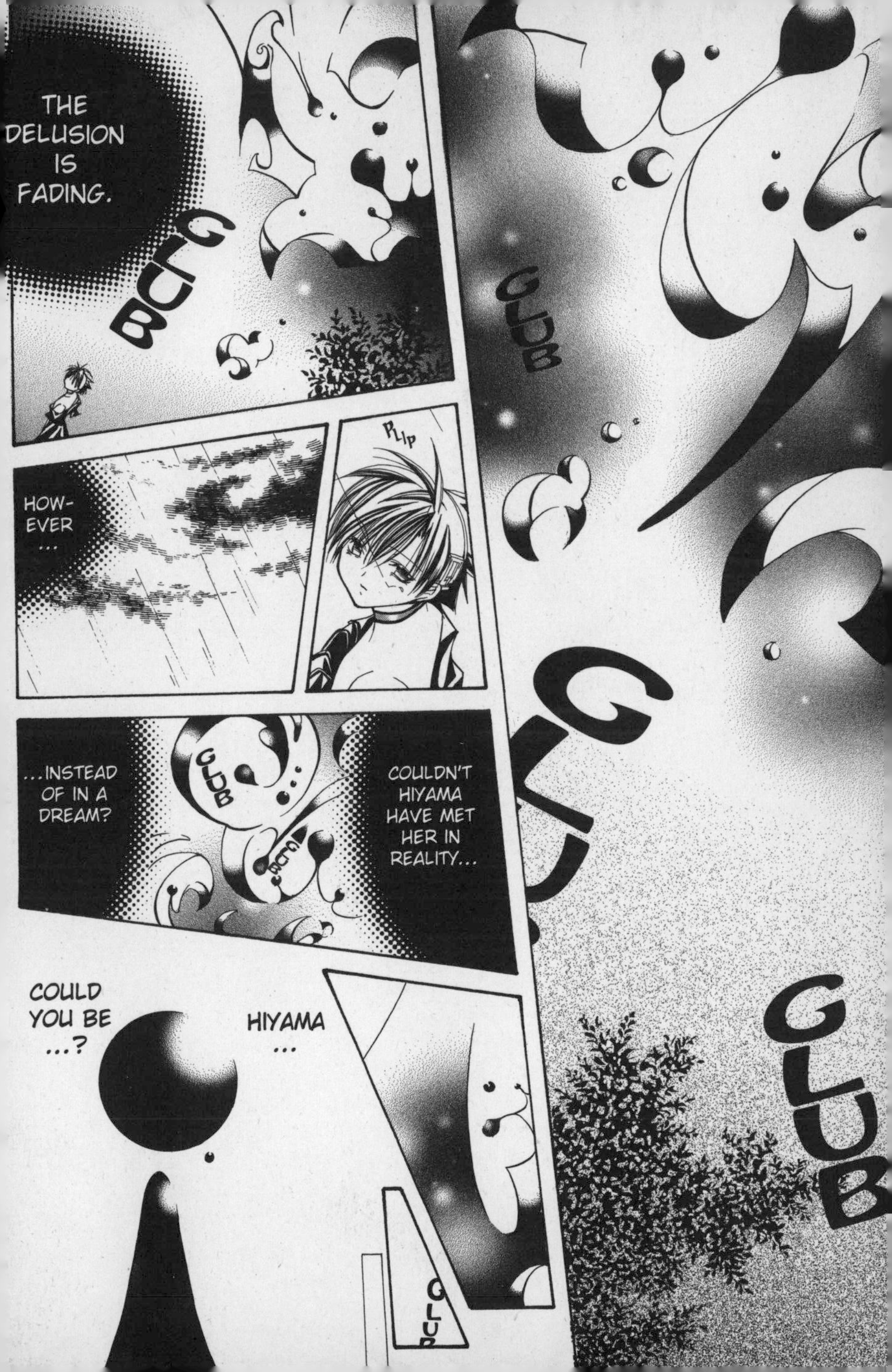
GLUB
GLUB
GLUB
GLUB
THE DELUSION IS FADING.
GLUB
PLIP
HOW-EVER ...
COULDN'T HIYAMA HAVE MET HER IN REALITY...
GLUB
GLUB
...INSTEAD OF IN A DREAM?
GLUP
HIYAMA ...
COULD YOU BE ...?

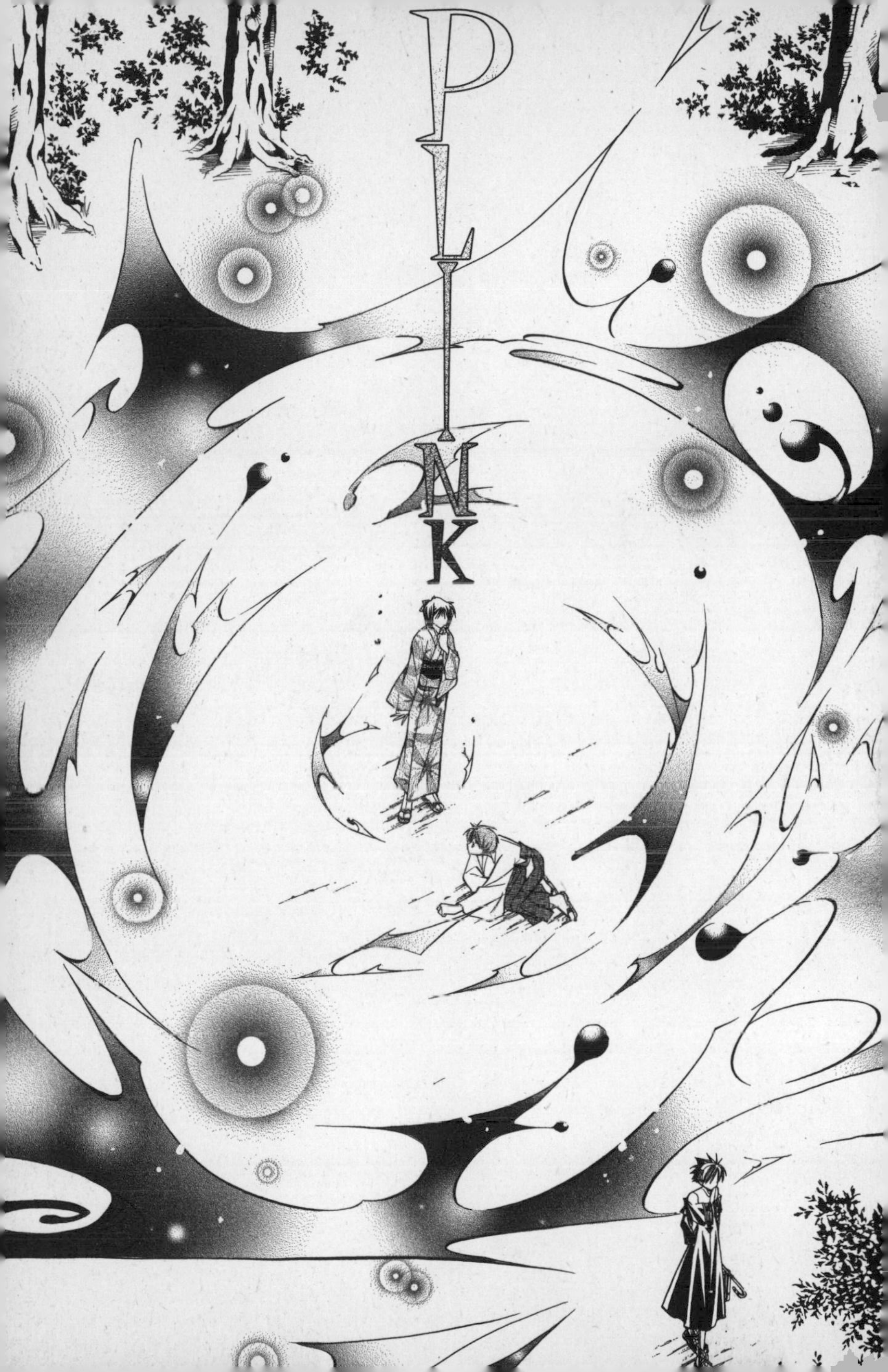
PLINK

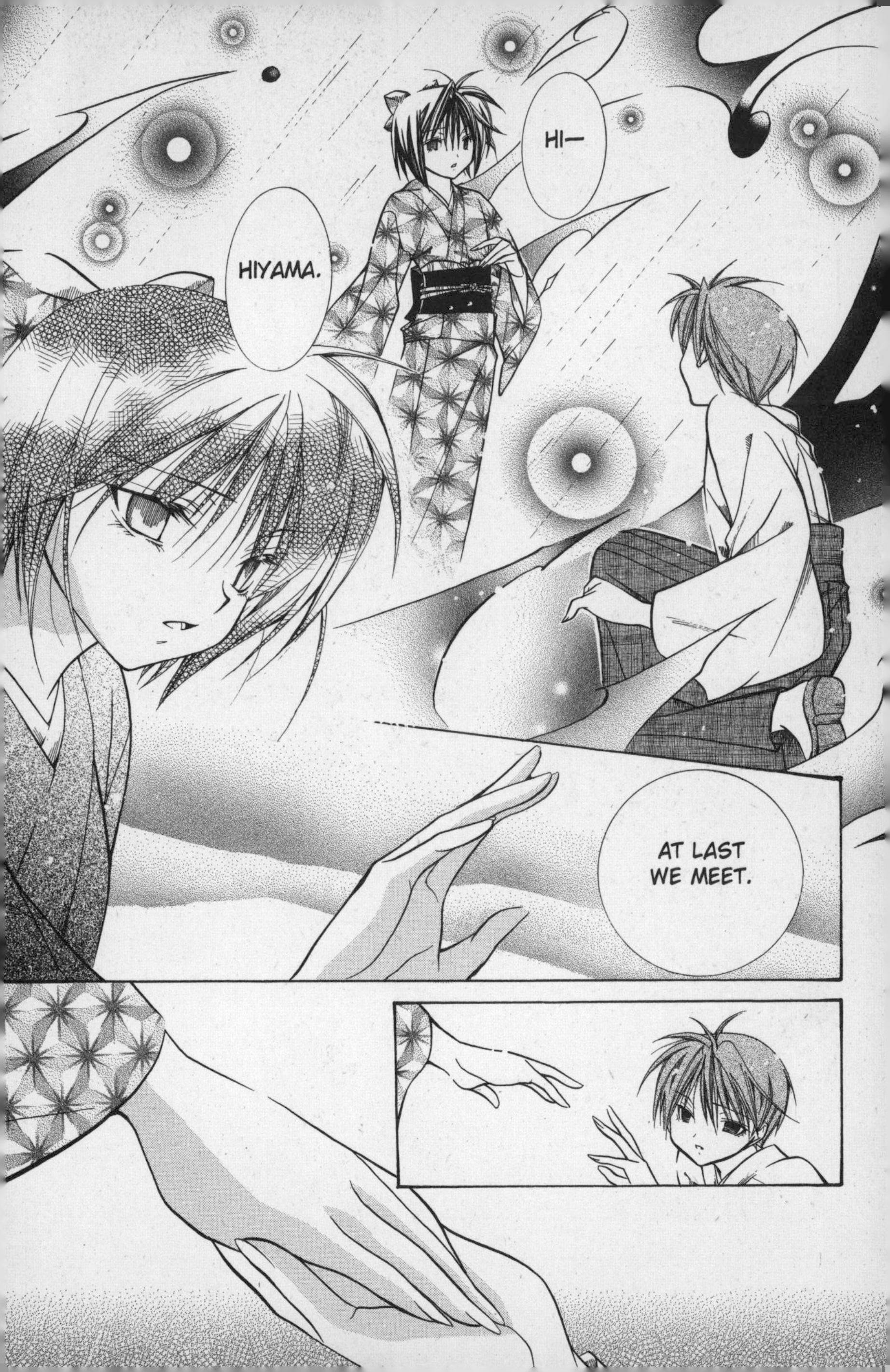
HI—
HIYAMA.
AT LAST WE MEET.

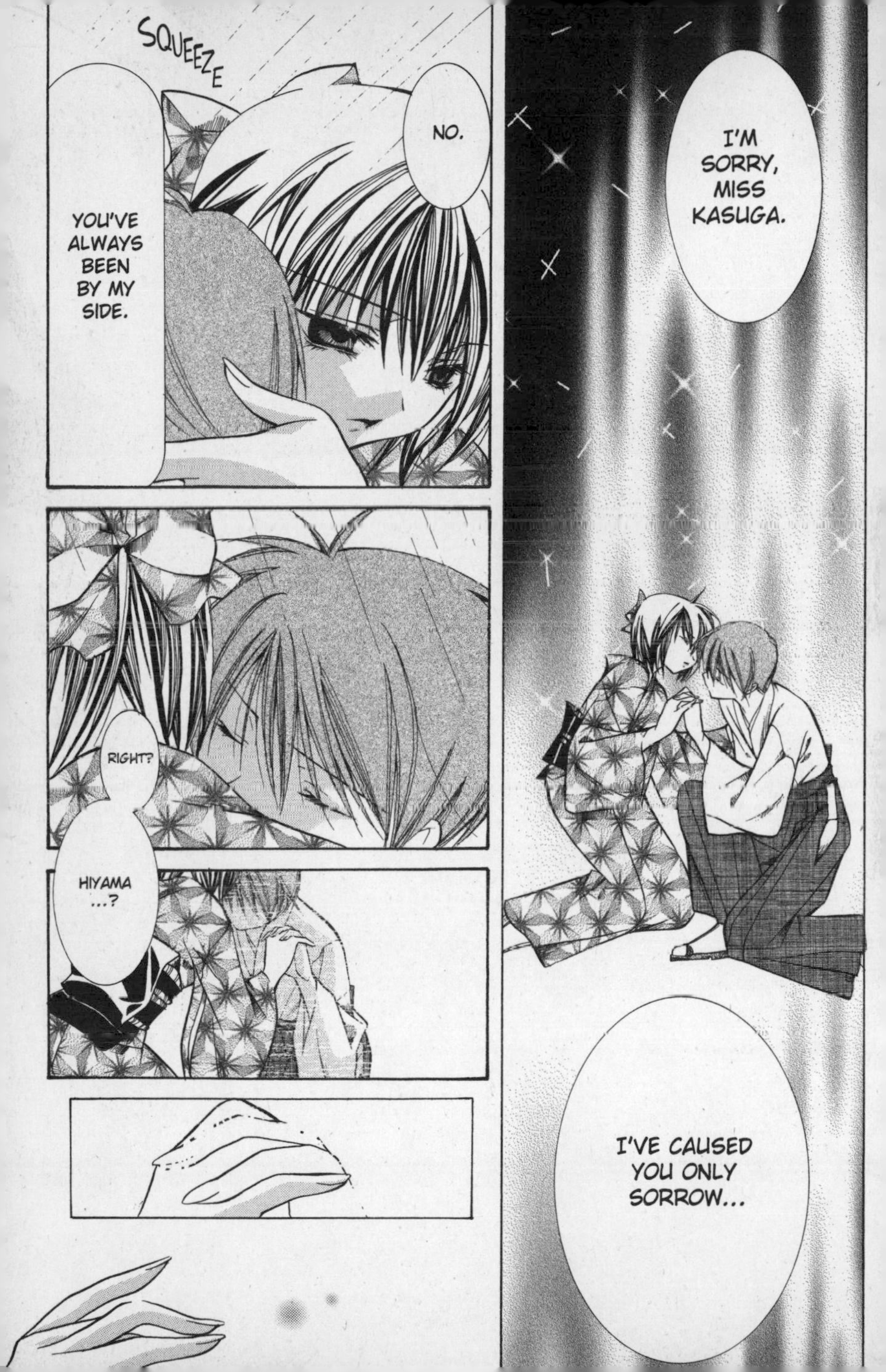
I'M SORRY, MISS KASUGA.
I'VE CAUSED YOU ONLY SORROW...
SQUEEZE
NO.
YOU'VE ALWAYS BEEN BY MY SIDE.
RIGHT?
HIYAMA ...?

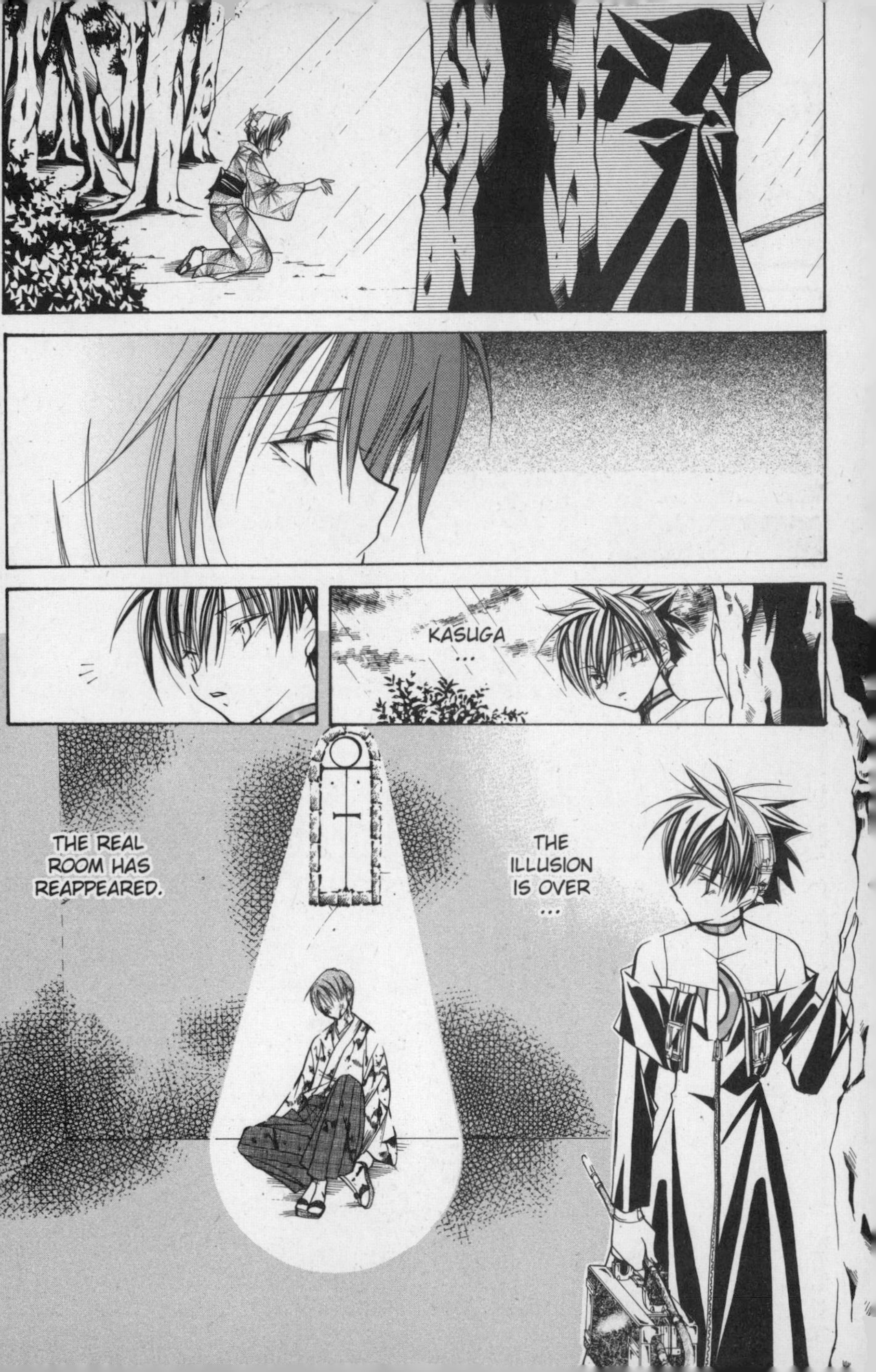
KASUGA ...
THE ILLUSION IS OVER ...
THE REAL ROOM HAS REAPPEARED.

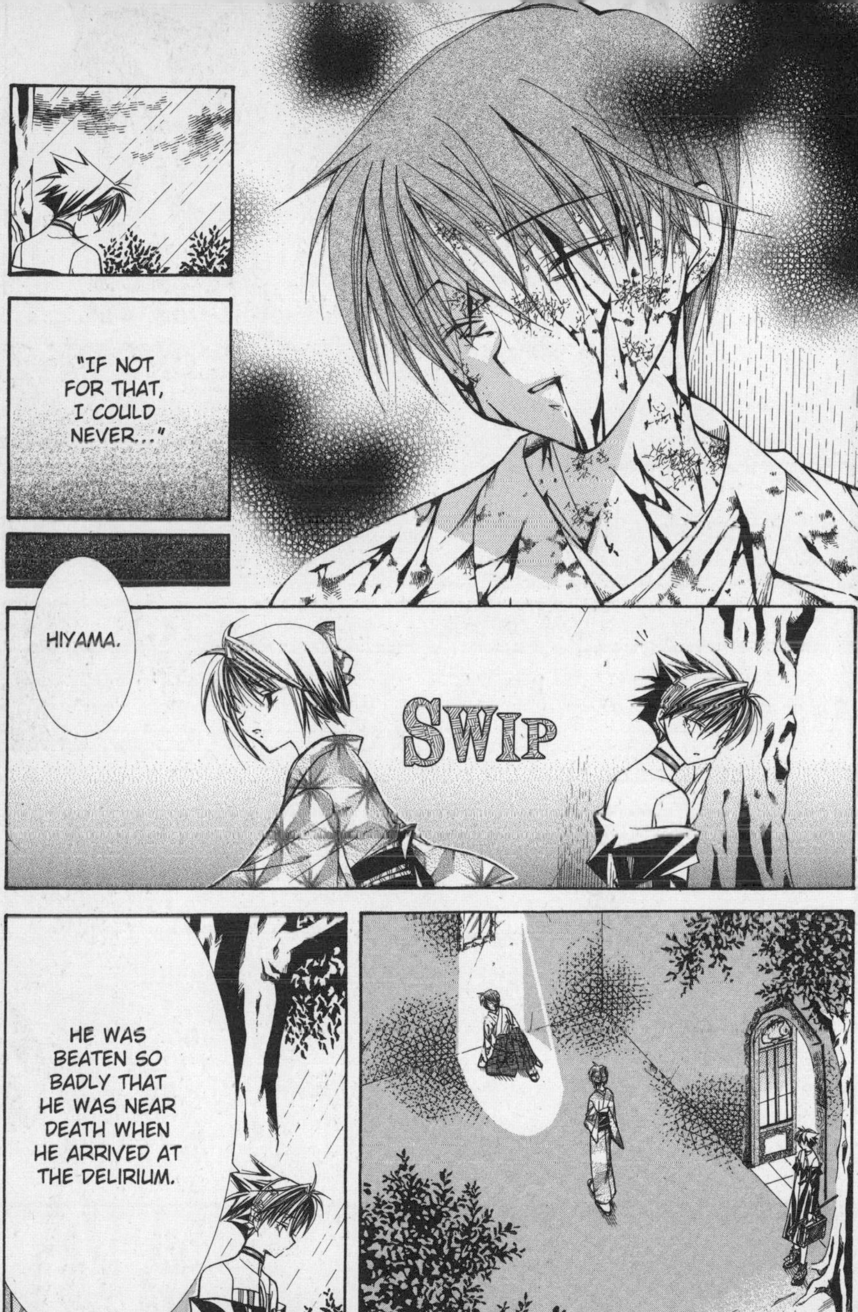
"IF NOT FOR THAT, I COULD NEVER..."
HIYAMA.
SWIP
HE WAS BEATEN SO BADLY THAT HE WAS NEAR DEATH WHEN HE ARRIVED AT THE DELIRIUM.

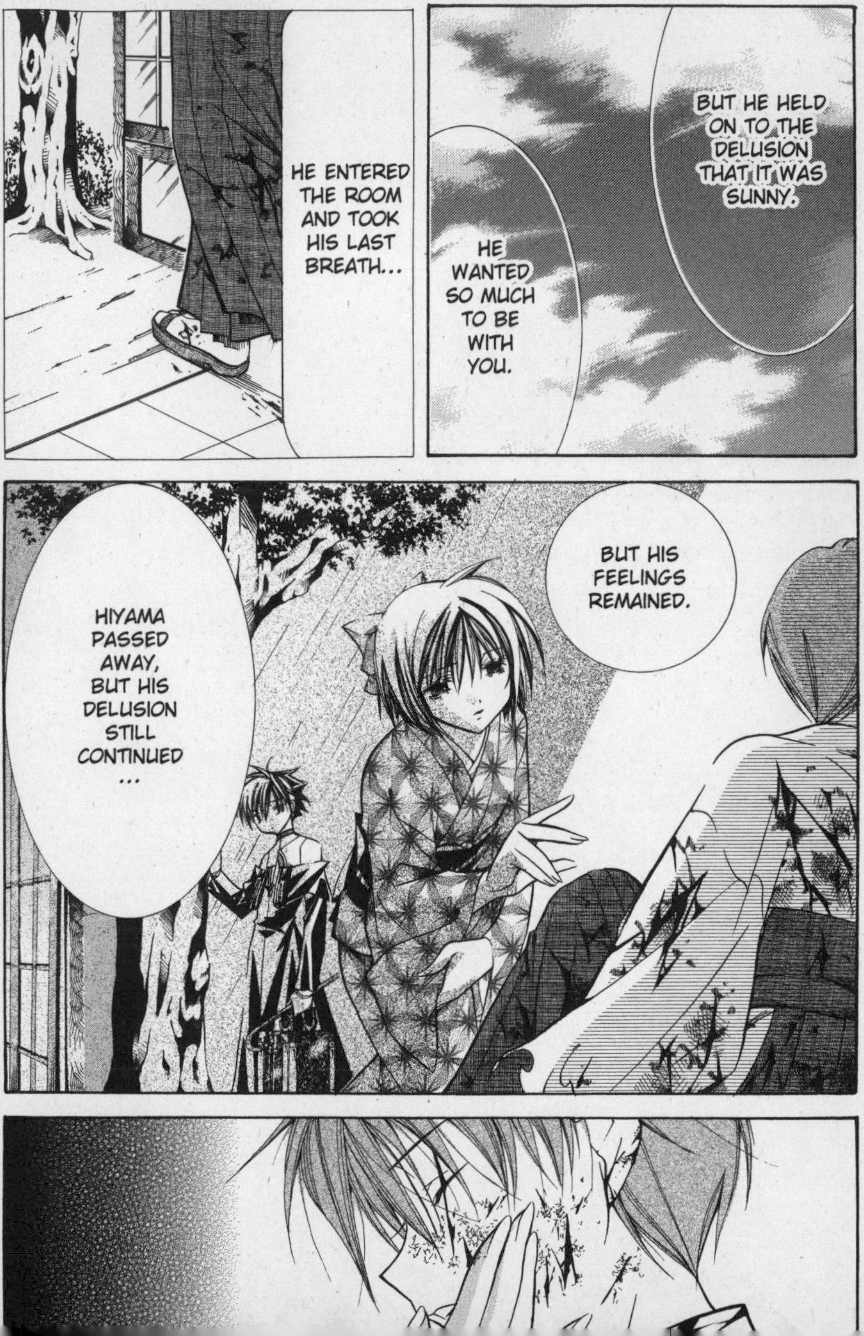
BUT HE HELD ON TO THE DELUSION THAT IT WAS SUNNY.
HE WANTED SO MUCH TO BE WITH YOU.
HE ENTERED THE ROOM AND TOOK HIS LAST BREATH...
BUT HIS FEELINGS REMAINED.
HIYAMA PASSED AWAY, BUT HIS DELUSION STILL CONTINUED ...

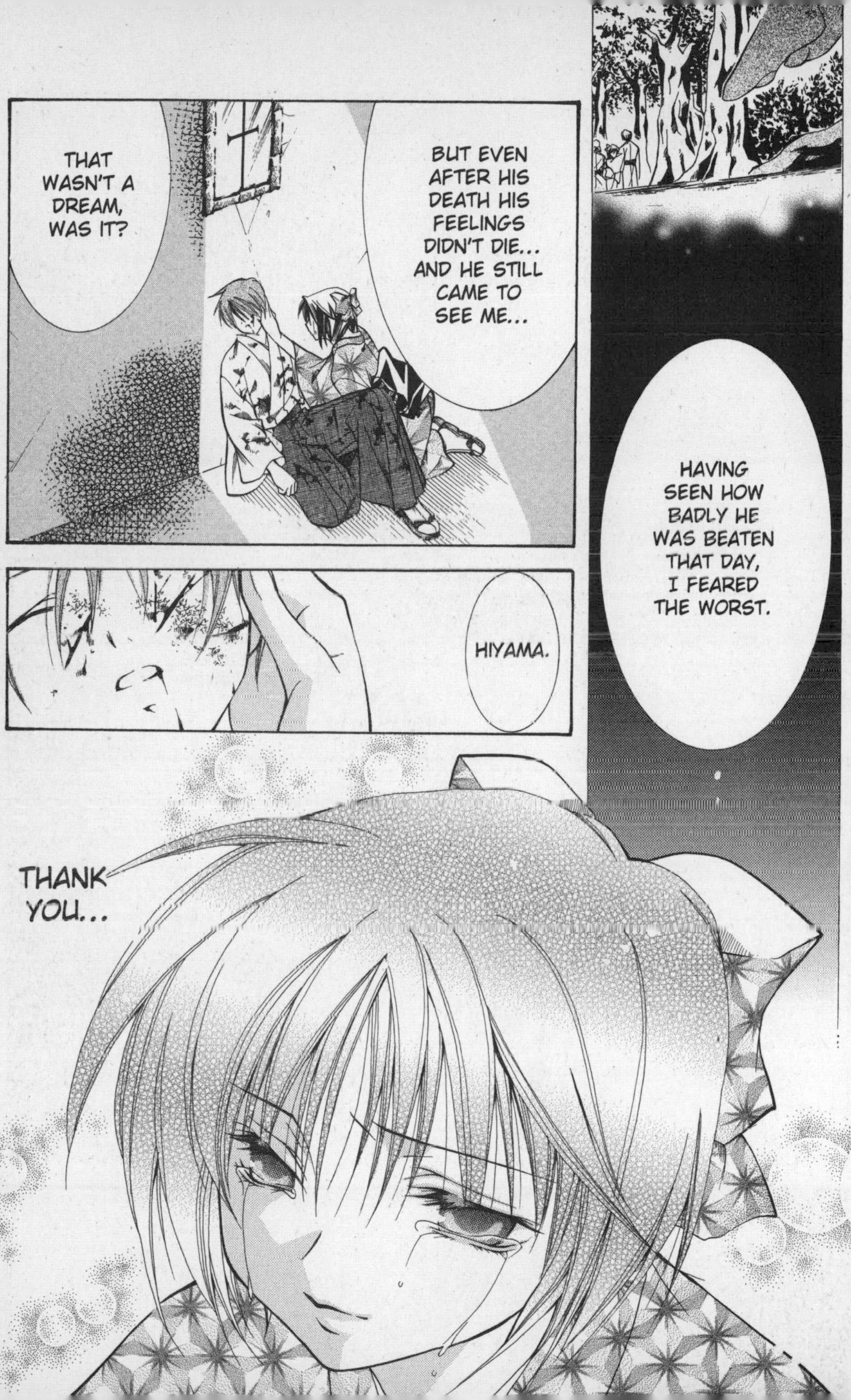
HAVING SEEN HOW BADLY HE WAS BEATEN THAT DAY, I FEARED THE WORST.
BUT EVEN AFTER HIS DEATH HIS FEELINGS DIDN'T DIE... AND HE STILL CAME TO SEE ME...
THAT WASN'T A DREAM, WAS IT?
HIYAMA.
THANK YOU...

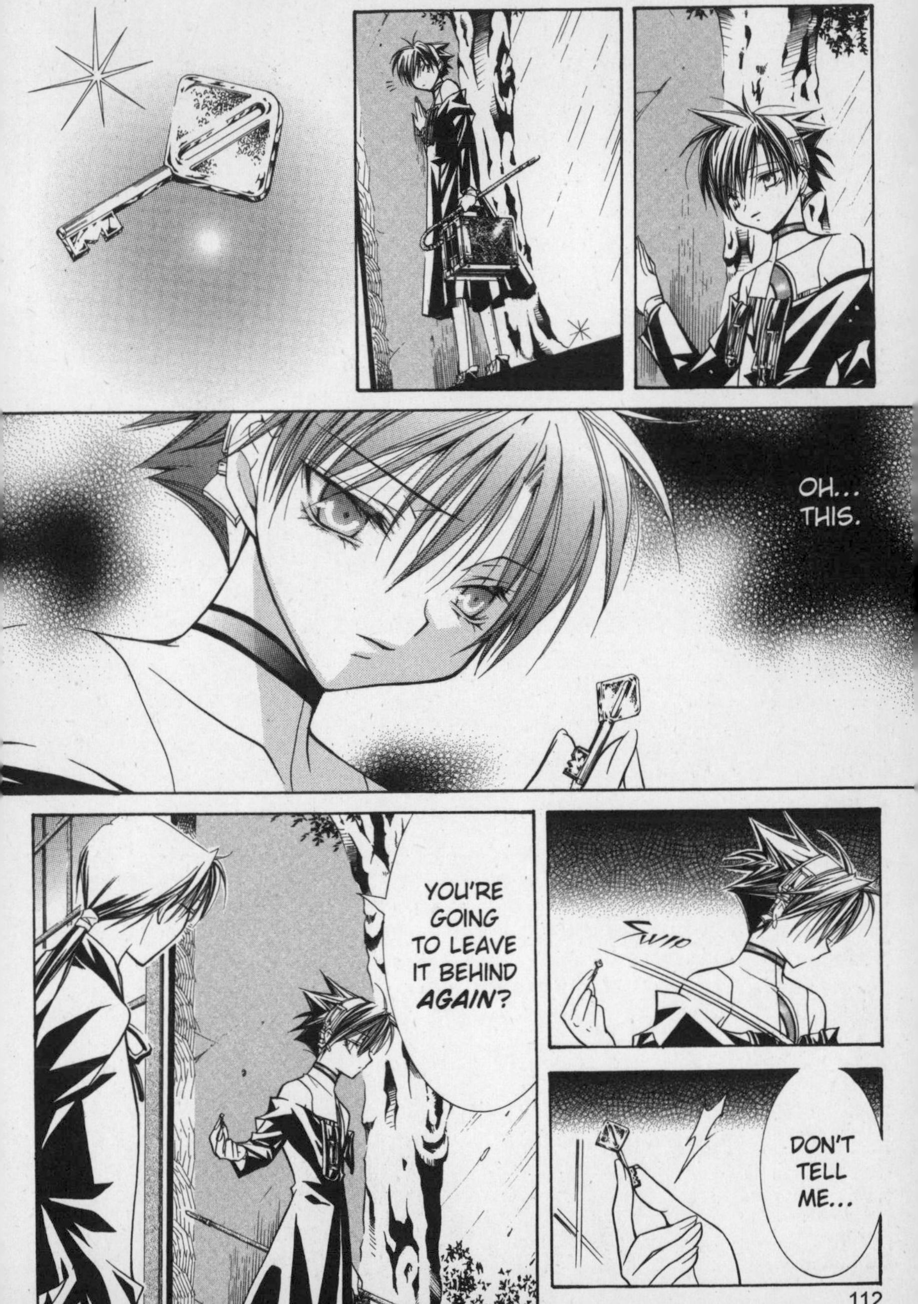
OH... THIS.
SWIP
DON'T TELL ME...
YOU'RE GOING TO LEAVE IT BEHIND *AGAIN*?

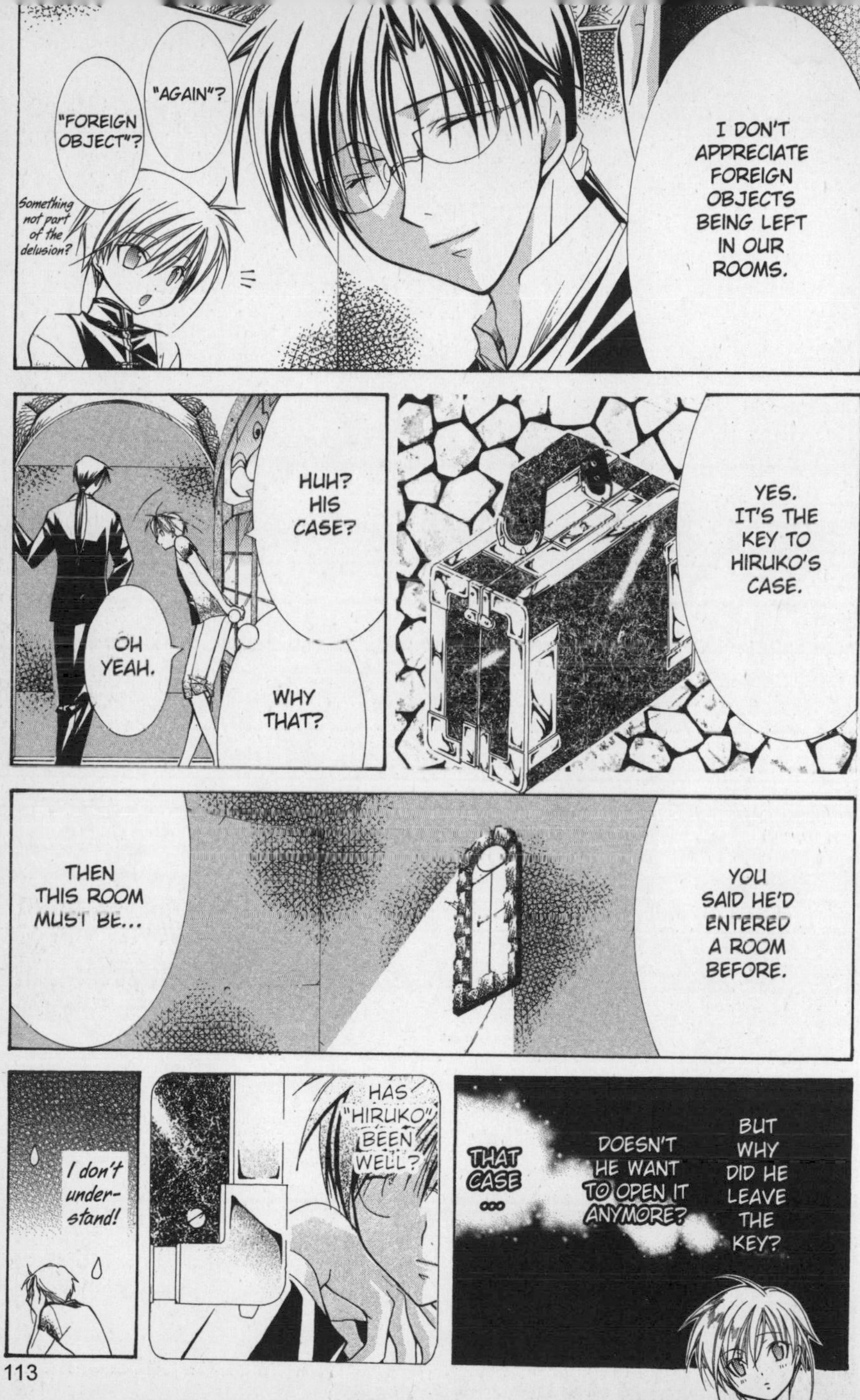
I DON'T APPRECIATE FOREIGN OBJECTS BEING LEFT IN OUR ROOMS.
"AGAIN"?
"FOREIGN OBJECT"?
Something not part of the delusion?
YES. IT'S THE KEY TO HIRUKO'S CASE.
HUH? HIS CASE?
WHY THAT?
OH YEAH.
YOU SAID HE'D ENTERED A ROOM BEFORE.
THEN THIS ROOM MUST BE...
BUT WHY DID HE LEAVE THE KEY?
DOESN'T HE WANT TO OPEN IT ANYMORE?
THAT CASE...
HAS "HIRUKO" BEEN WELL?
I don't under-stand!

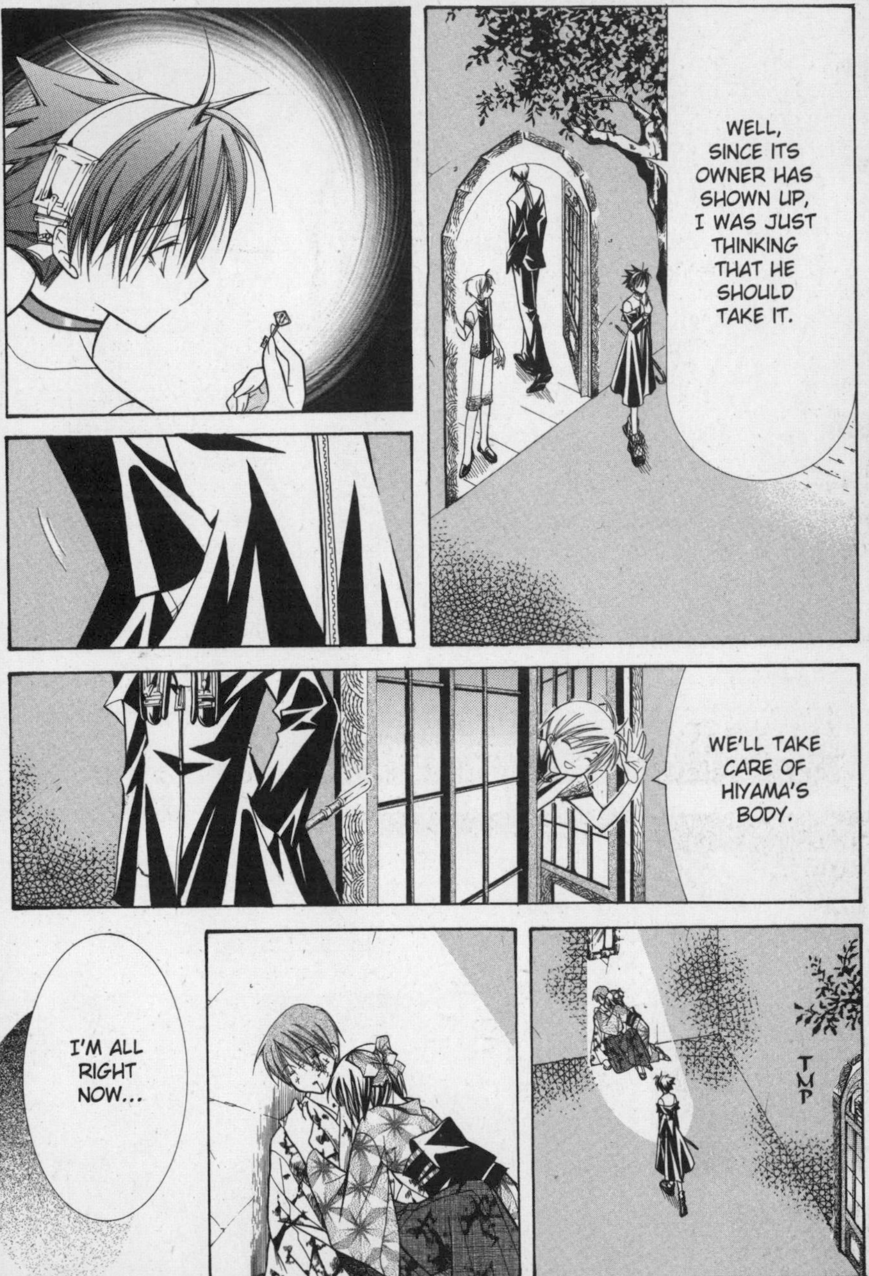
WELL, SINCE ITS OWNER HAS SHOWN UP, I WAS JUST THINKING THAT HE SHOULD TAKE IT.
WE'LL TAKE CARE OF HIYAMA'S BODY.
TMP
I'M ALL RIGHT NOW...

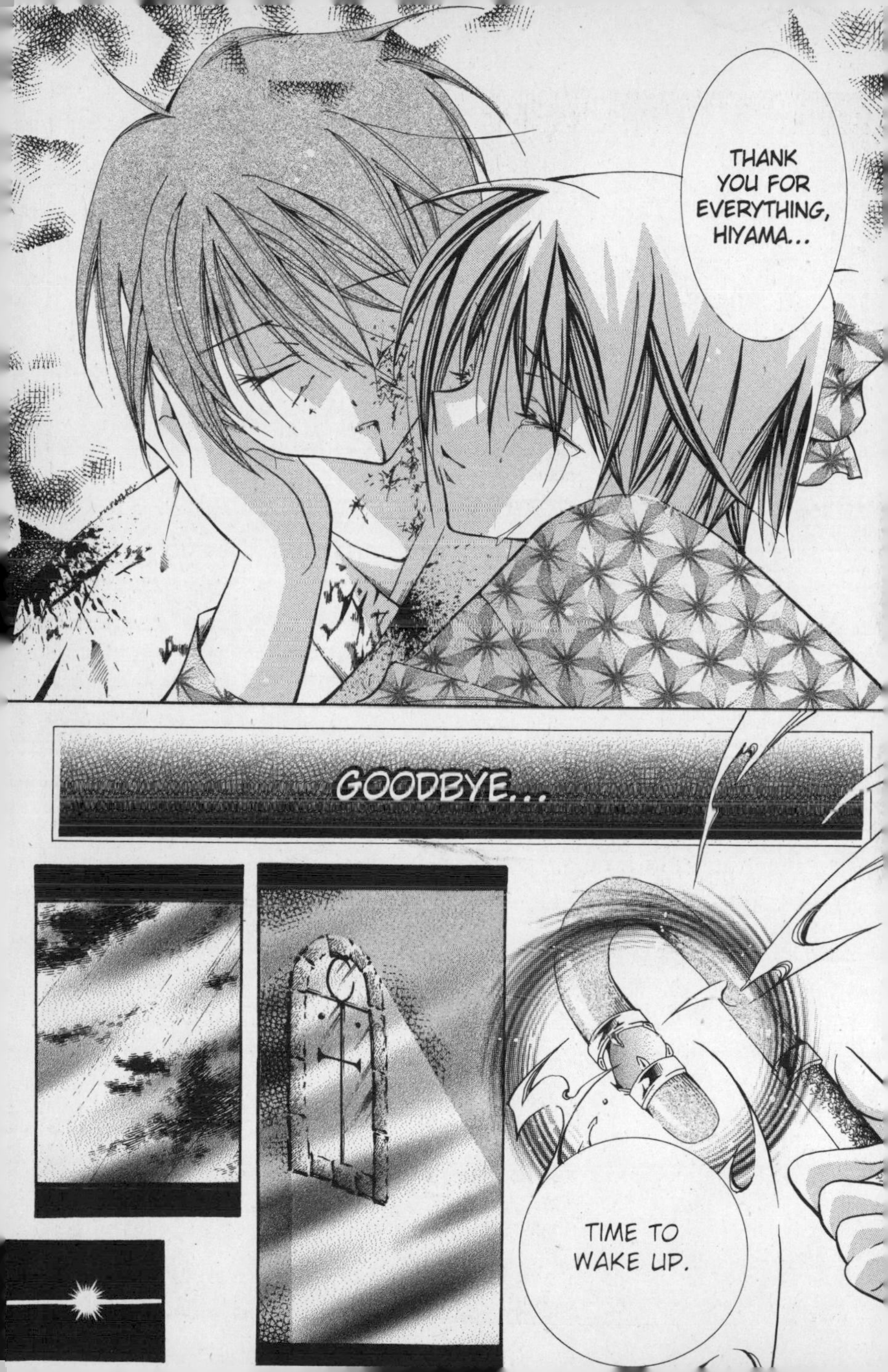
THANK YOU FOR EVERYTHING, HIYAMA...
GOODBYE...
TIME TO WAKE UP.

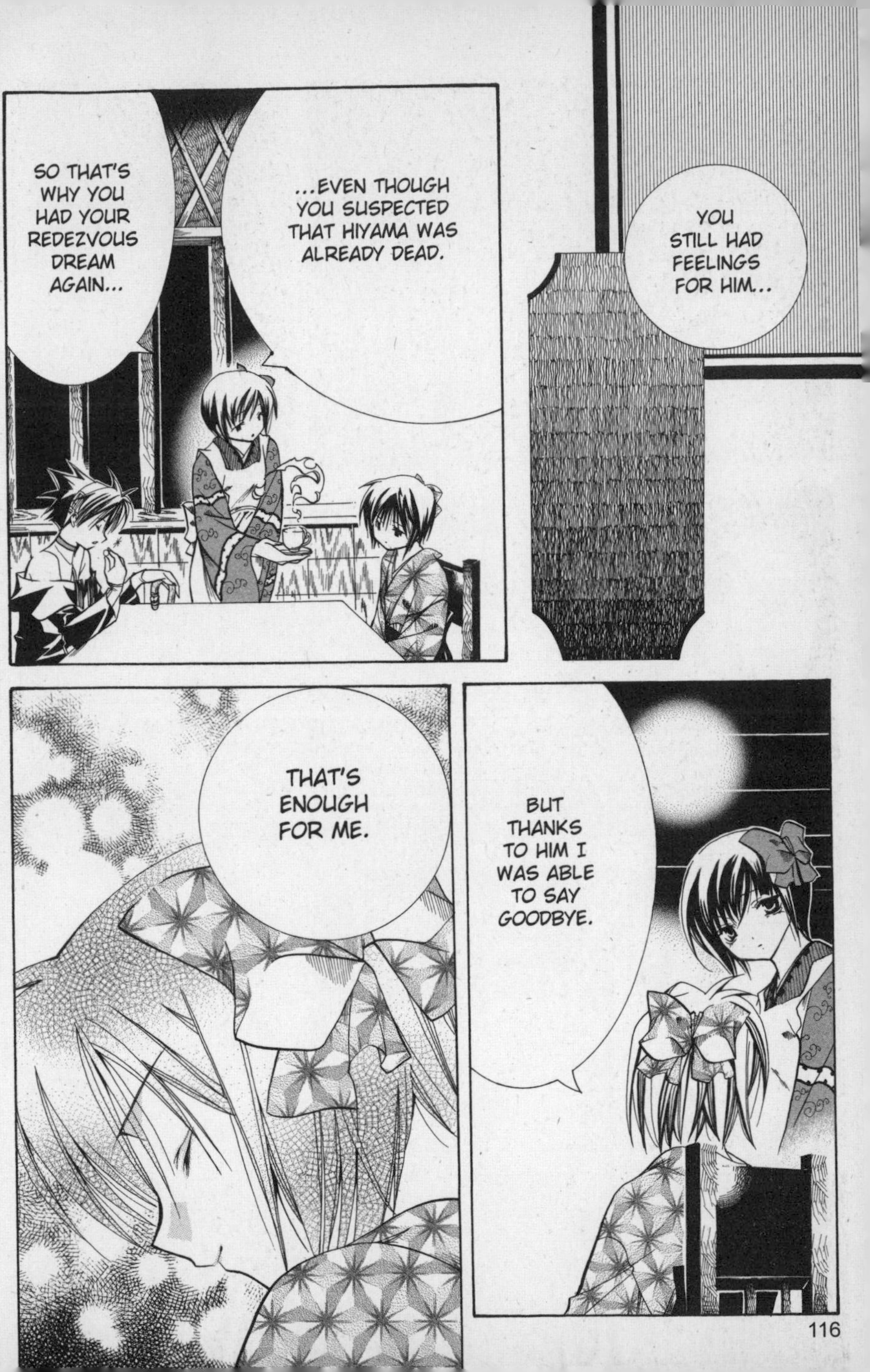
YOU STILL HAD FEELINGS FOR HIM...
...EVEN THOUGH YOU SUSPECTED THAT HIYAMA WAS ALREADY DEAD.
SO THAT'S WHY YOU HAD YOUR REDEZVOUS DREAM AGAIN...
BUT THANKS TO HIM I WAS ABLE TO SAY GOODBYE.
THAT'S ENOUGH FOR ME.

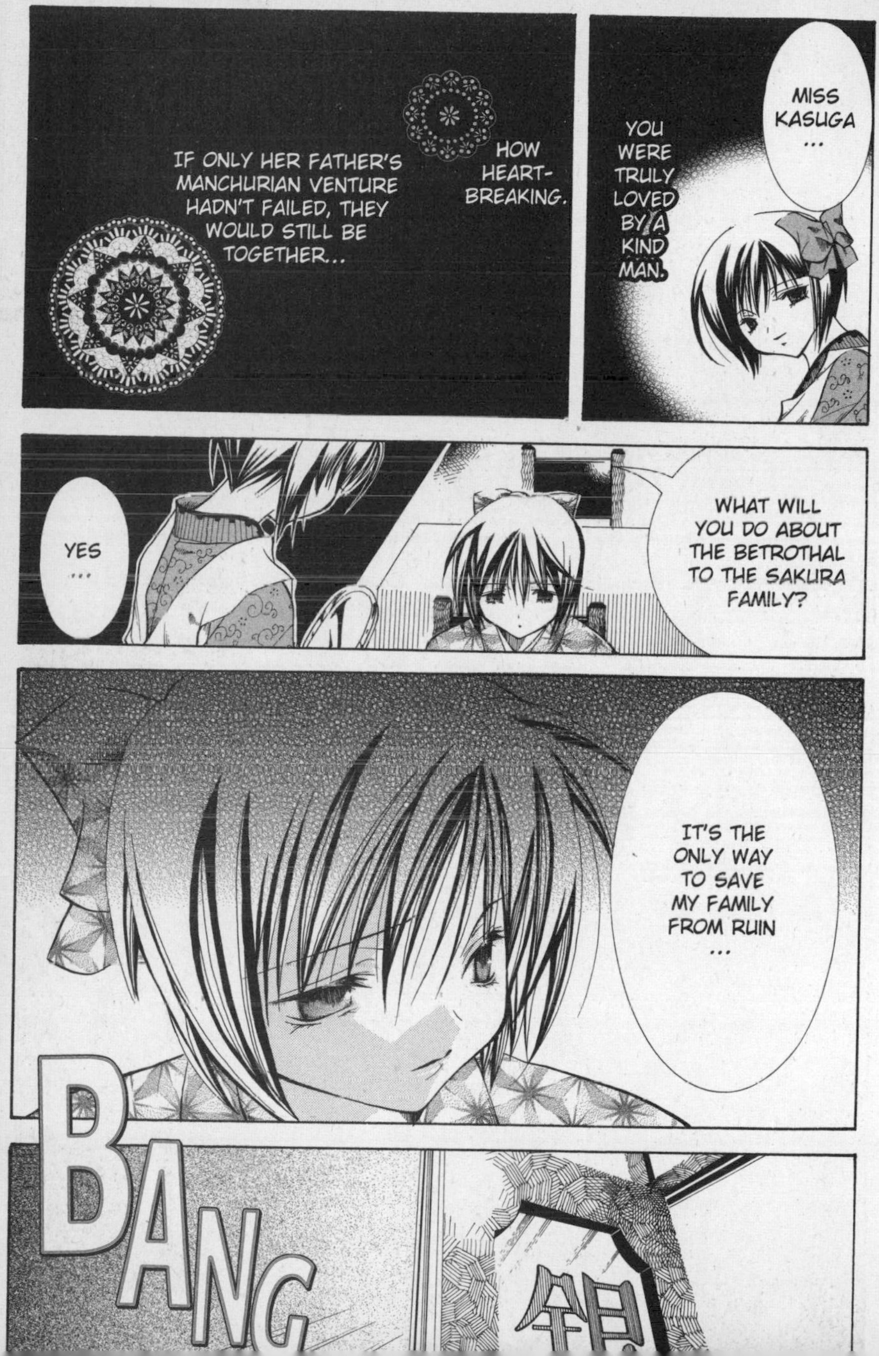
MISS KASUGA ...
YOU WERE TRULY LOVED BY A KIND MAN.
HOW HEART-BREAKING.
IF ONLY HER FATHER'S MANCHURIAN VENTURE HADN'T FAILED, THEY WOULD STILL BE TOGETHER...
WHAT WILL YOU DO ABOUT THE BETROTHAL TO THE SAKURA FAMILY?
YES ...
IT'S THE ONLY WAY TO SAVE MY FAMILY FROM RUIN ...
BANG

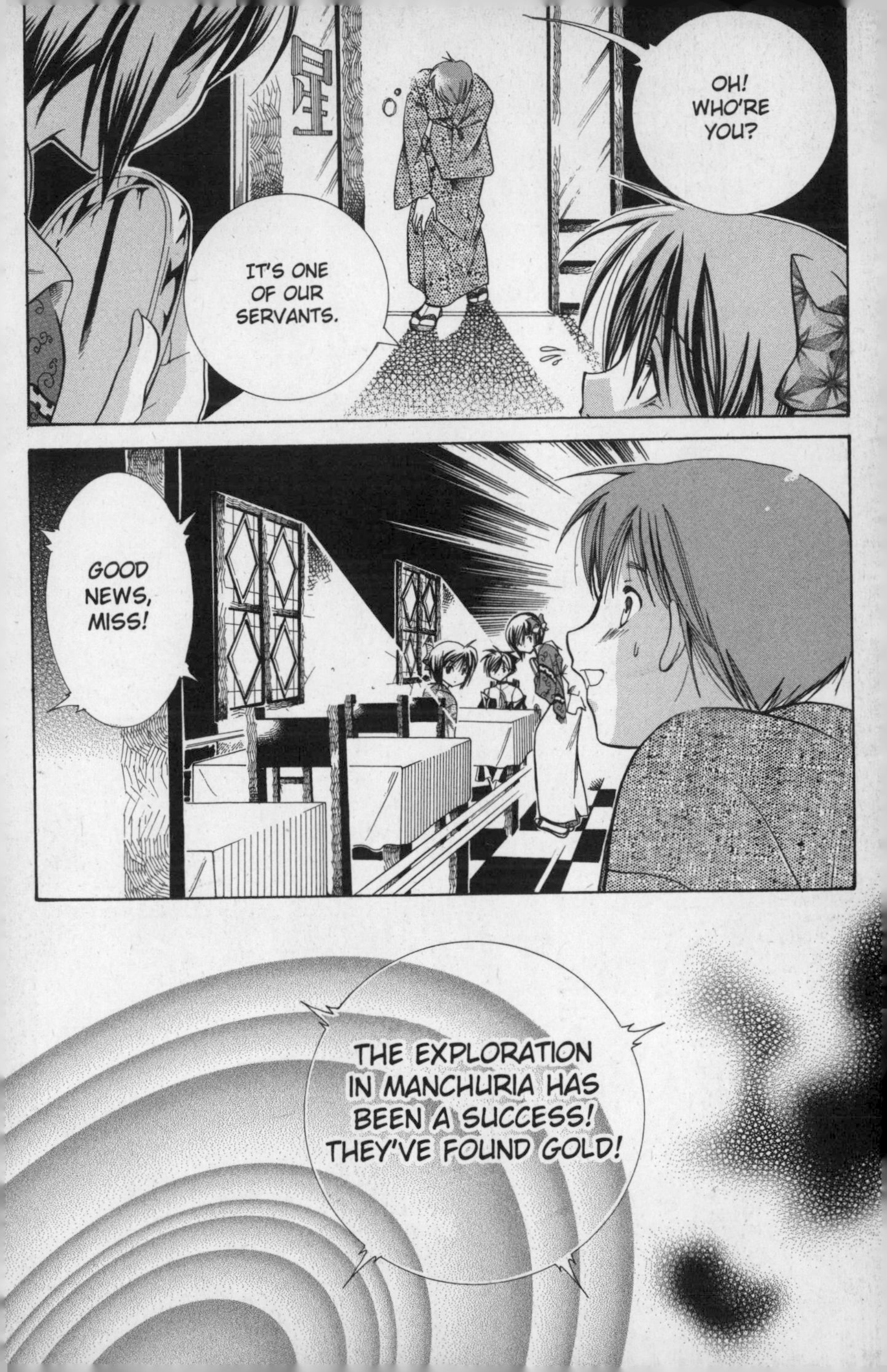
OH! WHO'RE YOU?
IT'S ONE OF OUR SERVANTS.
GOOD NEWS, MISS!
THE EXPLORATION IN MANCHURIA HAS BEEN A SUCCESS! THEY'VE FOUND GOLD!

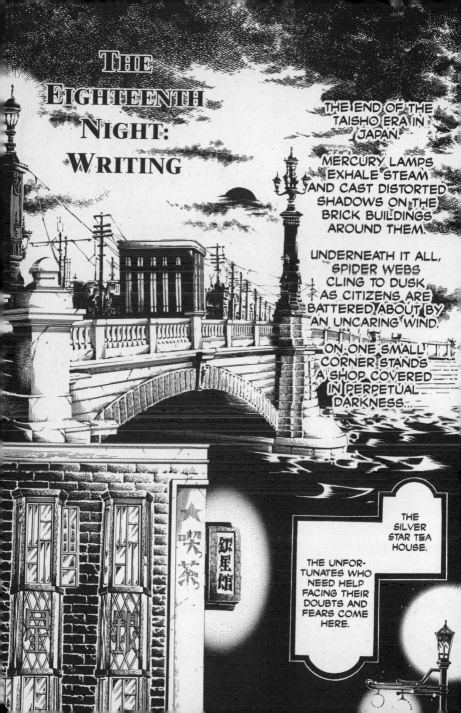

# THE EIGHTEENTH NIGHT: WRITING

THE END OF THE TAISHO ERA IN JAPAN.

MERCURY LAMPS EXHALE STEAM AND CAST DISTORTED SHADOWS ON THE BRICK BUILDINGS AROUND THEM.

UNDERNEATH IT ALL, SPIDER WEBS CLING TO DUSK, AS CITIZENS ARE BATTERED ABOUT BY AN UNCARING WIND.

ON ONE SMALL CORNER STANDS A SHOP COVERED IN PERPETUAL DARKNESS.

銀星館

喫茶

THE SILVER STAR TEA HOUSE.

THE UNFORTUNATES WHO NEED HELP FACING THEIR DOUBTS AND FEARS COME HERE.

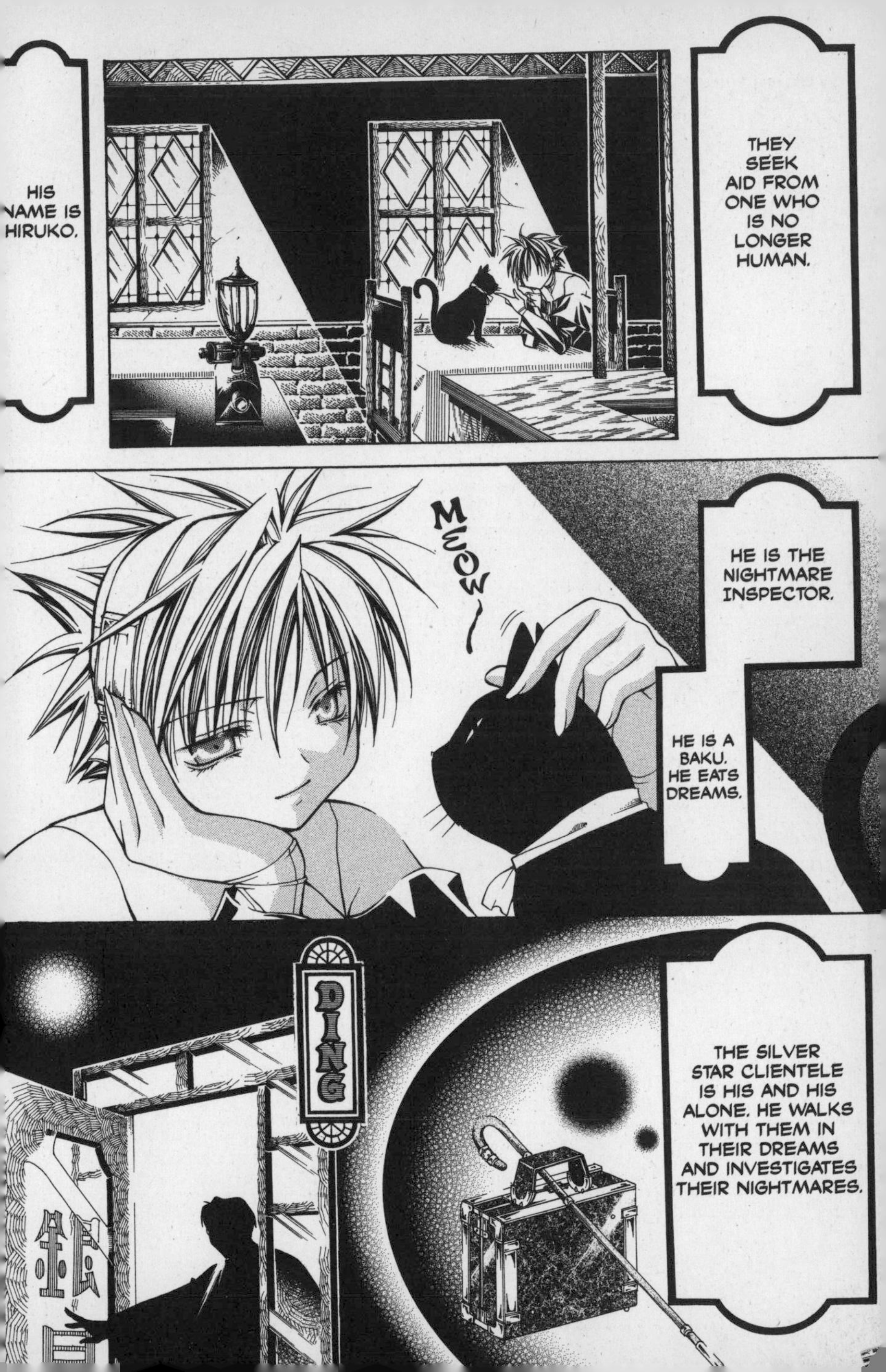
THEY SEEK AID FROM ONE WHO IS NO LONGER HUMAN.
HIS NAME IS HIRUKO.
HE IS THE NIGHTMARE INSPECTOR.
MEOW~
HE IS A BAKU. HE EATS DREAMS.
THE SILVER STAR CLIENTELE IS HIS AND HIS ALONE. HE WALKS WITH THEM IN THEIR DREAMS AND INVESTIGATES THEIR NIGHTMARES.
DING

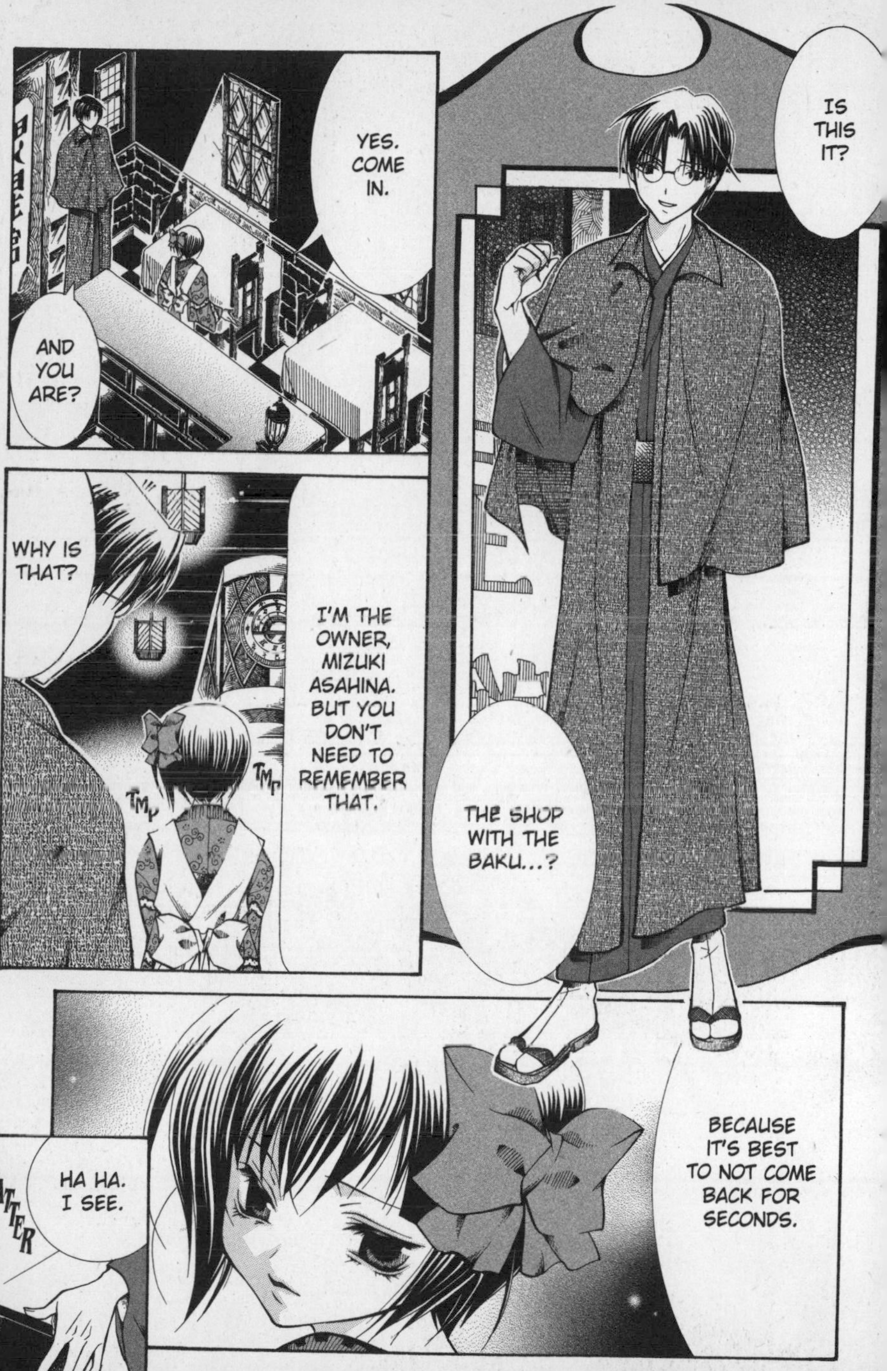
IS THIS IT?
THE SHOP WITH THE BAKU...?
YES. COME IN.
AND YOU ARE?
I'M THE OWNER, MIZUKI ASAHINA. BUT YOU DON'T NEED TO REMEMBER THAT.
TMP
TMP
WHY IS THAT?
BECAUSE IT'S BEST TO NOT COME BACK FOR SECONDS.
HA HA. I SEE.
CLATTER

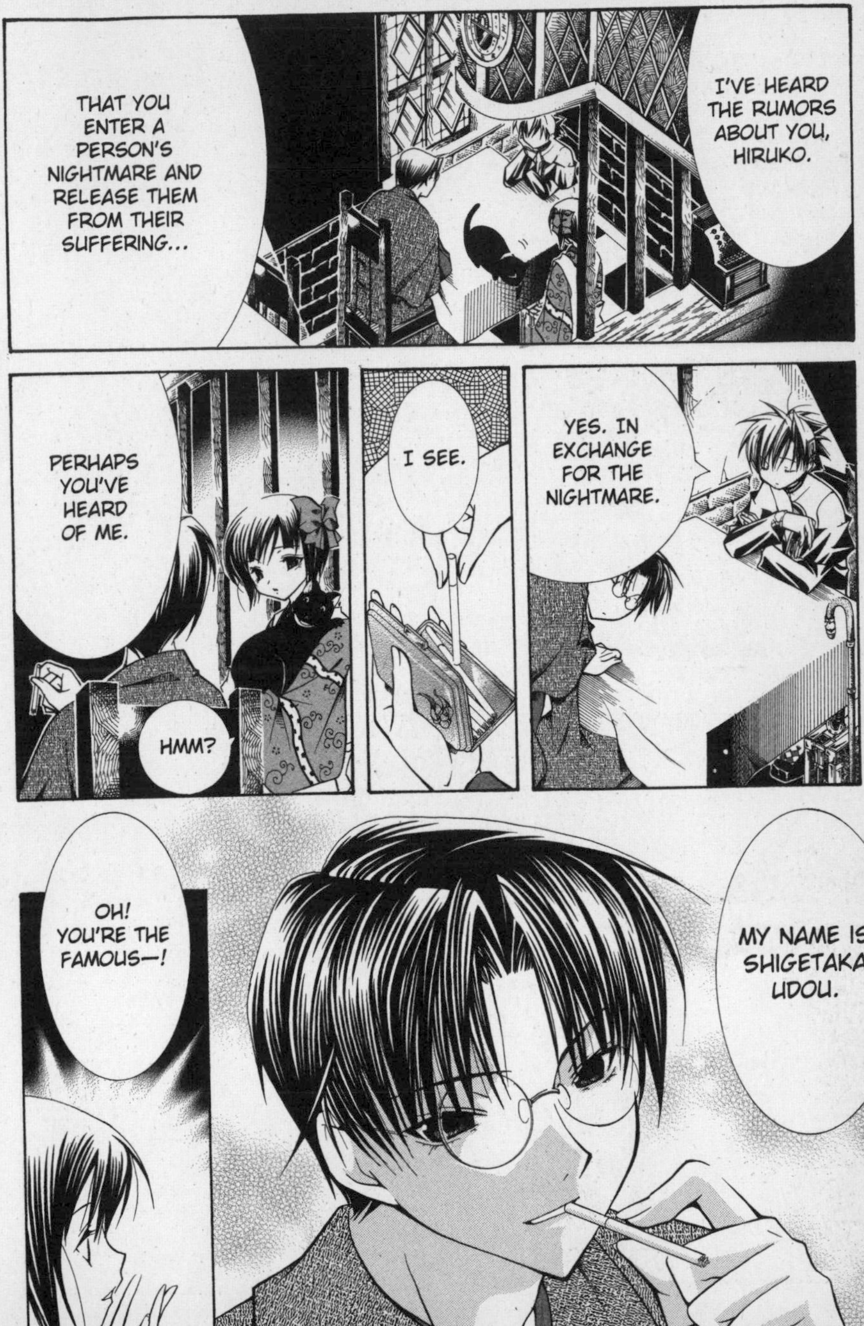
I'VE HEARD THE RUMORS ABOUT YOU, HIRUKO.
THAT YOU ENTER A PERSON'S NIGHTMARE AND RELEASE THEM FROM THEIR SUFFERING...
YES. IN EXCHANGE FOR THE NIGHTMARE.
I SEE.
PERHAPS YOU'VE HEARD OF ME.
HMM?
MY NAME IS SHIGETAKA UDOU.
OH! YOU'RE THE FAMOUS—!

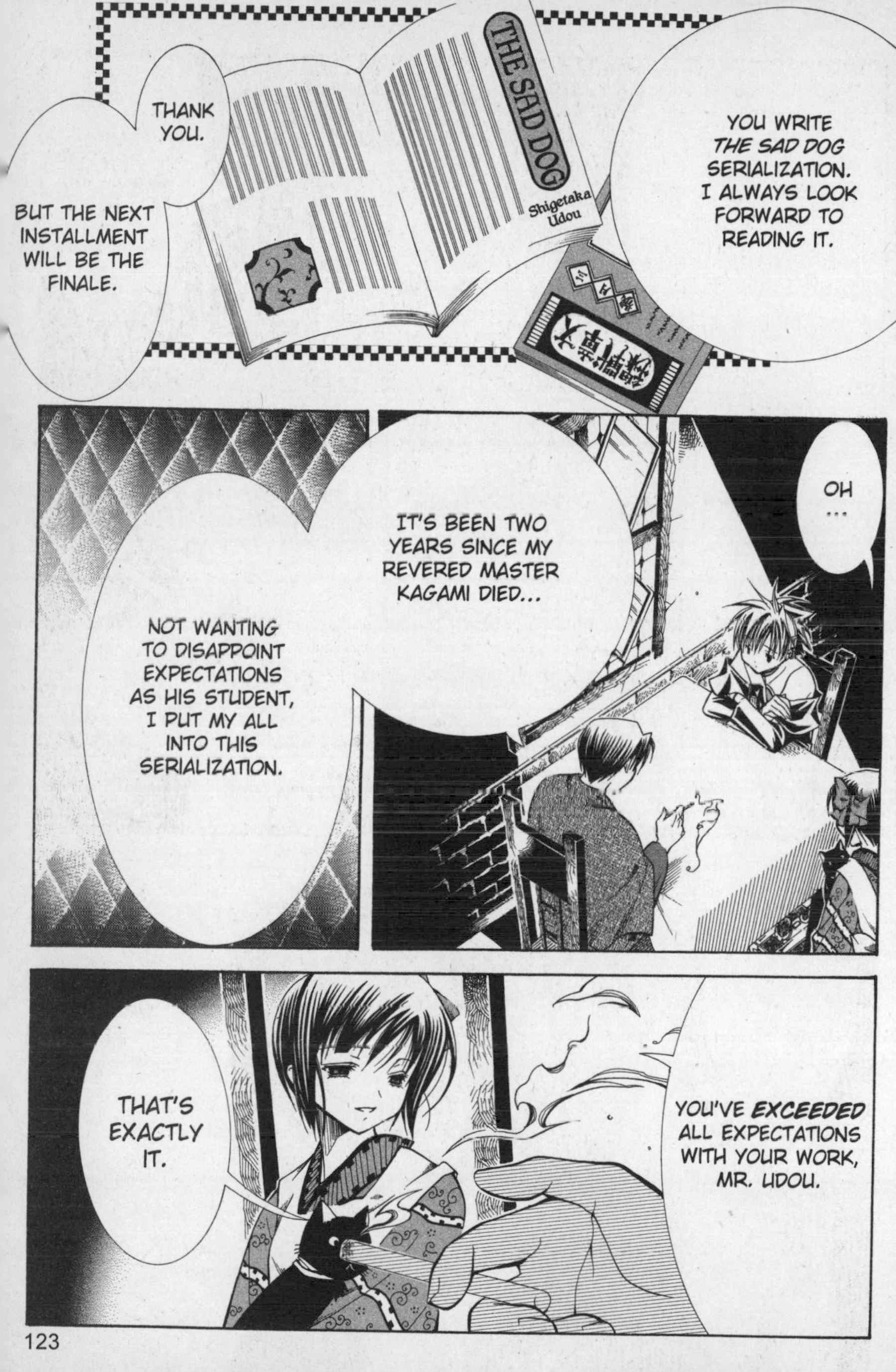
THE SAD DOG
Shigetaka Udou
YOU WRITE *THE SAD DOG* SERIALIZATION. I ALWAYS LOOK FORWARD TO READING IT.
THANK YOU.
BUT THE NEXT INSTALLMENT WILL BE THE FINALE.
OH ...
IT'S BEEN TWO YEARS SINCE MY REVERED MASTER KAGAMI DIED...
NOT WANTING TO DISAPPOINT EXPECTATIONS AS HIS STUDENT, I PUT MY ALL INTO THIS SERIALIZATION.
YOU'VE ***EXCEEDED*** ALL EXPECTATIONS WITH YOUR WORK, MR. UDOU.
THAT'S EXACTLY IT.

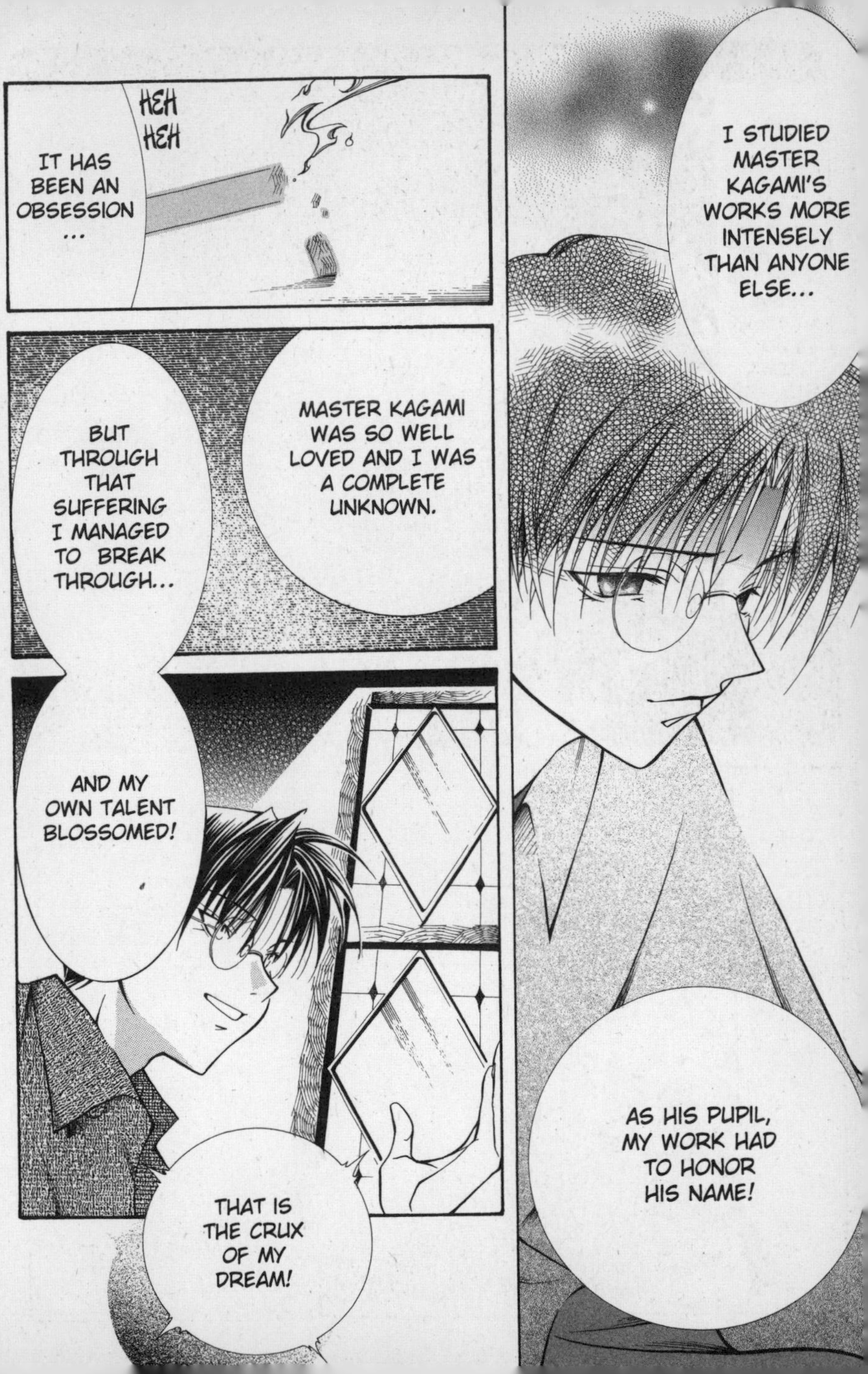
I STUDIED MASTER KAGAMI'S WORKS MORE INTENSELY THAN ANYONE ELSE...
AS HIS PUPIL, MY WORK HAD TO HONOR HIS NAME!
HEH HEH
IT HAS BEEN AN OBSESSION ...
MASTER KAGAMI WAS SO WELL LOVED AND I WAS A COMPLETE UNKNOWN.
BUT THROUGH THAT SUFFERING I MANAGED TO BREAK THROUGH...
AND MY OWN TALENT BLOSSOMED!
THAT IS THE CRUX OF MY DREAM!

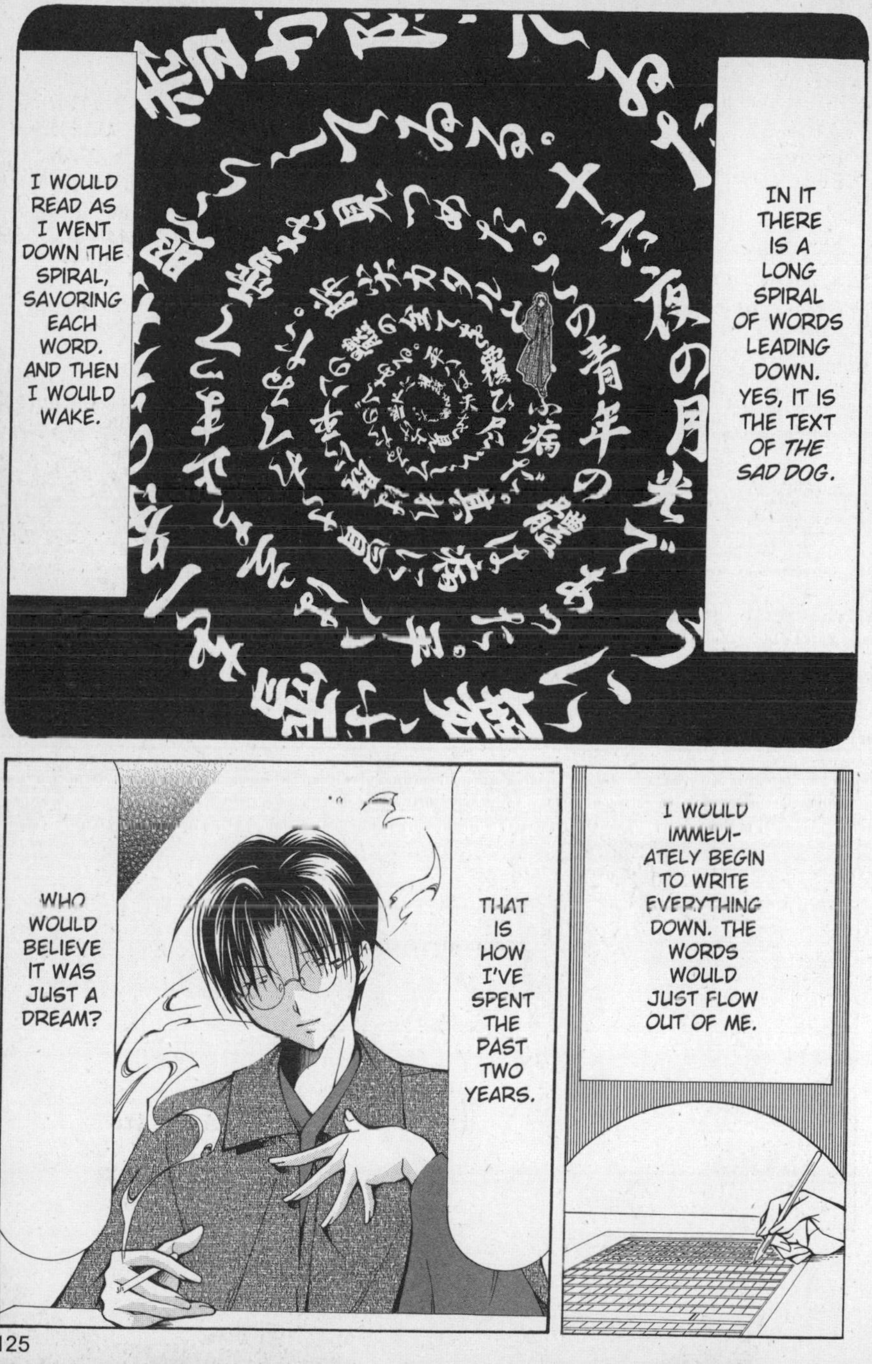
IN IT THERE IS A LONG SPIRAL OF WORDS LEADING DOWN. YES, IT IS THE TEXT OF *THE SAD DOG*.
I WOULD READ AS I WENT DOWN THE SPIRAL, SAVORING EACH WORD. AND THEN I WOULD WAKE.
I WOULD IMMEDI-ATELY BEGIN TO WRITE EVERYTHING DOWN. THE WORDS WOULD JUST FLOW OUT OF ME.
THAT IS HOW I'VE SPENT THE PAST TWO YEARS.
WHO WOULD BELIEVE IT WAS JUST A DREAM?

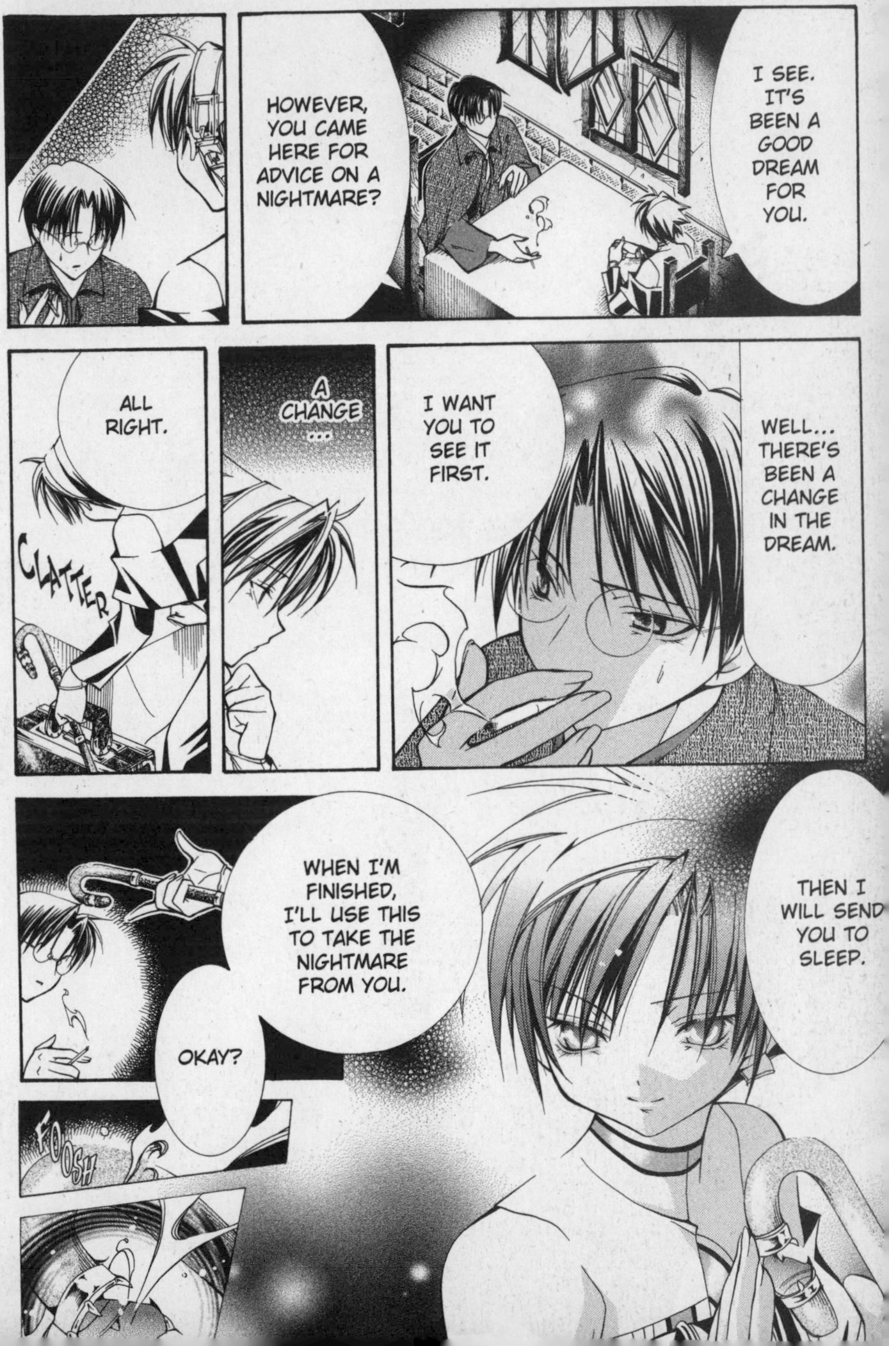
I SEE. IT'S BEEN A GOOD DREAM FOR YOU.
HOWEVER, YOU CAME HERE FOR ADVICE ON A NIGHTMARE?
WELL... THERE'S BEEN A CHANGE IN THE DREAM.
I WANT YOU TO SEE IT FIRST.
A CHANGE ...
ALL RIGHT.
CLATTER
THEN I WILL SEND YOU TO SLEEP.
WHEN I'M FINISHED, I'LL USE THIS TO TAKE THE NIGHTMARE FROM YOU.
OKAY?
FOOSH

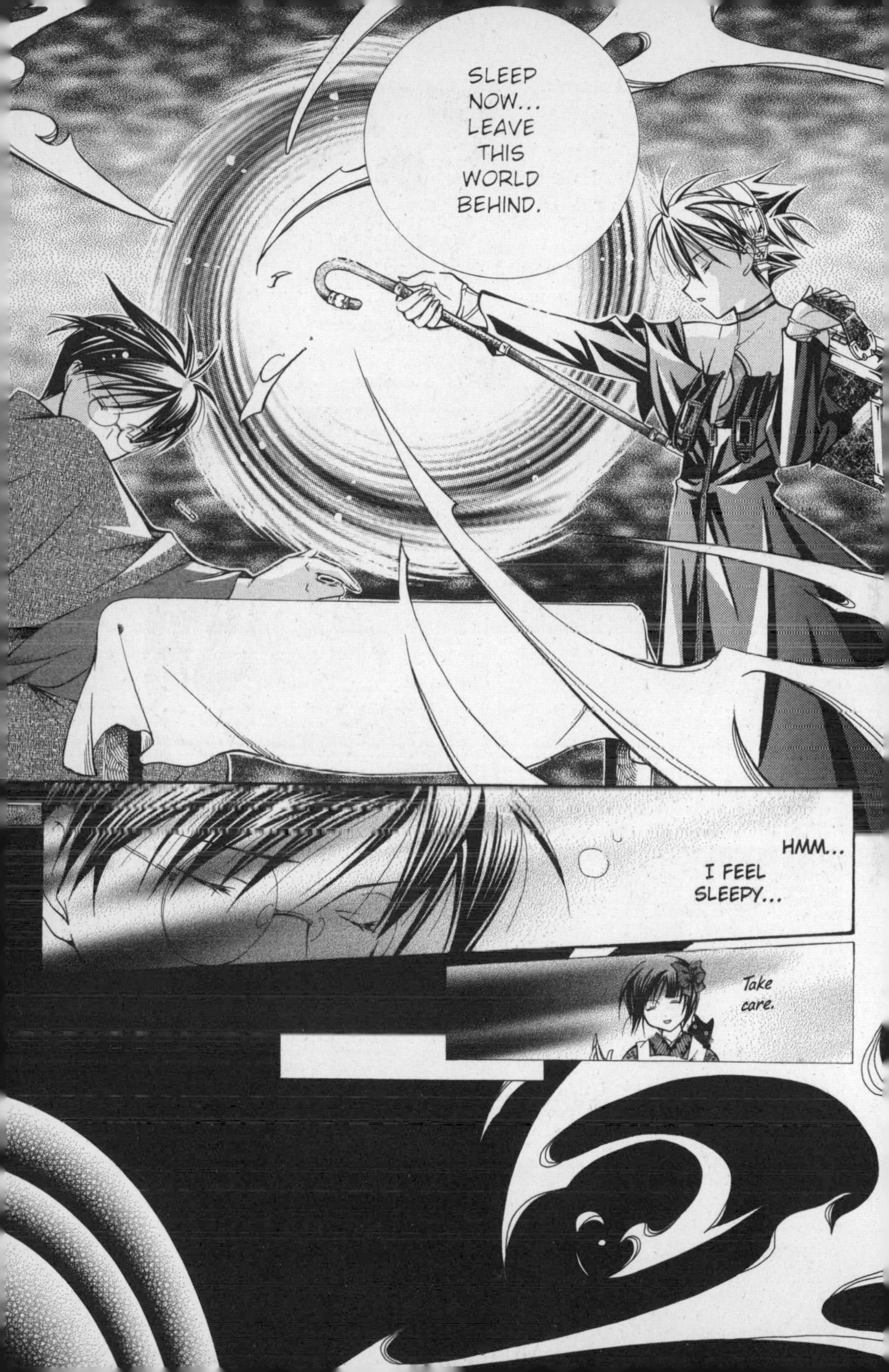
SLEEP NOW... LEAVE THIS WORLD BEHIND.
HMM...
I FEEL SLEEPY...
Take care.

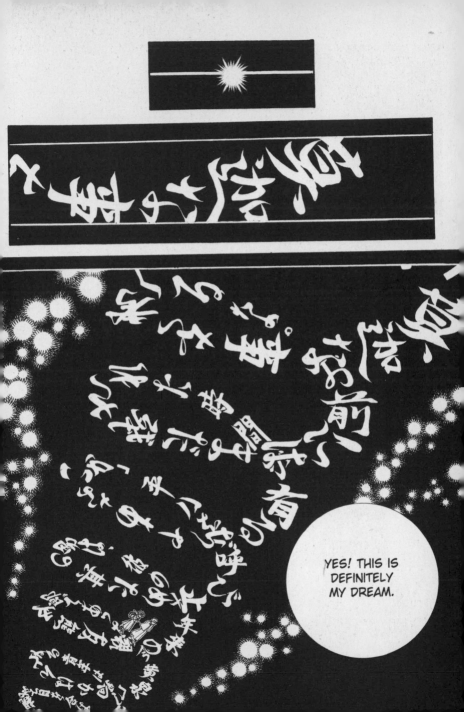

YES! THIS IS DEFINITELY MY DREAM.

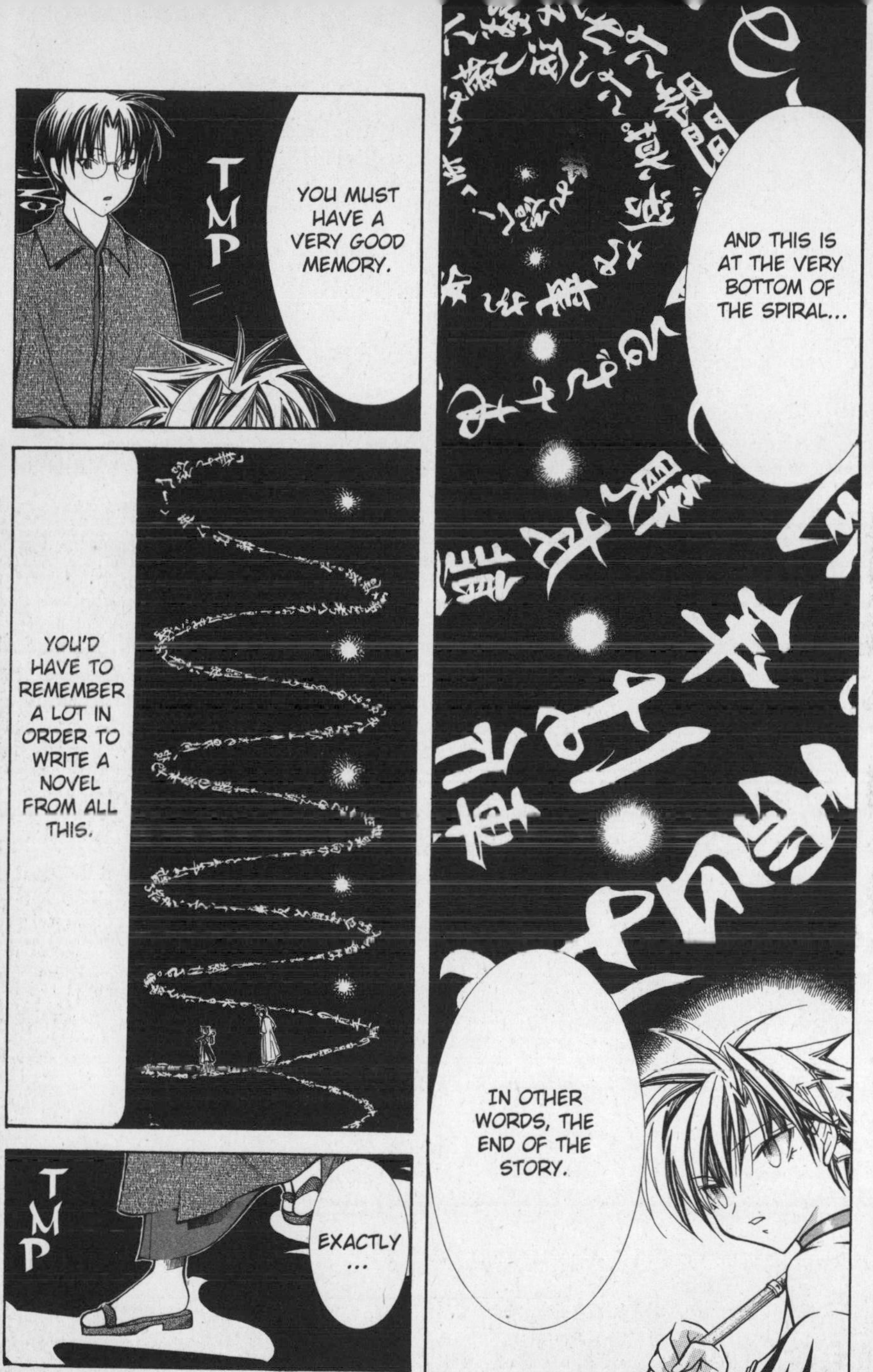
AND THIS IS AT THE VERY BOTTOM OF THE SPIRAL...
IN OTHER WORDS, THE END OF THE STORY.
TMP
YOU MUST HAVE A VERY GOOD MEMORY.
YOU'D HAVE TO REMEMBER A LOT IN ORDER TO WRITE A NOVEL FROM ALL THIS.
TMP
EXACTLY...

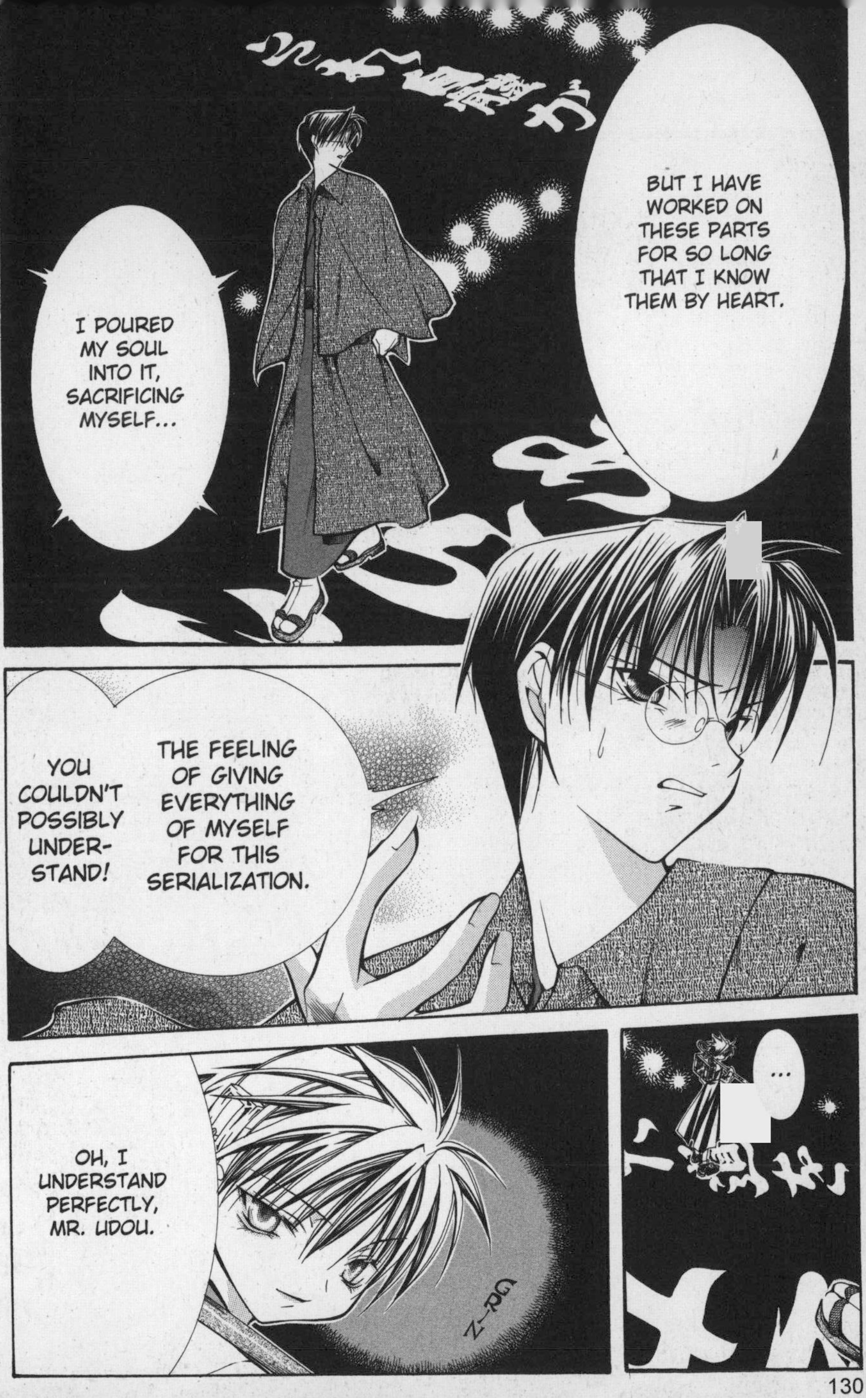
BUT I HAVE WORKED ON THESE PARTS FOR SO LONG THAT I KNOW THEM BY HEART.
I POURED MY SOUL INTO IT, SACRIFICING MYSELF...
THE FEELING OF GIVING EVERYTHING OF MYSELF FOR THIS SERIALIZATION.
YOU COULDN'T POSSIBLY UNDER-STAND!
...
OH, I UNDERSTAND PERFECTLY, MR. UDOU.
Z-RG

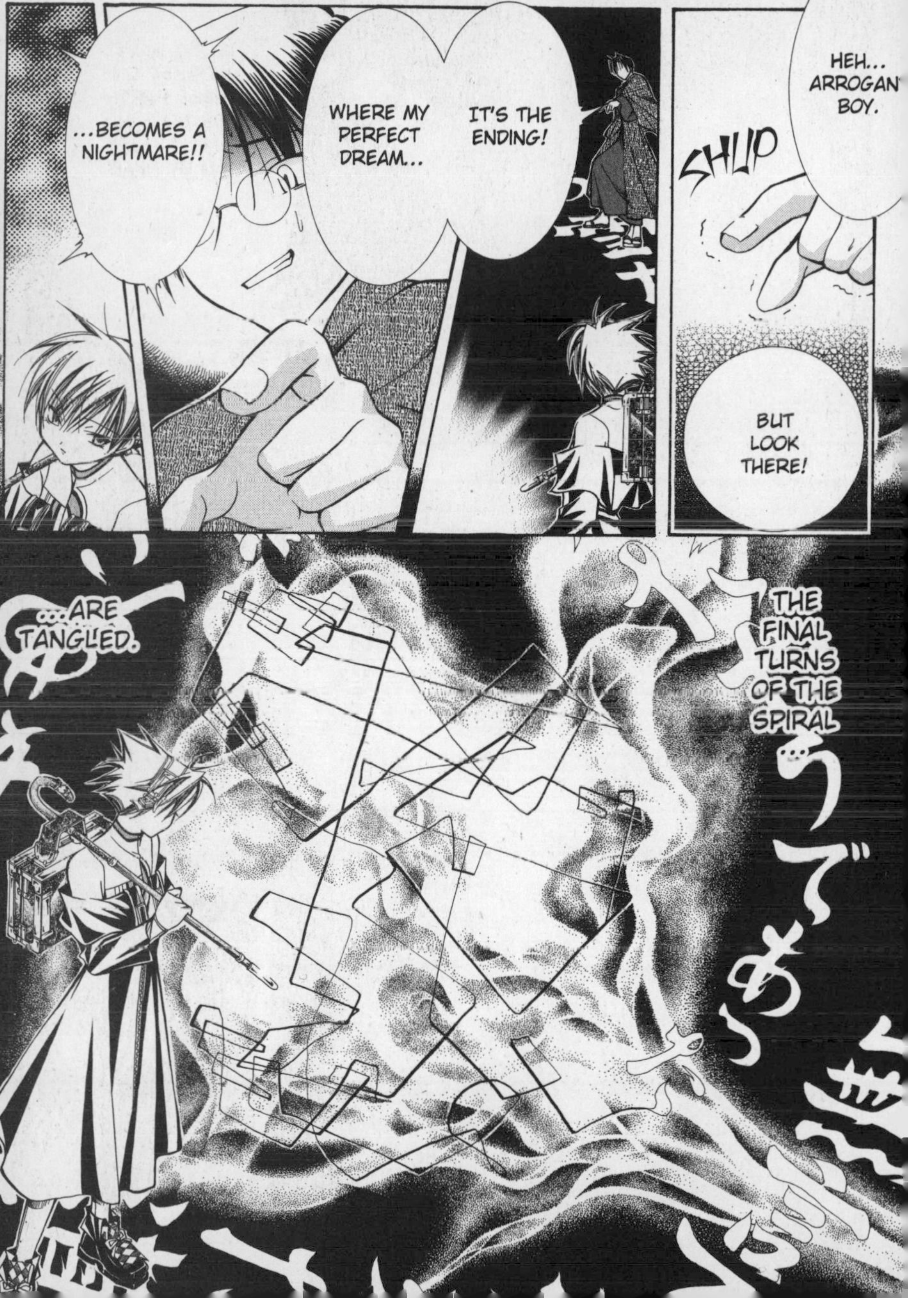
HEH... ARROGAN BOY.
SHUP
BUT LOOK THERE!
IT'S THE ENDING!
WHERE MY PERFECT DREAM...
...BECOMES A NIGHTMARE!!
THE FINAL TURNS OF THE SPIRAL
...ARE TANGLED.

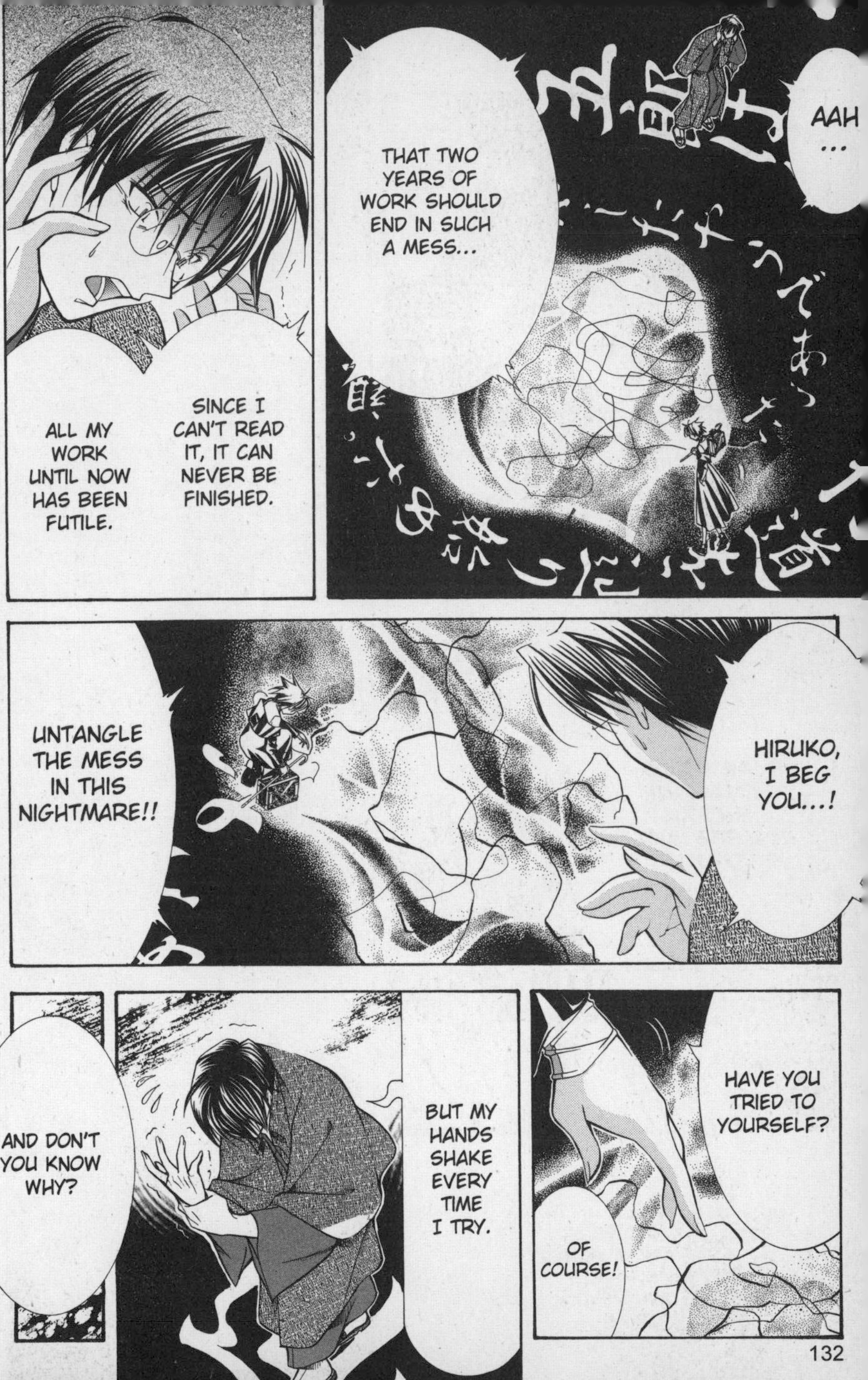
AAH...
THAT TWO YEARS OF WORK SHOULD END IN SUCH A MESS...
SINCE I CAN'T READ IT, IT CAN NEVER BE FINISHED.
ALL MY WORK UNTIL NOW HAS BEEN FUTILE.
HIRUKO, I BEG YOU...!
UNTANGLE THE MESS IN THIS NIGHTMARE!!
HAVE YOU TRIED TO YOURSELF?
OF COURSE!
BUT MY HANDS SHAKE EVERY TIME I TRY.
AND DON'T YOU KNOW WHY?

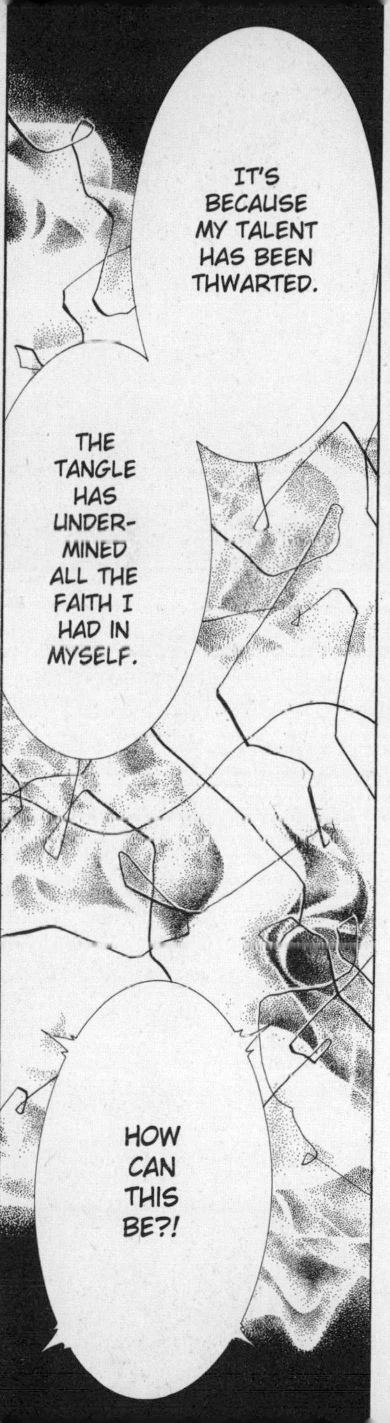
IT'S BECAUSE MY TALENT HAS BEEN THWARTED.
THE TANGLE HAS UNDER-MINED ALL THE FAITH I HAD IN MYSELF.
HOW CAN THIS BE?!
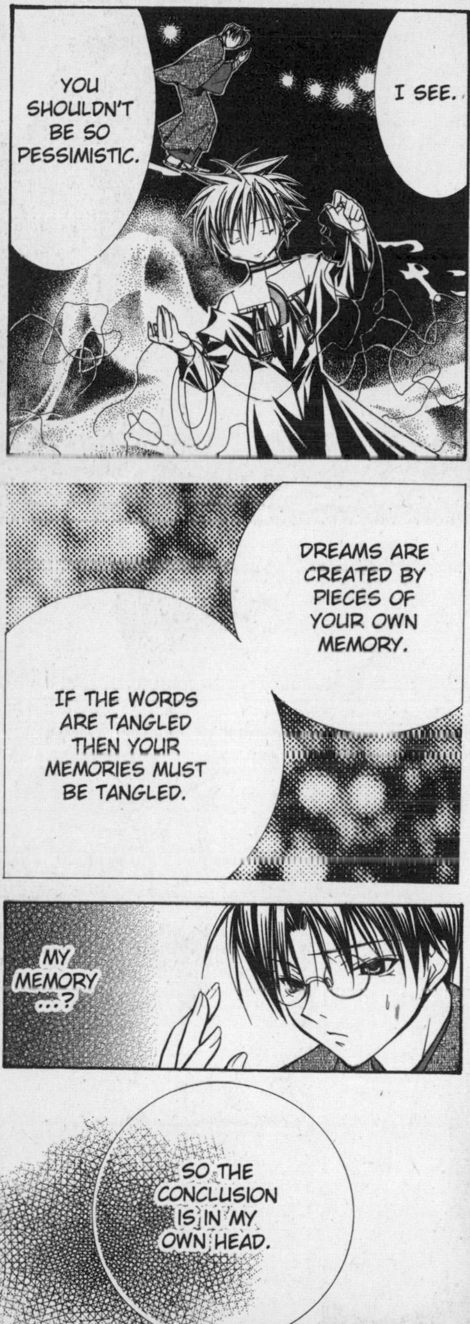
I SEE.
YOU SHOULDN'T BE SO PESSIMISTIC.
DREAMS ARE CREATED BY PIECES OF YOUR OWN MEMORY.
IF THE WORDS ARE TANGLED THEN YOUR MEMORIES MUST BE TANGLED.
MY MEMORY ...?
SO THE CONCLUSION IS IN MY OWN HEAD.

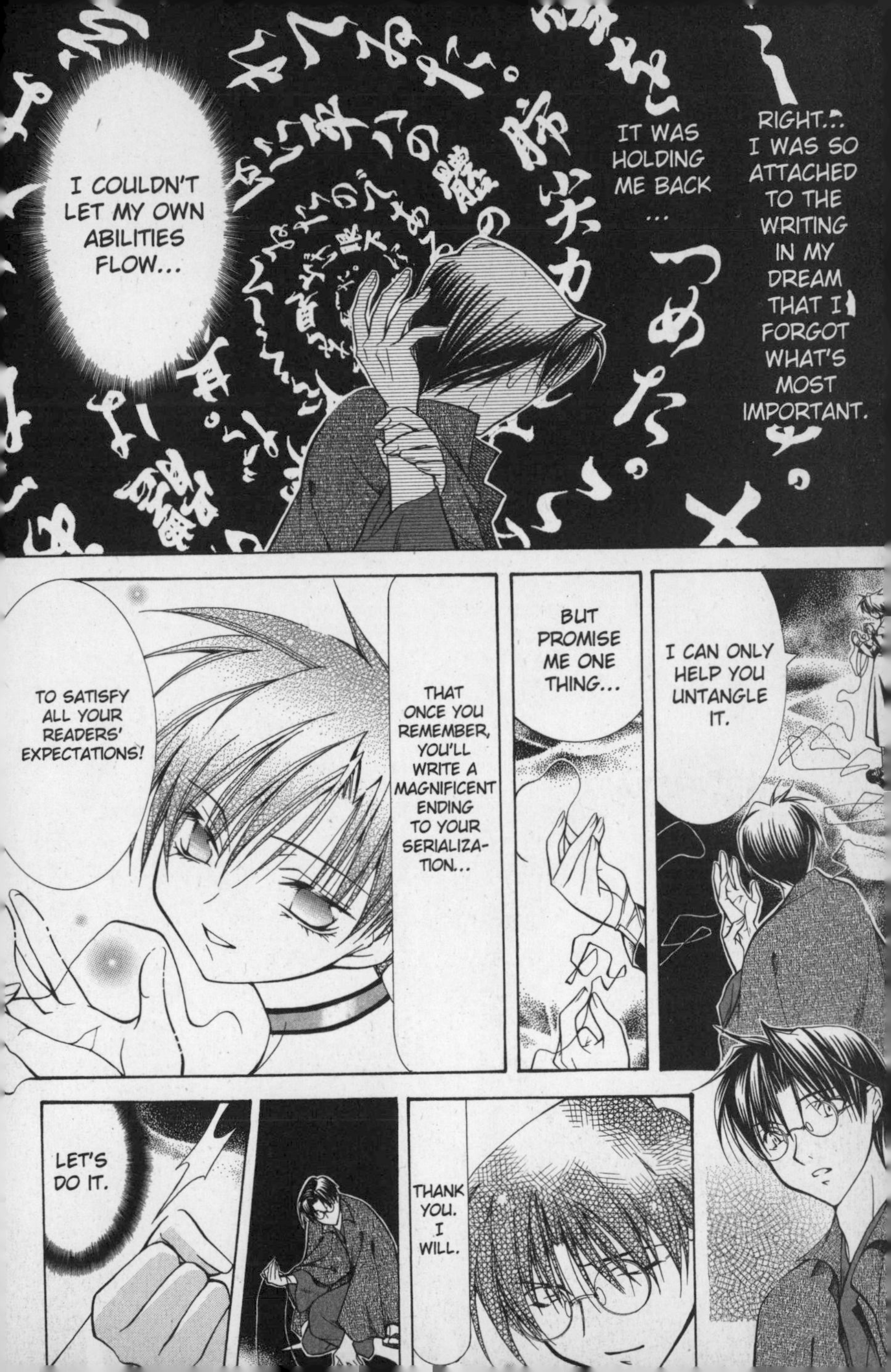
RIGHT... I WAS SO ATTACHED TO THE WRITING IN MY DREAM THAT I FORGOT WHAT'S MOST IMPORTANT.
IT WAS HOLDING ME BACK...
I COULDN'T LET MY OWN ABILITIES FLOW...
I CAN ONLY HELP YOU UNTANGLE IT.
BUT PROMISE ME ONE THING...
THAT ONCE YOU REMEMBER, YOU'LL WRITE A MAGNIFICENT ENDING TO YOUR SERIALIZATION...
TO SATISFY ALL YOUR READERS' EXPECTATIONS!
THANK YOU. I WILL.
LET'S DO IT.

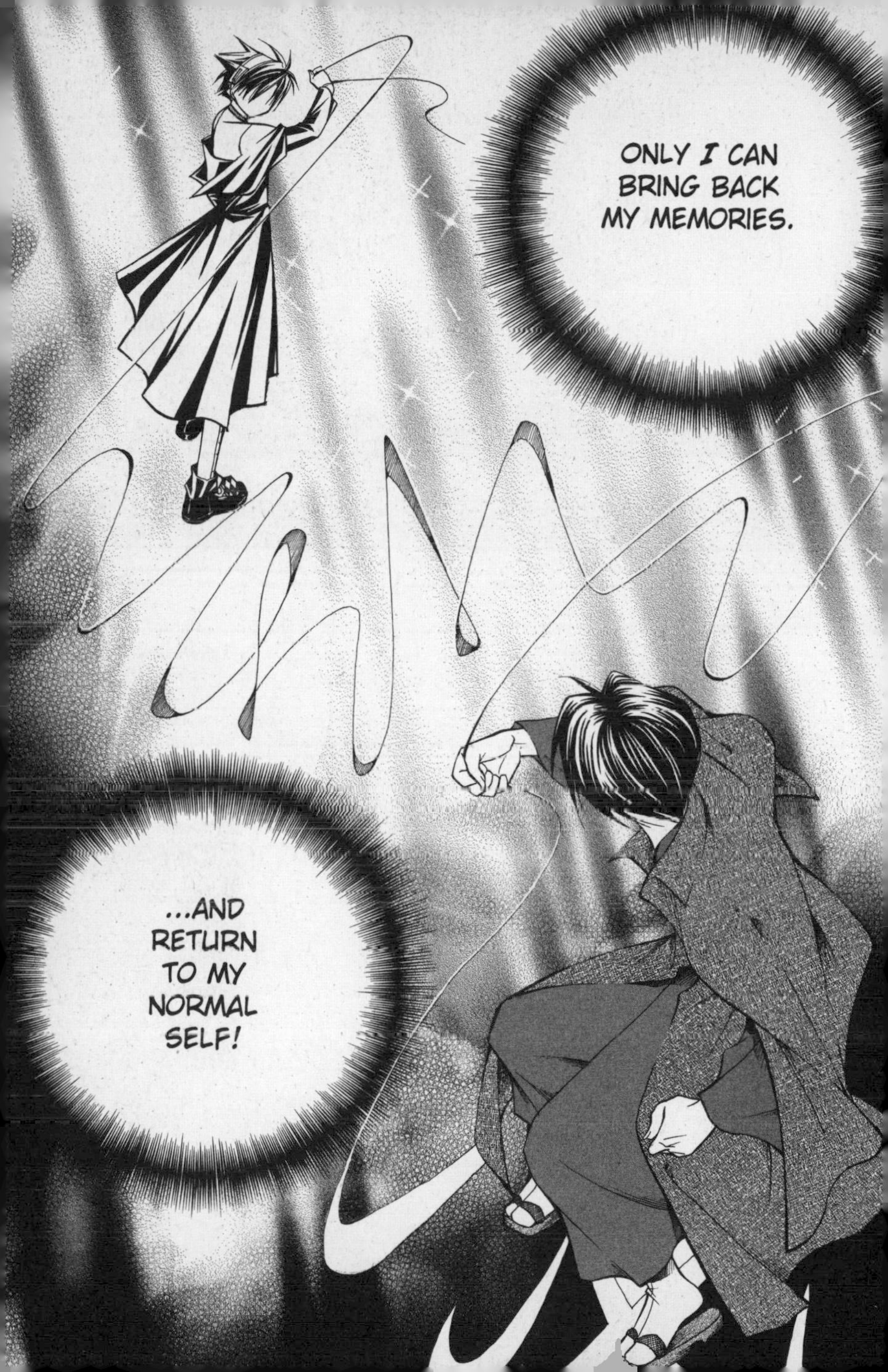
ONLY I CAN BRING BACK MY MEMORIES.
...AND RETURN TO MY NORMAL SELF!

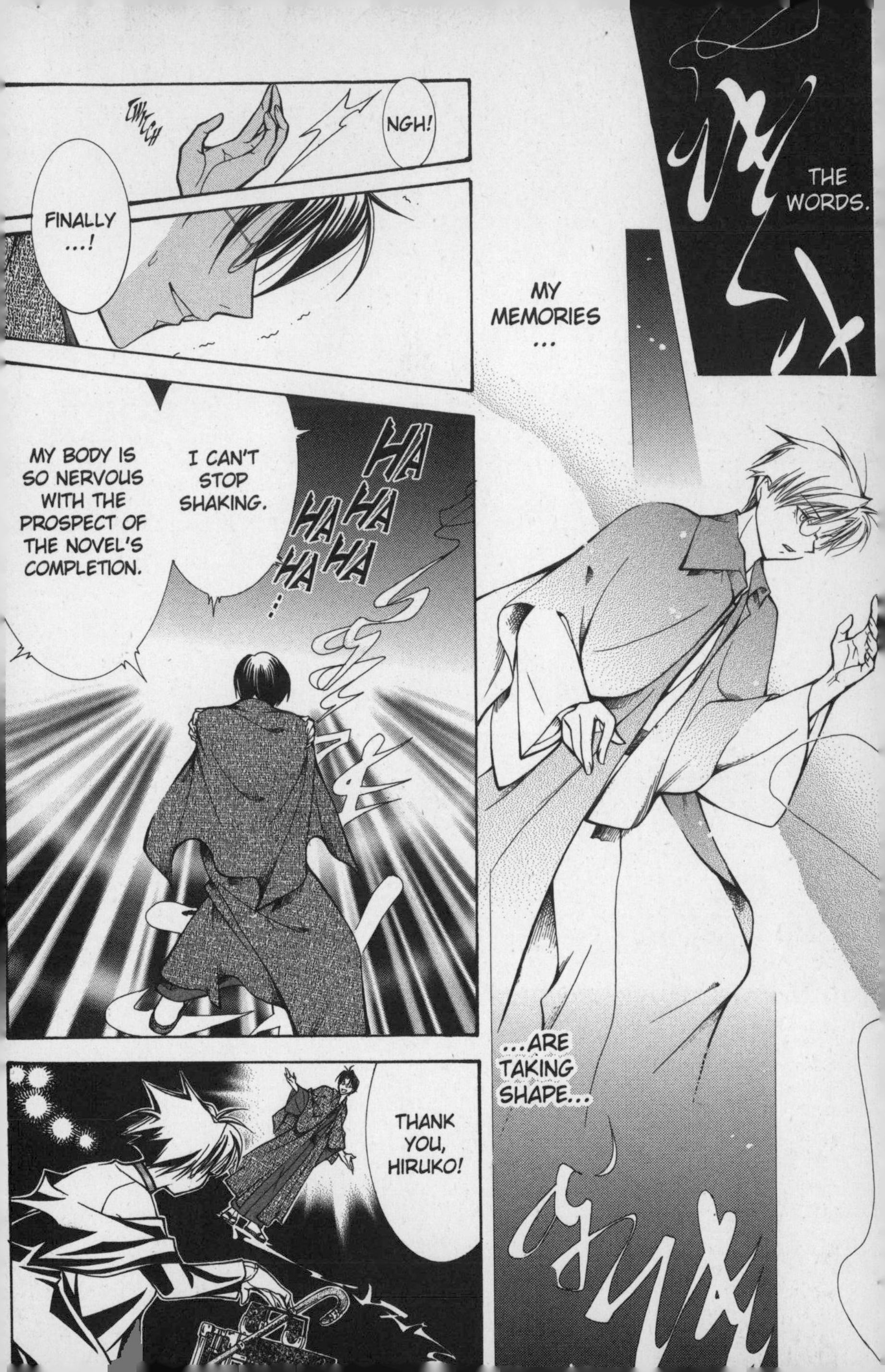
THE WORDS.
MY MEMORIES ...
...ARE TAKING SHAPE...
NGH!
TWITCH
FINALLY ...!
I CAN'T STOP SHAKING.
MY BODY IS SO NERVOUS WITH THE PROSPECT OF THE NOVEL'S COMPLETION.
HA HA HA HA HA HA ...
THANK YOU, HIRUKO!

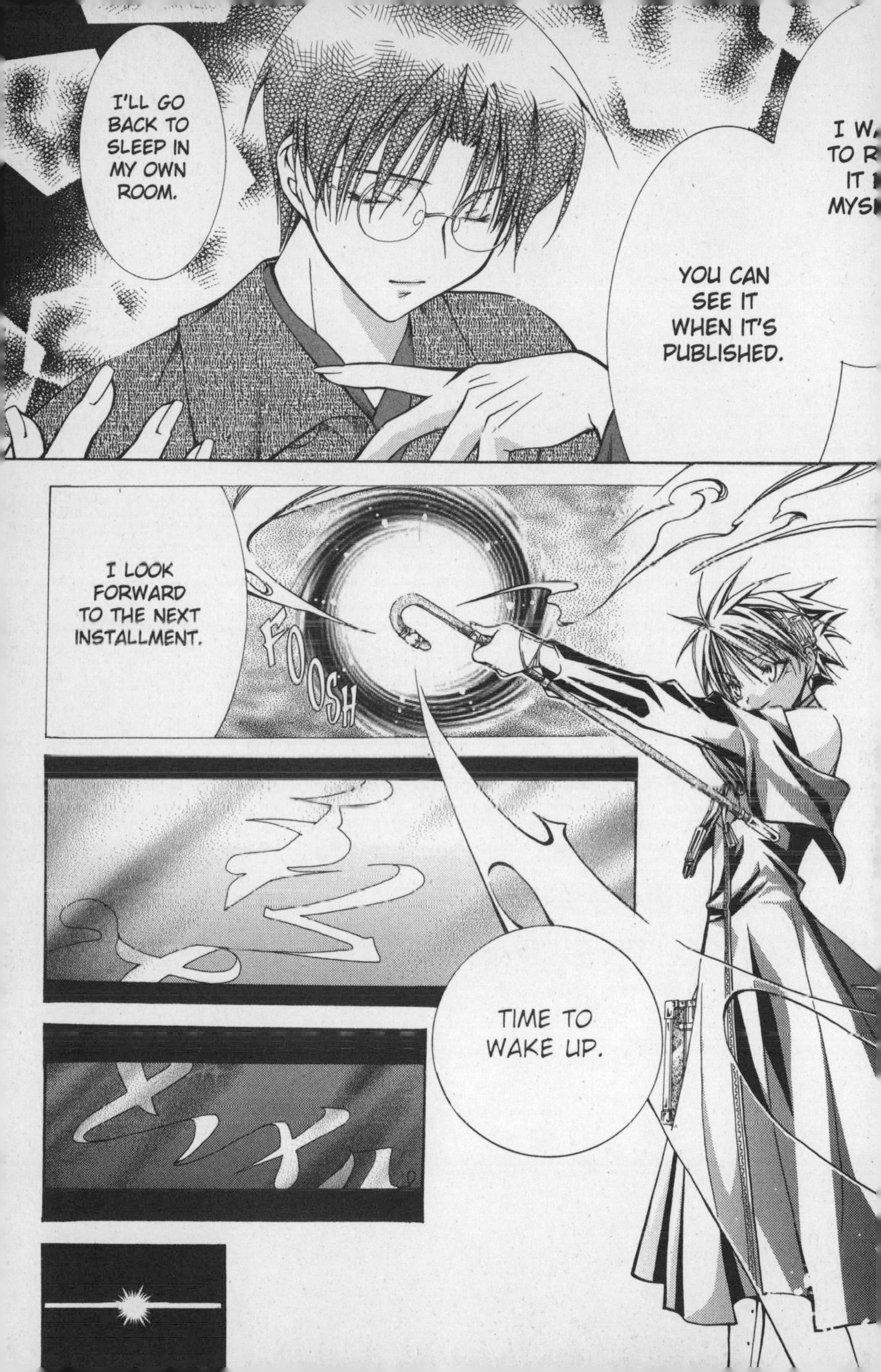
YOU CAN SEE IT WHEN IT'S PUBLISHED.
I'LL GO BACK TO SLEEP IN MY OWN ROOM.
I LOOK FORWARD TO THE NEXT INSTALLMENT.
FOOSH
TIME TO WAKE UP.

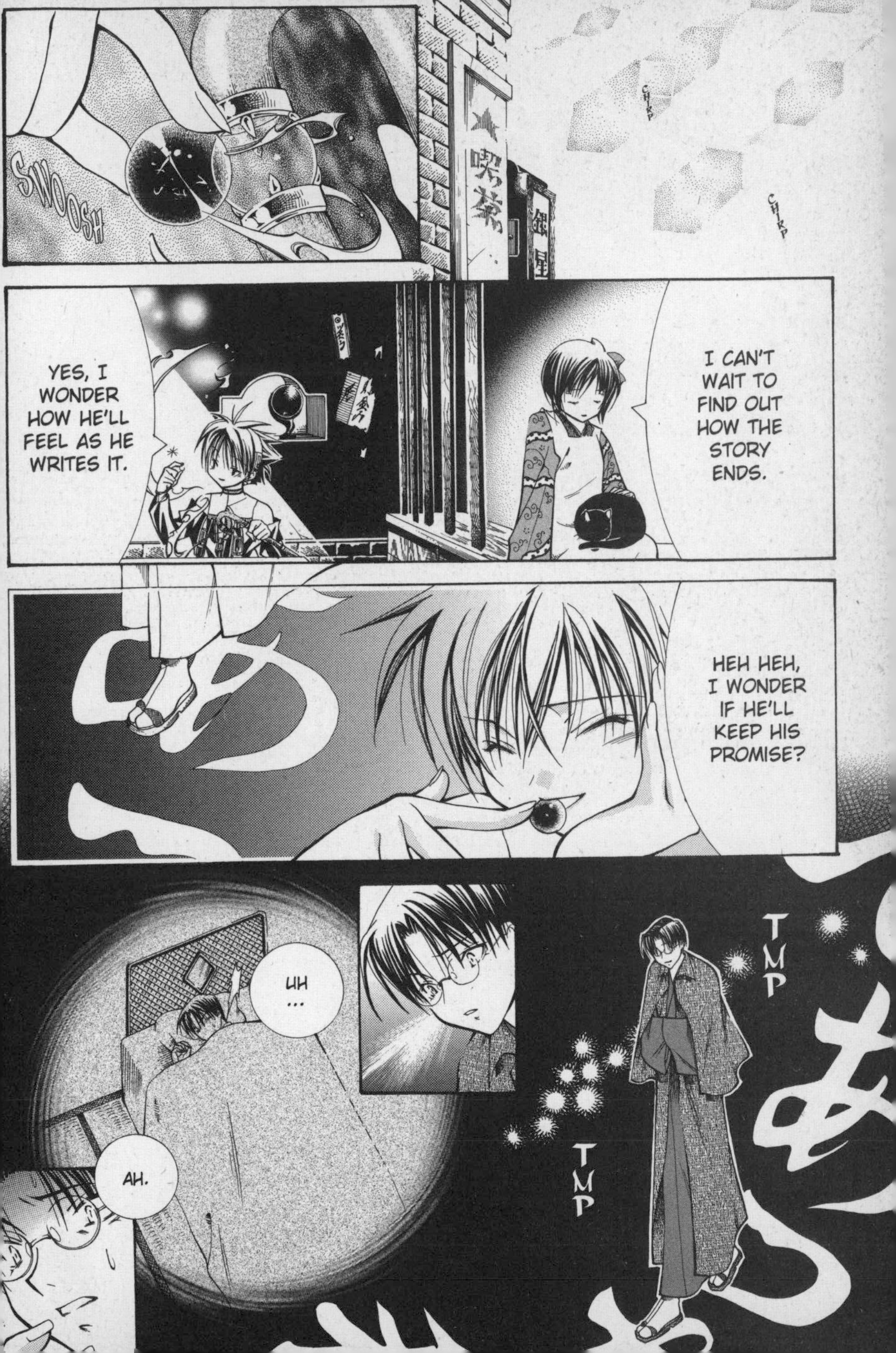
CHIRP
CHIRP
SWOOSH
I CAN'T WAIT TO FIND OUT HOW THE STORY ENDS.
YES, I WONDER HOW HE'LL FEEL AS HE WRITES IT.
HEH HEH, I WONDER IF HE'LL KEEP HIS PROMISE?
TMP
TMP
UH ...
AH.

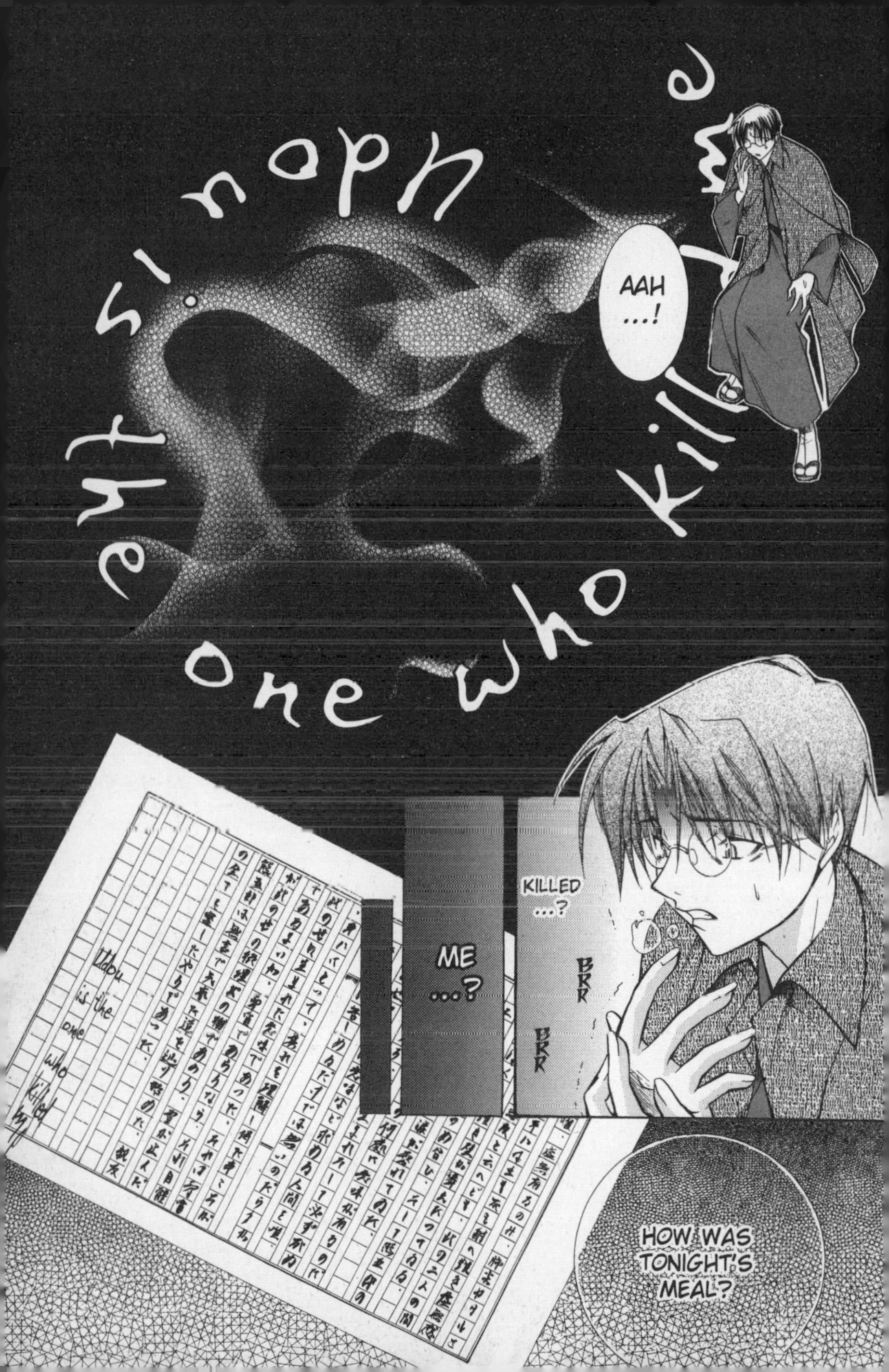
Udou is the one who kill me
AAH ...!
KILLED ...?
BRR
BRR
ME ...?
Udou is the one who killed my
HOW WAS TONIGHT'S MEAL?

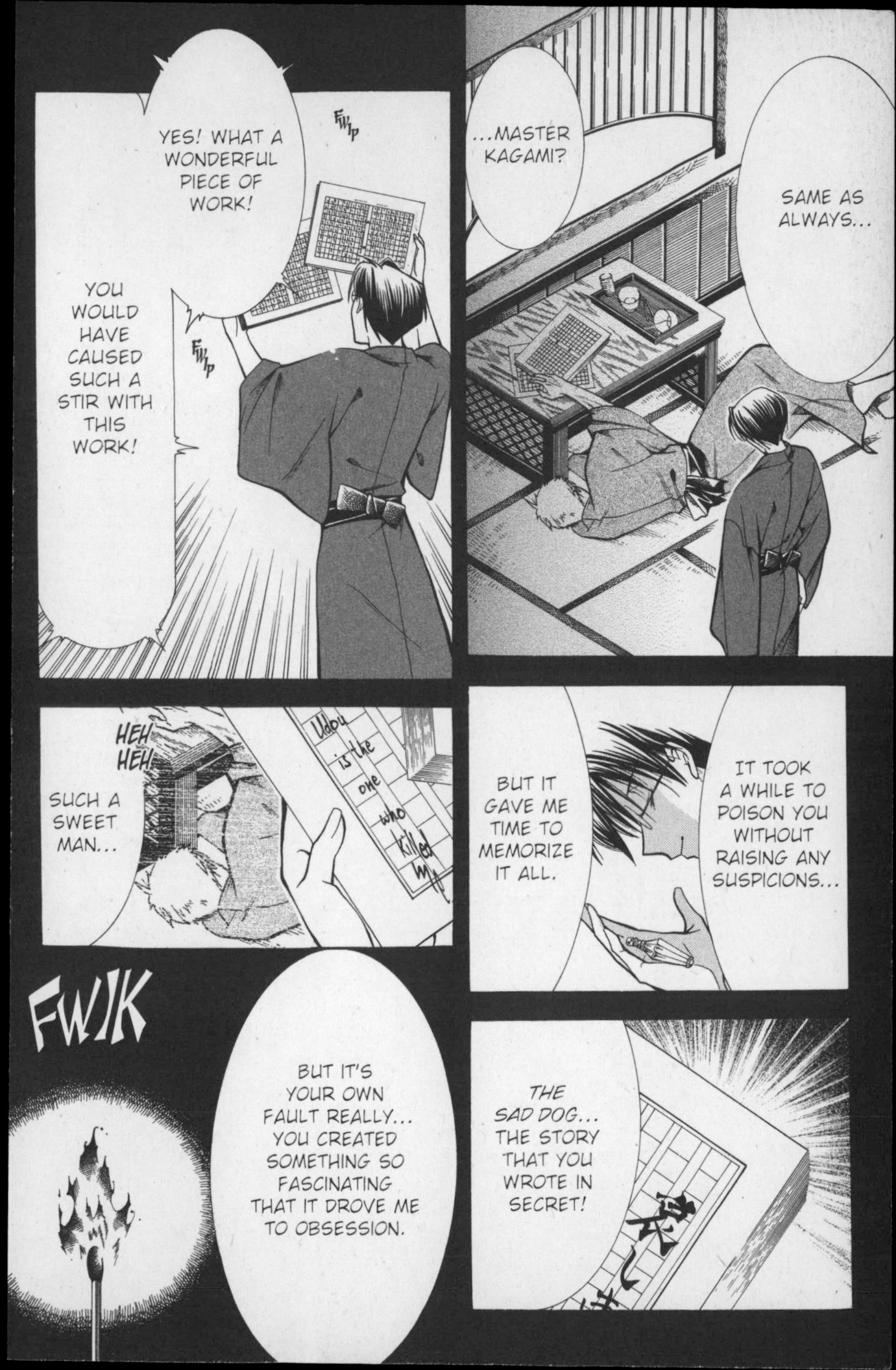
SAME AS ALWAYS...
...MASTER KAGAMI?
YES! WHAT A WONDERFUL PIECE OF WORK!
FWIP
YOU WOULD HAVE CAUSED SUCH A STIR WITH THIS WORK!
FWIP
IT TOOK A WHILE TO POISON YOU WITHOUT RAISING ANY SUSPICIONS...
BUT IT GAVE ME TIME TO MEMORIZE IT ALL.
HEH HEH
SUCH A SWEET MAN...
Udou is the one who killed
THE SAD DOG... THE STORY THAT YOU WROTE IN SECRET!
BUT IT'S YOUR OWN FAULT REALLY... YOU CREATED SOMETHING SO FASCINATING THAT IT DROVE ME TO OBSESSION.
FWIK

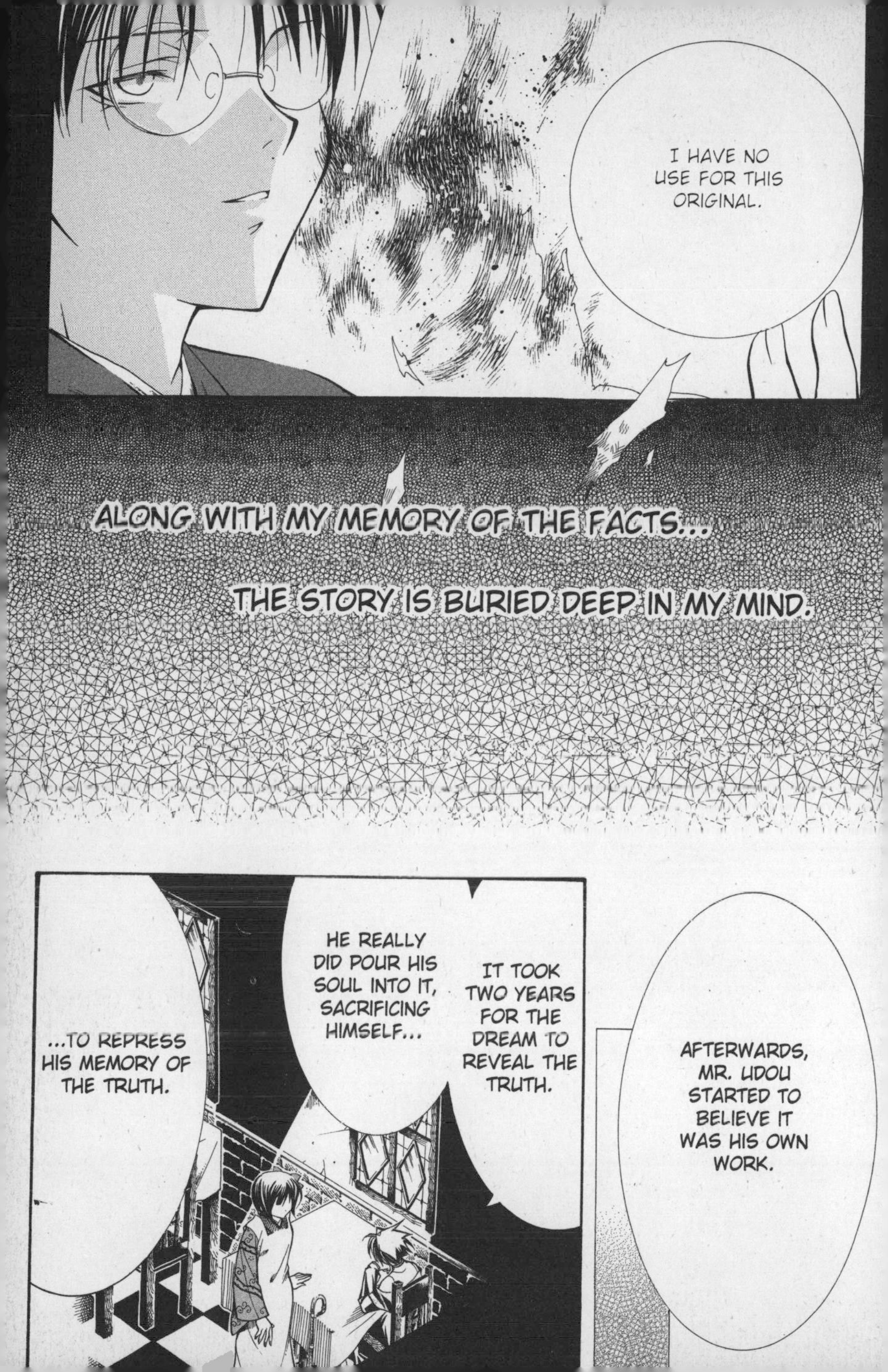
I HAVE NO USE FOR THIS ORIGINAL.
ALONG WITH MY MEMORY OF THE FACTS...
THE STORY IS BURIED DEEP IN MY MIND.
AFTERWARDS, MR. UDOU STARTED TO BELIEVE IT WAS HIS OWN WORK.
IT TOOK TWO YEARS FOR THE DREAM TO REVEAL THE TRUTH.
HE REALLY DID POUR HIS SOUL INTO IT, SACRIFICING HIMSELF...
...TO REPRESS HIS MEMORY OF THE TRUTH.

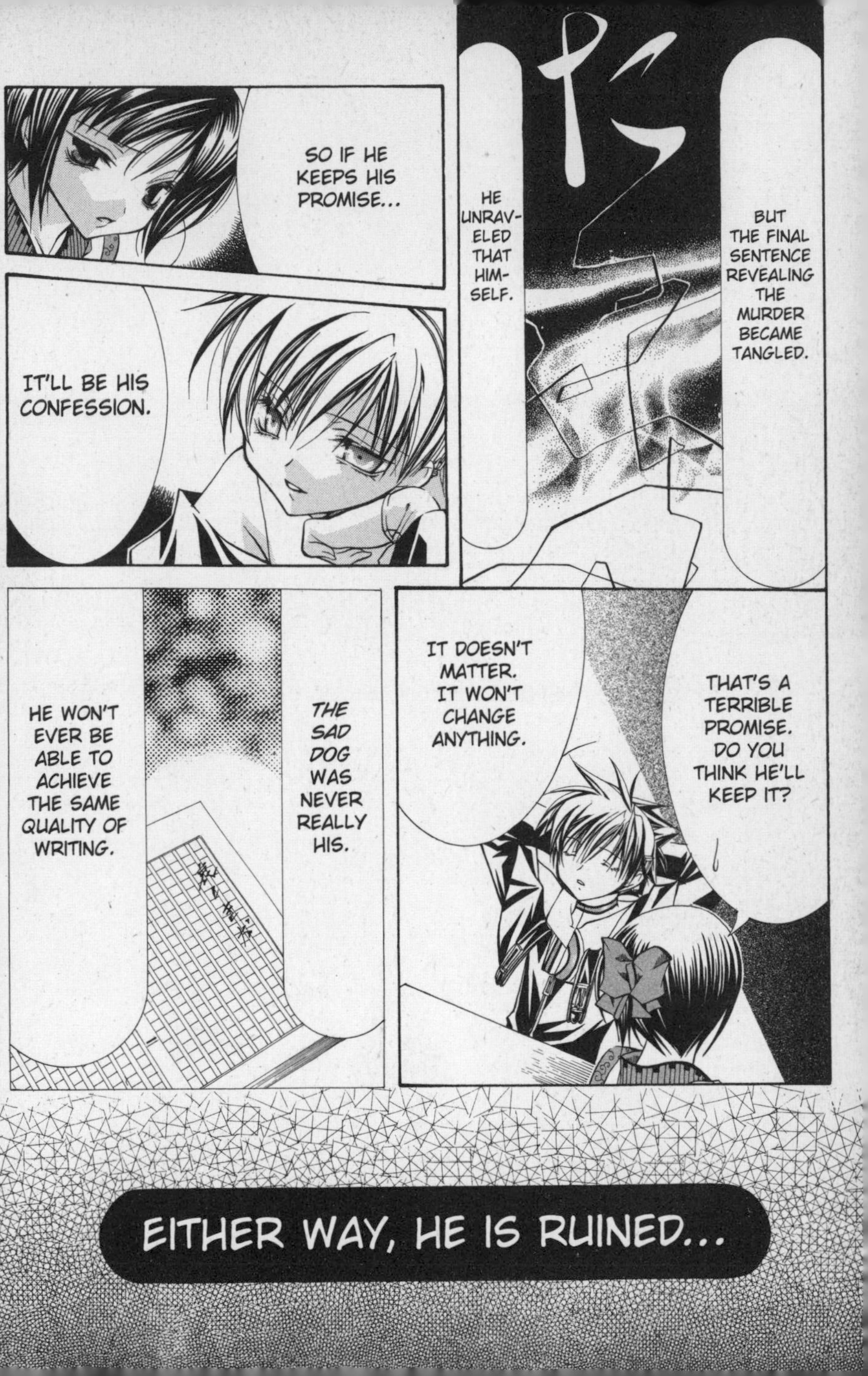
HE UNRAVELED THAT HIMSELF.
BUT THE FINAL SENTENCE REVEALING THE MURDER BECAME TANGLED.
SO IF HE KEEPS HIS PROMISE...
IT'LL BE HIS CONFESSION.
THAT'S A TERRIBLE PROMISE. DO YOU THINK HE'LL KEEP IT?
IT DOESN'T MATTER. IT WON'T CHANGE ANYTHING.
*THE SAD DOG* WAS NEVER REALLY HIS.
HE WON'T EVER BE ABLE TO ACHIEVE THE SAME QUALITY OF WRITING.
EITHER WAY, HE IS RUINED...

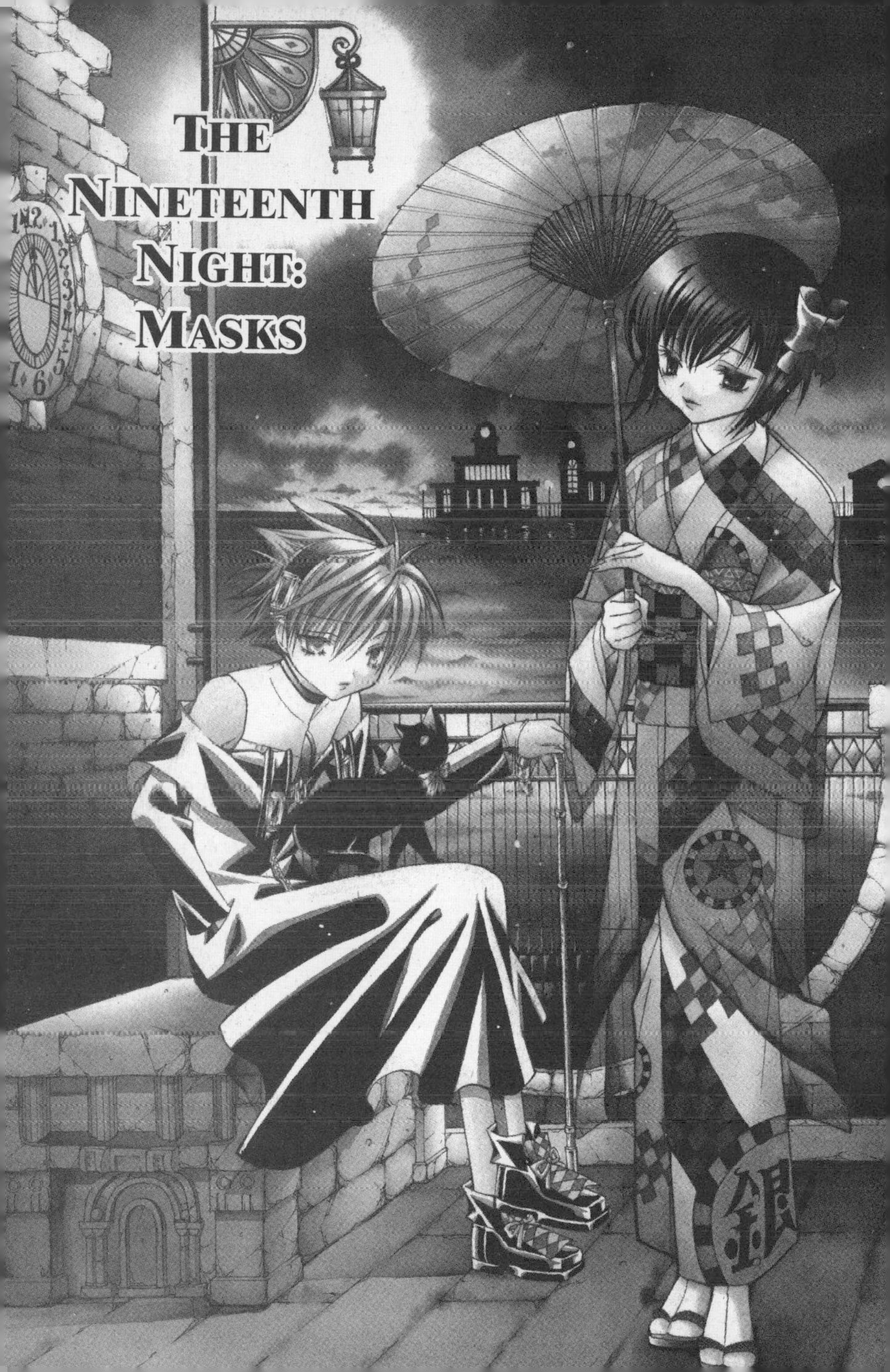
The Nineteenth Night: Masks

Q6:   Hiruko and Mizuki sent a letter to their favorite daily radio show.
      For what segment and what prize did they win?
      And what name did they use as an alias?

Q7:   Mizuki loves ribbons. What amazing thing has she made them out of?

Q8:   Hiruko and Mizuki once had a big fight over what they thought of Formalin (the cane) and didn't speak for two
      months. What does Hiruko think of Formalin?

Q9:   When Hifumi comes back from a Friday night out on the town, he reeks of something strange. What is it?

Q10:  Hiruko loves soda. He wants to collect soda marbles to conquer the world.
      How will he conquer the world with marbles?
      How many marbles would he need?

Looking
forward
to your
answers!

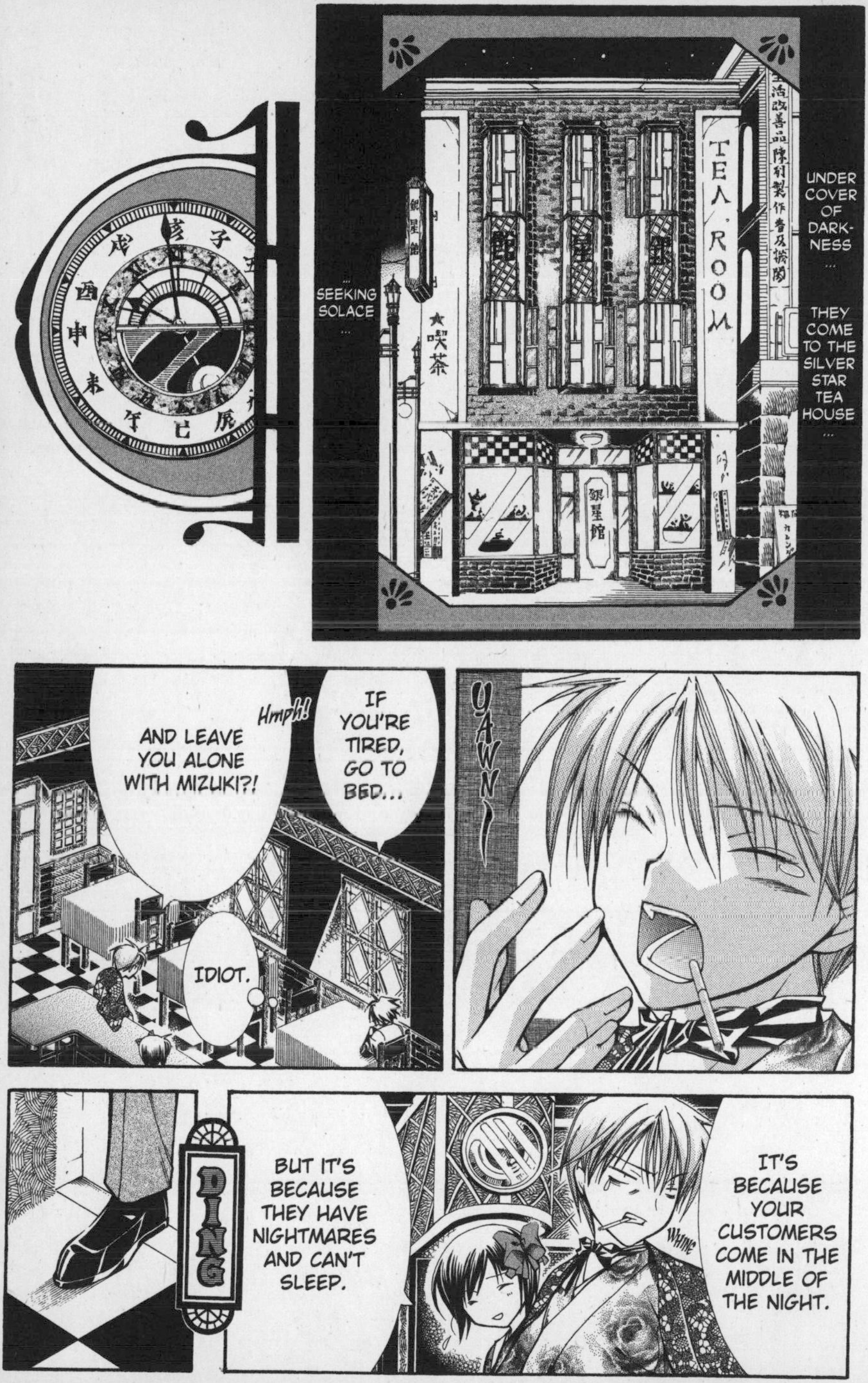
UNDER COVER OF DARKNESS...
THEY COME TO THE SILVER STAR TEA HOUSE...
TEA ROOM
銀星館
喫茶
...SEEKING SOLACE...
YAWN
IF YOU'RE TIRED, GO TO BED...
Hmph!
AND LEAVE YOU ALONE WITH MIZUKI?!
IDIOT.
IT'S BECAUSE YOUR CUSTOMERS COME IN THE MIDDLE OF THE NIGHT.
WHINE
BUT IT'S BECAUSE THEY HAVE NIGHTMARES AND CAN'T SLEEP.
DING

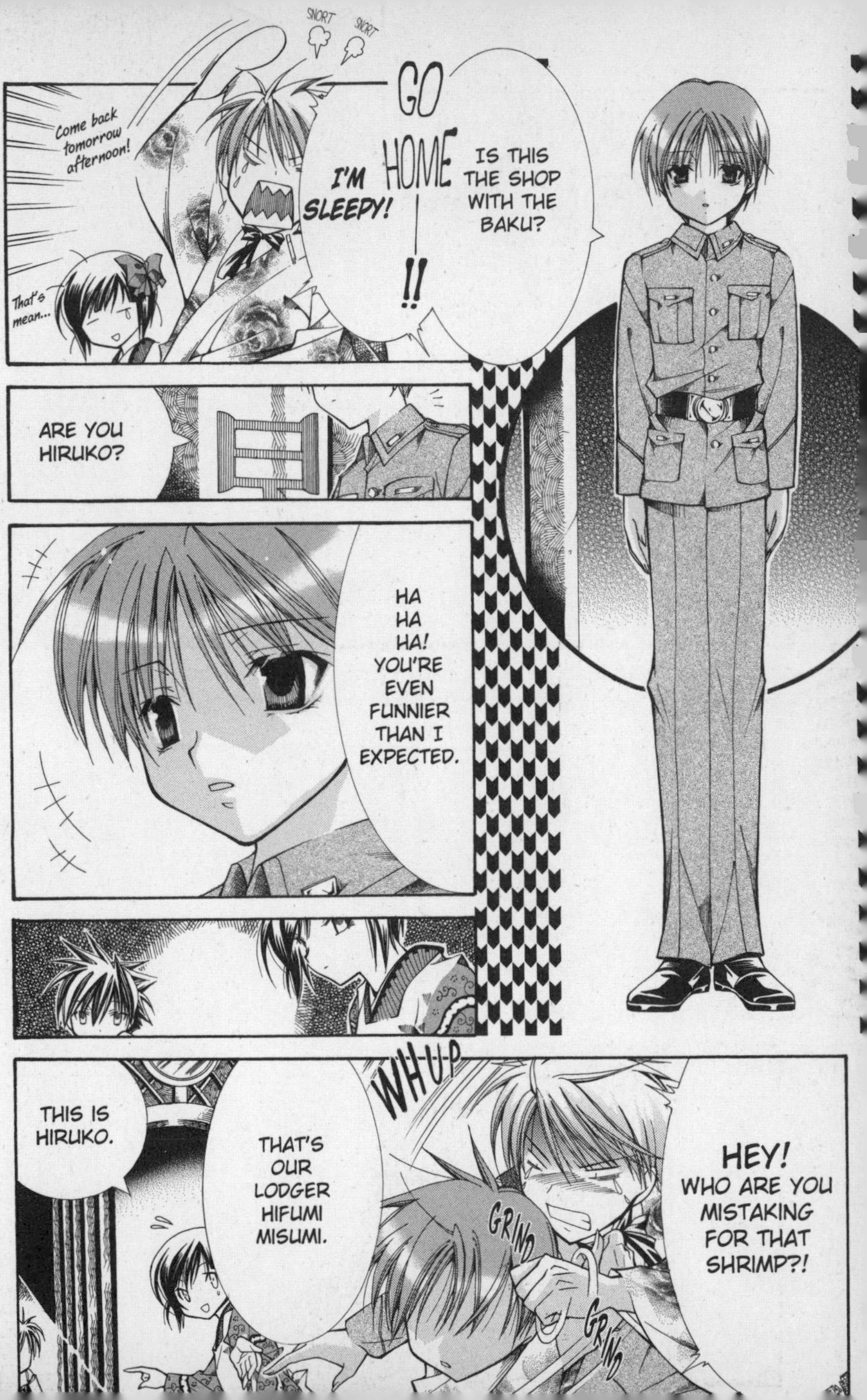

IS THIS THE SHOP WITH THE BAKU?
SNORT
SNORT
GO HOME!!
I'M SLEEPY!
Come back tomorrow afternoon!
That's mean...
ARE YOU HIRUKO?
HA HA HA! YOU'RE EVEN FUNNIER THAN I EXPECTED.
WHUP
HEY! WHO ARE YOU MISTAKING FOR THAT SHRIMP?!
GRIND
GRIND
THAT'S OUR LODGER HIFUMI MISUMI.
THIS IS HIRUKO.

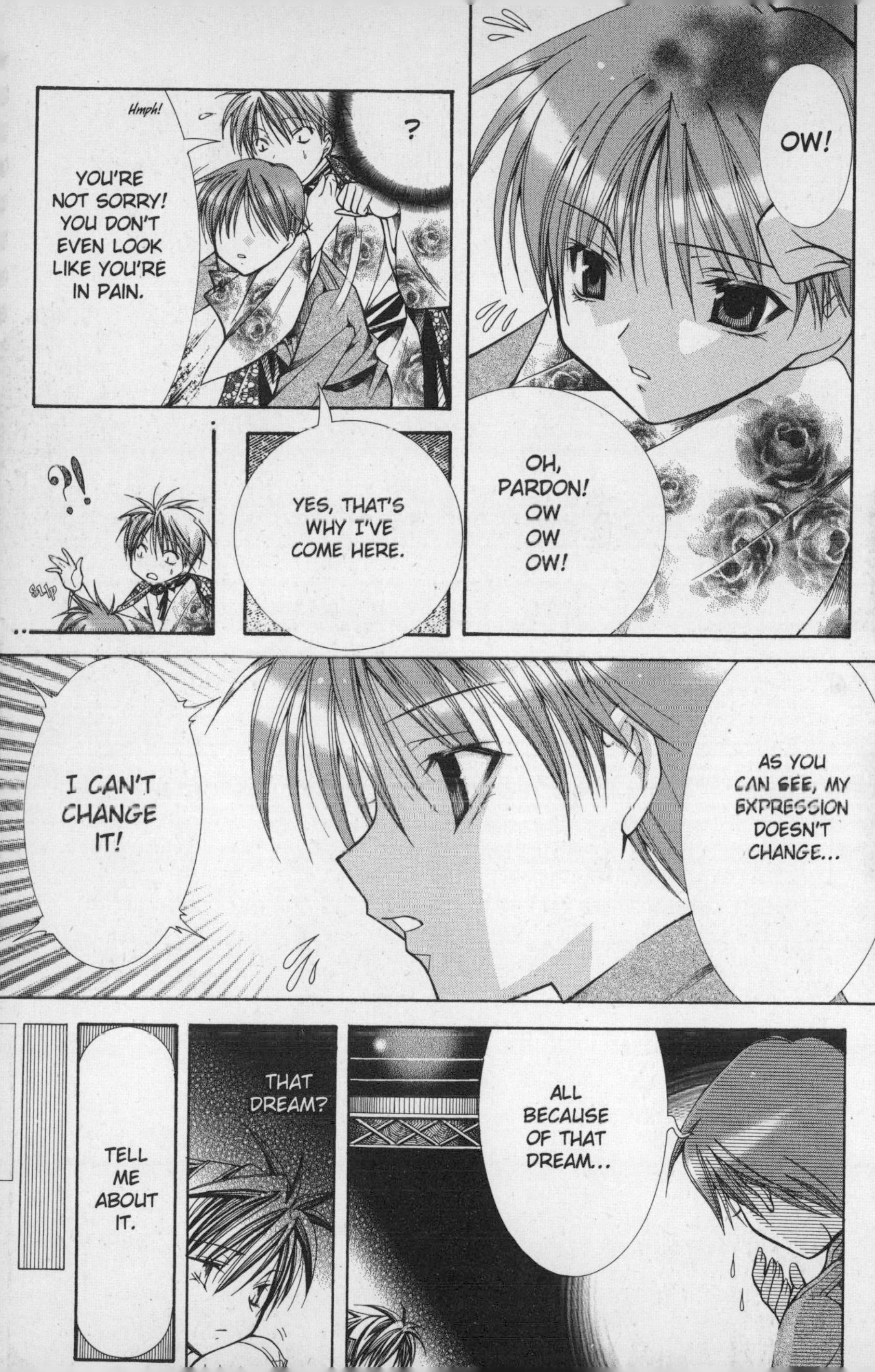
OW!
OH, PARDON! OW OW OW!
?
Hmph!
YOU'RE NOT SORRY! YOU DON'T EVEN LOOK LIKE YOU'RE IN PAIN.
YES, THAT'S WHY I'VE COME HERE.
?!
SLIP
AS YOU CAN SEE, MY EXPRESSION DOESN'T CHANGE...
I CAN'T CHANGE IT!
ALL BECAUSE OF THAT DREAM...
THAT DREAM?
TELL ME ABOUT IT.

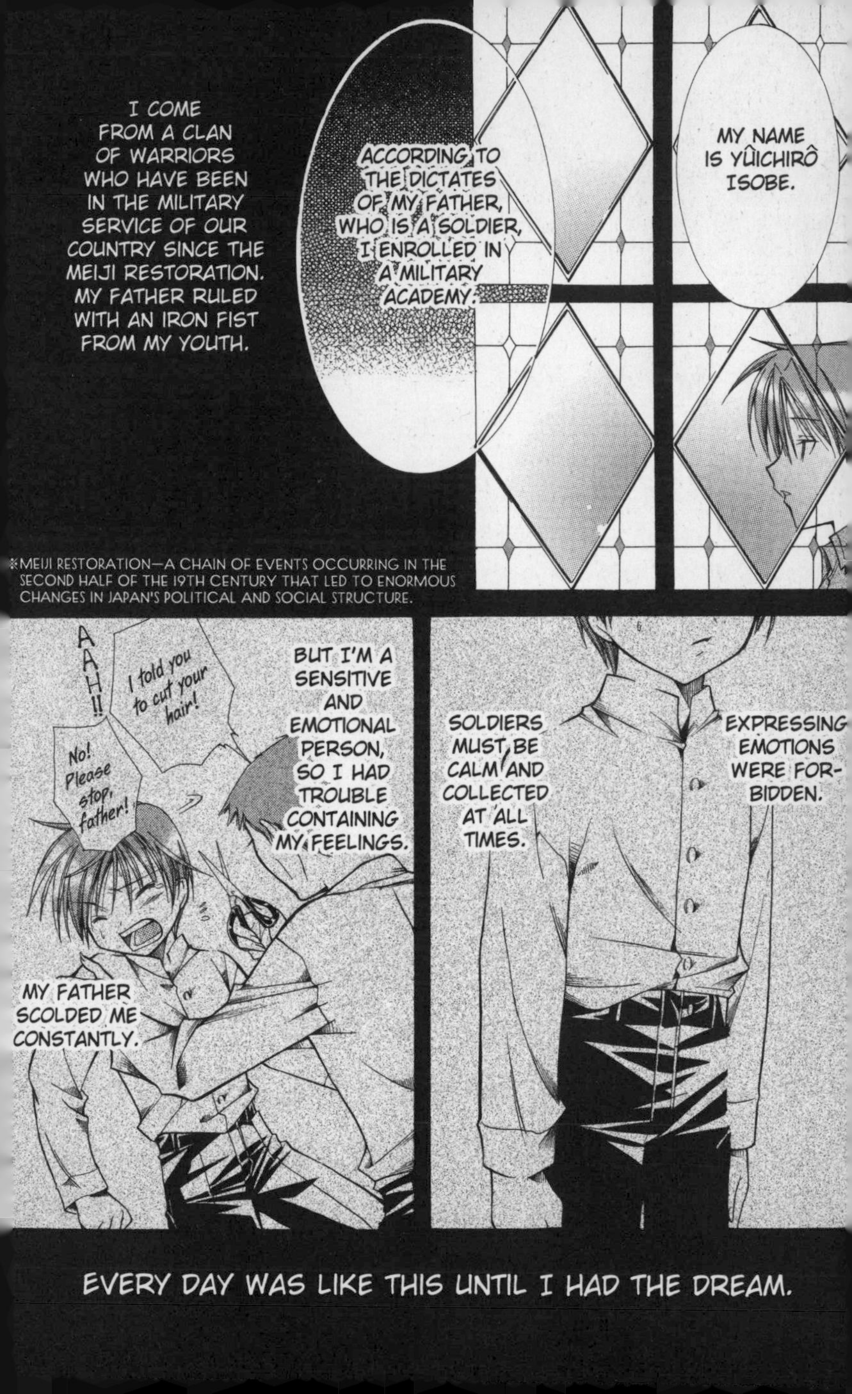
MY NAME IS YÛICHIRÔ ISOBE.
ACCORDING TO THE DICTATES OF MY FATHER, WHO IS A SOLDIER, I ENROLLED IN A MILITARY ACADEMY.
I COME FROM A CLAN OF WARRIORS WHO HAVE BEEN IN THE MILITARY SERVICE OF OUR COUNTRY SINCE THE MEIJI RESTORATION. MY FATHER RULED WITH AN IRON FIST FROM MY YOUTH.
※MEIJI RESTORATION—A CHAIN OF EVENTS OCCURRING IN THE SECOND HALF OF THE 19TH CENTURY THAT LED TO ENORMOUS CHANGES IN JAPAN'S POLITICAL AND SOCIAL STRUCTURE.
EXPRESSING EMOTIONS WERE FOR-BIDDEN.
SOLDIERS MUST BE CALM AND COLLECTED AT ALL TIMES.
BUT I'M A SENSITIVE AND EMOTIONAL PERSON, SO I HAD TROUBLE CONTAINING MY FEELINGS.
I told you to cut your hair!
AAH!!
No! Please stop, father!
MY FATHER SCOLDED ME CONSTANTLY.
EVERY DAY WAS LIKE THIS UNTIL I HAD THE DREAM.

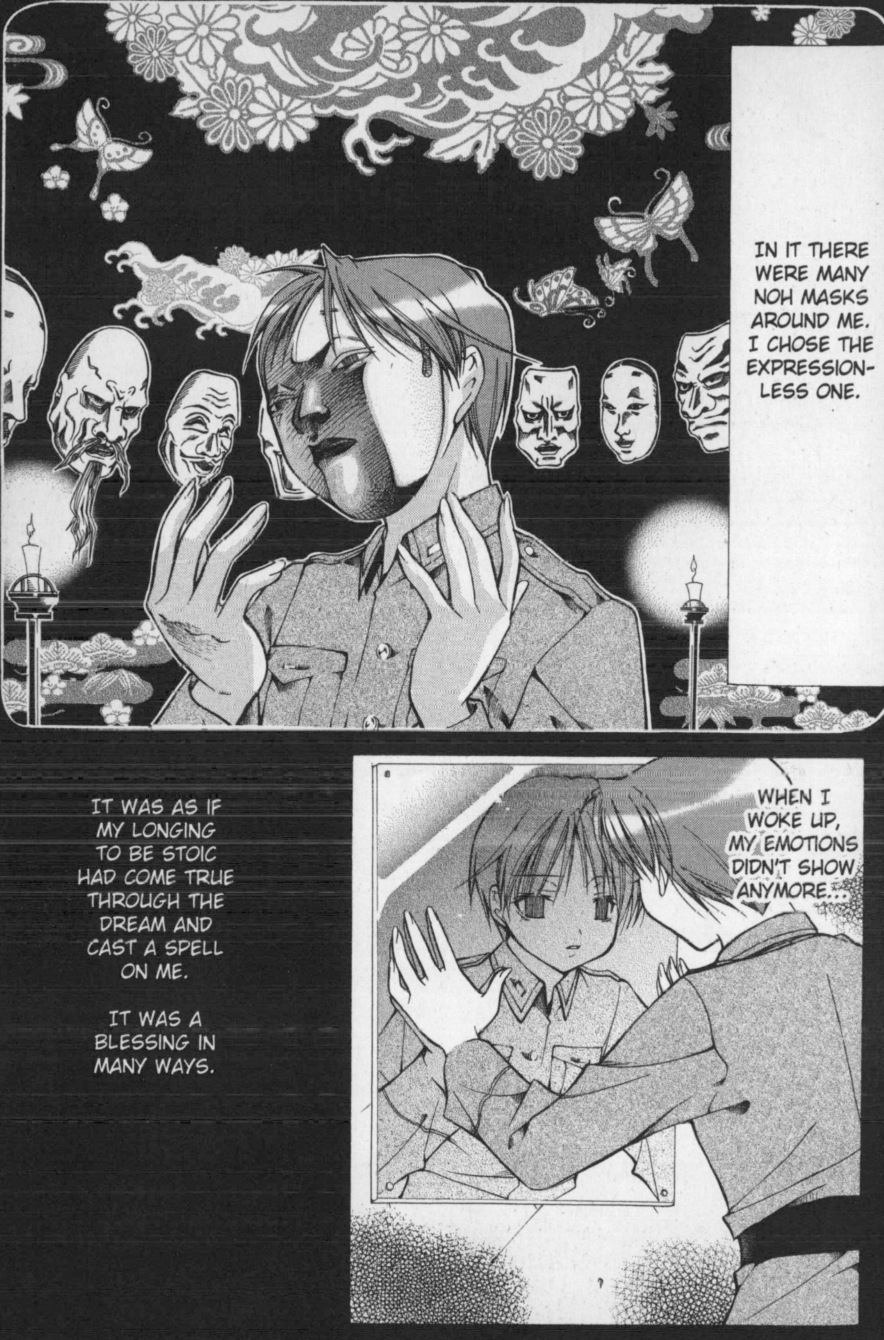
IN IT THERE WERE MANY NOH MASKS AROUND ME. I CHOSE THE EXPRESSIONLESS ONE.
WHEN I WOKE UP, MY EMOTIONS DIDN'T SHOW ANYMORE...
IT WAS AS IF MY LONGING TO BE STOIC HAD COME TRUE THROUGH THE DREAM AND CAST A SPELL ON ME.
IT WAS A BLESSING IN MANY WAYS.

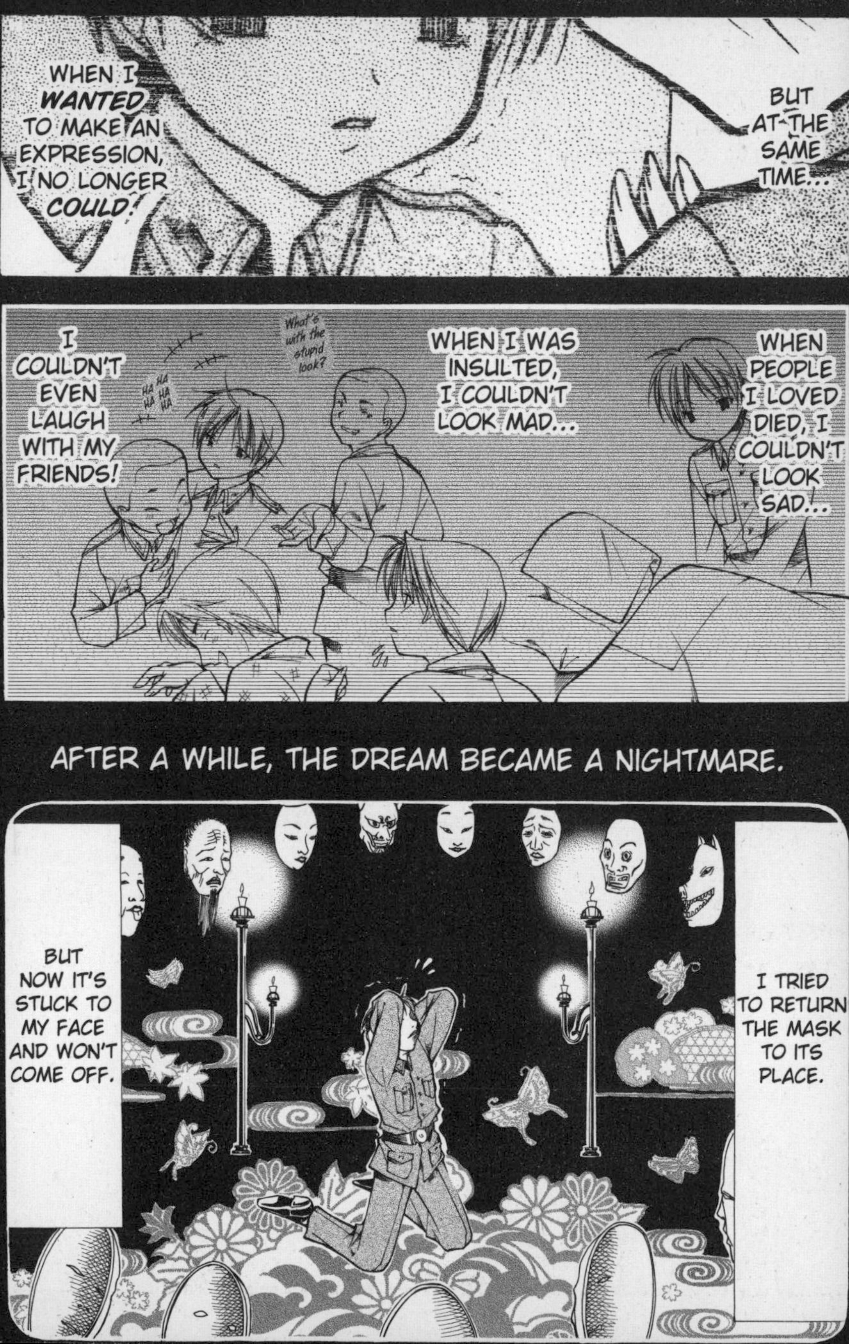
BUT AT THE SAME TIME...
WHEN I *WANTED* TO MAKE AN EXPRESSION, I NO LONGER *COULD*!
WHEN PEOPLE I LOVED DIED, I COULDN'T LOOK SAD...
WHEN I WAS INSULTED, I COULDN'T LOOK MAD...
What's with the stupid look?
HA HA HA HA HA
I COULDN'T EVEN LAUGH WITH MY FRIENDS!
AFTER A WHILE, THE DREAM BECAME A NIGHTMARE.
I TRIED TO RETURN THE MASK TO ITS PLACE.
BUT NOW IT'S STUCK TO MY FACE AND WON'T COME OFF.

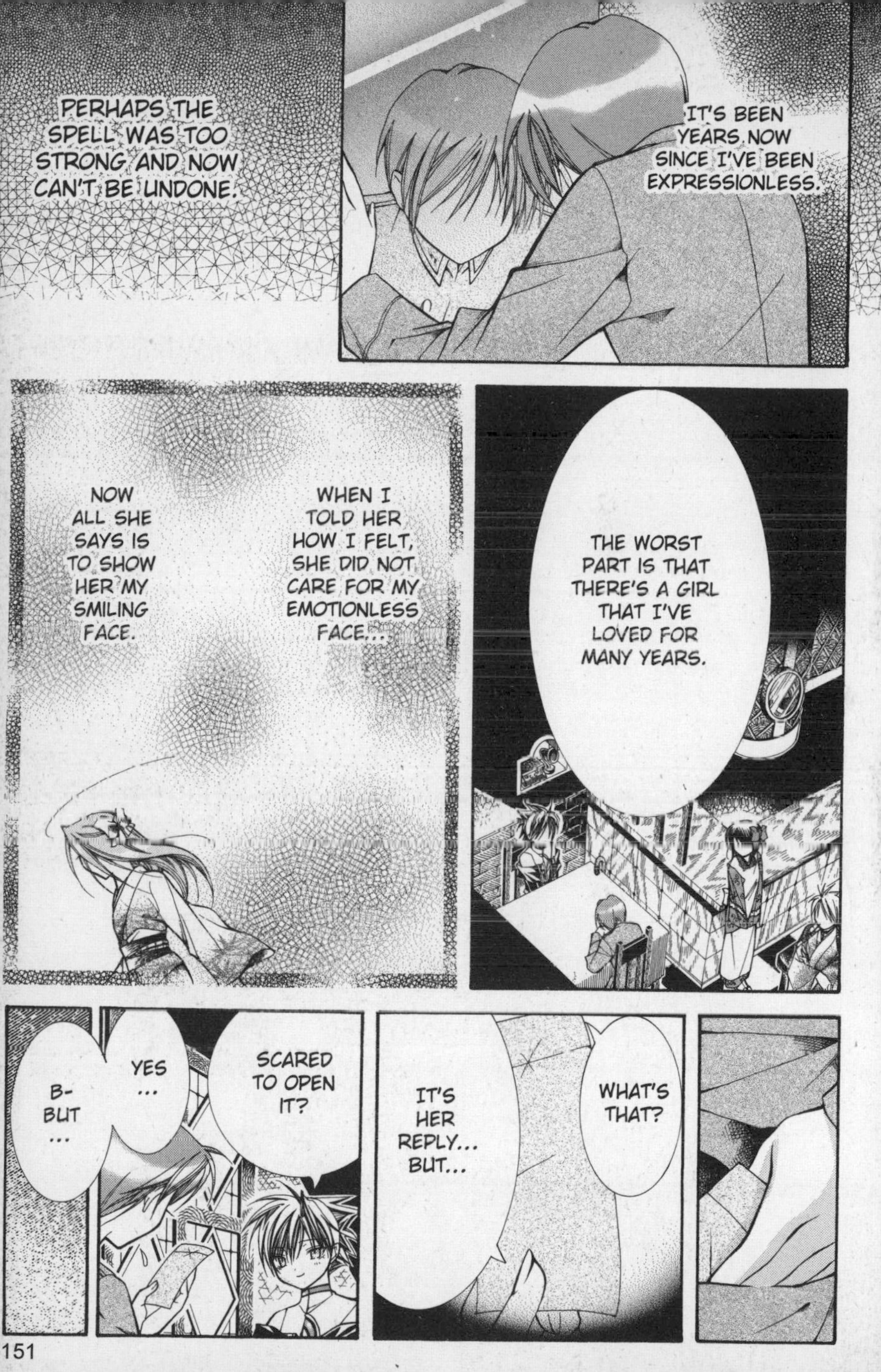
IT'S BEEN YEARS NOW SINCE I'VE BEEN EXPRESSIONLESS.
PERHAPS THE SPELL WAS TOO STRONG AND NOW CAN'T BE UNDONE.
THE WORST PART IS THAT THERE'S A GIRL THAT I'VE LOVED FOR MANY YEARS.
WHEN I TOLD HER HOW I FELT, SHE DID NOT CARE FOR MY EMOTIONLESS FACE...
NOW ALL SHE SAYS IS TO SHOW HER MY SMILING FACE.
WHAT'S THAT?
IT'S HER REPLY... BUT...
SCARED TO OPEN IT?
YES ...
B- BUT ...

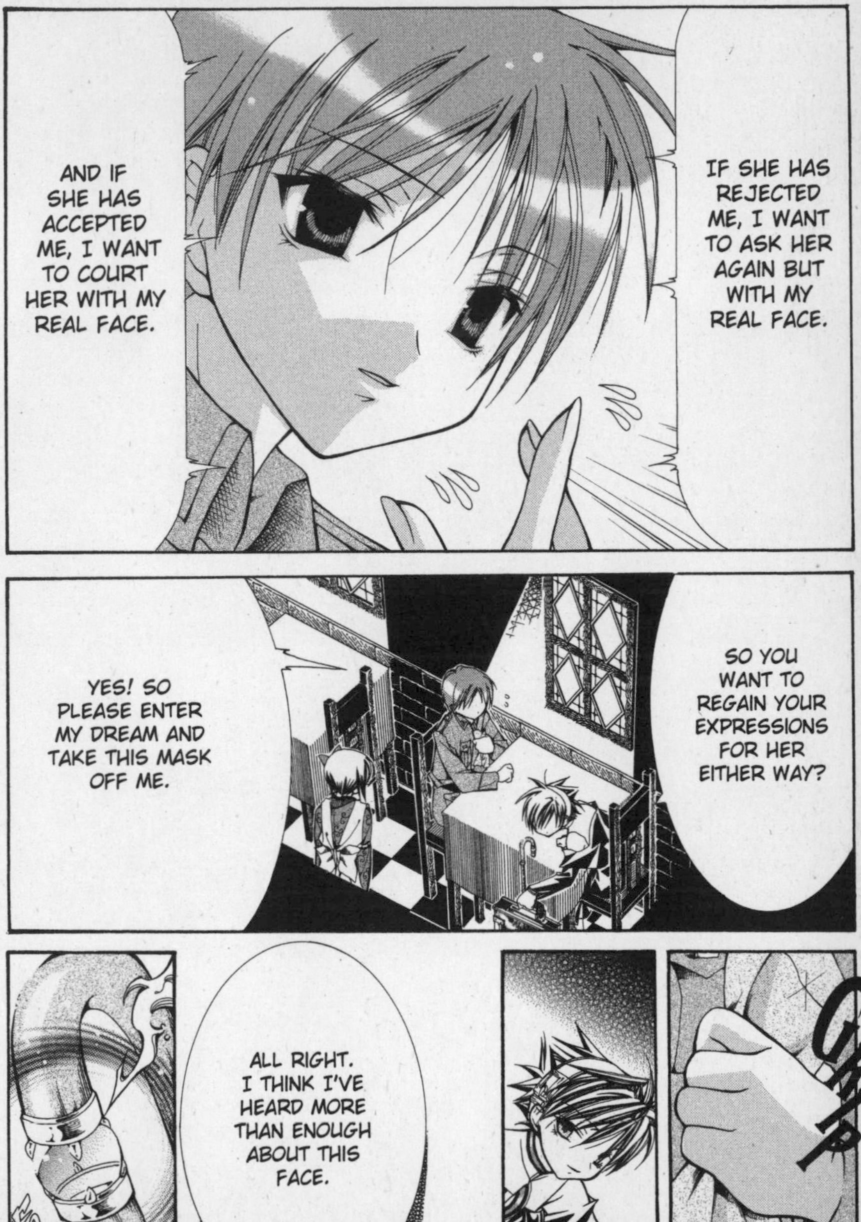
IF SHE HAS REJECTED ME, I WANT TO ASK HER AGAIN BUT WITH MY REAL FACE.
AND IF SHE HAS ACCEPTED ME, I WANT TO COURT HER WITH MY REAL FACE.
SO YOU WANT TO REGAIN YOUR EXPRESSIONS FOR HER EITHER WAY?
YES! SO PLEASE ENTER MY DREAM AND TAKE THIS MASK OFF ME.
GRIP
ALL RIGHT. I THINK I'VE HEARD MORE THAN ENOUGH ABOUT THIS FACE.
FOOSH

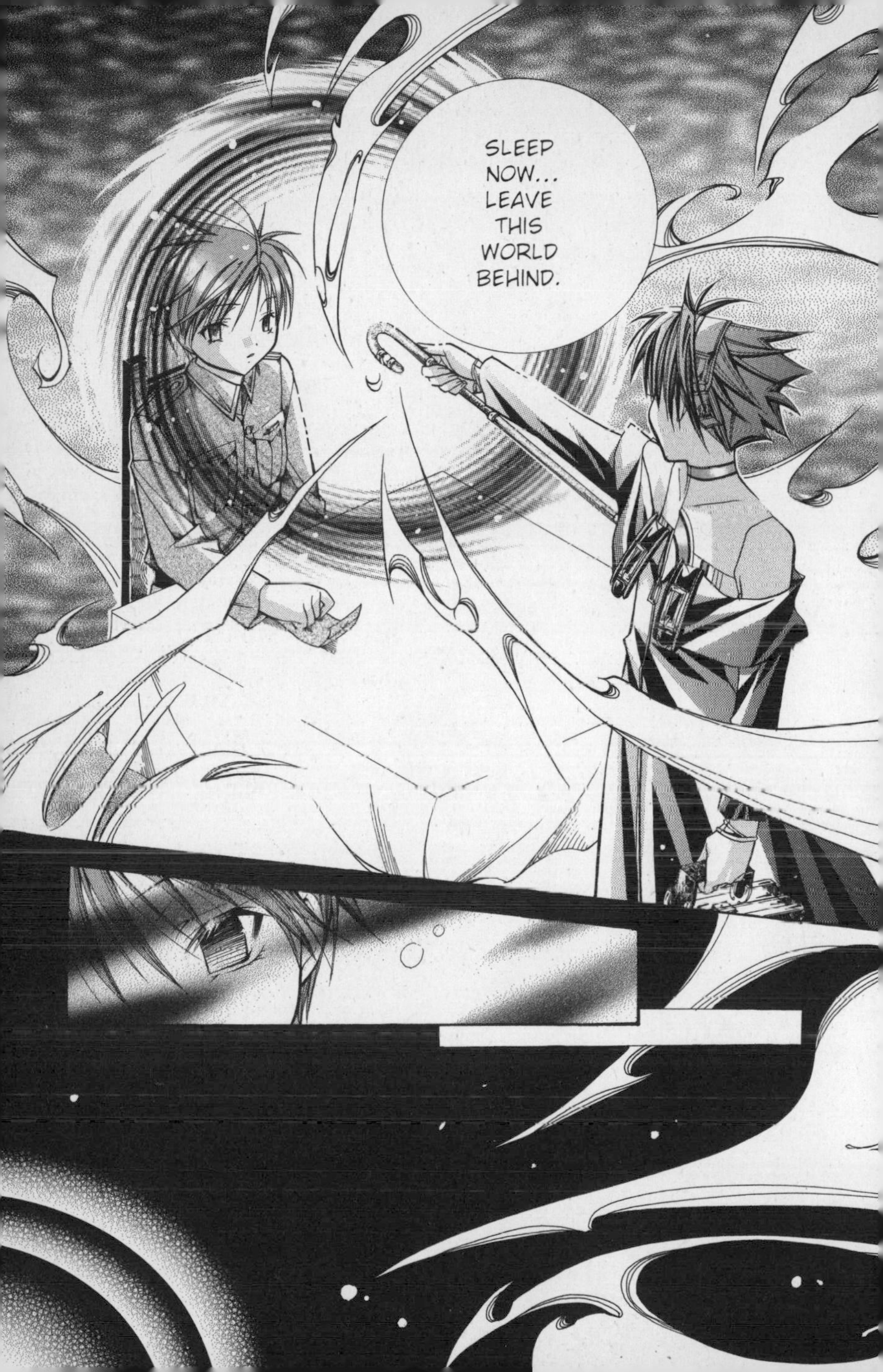
SLEEP NOW... LEAVE THIS WORLD BEHIND.

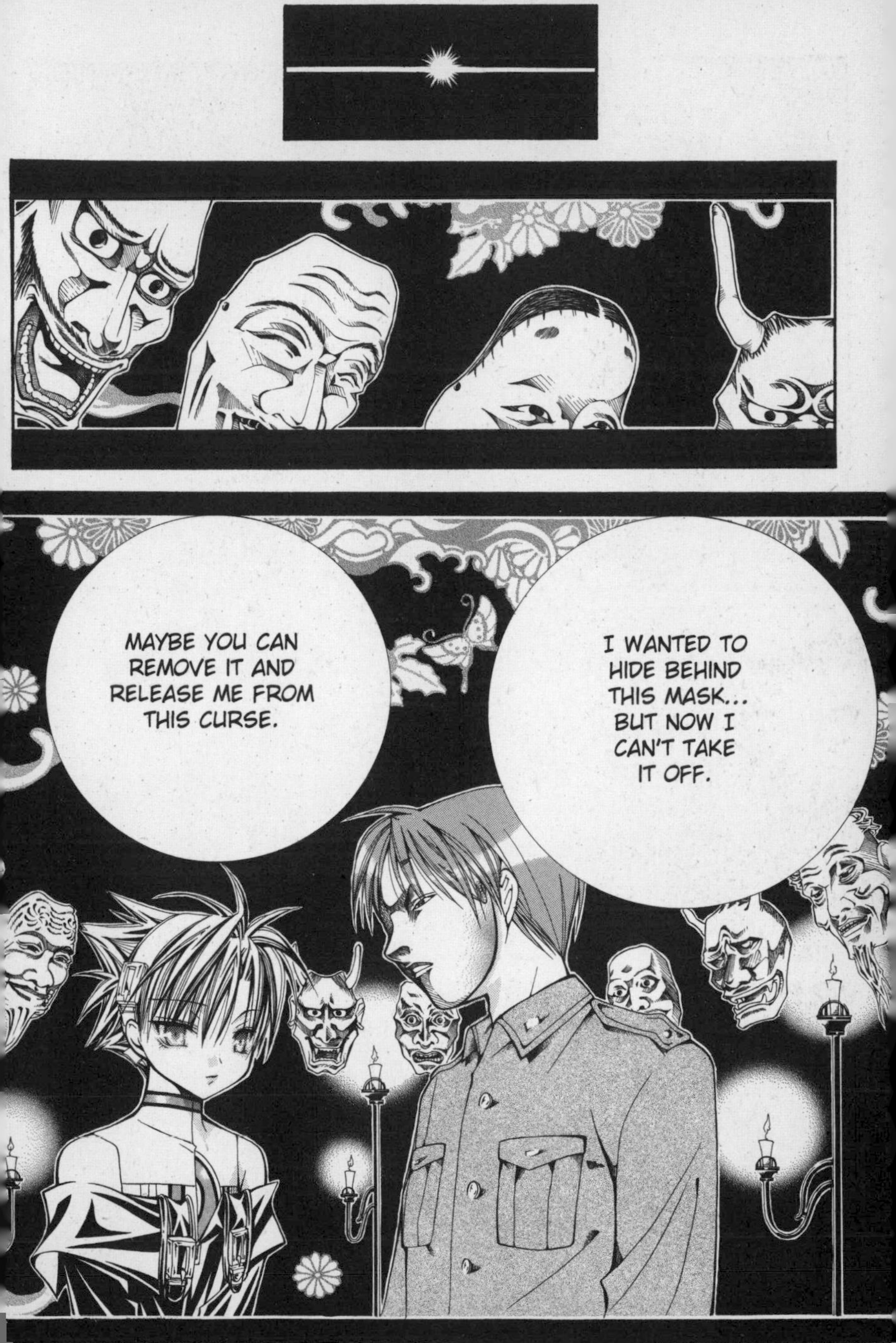
I WANTED TO HIDE BEHIND THIS MASK... BUT NOW I CAN'T TAKE IT OFF.
MAYBE YOU CAN REMOVE IT AND RELEASE ME FROM THIS CURSE.

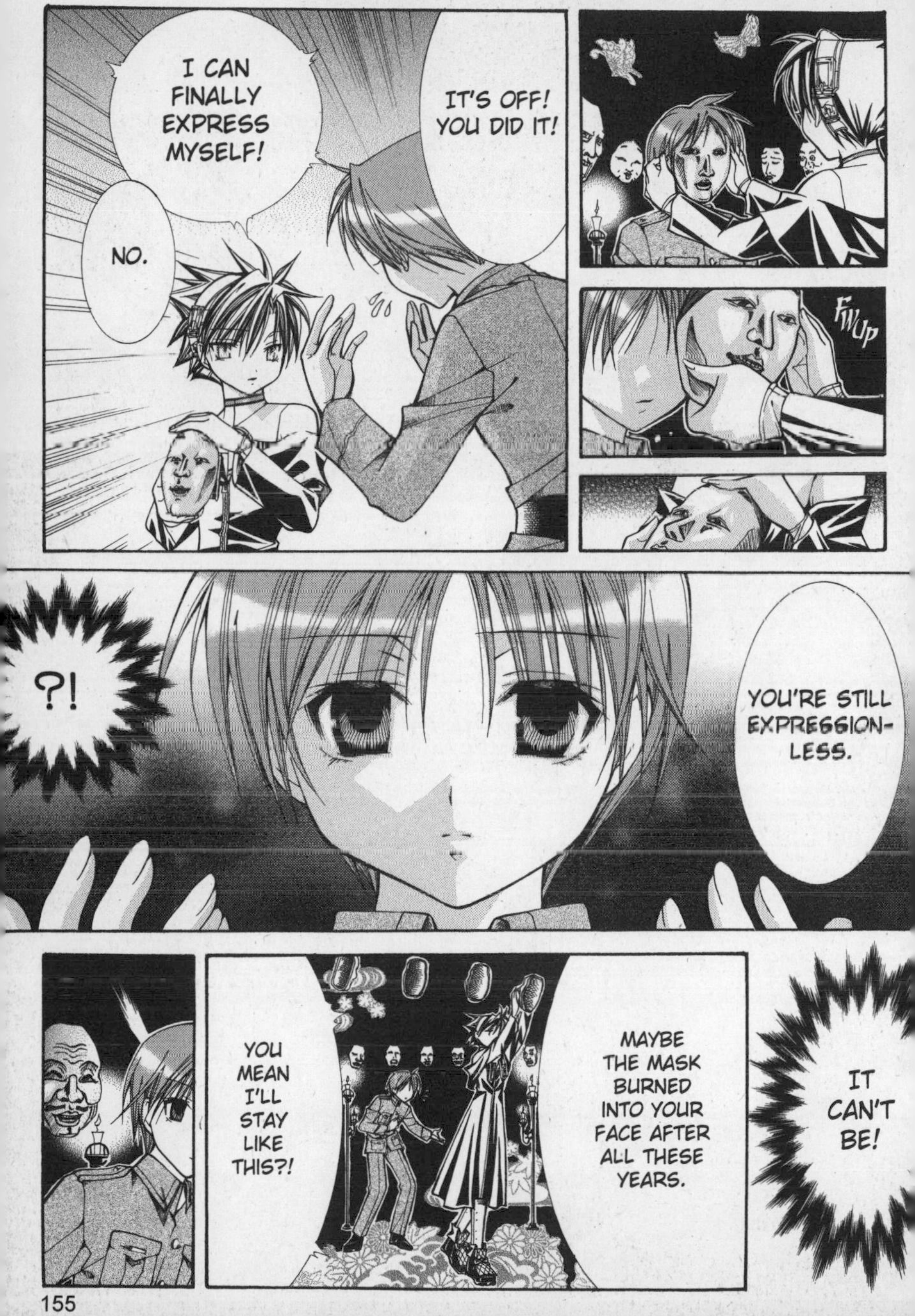
FWUP
IT'S OFF! YOU DID IT!
I CAN FINALLY EXPRESS MYSELF!
NO.
YOU'RE STILL EXPRESSION-LESS.
?!
IT CAN'T BE!
MAYBE THE MASK BURNED INTO YOUR FACE AFTER ALL THESE YEARS.
YOU MEAN I'LL STAY LIKE THIS?!

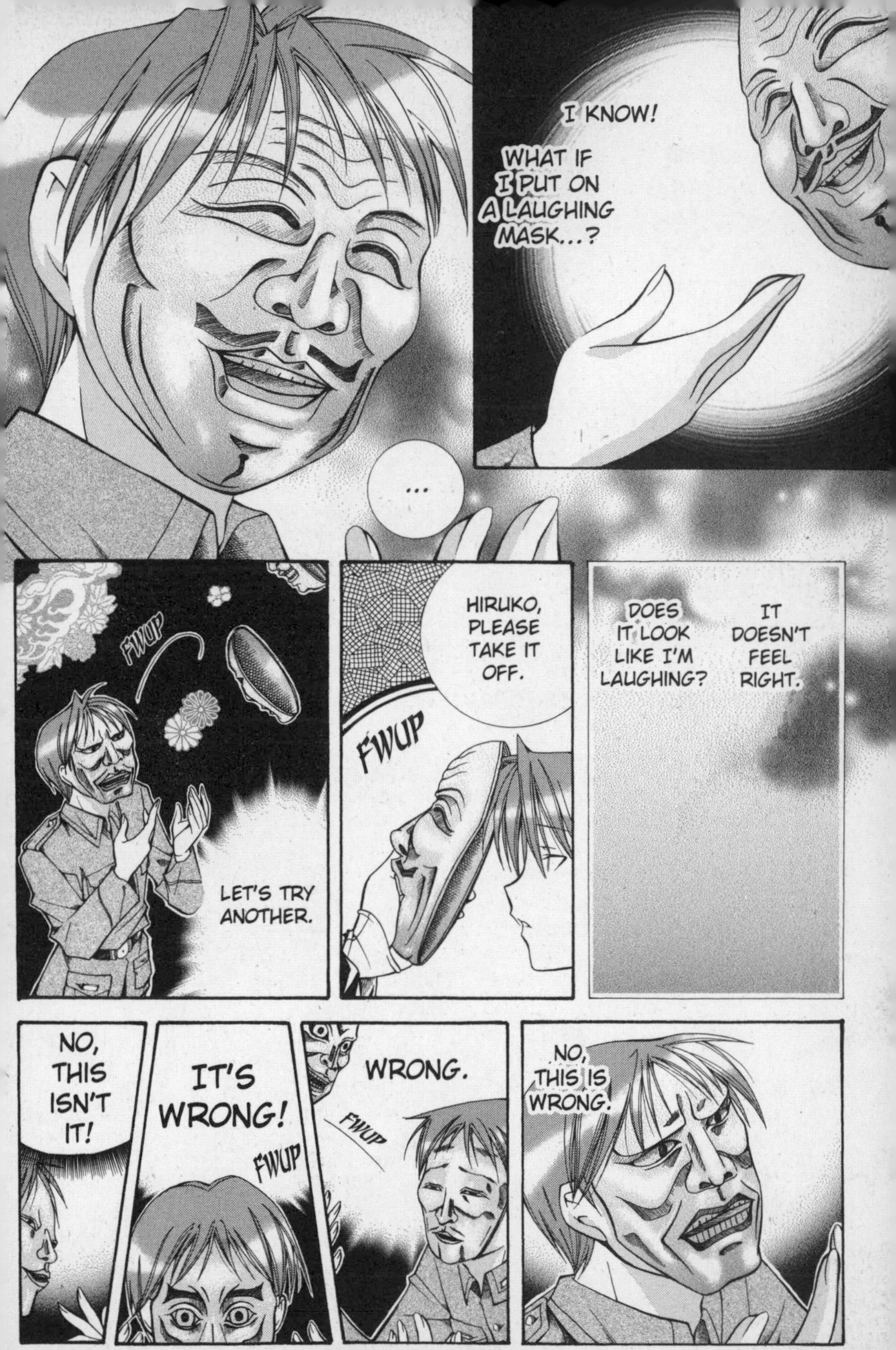
I KNOW!
WHAT IF I PUT ON A LAUGHING MASK...?
...
IT DOESN'T FEEL RIGHT.
DOES IT LOOK LIKE I'M LAUGHING?
HIRUKO, PLEASE TAKE IT OFF.
FWUP
FWUP
LET'S TRY ANOTHER.
NO, THIS IS WRONG.
WRONG.
FWUP
IT'S WRONG!
FWUP
NO, THIS ISN'T IT!

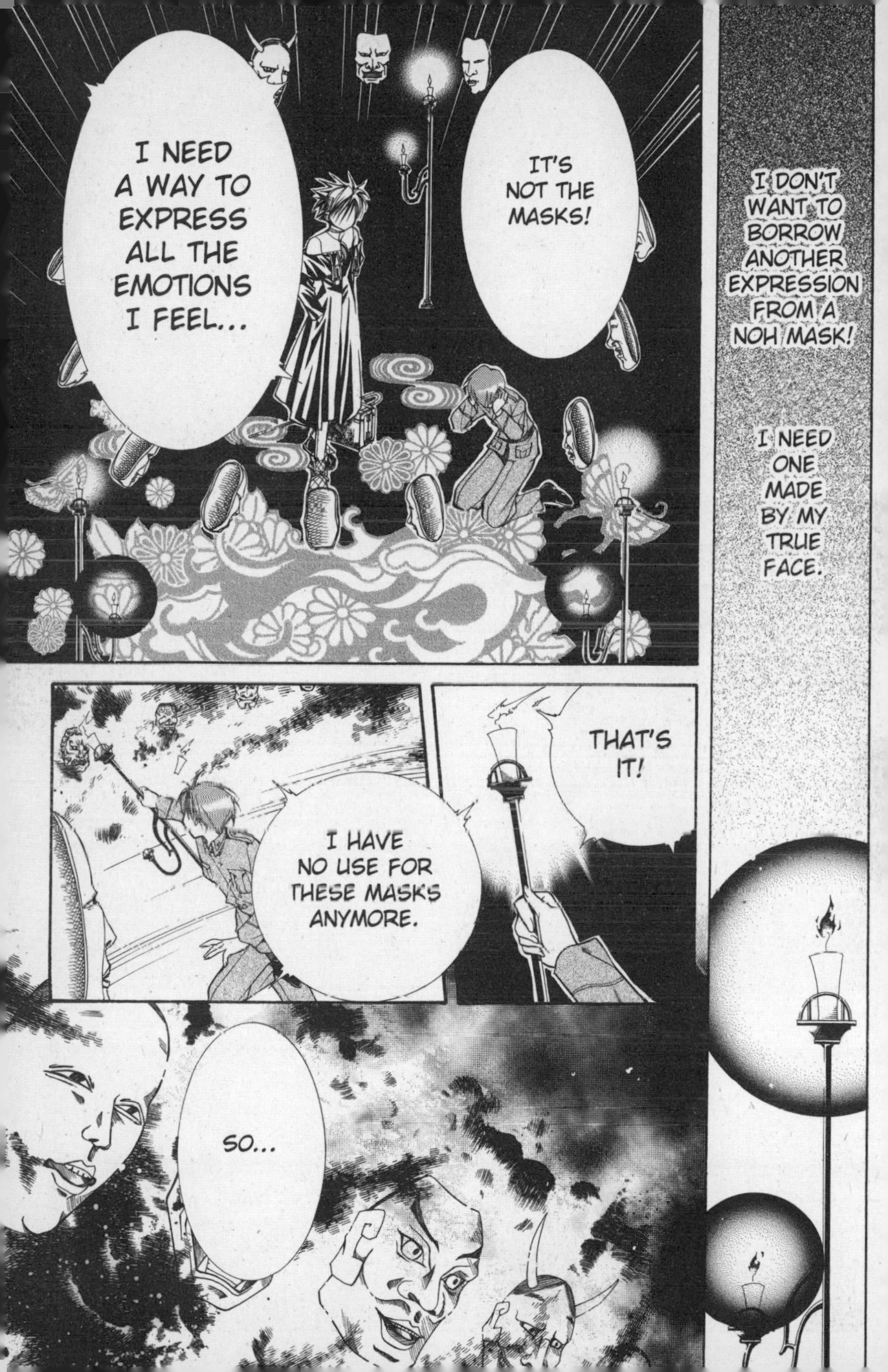
I DON'T WANT TO BORROW ANOTHER EXPRESSION FROM A NOH MASK!
I NEED ONE MADE BY MY TRUE FACE.
IT'S NOT THE MASKS!
I NEED A WAY TO EXPRESS ALL THE EMOTIONS I FEEL...
THAT'S IT!
I HAVE NO USE FOR THESE MASKS ANYMORE.
SO...

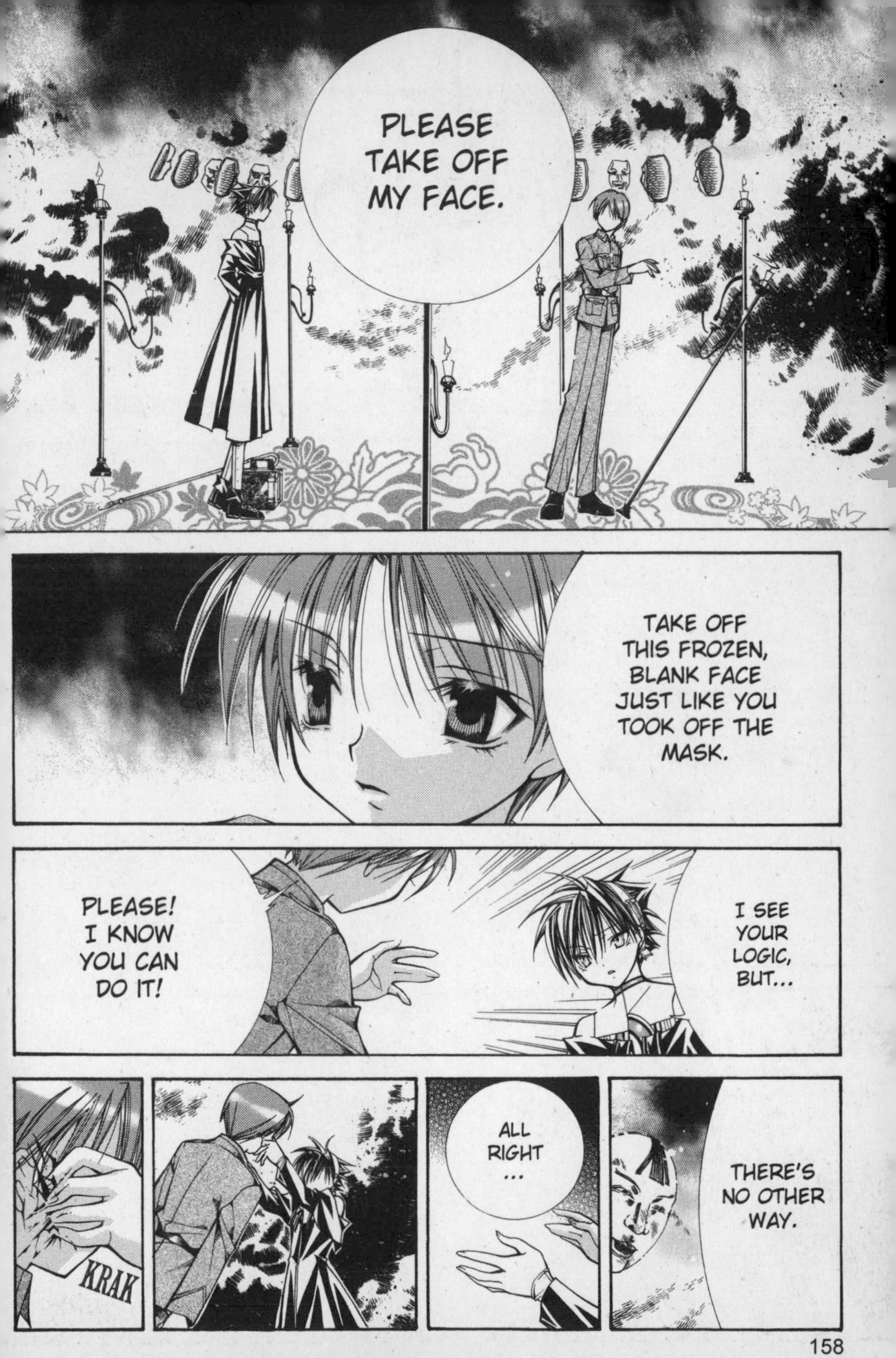
PLEASE TAKE OFF MY FACE.
TAKE OFF THIS FROZEN, BLANK FACE JUST LIKE YOU TOOK OFF THE MASK.
I SEE YOUR LOGIC, BUT...
PLEASE! I KNOW YOU CAN DO IT!
THERE'S NO OTHER WAY.
ALL RIGHT ...
KRAK

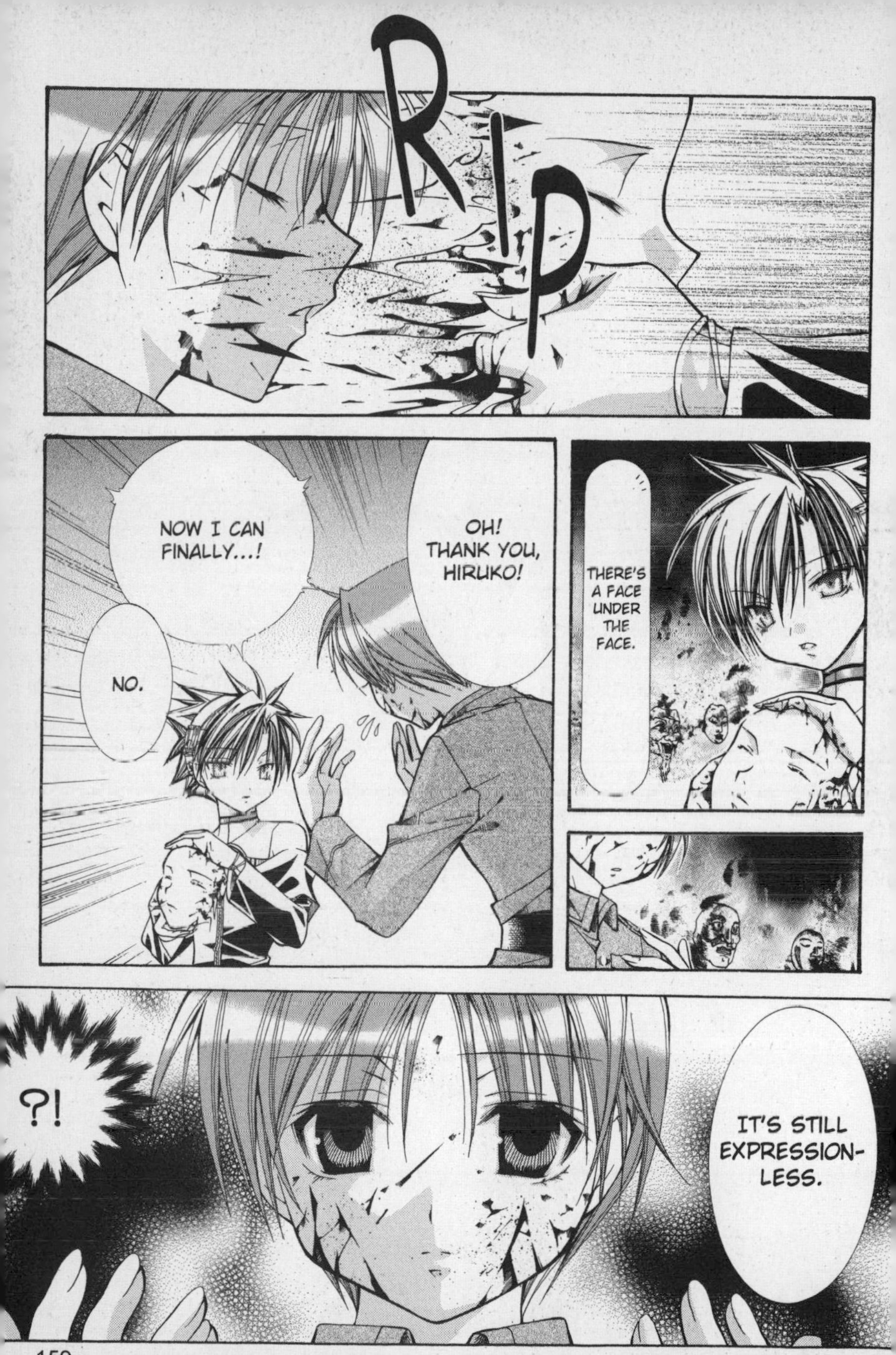
RIP
THERE'S A FACE UNDER THE FACE.
OH! THANK YOU, HIRUKO!
NOW I CAN FINALLY...!
NO.
IT'S STILL EXPRESSION-LESS.
?!

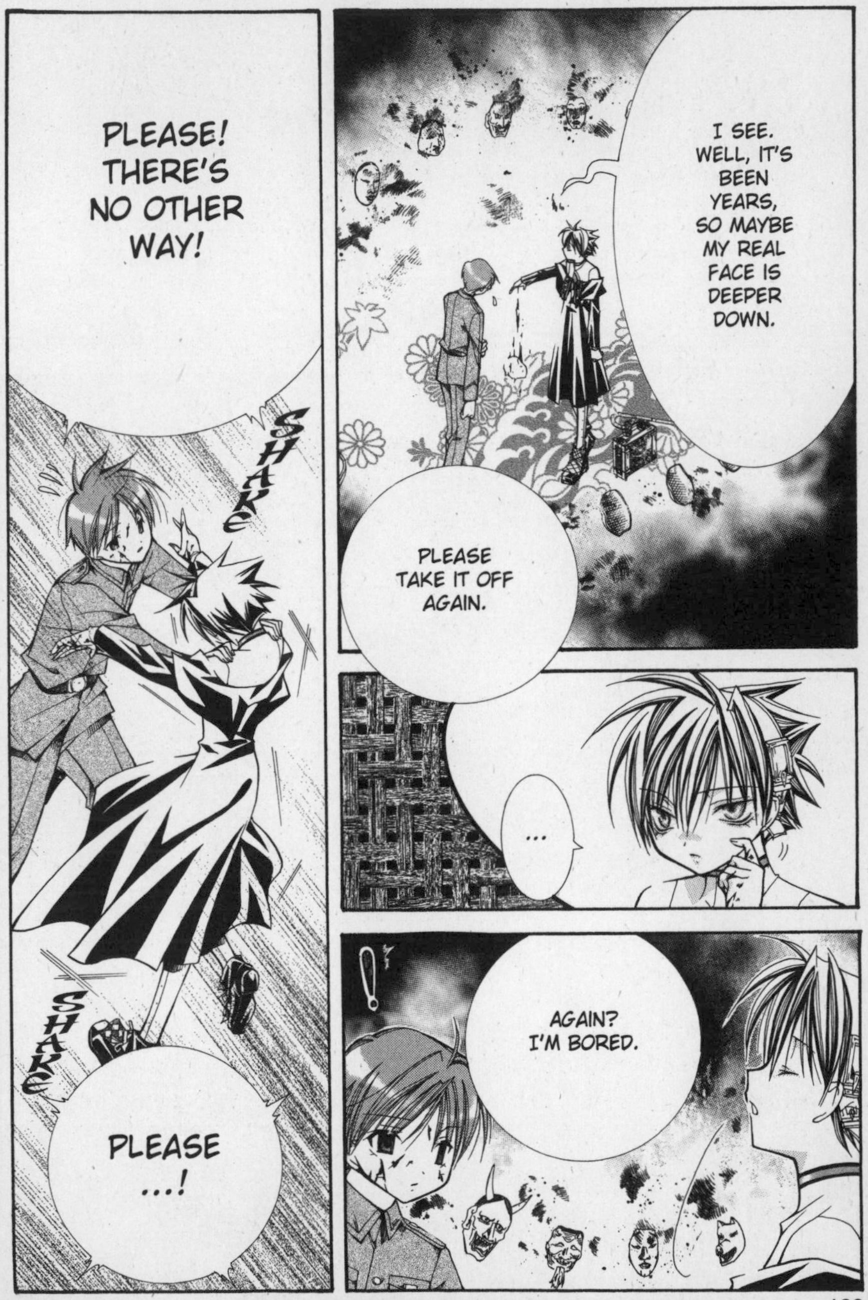
I SEE. WELL, IT'S BEEN YEARS, SO MAYBE MY REAL FACE IS DEEPER DOWN.
PLEASE TAKE IT OFF AGAIN.
...
AGAIN? I'M BORED.
!
PLEASE! THERE'S NO OTHER WAY!
SHAKE
SHAKE
PLEASE ...!

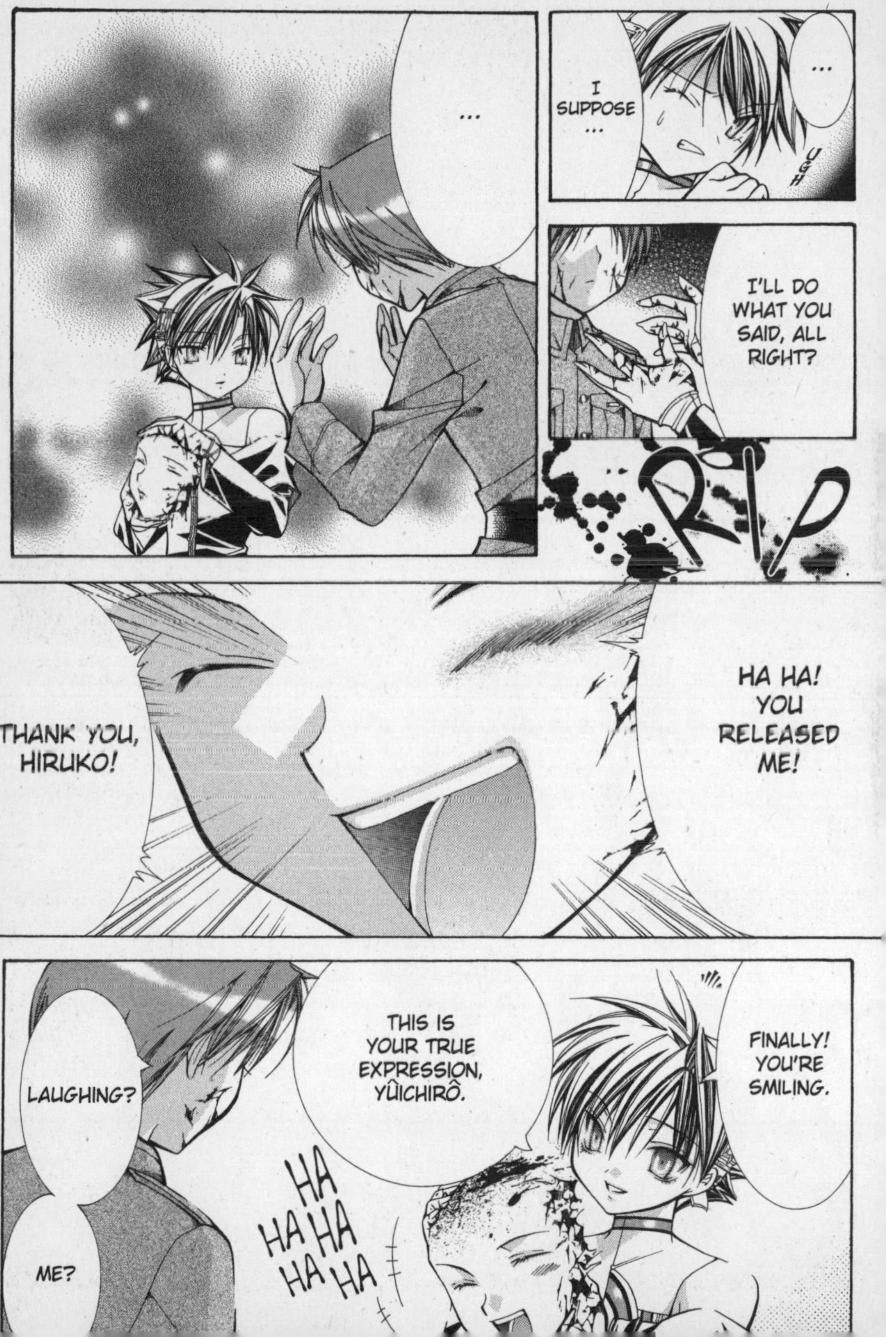
...
I SUPPOSE ...
UGH
I'LL DO WHAT YOU SAID, ALL RIGHT?
RIP
...
HA HA! YOU RELEASED ME!
THANK YOU, HIRUKO!
FINALLY! YOU'RE SMILING.
THIS IS YOUR TRUE EXPRESSION, YÛICHIRÔ.
HA HA HA HA HA HA HA
LAUGHING?
ME?

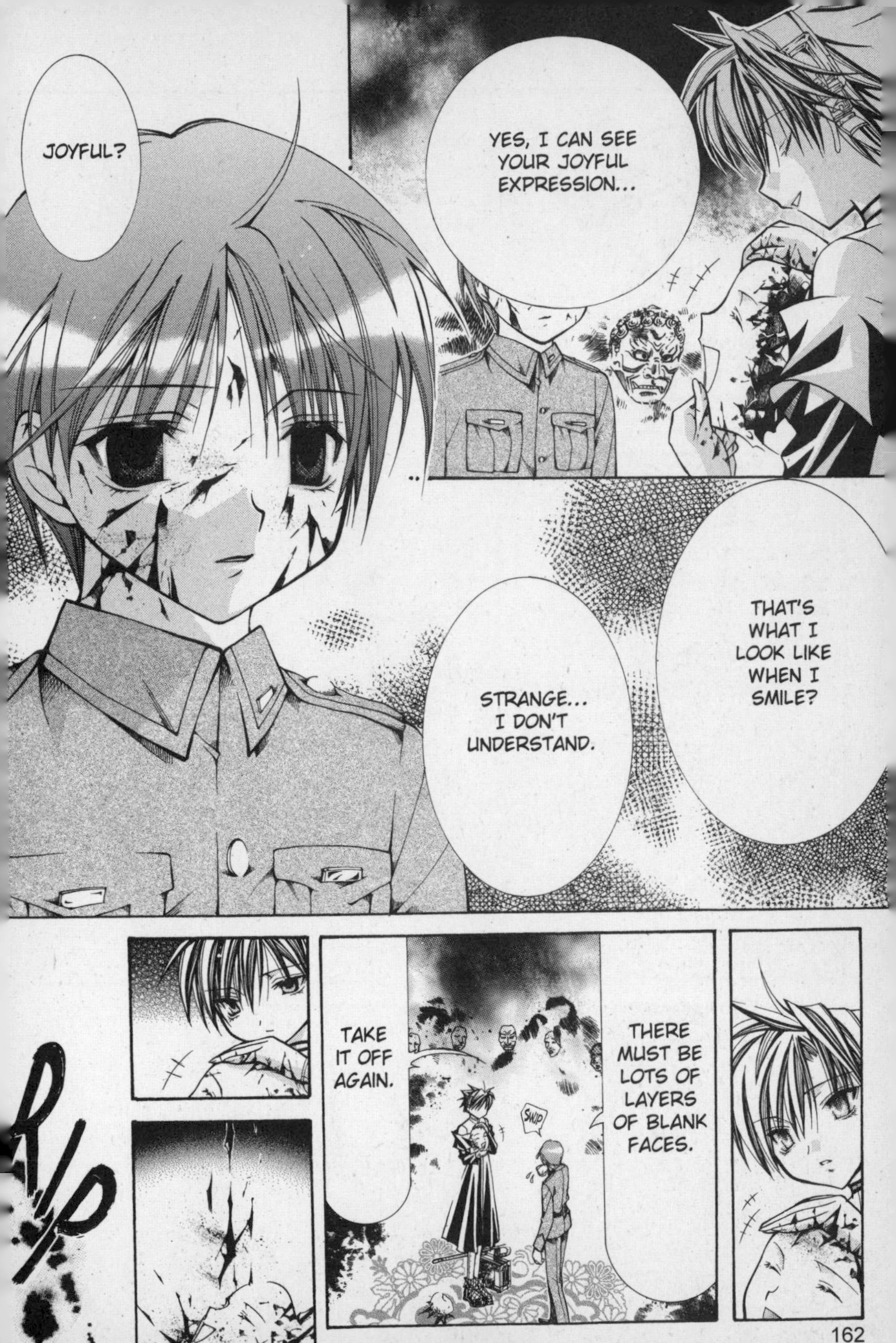
YES, I CAN SEE YOUR JOYFUL EXPRESSION...
JOYFUL?
THAT'S WHAT I LOOK LIKE WHEN I SMILE?
STRANGE... I DON'T UNDERSTAND.
THERE MUST BE LOTS OF LAYERS OF BLANK FACES.
SNIP
TAKE IT OFF AGAIN.
RIP

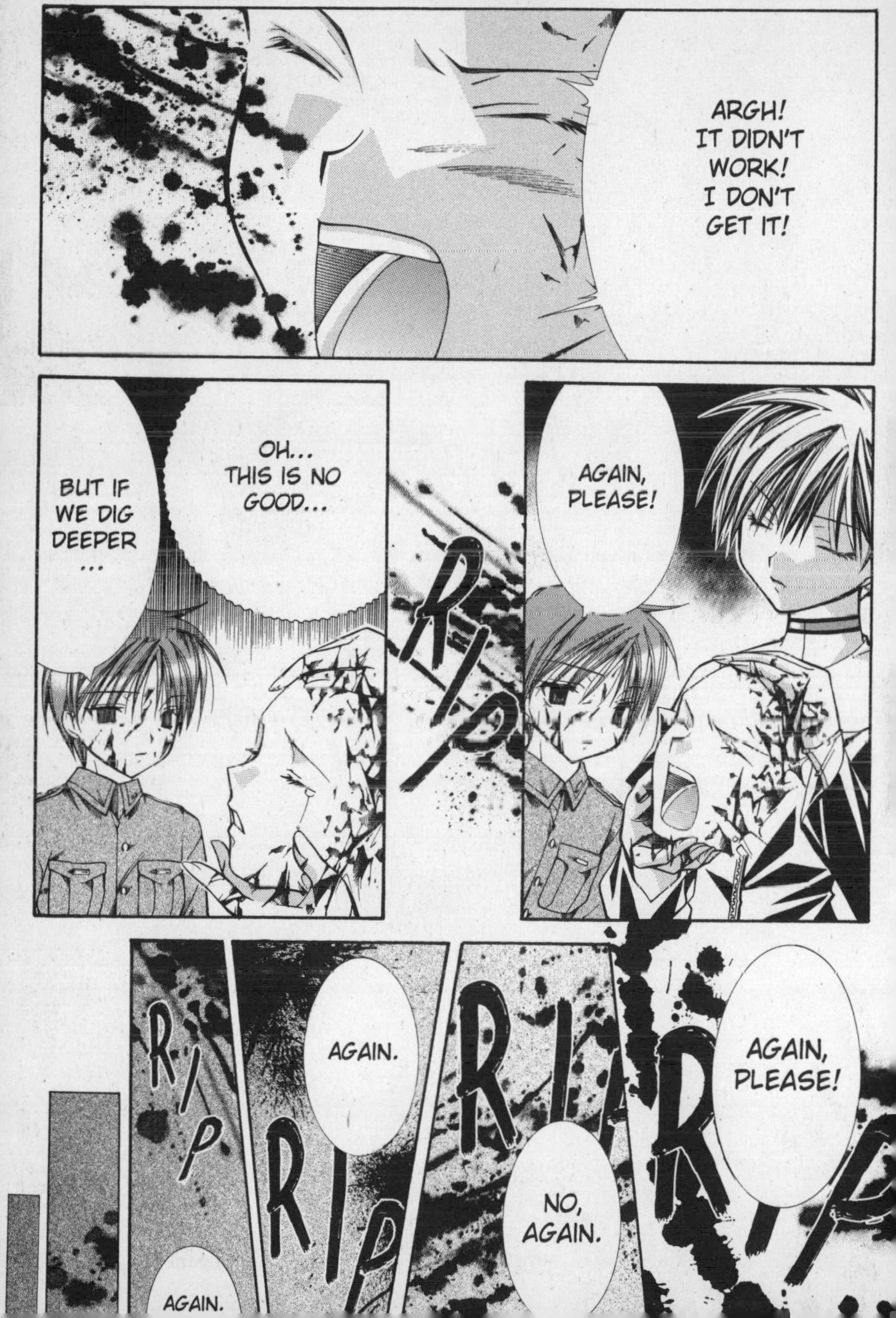
ARGH! IT DIDN'T WORK! I DON'T GET IT!
AGAIN, PLEASE!
RIP
OH... THIS IS NO GOOD...
BUT IF WE DIG DEEPER ...
AGAIN, PLEASE!
RIP
NO, AGAIN.
RIP
AGAIN.
RIP
AGAIN.

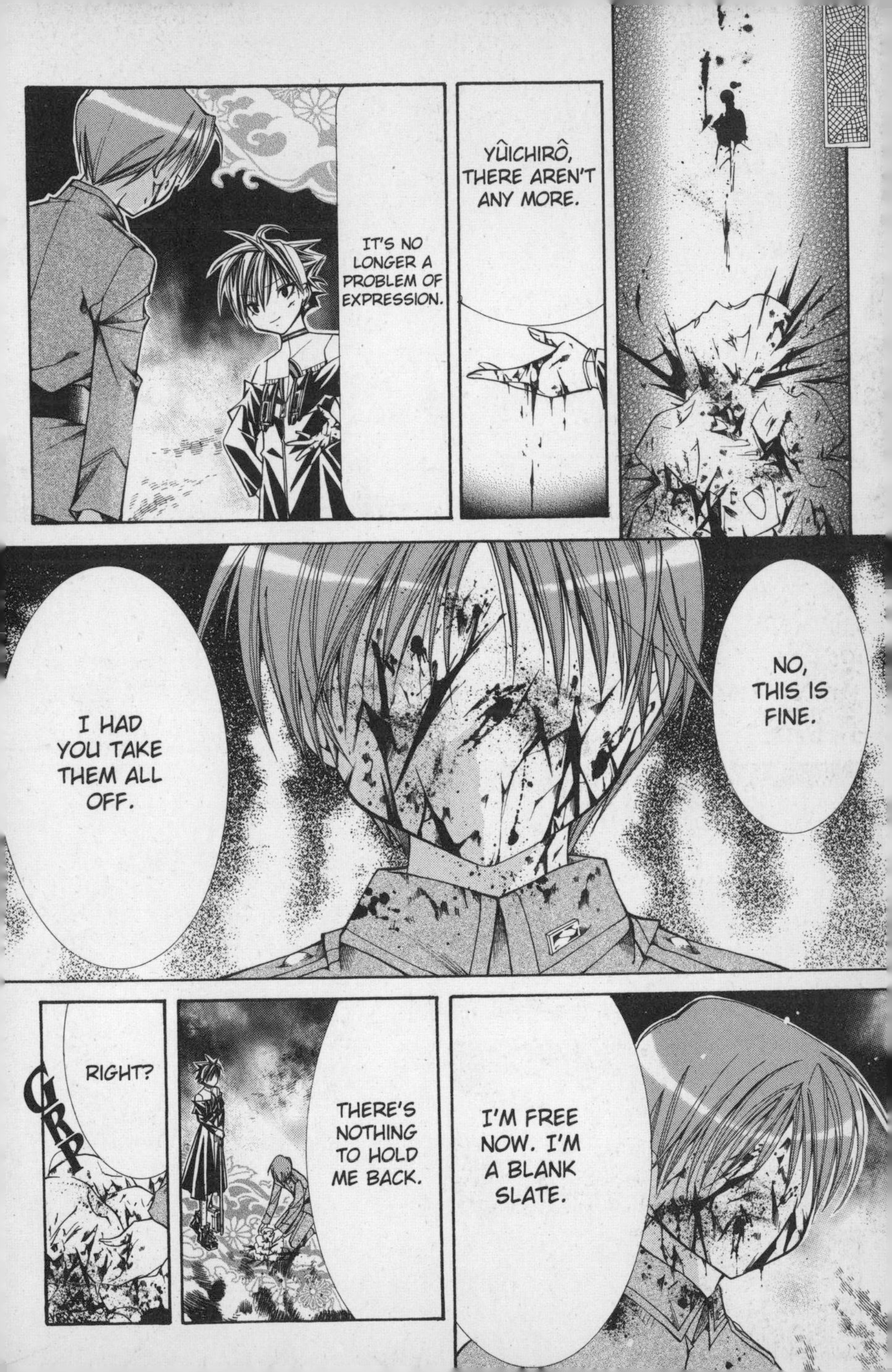
YÛICHIRÔ, THERE AREN'T ANY MORE.
IT'S NO LONGER A PROBLEM OF EXPRESSION.
NO, THIS IS FINE.
I HAD YOU TAKE THEM ALL OFF.
I'M FREE NOW. I'M A BLANK SLATE.
THERE'S NOTHING TO HOLD ME BACK.
RIGHT?
GRP

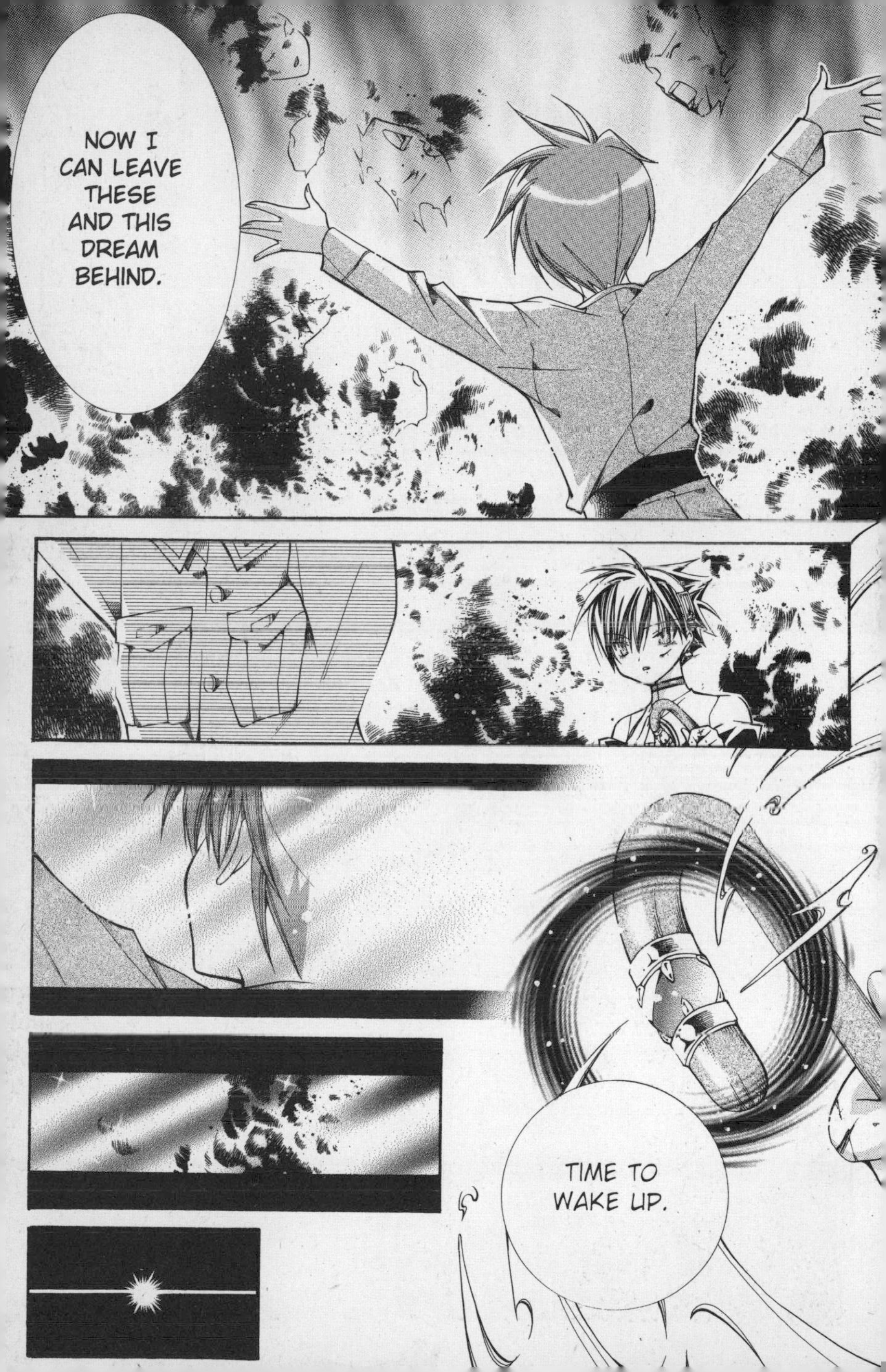
NOW I CAN LEAVE THESE AND THIS DREAM BEHIND.
TIME TO WAKE UP.

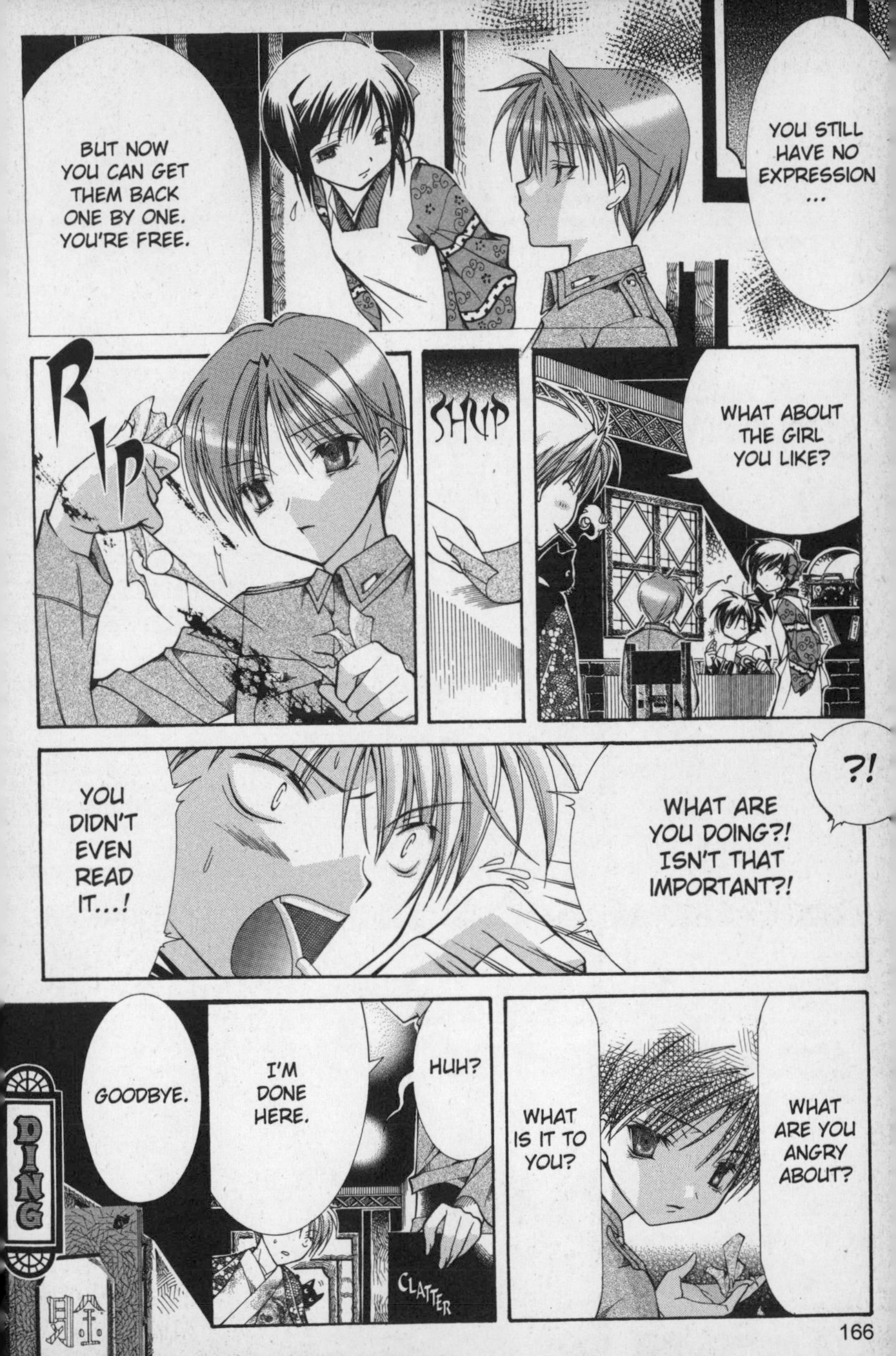

YOU STILL HAVE NO EXPRESSION ...
BUT NOW YOU CAN GET THEM BACK ONE BY ONE. YOU'RE FREE.
WHAT ABOUT THE GIRL YOU LIKE?
SHUP
RIP
?!
WHAT ARE YOU DOING?! ISN'T THAT IMPORTANT?!
YOU DIDN'T EVEN READ IT...!
WHAT ARE YOU ANGRY ABOUT?
WHAT IS IT TO YOU?
HUH?
I'M DONE HERE.
CLATTER
GOODBYE.
DING

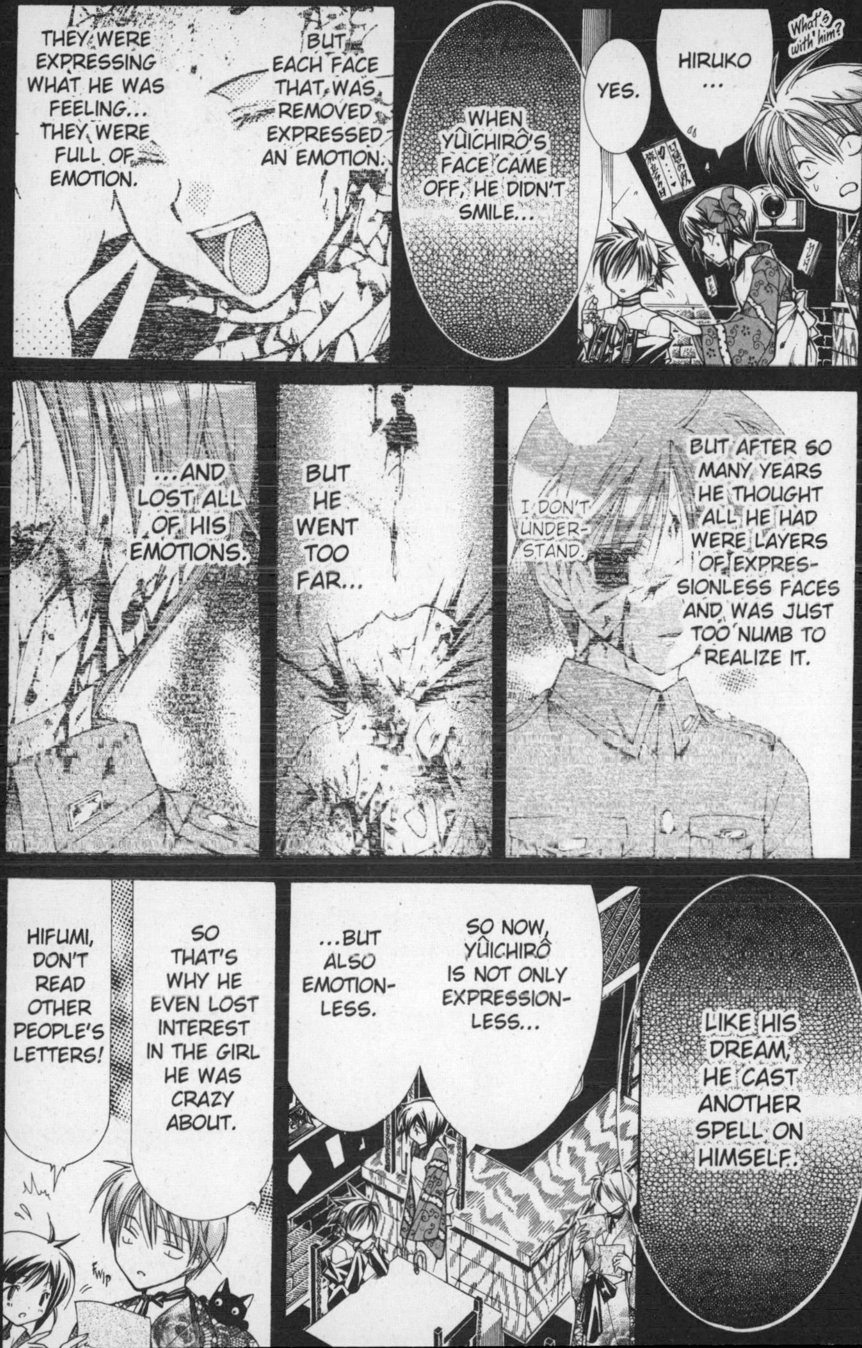
What's with him?
HIRUKO...
YES.
WHEN YÛICHIRÔ'S FACE CAME OFF, HE DIDN'T SMILE...
BUT EACH FACE THAT WAS REMOVED EXPRESSED AN EMOTION.
THEY WERE EXPRESSING WHAT HE WAS FEELING... THEY WERE FULL OF EMOTION.
BUT AFTER SO MANY YEARS HE THOUGHT ALL HE HAD WERE LAYERS OF EXPRESSIONLESS FACES AND WAS JUST TOO NUMB TO REALIZE IT.
I DON'T UNDERSTAND.
BUT HE WENT TOO FAR...
...AND LOST ALL OF HIS EMOTIONS.
LIKE HIS DREAM, HE CAST ANOTHER SPELL ON HIMSELF.
SO NOW, YÛICHIRÔ IS NOT ONLY EXPRESSIONLESS...
...BUT ALSO EMOTIONLESS.
SO THAT'S WHY HE EVEN LOST INTEREST IN THE GIRL HE WAS CRAZY ABOUT.
HIFUMI, DON'T READ OTHER PEOPLE'S LETTERS!
FWIP

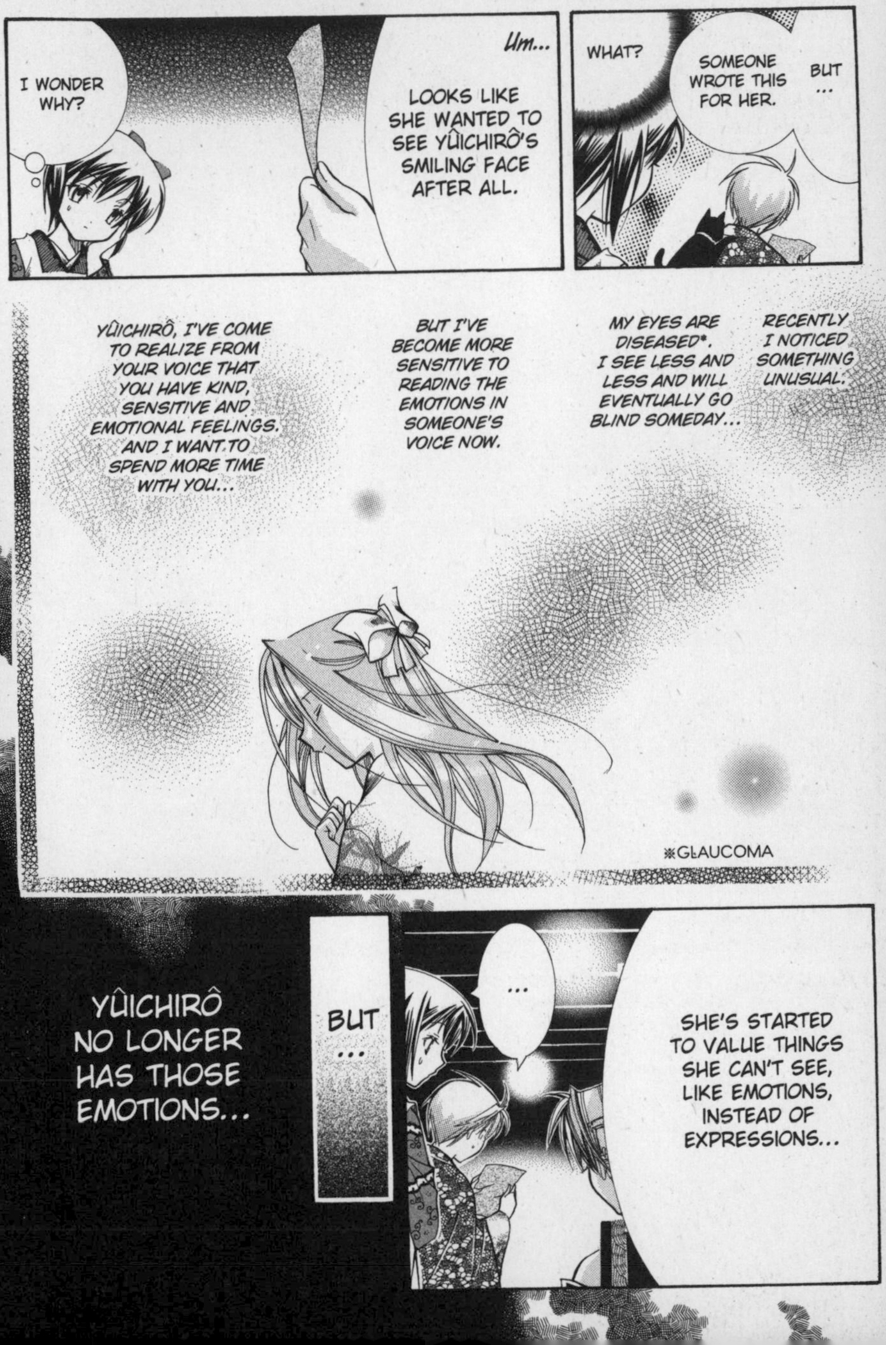
BUT ...
SOMEONE WROTE THIS FOR HER.
WHAT?
Um...
LOOKS LIKE SHE WANTED TO SEE YÛICHIRÔ'S SMILING FACE AFTER ALL.
I WONDER WHY?
RECENTLY I NOTICED SOMETHING UNUSUAL.
MY EYES ARE DISEASED*. I SEE LESS AND LESS AND WILL EVENTUALLY GO BLIND SOMEDAY...
BUT I'VE BECOME MORE SENSITIVE TO READING THE EMOTIONS IN SOMEONE'S VOICE NOW.
YÛICHIRÔ, I'VE COME TO REALIZE FROM YOUR VOICE THAT YOU HAVE KIND, SENSITIVE AND EMOTIONAL FEELINGS. AND I WANT TO SPEND MORE TIME WITH YOU...
※GLAUCOMA
SHE'S STARTED TO VALUE THINGS SHE CAN'T SEE, LIKE EMOTIONS, INSTEAD OF EXPRESSIONS...
...
BUT ...
YÛICHIRÔ NO LONGER HAS THOSE EMOTIONS...

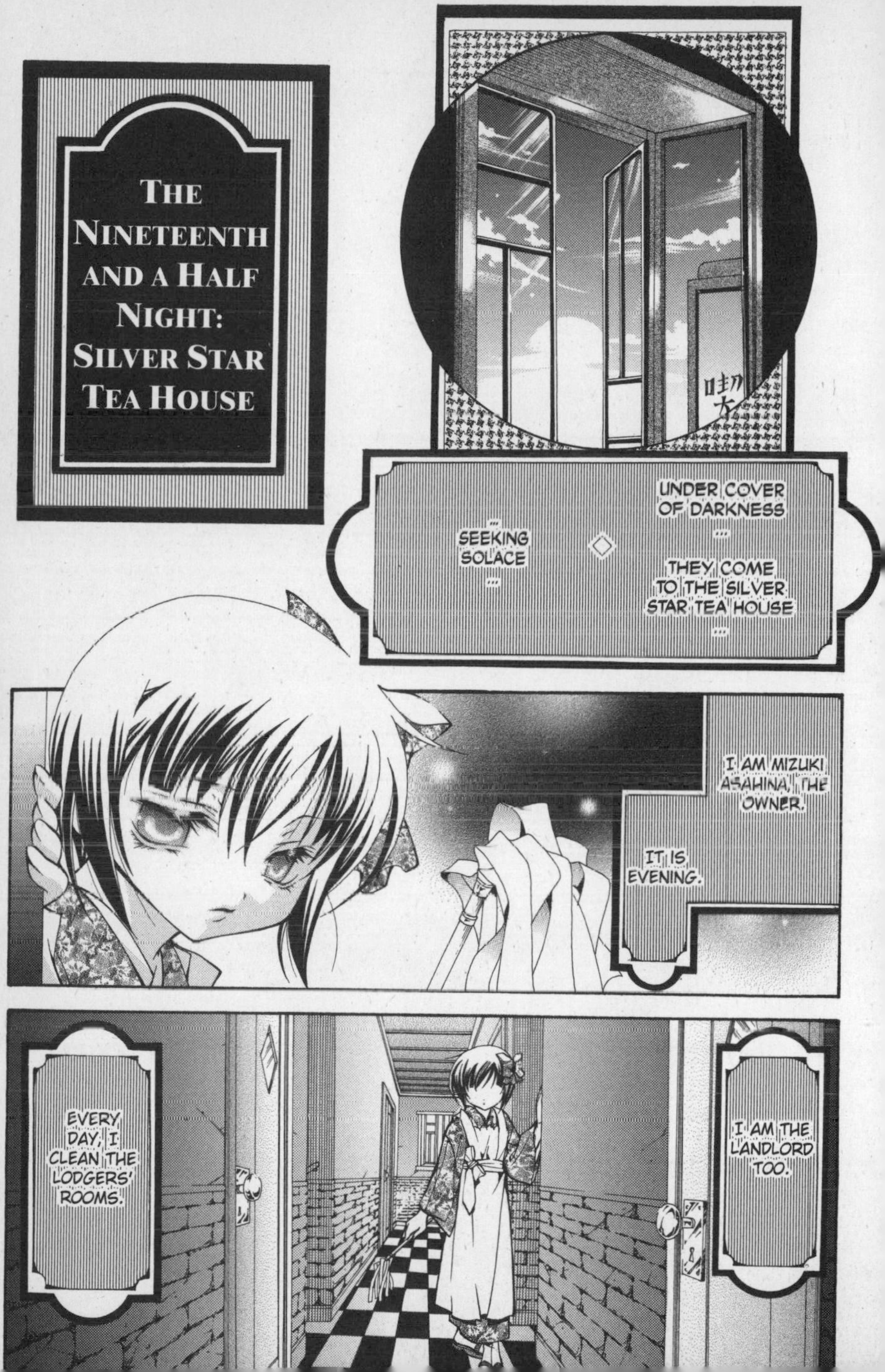
UNDER COVER OF DARKNESS ...
THEY COME TO THE SILVER STAR TEA HOUSE ...
... SEEKING SOLACE ...
THE NINETEENTH AND A HALF NIGHT: SILVER STAR TEA HOUSE
I AM MIZUKI ASAHINA, THE OWNER.
IT IS EVENING.
I AM THE LANDLORD TOO.
EVERY DAY, I CLEAN THE LODGERS' ROOMS.

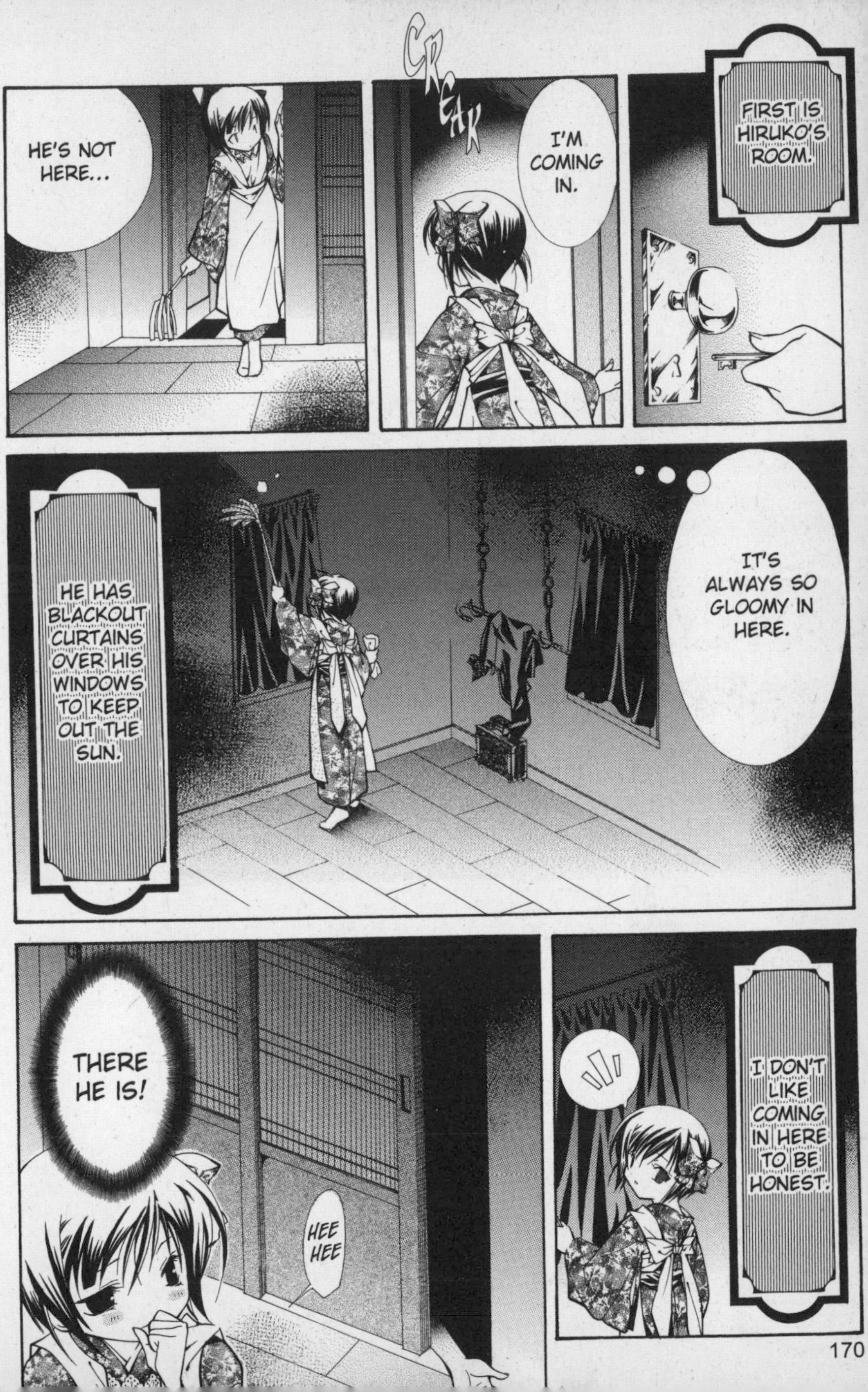
FIRST IS HIRUKO'S ROOM.
CREAK
I'M COMING IN.
HE'S NOT HERE...
IT'S ALWAYS SO GLOOMY IN HERE.
HE HAS BLACKOUT CURTAINS OVER HIS WINDOWS TO KEEP OUT THE SUN.
I DON'T LIKE COMING IN HERE TO BE HONEST.
THERE HE IS!
HEE HEE

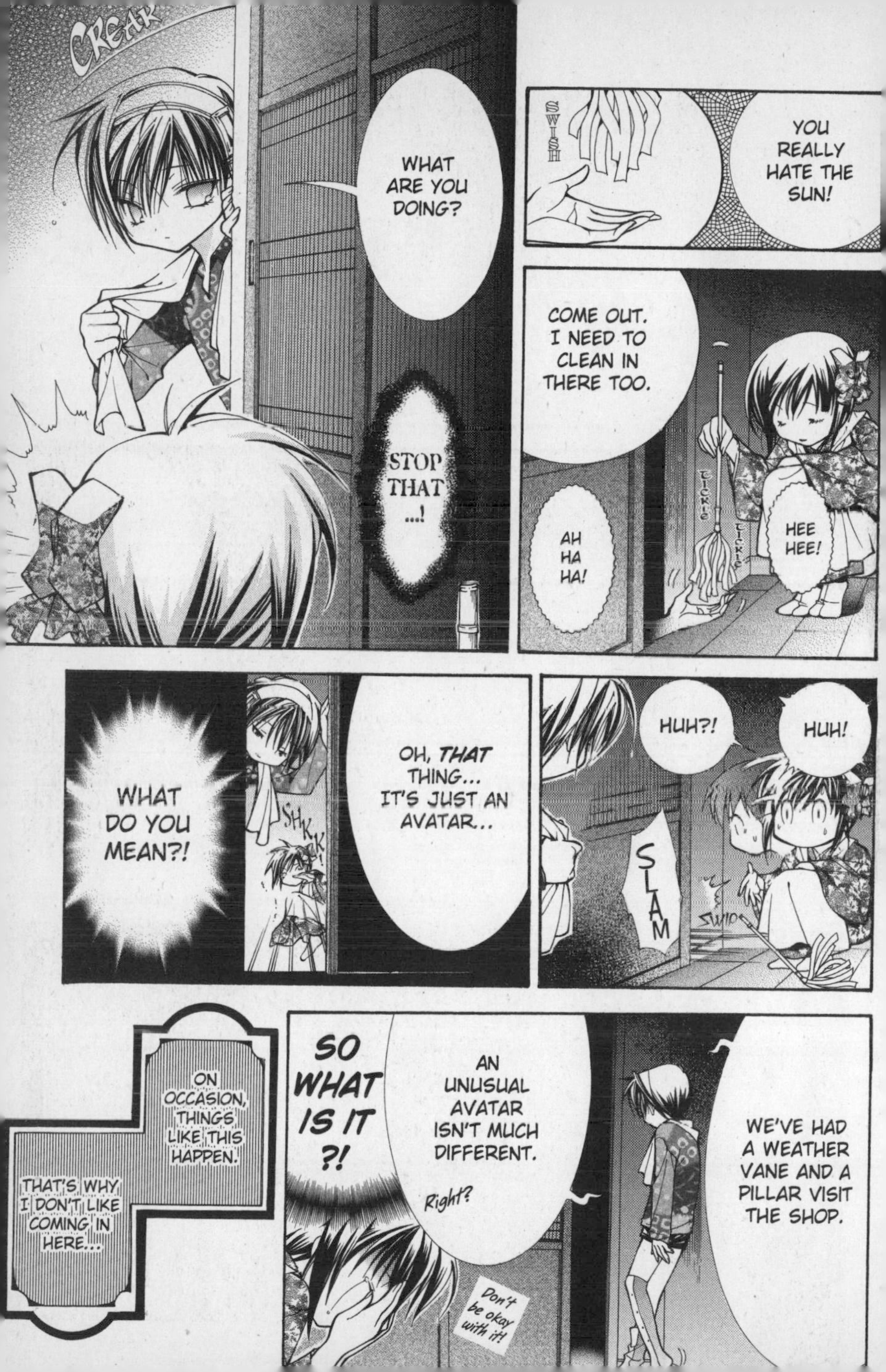
SWISH
YOU REALLY HATE THE SUN!
COME OUT. I NEED TO CLEAN IN THERE TOO.
HEE HEE!
TICKLE
TICKLE
AH HA HA!
CREAK
WHAT ARE YOU DOING?
STOP THAT ...!
HUH!
HUH?!
SLAM
SWIP
OH, *THAT* THING... IT'S JUST AN AVATAR...
WHAT DO YOU MEAN?!
WE'VE HAD A WEATHER VANE AND A PILLAR VISIT THE SHOP.
AN UNUSUAL AVATAR ISN'T MUCH DIFFERENT.
Right?
SO WHAT IS IT ?!
Don't be okay with it!
ON OCCASION, THINGS LIKE THIS HAPPEN.
THAT'S WHY I DON'T LIKE COMING IN HERE...

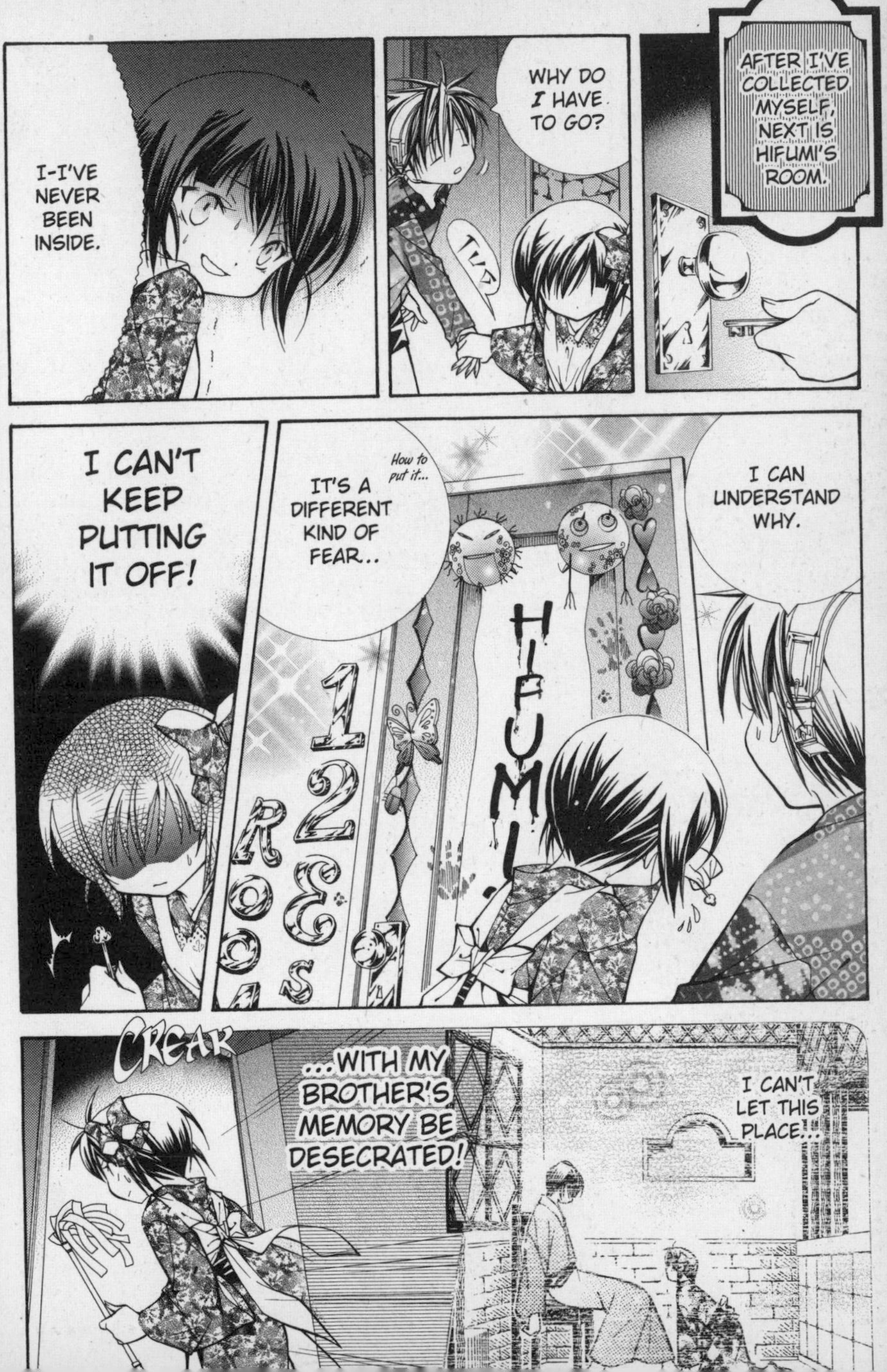
AFTER I'VE COLLECTED MYSELF, NEXT IS HIFUMI'S ROOM.
WHY DO I HAVE TO GO?
TUG
I-I'VE NEVER BEEN INSIDE.
I CAN UNDERSTAND WHY.
How to put it...
IT'S A DIFFERENT KIND OF FEAR..
HIFUMI
I CAN'T KEEP PUTTING IT OFF!
I CAN'T LET THIS PLACE...
...WITH MY BROTHER'S MEMORY BE DESECRATED!
CREAK

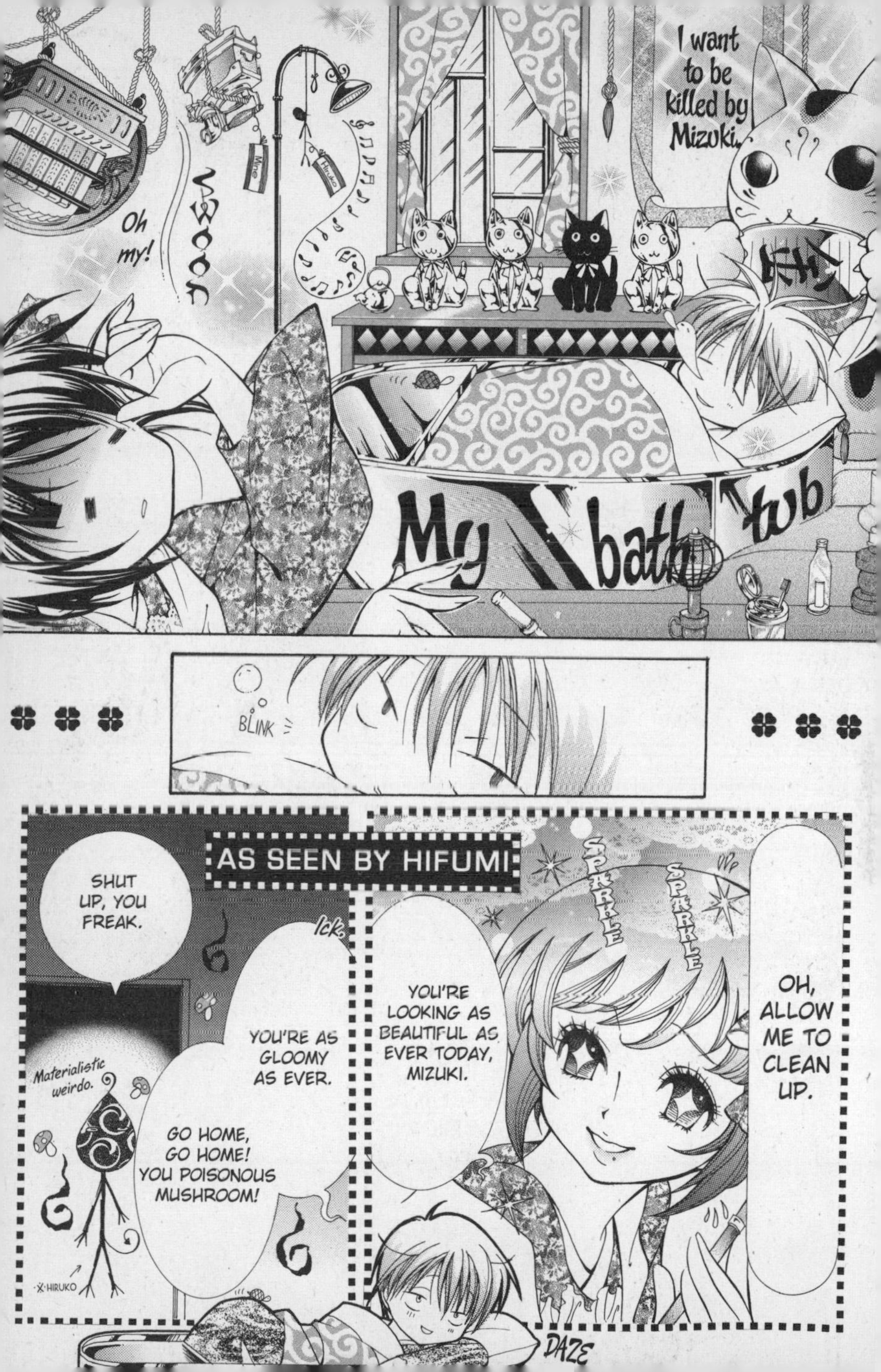
I want to be killed by Mizuki.
Hiruko
Mine
My bath tub
SWOON
Oh my!
BLINK
AS SEEN BY HIFUMI
OH, ALLOW ME TO CLEAN UP.
SPARKLE
SPARKLE
YOU'RE LOOKING AS BEAUTIFUL AS EVER TODAY, MIZUKI.
DAZE
Ick
SHUT UP, YOU FREAK.
YOU'RE AS GLOOMY AS EVER.
GO HOME, GO HOME! YOU POISONOUS MUSHROOM!
Materialistic weirdo.
HIRUKO

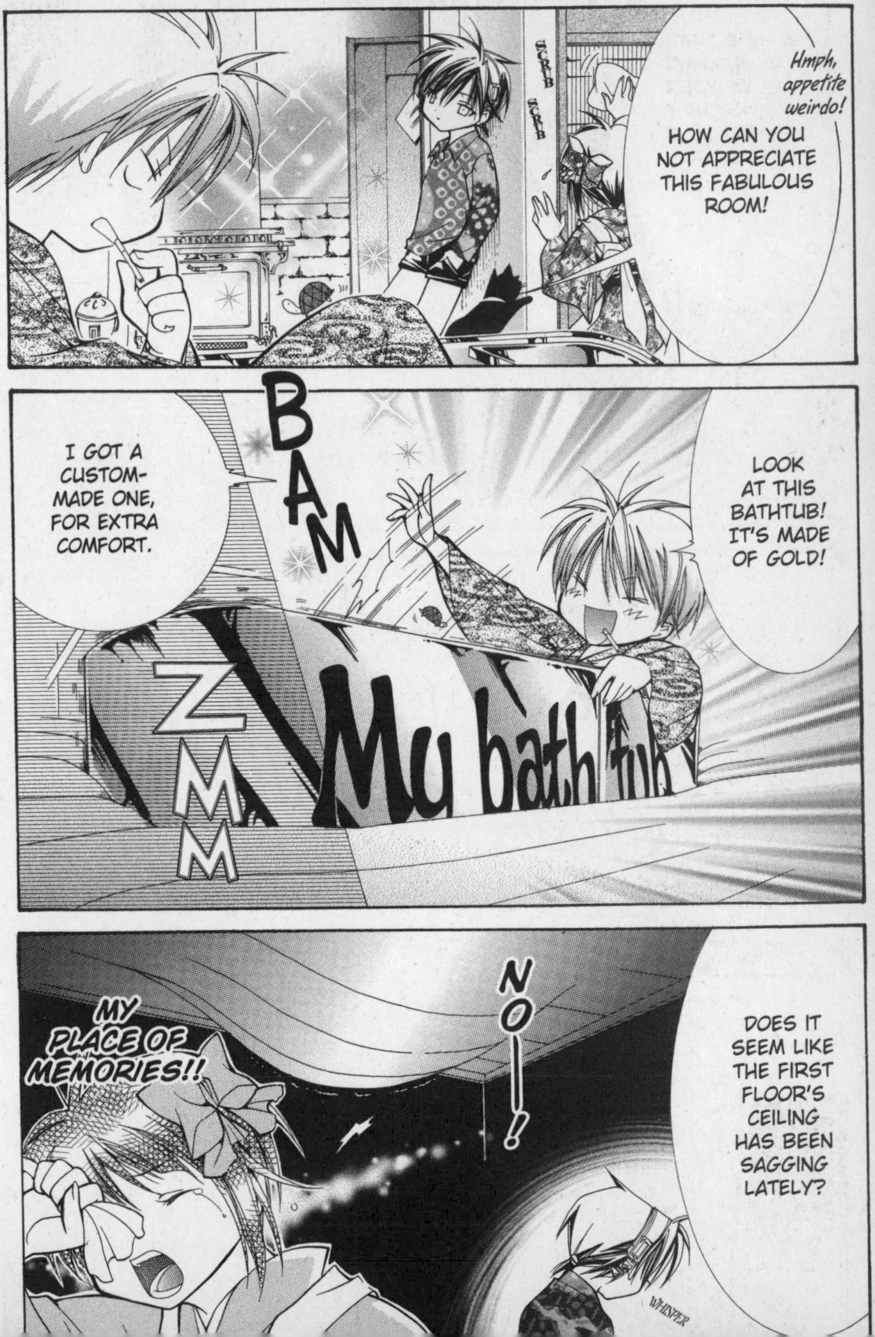
Hmph, appetite weirdo!
HOW CAN YOU NOT APPRECIATE THIS FABULOUS ROOM!
SCRUB SCRUB
LOOK AT THIS BATHTUB! IT'S MADE OF GOLD!
BAM
I GOT A CUSTOM-MADE ONE, FOR EXTRA COMFORT.
My bath tub
ZMMM
DOES IT SEEM LIKE THE FIRST FLOOR'S CEILING HAS BEEN SAGGING LATELY?
WHISPER
NO—!
MY PLACE OF MEMORIES!!

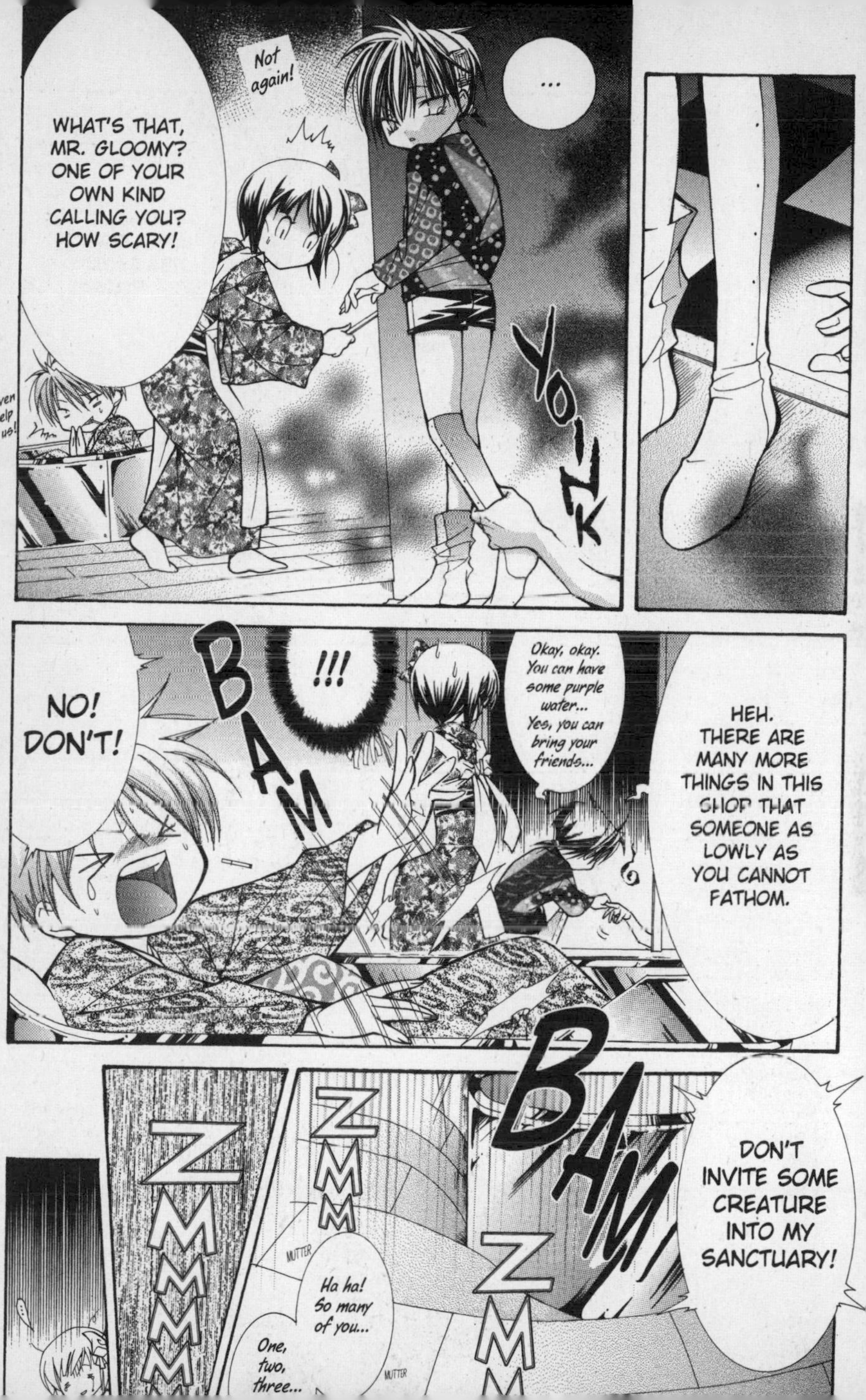
...
Not again!
WHAT'S THAT, MR. GLOOMY? ONE OF YOUR OWN KIND CALLING YOU? HOW SCARY!
YOINK
Heaven help us!
HEH. THERE ARE MANY MORE THINGS IN THIS SHOP THAT SOMEONE AS LOWLY AS YOU CANNOT FATHOM.
Okay, okay. You can have some purple water... Yes, you can bring your friends...
!!!
BAM
NO! DON'T!
DON'T INVITE SOME CREATURE INTO MY SANCTUARY!
BAM
ZMM
ZMMM
ZMMMMM
MUTTER
Ha ha! So many of you...
One, two, three...
MUTTER

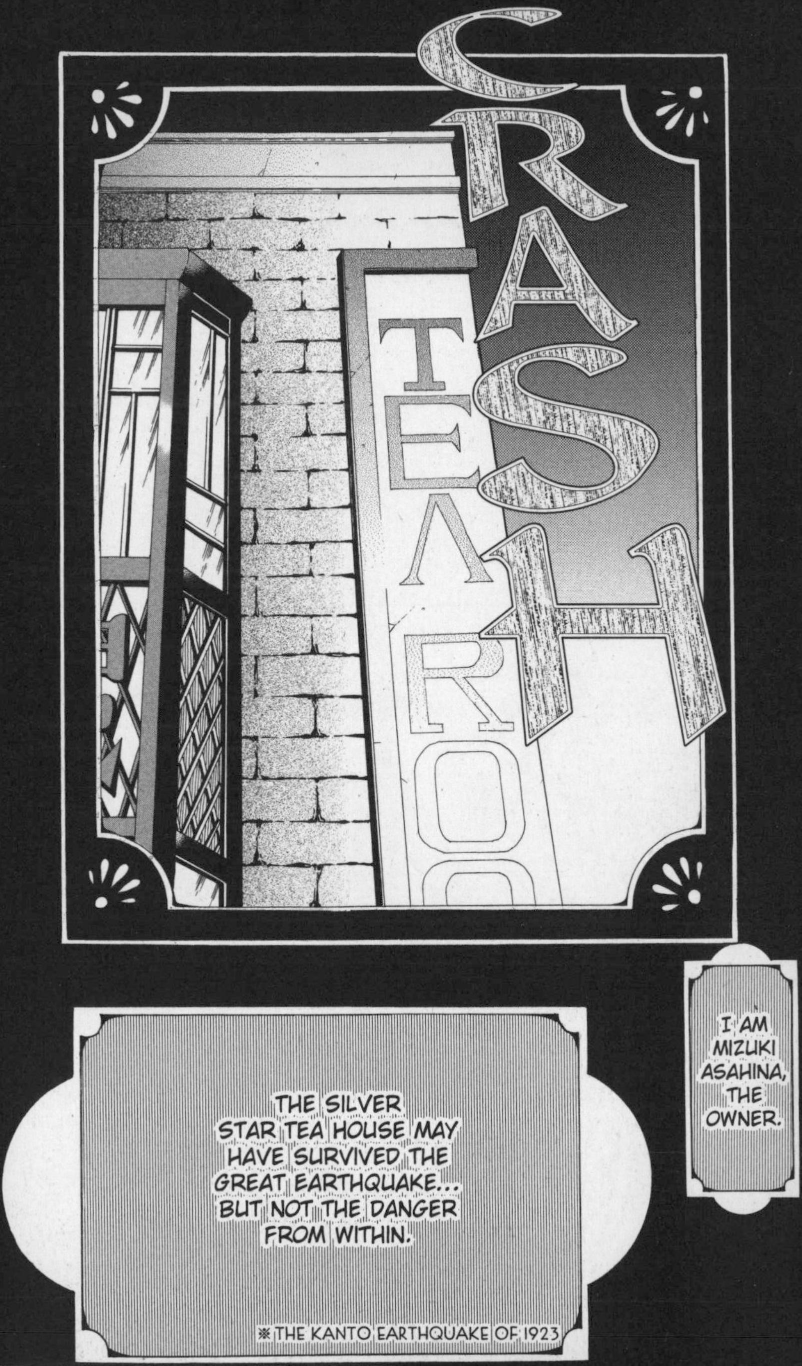
CRASH
TEA ROO
I AM MIZUKI ASAHINA, THE OWNER.
THE SILVER STAR TEA HOUSE MAY HAVE SURVIVED THE GREAT EARTHQUAKE... BUT NOT THE DANGER FROM WITHIN.
※THE KANTO EARTHQUAKE OF 1923

**NIGHTMARE INSPECTOR 3: END**

Hello. Shin Mashiba here. Thanks to you we're now up to volume 3. I want to thank from the bottom of my heart my very supportive editor who I've been a mental and physical strain on and all the readers who've followed me this far.

With The Nineteenth Night "Masks," we moved over to a different anthology—G Fantasy. (That's the reason for the different composition, etc.)

I still have a lot to improve upon, but please support me in this endeavour.

To everyone who has helped me.

* My editor Yuki Saeki and my former editor Masataka Matsushita
* My special friends who've helped out: Wan Wan Shiroi, Riru Shirayuki and Nema
* All my kind assistants: Katsumi Arai, Mieko Araki, Mai Tanaka, Mano, MOAI
* All the people at Square Enix.

Special Guest
Wan Wan Shiroi
Thank you for taking time out of your busy schedule to draw four pages for me. I hope to get you proper pages in the next volume.♥

To my friends who created the writing for The Eighteenth Night (*also continued on the next page), thank you so much for the beautiful writing. You really came to my rescue...

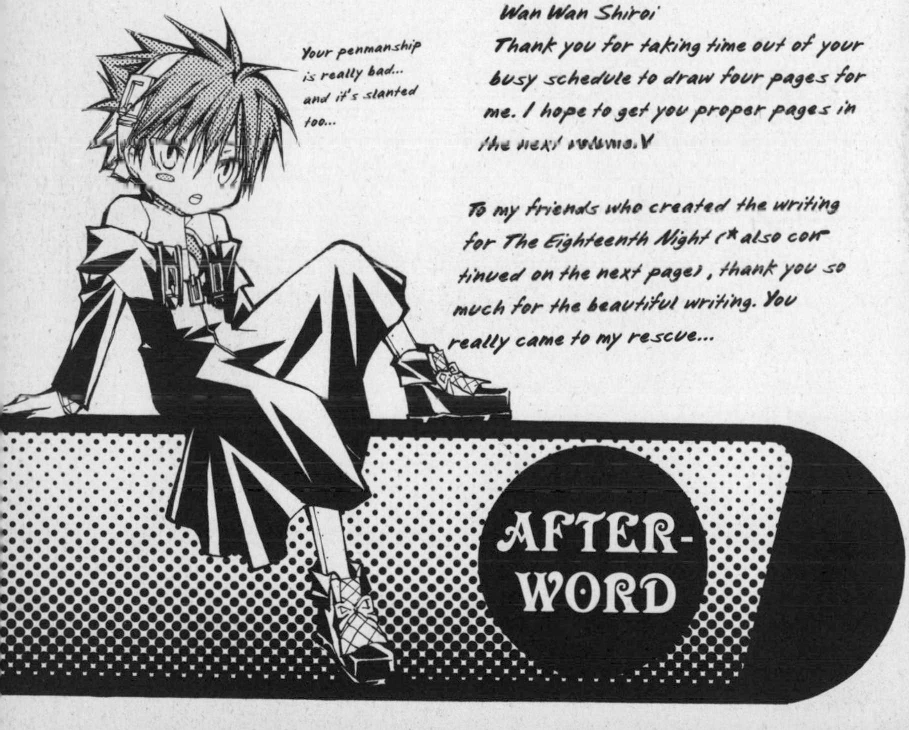
Your penmanship is really bad... and it's slanted too...
AFTER-WORD

# The Sad Dog

It was snowing. The snowflakes, dancing like tiny white butterflies in the night sky, were illuminated by a single shaft of light. It was just after the full moon. Heihachi stood gazing at the snow. His ravaged body, infected with tuberculosis, seemed even less substantial in the cold moonlight. He looked up towards the sky and then lowered his eyes, taking in the waterfall cascading at his feet.

"I'm hardly more than a skeleton as it is," he said. "What should it matter if I throw myself to my death now?"

He heard a voice call out to him.

"Stop!"

Heihachi turned around.

"Don't be so rash! You still have some time left."

Kumagorou, Heihachi's dear friend of many years, came into sight. As a man who was just at the brink of throwing his life away, Heihachi kept his eyes glued to the ground. Finally he looked up and met his friend's gaze. The snow continued its silent drifting. For Heihachi, nothingness was inevitable; the roar of the waterfall merely evidence that he continued to exist. Heihachi's struggle with tuberculosis had taught him the utter meaninglessness of life and death. How could Kumagorou possibly understand what he was going through? Kumagorou might be his closest friend, but this wall between them was simply insurmountable.

The two continued to stare at each other. Tears trailed down Kumagorou's cheeks.

"What is the meaning of life?" he wondered. Everything that is born will eventually die. Those who seek meaning in this world will only find disillusionment and pain. Heihachi had already discovered this truth, the true meaning of existence. It was a contradiction in itself. It was the inevitable.

The snowfall stopped. Silently, Kumagorou turned around and began his trek back the way he came. He finally understood his dear friend.

## COMING NEXT VOLUME

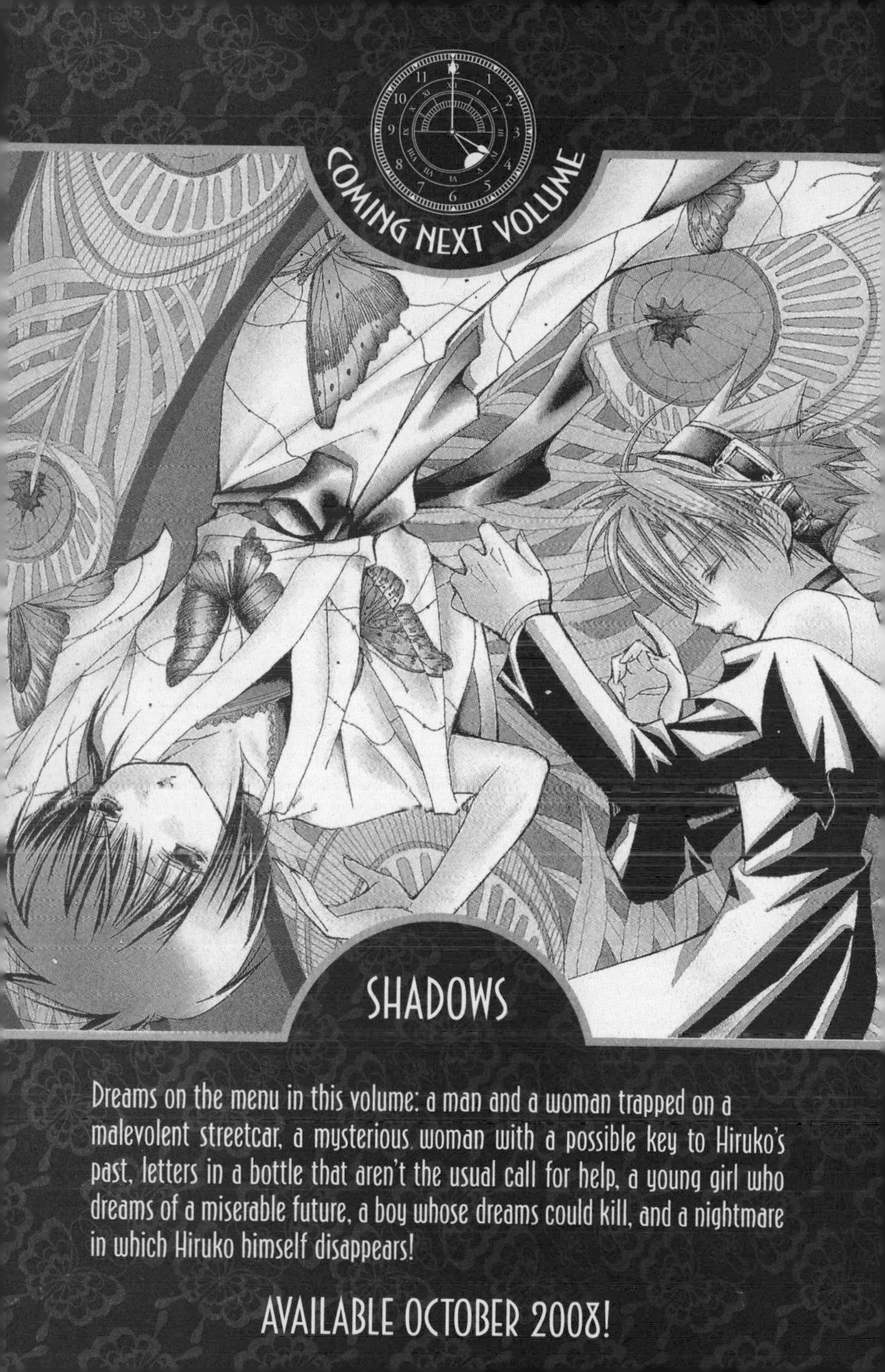

# SHADOWS

Dreams on the menu in this volume: a man and a woman trapped on a malevolent streetcar, a mysterious woman with a possible key to Hiruko's past, letters in a bottle that aren't the usual call for help, a young girl who dreams of a miserable future, a boy whose dreams could kill, and a nightmare in which Hiruko himself disappears!

## AVAILABLE OCTOBER 2008!

## SHIN MASHIBA

Recently I've had a recurring nightmare that I'm being chased.
It's probably about time management...
Can you remember the first dream you ever had?

Shin Mashiba's first manga, *Yumekui Kenbun* (Nightmare Inspector), premiered in *Monthly Stencil*, a shojo magazine, in December 2001 and was then serialized in *Monthly G Fantasy* from 2003 to 2007. Mashiba-san's own nightmares include being forced to eat 50 living slugs.

# NIGHTMARE INSPECTOR

## YUMEKUI KENBUN: NIGHTMARE INSPECTOR
## VOL. 3
### The VIZ Media Edition

### STORY AND ART BY
### SHIN MASHIBA

Translation/Gemma Collinge
English Adaptation/Kristina Blachere
Touch-up Art & Lettering/James Gaubatz
Cover Design/Sam Elzway
Interior Design/Julie Behn
Editor/ Yuki Murashige

Editor in Chief, Books/Alvin Lu
Editor in Chief, Magazines/Marc Weidenbaum
VP of Publishing Licensing/Rika Inouye
VP of Sales/Gonzalo Ferreyra
Sr. VP of Marketing/Liza Coppola
Publisher/Hyoe Narita

YUMEKUIKENBUN vol. 3 © 2003 Shin Mashiba/SQUARE ENIX All rights reserved.
First published in Japan in 2003 by SQUARE ENIX CO., LTD. English translation rights
arranged with SQUARE ENIX CO., LTD. and VIZ Media, LLC.

Printed in the U.S.A.

Published by VIZ Media, LLC
P.O. Box 77010
San Francisco, CA 94107

VIZ Media Edition
10 9 8 7 6 5 4 3 2 1
First printing, August 2008

store.viz.com

www.viz.com

## The Art of Fullmetal Alchemist

Contains all the manga artwork from 2001 to 2003!
- Gorgeously painted illustrations
- Color title pages, Japanese tankobon and promotional artwork
- Main character portraits and character designs from the video games

And a special two-page message from series creator Hiromu Arakawa!

**Hardcover $19.99**

## The Art of Fullmetal Alchemist: The Anime

Includes art inspired by the popular anime series!
- Initial character designs
- Cel art
- Production notes

Plus, an interview with Yoshiyuki Ito, character designer for the anime!

**Hardcover $19.99**

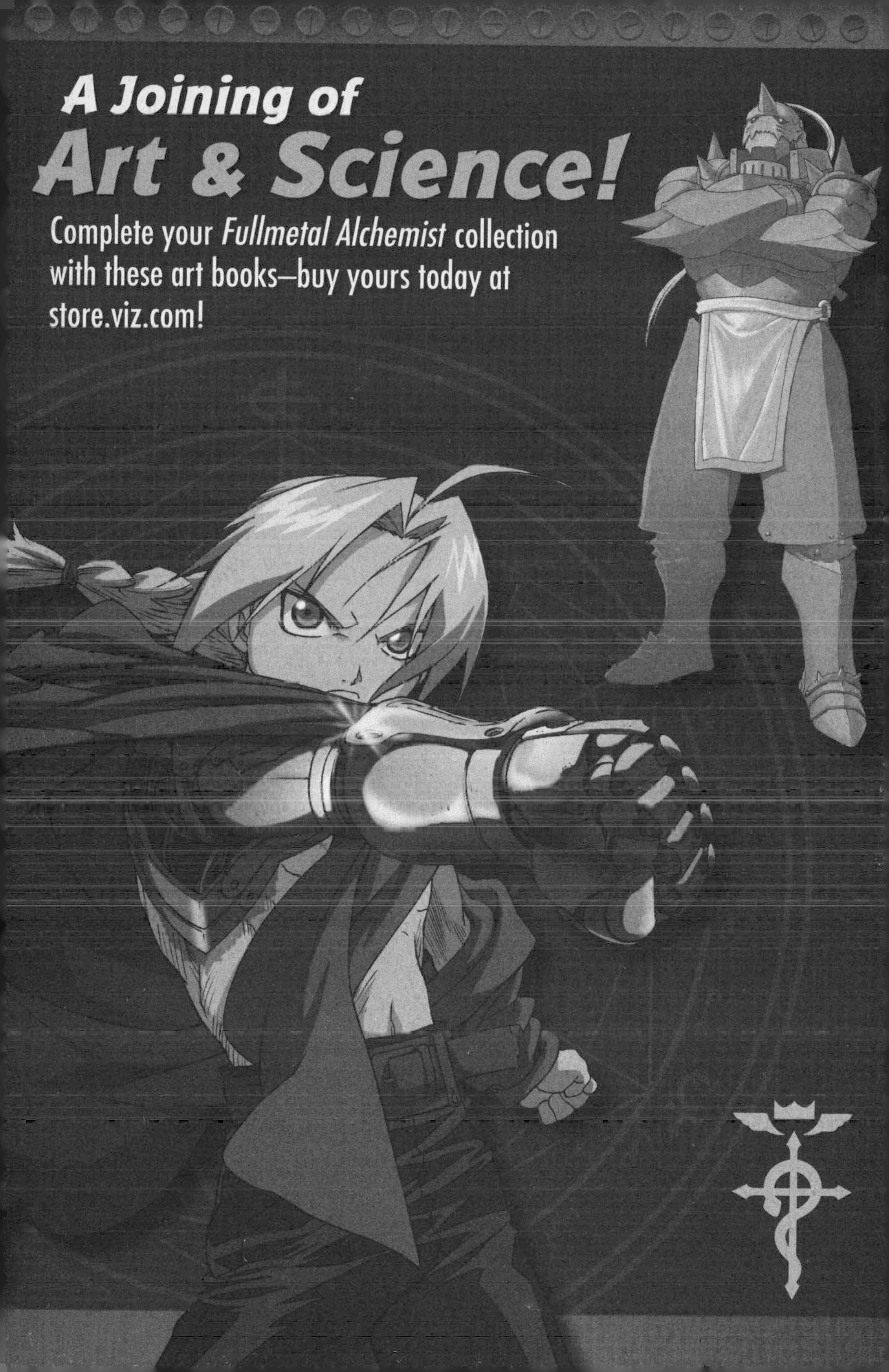

A Joining of
Art & Science!
Complete your *Fullmetal Alchemist* collection with these art books—buy yours today at store.viz.com!